Frontier Cities

FRONTIER CITIES

Encounters at the Crossroads of Empire

Edited by

JAY GITLIN

BARBARA BERGLUND

and

ADAM ARENSON

PENN

UNIVERSITY OF PENNSYLVANIA PRESS

PHILADELPHIA

Copyright © 2013 University of Pennsylvania Press

All rights reserved. Except for brief quotations used for purposes of review or scholarly citation, none of this book may be reproduced in any form by any means without written permission from the publisher.

Published by
University of Pennsylvania Press
Philadelphia, Pennsylvania 19104-4112
www.upenn.edu/pennpress

Printed in the United States of America
on acid-free paper

10 9 8 7 6 5 4 3 2 1

Library of Congress Cataloging-in-Publication Data
Frontier cities : encounters at the crossroads of empire / edited by Jay Gitlin, Barbara Berglund, and Adam Arenson. — 1st ed.
   p. cm.
Includes bibliographical references and index.
ISBN 978-0-8122-4468-7 (hardcover : alk. paper)
  1. Frontier and pioneer life—North America—History. 2. City and town life—North America—History. 3. Borderlands—North America—History. I. Gitlin, Jay. II. Berglund, Barbara. III. Arenson, Adam
E46.F76 2013
970—dc23   2012022789

CONTENTS

Introduction: Local Crossroads, Global Networks, and Frontier Cities
    Jay Gitlin, Barbara Berglund, and Adam Arenson   1

I. PRECEDENTS: IMPERIAL PLANS
AND COMMERCIAL VENTURES   9

1. The European Frontier City in EarlyModern Asia:
Goa, Macau, and Manila
    Alan Gallay   11

2. Colonial Projects and Frontier Practices: The First Century
of New Orleans History
    Daniel H. Usner, Jr.   27

II. URBAN SPACE AND FRONTIER REALITIES
IN THE EIGHTEENTH CENTURY   47

3. Insinuating Empire: Indians, Smugglers, and the Imperial
Geography of Eighteenth-Century Montreal
    Brett Rushforth   49

4. On the Edge of the West: The Roots and Routes
of Detroit's Urban Eighteenth Century
    Karen Marrero   66

5. People of the Pen, People of the Sword: Pittsburgh in 1774
    Carolyn Gilman   87

III. NETWORKS AND FLOWS: THE FRONTIER CITY IN THE NINETEENTH AND TWENTIETH CENTURIES — 105

6. Grain Kings, Rubber Dreams, and Stock Exchanges: How Transportation and Communication Changed Frontier Cities
   ELLIOTT WEST — 107

7. Frontier Ghosts Along the Urban Pacific Slope
   MATTHEW KLINGLE — 121

IV. RENDERINGS: VISUALIZING AND READING THE FRONTIER CITY — 147

8. Locating the Frontier City in Time and Space: Documenting a Passing Phenomenon
   TIMOTHY R. MAHONEY — 149

9. Mapping the Urban Frontier and Losing Frontier Cities
   PETER J. KASTOR — 165

10. Private Libraries and Global Worlds: Books and Print Culture in Colonial St. Louis
    JOHN NEAL HOOVER — 190

Epilogue: Frontier Cities and the Return of Globalization
   JAY GITLIN, BARBARA BERGLUND, AND ADAM ARENSON — 200

Notes — 209

List of Contributors — 253

Index — 255

Acknowledgments — 267

INTRODUCTION

Local Crossroads, Global Networks, and Frontier Cities

Jay Gitlin, Barbara Berglund, and Adam Arenson

In 1800, a Kansas chief known as Coeur qui Brule wrote to the lieutenant governor of Spanish Louisiana, expressing his desire to visit St. Louis: "*depuis longtemps je désire voir la ville* [for a long time I have wanted to see the town]."[1] Understanding that St. Louis was a place of French manners and values that explicitly equated civilization with urbanity, this native leader was eager for a chance to tour and experience the newest French city in North America. Coeur qui Brule recognized the significance of the cities European Americans built on North American frontiers. With his French name and apparent French language skills, Coeur qui Brule also embodied the kind of social and cultural mixing that occurred in frontier cities, at the heart of the imperial encounter.[2] He further remarked that he did not want to visit, like some chiefs, to seek presents. On the contrary, he said, "I have the heart of a Frenchman (*j'ai le coeur d'un français*)."[3]

Coeur qui Brule, however, would also have been acutely aware that he would always be a visitor in St. Louis: that the city was, from its inception, a French home, not an Indian one. When a group of 150 Missouri Indians arrived in 1764, while Auguste Chouteau and Pierre de Laclède's workmen were first laying out the town, Laclède hurried back to the site and carefully explained why the Missouri had to leave, disabusing them of their notion to settle in the heart of the new post. Revealingly, before they left, the women and children of the group were engaged to dig a cellar for the company's main building. Yet despite this exclusionary gesture, St. Louis, like other frontier cities, quickly established itself as a place of both enduring interest and influence within Indian country—to Coeur qui Brule and so many others.[4]

Fifty years ago, Richard C. Wade provided an insight that continues to generate surprise: "Towns were the spearheads of the frontier," he declared in the first sentence of *The Urban Frontier* (1959). "Planted far in advance of the line of settlement, they held the West for the approaching population."[5] As Coeur qui Brule had experienced one hundred and fifty years before that, towns and cities typically preceded rural settlements throughout early North America.

This volume is dedicated to documenting encounters like Coeur qui Brule's, and to explicating Wade's still-surprising insight that the phrase *frontier city* is not an oxymoron, not a contradiction in terms. We renew conversations about what the juxtaposition of *frontier* and *city* reveal, exploring these fascinating, if unexpected, locales.

Frontier cities are urban settlements that emerge from an initial frontier encounter. They are defined by the interplay between their global contexts—economic, cultural, and political ties, as well as the regulations of uninformed and distant policymakers—and their diverse local actors.[6] In frontier cities, natives and newcomers, hemmed in by practical considerations as they shared streets, buildings, and interwoven lives, created the earliest matrix of the American urban experience.

In these urban spaces of encounter, natives and newcomers alike were shaped by both front-door policy decisions and back-door intimacies and interactions. Even the most basic urban places contained many homes, sites of exchange, and roads that entered into, crossed, and left town. Its residents held connections to a wider world, whether through national or linguistic ties, economic networks, or memories of places across the seas or across the mountains that shaped their lives. These qualities gave rise to the Chinese migrants who established fishing camps on the eastern shores of San Francisco Bay in the early 1850s, to the French traders bypassing imperial regulations by throwing casks of brandy over the wall to Indian customers on the Rue St. Paul in eighteenth-century Montreal, and to a young indigenous boy named Elvis playing his air guitar outside the contemporary frontier city of Manaus in Brazil.

Frontier cities thus emerge as ideal places to see the intimate personal interactions of new settlements, their world-changing importance in the process of state-making, and how the legacies of these patterns of global and local interaction continue to shape cities to this day. They have much to teach us about the complex interactions between diverse peoples and nations; about the power of symbols and metaphors; and about productively reframing the dialogue between the fields of urban, early American, postcolonial, and American western history.

* * *

Recognizing that our key terms, *frontier* and *city*, have a long history of varied and multiple usages, we begin by offering some broad parameters that reflect the ways frontier and city are conceptualized in this volume. The expansiveness of these concepts is what, in large measure, gives them their appealing and ongoing explanatory power, but we want to make sure that we can all understand how we, and our contributors, are using these simple yet profound terms.

A *frontier* is fundamentally an edge and thus a potential meeting ground, a place of convergence. Although the word's first uses appear in early modern Europe, its contemporary resonance comes from association with the history of the American West—and with westering writ large. Within western history, the term has a contentious yet vitally productive past—rooted in the work of Frederick Jackson Turner and, in particular, his 1893 essay, "The Significance of the Frontier in American History." Turner viewed the frontier as an east-to-west moving line where "savagery and civilization" met—where hardy pioneers confronted indigenous peoples and the natural environment, and where they established mostly rural settlements whose residents and institutions manifested characteristics, such as individualism and democracy, which Turner perceived as central to American national identity.

While Turner's ideas about the frontier are plagued by sentiments common for his time, his positioning of the frontier as the crucible that forged characteristics central to the making of the American nation and his identification of the frontier as a process through which Euro-Americans conquered the American West and built a landed empire can still be very useful analytical frameworks. Recognizing this, we join those scholars who have reconceptualized frontiers as varied and multifarious zones of encounter, produced by the global push of empire-building nation-states. In these spaces, different peoples worked together—willingly or unwillingly—as they shaped the environment, created mechanisms of economic and cultural exchange, and established some principles for governance in situations typically structured by unequal power relations.[7]

Seen in this way, frontiers illuminate the centrality of empire-building and nation-making to North American and global expansion because they are among the most significant places where those processes occur. Imperial ambitions and realities among the English, Spanish, French, and Russians drove settlement in North America, and imperial aims fueled the expansion of the United States from early on. By defining frontier cities in ways that actively link them to empire-building and nation-making across North America and beyond, our goal is to both re-energize the concept of the frontier within the historiography of the American West and to simultaneously dislodge it from that tradition—to show that frontiers are not unique to the American West— and to demonstrate how the concept of the frontier has relevance for other fields dealing with intertwined histories of conquest and encounter.

In this sense, *frontier* is meant to possess analytical breadth, providing an opportunity for both the questioning and connecting of our common assumptions. It brings forth all the messiness, occasional beauty, and terrible violence wrought by processes of change and transformation that accompanied the waves of empire- and nation-making that stretched across the globe. And it reminds us as well that within North America, westering was not contained in the West—a frontier was both a moving target and a space shaped by many perspectives.[8]

If, in spatial terms, a *frontier* is an edge and a meeting ground, a *city* is similarly a point of convergence and connection. A city is also distinct from its surroundings. Whether it is its size, density, the number of specialized, nonagricultural workers, or some other factor, a city is defined, in part, by its contrast with that which is not urban—the countryside, the farm, the woods. As planning texts back to classical times and scholarship dating back to Raymond Williams's 1973 work *The Country and the City* make evident, this contrast is freighted with centuries of cultural as well as political and economic meaning. Cities might be defined by kingly decree or bureaucratic jurisdiction, by the realities of urban life or merely the aspirations of urbanity.[9]

As every city dweller knows, cities are places where order is beyond individual control, self-sufficiency is neither possible nor desired, and intercultural conversations are a fact of life. The medievalist and urban historian Roberto Lopez noted that the earliest "ideogram meaning 'city' consist[ed] of a cross enclosed in a circle." Both a home (the circle) and a place of convergence (the crossroads), with that convergence entailing "a quickening of communication,"[10] a city allows for and encourages exchange within a relatively safe haven. Even before large numbers of people reside there, a critical mass of skills and specialized roles is usually present. Urban space facilitates a range of social relationships and, reciprocally, the social needs of a city direct the creation of urban space.[11] The cities that result from these processes exist as both concrete structures and as powerful symbols, laden with social and cultural meanings. They hold tremendous innovative power, existing along geographic fault lines and within networks of trade, politics, and culture, but few realize how deep these dynamic forces reach. Cities—in all their social, spatial, economic, and temporal variations—contain both buildings and peoples with many stories. Built to manage complexity, cities provide a distinctive framework for viewing frontier encounters.

Frontiers, however, are still generally conjured up as rural spaces—where one finds pioneer farming families, lone miners, and cowboys—not urban ones. More often than not, "the frontier" is imagined as a line of rugged, rural outposts, despite the fact that urban frontiers are actually central to the way people imagine the West. Western-themed amusements are often quintessentially urban spaces that replicate a town's commercial strip containing the iconic western saloon; and real mining camps were some of the most urban spaces around in terms of population density and economic activity.

* * *

By reclaiming frontiers as urban phenomena, we are self-consciously stretching the way "the city" and "the urban" have increasingly come to be defined in two crucial ways. First, we seek to make an important temporal correction to what has become a trend in both urban western history and U.S. urban history writ large. Increasingly, historians have focused their attention on analyzing and describing a post–World War II America of suburban sprawl, framed powerfully by the racial politics refracted through the "urban crisis" of those decades, without considering the distinctive patterns of urban living, in the West and other regions, that stretch centuries before.[12]

By bridging the gap between early American history and studies of the infrastructure and politics of modern cities, we make a crucial intervention in the way processes of urbanization are understood. The frontier cities described and analyzed in this volume—with their stories of native-newcomer interactions, gendered and racialized spaces, and global-local networks—are utterly relevant to the issues that animate studies of contemporary cities.

Moreover, within urban history, there is a tendency to conceive of cities as completely belonging to newcomer societies, part and parcel of tidy forms of settler colonialism that tend to make invisible processes of displacement and removal.[13] The early histories of these places belie such assumptions, revealing the importance of cross-cultural interactions in city locations and design, social and economic structure, and remembered origins. We know that contemporary native peoples all over the world live, as often as not, in urban areas. What we have not acknowledged is that native peoples have been living in such places all along. Just as we have conceived of frontiers as zones that could not have contained cities, so have we been determined to deny that native people could live urban lives; rather, they must somehow reside in spaces that are remote, backwards, and lacking the civility we attribute to the very notion of the city.[14]

This has limited our ability to see, for example, the existence of native and métis satellite villages—or, dare we say, suburbs—in some of the frontier cities described on these pages. It is impossible to comprehend early St. Louis without observing its nearby villages of St. Charles, St. Ferdinand de Florissant, Carondelet, and Portage des Sioux. Over half the residents of the St. Louis metropolitan area lived in these satellite villages in 1800, and it was in this suburban periphery that many of the most fascinating social, cultural, and economic exchanges occurred. The failure to broaden our view of what constitutes urban space on past frontiers has thus hindered our ability to find points of connection between scholarship on modern cities and that of earlier frontier cities.[15]

Second, as we assert, frontiers are deeply connected to empire and crucial sites of urban development; yet in the tradition of U.S. historiography, the imperial, nation-making function of cities has typically been overlooked. By focusing on processes of urbanization in a frontier context, we bring to the forefront the ways in which urbanization both was fueled by empire and was an engine of it. For example, in the context of the diverse, rapidly growing instant city of nineteenth-century San Francisco, an important aspect of empire-building involved creating a recognizably American social order in a fluid population that was predominantly male and immigrant, thanks to the gold rush. In part this was done through politics and laws that linked citizenship to whiteness, and thus codified who had rights by defining who was white. But in a far-flung place where the arm of the state could reach only so far, an American social order was also asserted and contested in the kinds of cultural venues typically found only in urban areas: hotels and restaurants; places of amusement; tourist attractions; fairs and exhibitions. These were places where people came face-to-face with one another and, through the prisms of race, class, and gender, articulated varied and competing views of themselves and those around them.[16]

The absence of empire from the study of U.S. cities detracts from the ability of urban history to recover its comparative and intercultural roots and tell stories connected to larger, global contexts. By reasserting the urban nature of frontier places, we highlight a North America shaped by imperial agendas, global markets, and diffuse urban models and connections. This focus provides a crucial untold chapter in the history of the construction of place, by and for North Americans, interacting in the first great age of globalization. The stories this volume reveals about Montreal, St. Louis, Pittsburgh, San Francisco, Seattle, and other cities are not, moreover, about these places as we know them today. Instead, we are focused less on the stories of metropolises and more on the stories of how these cities came to be established, how their residents maintained a double focus on the local environment and distant, more global worlds, and what conditions existed so that these sites would not be among the countless abandoned settlements across human history.

Our conceptualizations of *frontier* and *city* thus allow us to see the two terms as a productive analytical fit. The early histories of frontier cities are the local stories of encounters and negotiation, set into larger global and hemispheric contexts. Their struggles, compromises, and legacies then shape and influence the making and remembering of that place even after that initial frontier is long gone. In their development, frontier cities followed no mythic line of settlement, nor did they all move in lockstep through a certain pattern of evolution.

Frontier cities connected people, and hence we are concerned with connecting histories. Colonial spaces and the frontier; global history and the history of the American West; urban studies and postcolonial theory; the re-invigorated interest in indigenous politics and culture—these disciplines and studies need to be connected, and the analysis of frontier cities offers one very fruitful way to make those connections. In the existing scholarship, too much is separated. Histories of American Indians or the environmental impact of colonization rarely consider cities and their dense political, market, and material interconnections.[17] And insights of postcolonial analyses of power networks and empire—so important to studies of India, Africa, Latin America, the Caribbean, and the Pacific—have been only loosely applied to North America.[18] Comparative works seeking to define the global frontier or the character of western expansion have been even scarcer.[19] We recognize, of course, that the historiography of urbanization in the American West is rich and contains innovative studies of the interdependency of city and country, the role of western cities in the national economy, and the contribution of the West to changing American notions of community and urban form itself.[20] Many of these studies, however, are too easily contained within the standard narratives of settler colonialism and nation building. What we are arguing for here are studies of frontier cities that include imperial and indigenous perspectives and have a transnational and comparative vision that can connect backward and forward in time.

Despite the attempts of new western historians to pay more attention to cross-cultural interaction, markets, and the changing modes of communication and transportation on various frontiers, the field of western history today seems outflanked by the innovations in colonial history, which has broadened its inquiries to include native communities, and re-imagined its subject as part of an Atlantic World that includes early modern Europe, Africa, and America.[21] Yet western historians have also always been cognizant of borders and those who cross them—the margins of political, economic, and cultural communities. In this age of re-globalization, as national and geographic boundaries become ever more fluid, the insights of earlier generations of western history seem ready for application for a wider world, one that reaches back into the origins of European settlements around the world.[22] At the same time, too many histories of early American cities tell a "colonial" story, focused only on stories of self-shaping distinctiveness or provincial emulation. When the word *frontier* is substituted for *colonial*, new kinds of social relations, both local and global—before relegated to the periphery—magically appear.

If we maintain, as did the inhabitants of frontier cities themselves, a double focus that captures the immediate and intimate along with the distant and global, we will see—with the open eyes of a Coeur qui Brule—a frontier with cities and cities with intriguing and important edges that we simply have not noticed. We have missed not only local stories but also stories of empires and far-reaching commercial networks. Their absence from the study of urban North America detracts from our ability to recover the comparative and intercultural roots of current U.S. cities, born within global networks of trade, culture, and politics.

I.

Precedents: Imperial Plans and Commercial Ventures

CHAPTER 1

The European Frontier City in Early Modern Asia: Goa, Macau, and Manila

Alan Gallay

> Hear the proclamation of the alderman and offices of the
> Council of this City of Goa, that every citizen and any
> other head of a household of any quality nation who is
> Portuguese, should come next Monday morning very
> early to the council chamber, since this is needful for the
> good of the common weal of the city: under penalty that
> anyone who does not turn up in the said council chamber
> must accept whatever is decided there on the said day
> by a majority vote of the people and leading men of the
> municipality, and he cannot plead that he was not informed
> that the meeting was held. (April 21, 1535)[1]

Those of us who study the English colonies on the Atlantic are apt to overlook the importance of the frontier city in the early modern world. We tend to emphasize towns in New England, plantations in the American South and the West Indies, and view the urban life of New Amsterdam as a Dutch anomaly. But in the larger context of European overseas expansion, the city was critical, providing the foundation of empire.

The European frontier cities in Asia preceded and coincided with the building of frontier towns and cities in the Americas. These cities were the entrepôts for world trade, the way stations for ships traversing the oceans, and the nodes through which Europeans conducted diplomacy and undertook military affairs. This essay focuses on three of the most significant European cities in Asia: Portuguese Goa in India and Macau in China, and Spanish Manila in the Philippines. Examining why the Iberians established and defined cities in Asia, and how these cities functioned, gives us a better context for understanding the form and function of frontier cities around the globe. As the proclamation above makes clear, the early modern frontier city practiced self-government; householders possessed a say in shaping the city's life. With the mother country so far away, the people who inhabited these frontier cities shaped the contours of empire.

First, a bit of important context on European expansion in the east. The European empires in the Pacific and Indian Oceans involved less territorial occupation than in the west. The focus was maritime and mercantile, securing trade by dominating sea-lanes and connecting urban bases in Asia and East Africa. The crux, and the most profitable aspect of their eastern empires, was trade that revolved around spices from a variety of islands, horses from Persia and Arabia, gold from East Africa and Sumatra, amber and precious stones from India and the Indian Ocean area, cotton textiles and rice from several places, musk, rhubarb, China-root, porcelains, silk, lacquers, paper, and furniture from China, and silk and copper from Japan. The most desired items were silks and spices, as well as gold.[2] The key European problem: the lack of commodities to exchange for Asian goods. Portugal, the first European power to construct an Asian empire, solved the problem by carrying goods between China and Japan, becoming middlemen in Asia trade. The key item in making the whole Asian trade work, and which by extension incorporated Europe and the Americas into the Asian economic system, was silver.[3]

China had converted to a silver standard by the second half of the sixteenth century; and when we include the kingdoms that paid tribute to China, one-third of the world was on the silver system. China's creation of the Single Whip Tax in the 1570s, which consolidated numerous taxes into one empirewide tax, was payable only in silver. Even peasants paid taxes in silver. To earn silver, Chinese manufactured silk in household production. China became a vacuum sucking silver from other parts of the world. From the 1570s to the 1640s, silver had twice the value in China that it had in Europe. After the price evened out in the 1640s, silver continued to flow to China to meet demand. In the eighteenth century, the value of silver in China again rose until about 1750.[4]

In return for silver, the Chinese produced 2,500 tons of silk per year in the early seventeenth century. One-third went to Japan, India, and the Americas through the Philippines. From the Japanese, the Chinese obtained silver. Hence, Portugal conducted a silver-for-silk trade between Japan and China. The Portuguese earned about 275 percent profit for silks carried from China to Japan, and around 180 percent on raw silk. The Portuguese also carried silver from the Spanish Philippines, which came across the Atlantic from Acapulco. From 1500 to 1800, Latin America produced 80 percent of the world's silver. The greatest source was the silver mines at Potosí in Peru (modern-day Bolivia).[5] Potosí silver was carried overland to Lima in a two-and-a-half month journey, then transported to Acapulco, and from there across the Pacific to Manila. Manila became one of the great marts of Asia as Portuguese from Macau, Chinese junks, and other Asian vessels arrived to pick up the silver, and additional items, such as sweet potatoes and maize, which largely made their way to China where they became a staple among the peasants, helping China meet the demands of intensive population growth in the seventeenth century. After Potosí's decline, other areas picked up production, especially Mexico. The Acapulco-Manila connection became the prime link in the silver-for-silk trade, allowing Macau to survive as a major entrepôt after it lost the Japanese trade in 1639. Chinese imports saturated the Latin American market: Chinese porcelains could be found in small shops throughout South America and Mexico.[6] Even Japanese exports made their way across the Pacific, and a recent five hundred-plus-page dissertation documents the influence of Japanese silk screens upon Mexican art in the seventeenth century.[7] For the Portuguese, the intra-Asian trade was far more profitable than the trans-Oceania trade that extended around the Cape Route between Europe and Asia, but the crown made its money from that route, approximately 65 to 70 percent of its income in the seventeenth century.[8] Similarly, Mexican and Manila merchants were the greatest beneficiaries of the Manila trade, though the Spanish crown made money off the portion of the Manila trade that was carried across Mexico to Vera Cruz then shipped to Spain.[9] The result of this global trade network that connected Asia to Europe and the Americas was the development of frontier cities in Asia.

Goa

Goa was a small city on the western coast of India on the dividing line between Hindu and Muslim India. (India already had several large cities, three with populations of over five hundred thousand people and several others over two hundred thousand.) The small port of Goa changed hands three times from 1356 to 1471 before the Portuguese took it in 1510. Goa initially was desirable for its access to one item: horses—it was the port at which horses were imported from Hormuz. It was not Portugal's only city on the Indian subcontinent, and not especially significant for European trade with India, but it was the most important Portuguese city in India. The Portuguese captured Goa for its fertile hinterlands, the city serving as the place to victual their Asian fleet before the long journey home around Africa, and it became the administrative capital for the "State of India," the Portuguese designation for their Asian empire. It became the religious capital as well, earning the nickname "the Rome of the Orient." Nevertheless, Goa's reach into Asia was limited.[10] To the east, the Portuguese merchants and local officials in China, Japan, and numerous other locales in the Spice Islands conducted trade and diplomacy, governing their cities with little interference from Goa. The Portuguese simply did not have the military power to assert themselves over their far-flung settlements, let alone against East Asians. The Indian Ocean was another matter. There, Portuguese officials used a deep ocean fleet to try to force Indians, East Africans, and others to trade only with them, and Goa had much administrative reach. Two other deep ocean fleets patrolled key locales in the Spice Islands, but these were more for protection of sea-lanes and trading communities than for use as offensive weapons.[11]

Both the Portuguese and the Spanish, unlike the French and English, perceived cities as essential to empire, providing the institutional and cultural framework for political and ecclesiastic administration.[12] By point of comparison, New England Puritans promoted the town structure, which came to define in many ways their course of settlement, but where Puritans did not predominate, as in the Chesapeake colonies, cities and towns had little importance. English urban building was largely a religio-cultural decision made by colonists, not a directive from the imperial government. In Pennsylvania, William Penn, of course, saw Philadelphia—a planned urban environment—as central to colony building, and later, Savannah, Georgia, was a planned urban environment; but outside of these two, cities were an inconsiderable part of English imperial designs, and in both of the aforementioned cases the choice to create a city was made by the colonies' private proprietors and not the crown.[13]

In the Portuguese empire, even where private interests predominated, the Portuguese established themselves by building cities. Outside of Brazil and

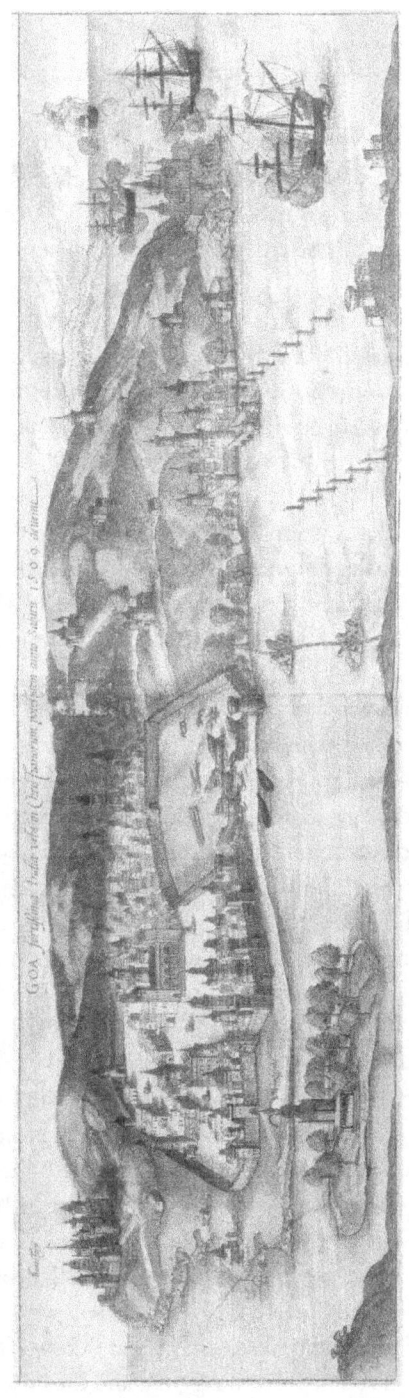

Figure 1.1. Goa, India, in 1509. From Georg Braun and Franz Hogenberg, *Civitates orbis terrarum* (Cologne, 1572–1617), I:57.

West Africa, these cities were not intended to command large areas of territory. The Portuguese imperial concern in Asia was to secure or create cities, and then connect one urban area to the next by sea. They usually began with fortified outposts (and not all of these evolved into cities). In Portuguese terms, a city must include an array of buildings: churches, convents, seminaries, a town council, but also the creation of a *câmara*, a municipal senate or council.[14]

Relatively few Portuguese inhabited these outposts and cities; only through mixed marriages could subsequent generations maintain a "Portuguese" population. Afonso de Albuquerque, who had conquered Goa, encouraged mixed marriage from the start.[15] In Goa, the new people became known as the Goans, though they called themselves "the descendants."[16] In essence, there were few "pure" Portuguese in their Asian empire—maybe 10,000 permanent residents, supplemented yearly by soldiers and sailors—some of whom were transient, some of whom remained. The Portuguese provided that a man could opt out of military service after two three-year terms if he married and became a local trader—he had to become a *casado*, a married householder.

Where fortifications evolved into cities, they became very much Portuguese cities. They modeled themselves on cities in Portugal in a variety of ways. They applied to Portugal for municipal status—forming a *câmara* and asking for the same privileges as those possessed by one of three cities in Portugal. For instance, Goa, which established a city government within months of conquest, asked for the rights of Lisbon, which they received.[17] The *câmara* of Goa wrote the Lisbon *câmara* for details on how to carry out their civic duties: Goa thus became the city most like Lisbon within the Portuguese empire. The *câmara* ran the Portuguese frontier city, but the crown appointed a Captain-General to command the city's military. He could attend council meetings and possessed two votes, but he was required to respect the rights and privileges of the citizens and could not interfere with the daily administration of the city. In practice, the *câmara* greatly influenced the military by offering advice and supplies. The *câmara* brooked little outside interference in local matters. Goa had a viceroy to oversee the State of India's affairs, but even he could interfere little with the city. In disputes taken to the crown, the *câmara* was likely to prevail, as when the viceroy tried to debase the currency. The *câmara* even challenged the Society of Jesuits and won.[18]

Within the city, all those who were *casados* were allowed to vote. Elections were scrupulously observed to prevent rigging, and the crown even reviewed results. After 1688, city officials were appointed by the crown, but the city sent forth a list to Lisbon of whom they would like appointed and the crown complied. Unlike in Lisbon, lawyers did not play a significant role in Goa's *câmara*, where merchants predominated.

What did the *câmara* do? It kept the speculators in line who controlled food supplies to the city, preserved public spaces, and oversaw the construction of shipyards and hospitals, as well as the collection of customs and the operation of the mint. Portuguese frontier cities, like Spanish ones, were highly regulated in terms of their architectural design. In Goa, the *câmara*, along with the ecclesiastics, saw to the transformation of buildings—both pre-conquest and post-conquest buildings—to make them conform architecturally. The *câmara* prescribed what building materials could be used. City houses were typically two stories, built of mortar and a tiled roof and painted red and white. The lower front had windows of polished oyster protected by railings. Each house had a yard. The beautiful city had a spectacular cathedral, built from 1562 to 1631, and many other impressive religious institutions. Within a decade the city was completely full of buildings, and people had to move outside the city walls. But the city also had two grave problems: water and refuse. City ponds and wells had bad water. There was no rubbish collection. Lagos (lakes), public squares, roads, and the riverbank became filled with filth. In the city's lagoon, an elephant was killed and left to rot, leading to the first, and one of the most severe, epidemics that struck the city nearly constantly. The population, which reached two hundred thousand in the seventeenth century, fell to twenty-two thousand by the end of that century—almost a 90 percent decline.[19] Part of this reduction was due to the economic decline of the Portuguese empire, particularly from the loss of the southern spice trade to the Dutch and later to the British. But many residents left the city to move to healthier sites. By 1834 only one thousand people were left in Goa, mostly the religious. Nevertheless, Goa and two other Indian cities, Daman and Diu, were kept by the Portuguese until annexed by India in 1961.

Macau

The origins of Macau in Southeast China are obscure. largely because the Portuguese who established the city were not acting in any official capacity, but were private traders. The Portuguese first entered China by 1519 but were pushed out in 1521. Traders continued to arrive for another thirty-plus years before reaching the sleepy fishing village that became Macau in 1553. Portuguese tradition posits that the Ming emperor allowed the Portuguese to stay because they had effectively defeated Chinese pirates, but it is unclear when the Chinese leadership actually learned that the Portuguese had established themselves at Macau.[20]

A *câmara* was not established until the early 1580s, which was approved by Goa, as Macau was part of the State of India. Yet Macau was not subservient to Goa, let alone Lisbon. The municipal authorities at Macau held more powers than any other city in the State of India, or even in Portugal, as the city effectively conducted its own foreign relations with the Chinese, Japanese, Dutch, and several Asian kings. Chinese officials refused to negotiate with the Portuguese Captain-General assigned to Macau; they would only treat with the *câmara*.

Was Macau even part of the Portuguese empire, or of China? Macau operated as a sovereign Portuguese city until the end of the twentieth century, but the realities of its location forced it to accede to Chinese demands in ways that undermined sovereignty. The Chinese believed they owned Macau, and the Portuguese lived there only by permission. The Chinese collected anchorage duties on all ships at Macau, and duties on all Chinese ships going in or out, and on Portuguese exports. Portuguese ships, however, did not pay duties on what they brought in; Macau charged those duties, which supported the city.

Just as the Chinese had allowed Persian and Arab trading communities a large degree of self-rule in the Middle Ages, the Portuguese largely governed themselves. Portuguese officials in Lisbon and Goa criticized Macau's subservience to China, but Macau knew what it had to do to survive. They paid land fees to the Chinese, and deftly handled the Chinese as they did their Portuguese masters. For instance, in 1621, the Chinese demanded the closure of a Jesuit college. The Portuguese at home and at Goa were militantly opposed. The Macaoans handled the situation as they usually did to reach a successful conclusion—they "simulated obedience," employed bribes, and negotiated compromise. The college stayed and life went on.[21]

The Portuguese crown provided almost no interference with Macau. Macau maintained the military, civil, and ecclesiastical presence with its own funds. It was largely politically independent because it did not rely economically on Portugal or the State of India. When Macau needed money, the *câmara* called on the householders for funds and borrowed from Chinese entrepreneurs. Even the King of Siam lent money to Macau in 1660.

Alternatively, Macau helped the Portuguese crown, as when it outfitted an expedition to relieve Malacca from Dutch attacks in 1640.

Why did the Chinese tolerate Portuguese Macau? For one, the Portuguese were no threat to the Chinese. As António Bocarro observed in 1635: "The peace that we have with the King of China is as he likes it, for since the place is so far from India, and since he has such vastly greater numbers of men than the most that the Portuguese could possibly assemble there, never did we think of breaking with him whatever serious grievances we may have had; because the Chinese have only to stop our food-supplies to ruin our city, since there is no other place nor means of obtaining any."[22] Macau utterly relied on commerce—its strength and its weakness. As a resident Jesuit noted in 1664, "The wealth of Macau consists of the sea . . . there being nothing of value other than what is brought by the wind and tides. If these fail, then everything else fails, nor is it possible for this Province with its missions to maintain itself in any other way."[23] The Chinese permitted Macau's existence as a Portuguese city because of trade.

Most important was the refusal of China and Japan to trade with one another in 1530. The Portuguese filled the void for almost a century, from the 1540s until 1639. Private Portuguese traders reached Japan in 1543. They introduced guns, which were rapidly reproduced. The Jesuits arrived in 1548 from Goa. Three years later the first Portuguese text was written about the Japanese. Jesuits became advisors to the Shogun, and the Japanese sent an embassy to the Pope. The Portuguese settled at the port of Nagasaki in 1571. Missionaries followed but were expelled in 1639. The unification of Japan into one nation and the change from the Ming to the Manchu dynasty in China led to the reopening of direct trade between China and Japan. The Japanese no longer needed the Portuguese. But with the drying up of the Japanese silver mines, the Portuguese no longer needed the Japanese, especially with silver from America arriving in Spanish Manila.[24]

Manila

Although the Spanish made a few inroads into Asia, such as at Formosa and Mindanao, they largely confined colony building to the Philippines, where they built the city of Manila.[25] Even more than the Portuguese, the Spanish perceived cities as both the starting point and the bastion of empire. Manila was the third attempt by the Spanish to build a city in the Philippines: the first lacked sufficient food supplies and was harassed by the Portuguese, the second was in a fertile area but difficult to supply. Manila was chosen in 1571 and proved an immense success with its ready supply of food and its superb harbor—one of the world's best, with secure anchorage for both domestic and international trade.[26]

At Manila the Spanish tapped into the traditional trade between China and the Philippines, but also between Japan and the Philippines. From a small town of two thousand Muslim Malaysians and a few Chinese, Manila grew to forty thousand by 1630. The largest growth was in the Chinese population, which reached twenty thousand in 1600, but fluctuated wildly in the seventeenth century between five thousand and thirty thousand residents because of periodic massacres by the Spanish and expulsions of non-Christian Chinese.[27]

The Japanese population in Manila was about three thousand in the 1620s, facilitating trade with Japan.[28] Few Filipinos lived in Manila, though they were periodically brought in as draft labor and, much later, as wage labor. The Spanish worked to organize Filipinos into Spanish-designed communities. Philip II issued ordinances in 1573 that provided the outline, as well as some detail, for establishing these communities. It took the Spanish three hundred years, but ultimately they succeeded by the late nineteenth century in forming over one thousand communities based on the original 1573 model.

Manila itself was organized on the standard Spanish grid pattern, boasting a great cathedral, many impressive pubic buildings, hundreds of two-story houses, and several monastic estates. A segregated city, the Spanish section of Manila was walled and heavily fortified and protected by a deep moat. In a single generation, Manila had become an impressive city. The Chinese lived in two quarters outside the walled Spanish section; the Spanish artillery kept their guns trained upon the main streets of the primary Chinese quarter of the city.[29] City ordinances provided that Chinese had to leave the walled enclave at night, though many did not do so, if for no other reason than their job needs. Chinese provided the bulk of the city's labor. They were the butchers and bakers, the domestics and farmers. They also were essential as translators and merchants for the Chinese junks that arrived to trade. The city could not function without its Chinese population, and thus, despite the periodic expulsions, violence, and massacres, the Chinese never left the Philippines. Non-Christian Chinese paid a tax to Manila officials that helped keep the city government afloat. It was no wonder that city officials opposed the home government's periodic expulsion of non-Christian Chinese. Moreover, the

Christian Chinese and the Chinese *mestizos* were highly valued by the city, and even won a land dispute against the Jesuits in 1667.[30]

Manila emerged as arguably the most important point in Asia, linking Europe and the Americas to the Far East. It quickly became the largest port in the world for Chinese goods and remained so for almost two hundred years until the last quarter of the eighteenth century. The end of the Spanish galleon trade from Mexico in 1815 effectively ended Manila's importance to China. Two to three million pesos of silver had arrived yearly from the Americas, with a peak of twelve million in 1597.[31] Yet from the viewpoint of Spanish imperial officials and merchants, the trade seemed almost disastrous, as the riches of the Americas were funneled to Asia, not to Spain, though some assured themselves that at least the silver was not going to European competitors. Twice, in 1593 and 1631, the king banned the China trade; the order was disregarded and ultimately rescinded. The Manila-Acapulco trade was the most highly regulated trade in the Spanish empire, but the regulations were poorly enforced. To prevent the drain of silver to China, the king banned the shipment of Peruvian silver to Mexico six times from 1640 to 1706.[32] The repetition of restrictions and regulations points to basic facts—the continued smuggling of silver from Peru to Mexico and the disregard of regulations for shipping silver from Mexico to the Philippines.[33]

The Spanish government and private interests opposed the silver drain to Manila because they did not benefit from it. The Philippines were administered by the Vice-Royalty of Mexico, which was responsible for the annual *situado*, the government funds that supported the Philippines, which were largely drawn from the import taxes collected at Acapulco on Manila's trade and thus were a remittance of Manila's money to Manila. Mexico both administered the Philippines and benefited from the Manila trade. Mexican merchants capitalized the silver-for-silk trade. Spain was too preoccupied and too distant from Manila to exert effective control.[34]

Spain occasionally considered giving up Manila. One proposal was to trade it to Portugal for Brazil, but elements of the church insisted on maintaining the Philippines as the base to effect the conversion of Asians. Ironically, in the early years, missionary efforts were not focused on Filipinos, but more on the Chinese, Japanese, and other Asians; thus Manila was seen as merely a jumping-off point for sending missionaries elsewhere in Asia. So many of the early missionaries sought martyrdom by going into improbable places to convert that church officials repeatedly had to instruct those going to Asia to not seek martyrdom and to pursue long-term success through a "long" life commitment to conversion.³⁵ Eventually, the missionaries had to be directed to forego their forays into China, Japan, and elsewhere and focus on the Philippines.

As noted above, smuggling was rampant, conducted by the yearly galleons that traveled between the Philippines and Mexico. There is some anecdotal evidence to suggest its extent. In 1635 and 1637 the Spanish crown decided to enforce its limitations on trade by actually inspecting the cargoes that arrived in Acapulco to see if they fell within the prescribed limits. Two ships per year were supposed to carry 250,000 pesos of value to Manila, with a return of 500,000 pesos for a 100 percent profit expected from Asia. But the 1637 inspection showed that the cargo was nearly four times the government-imposed limit. The Acapulco and Manila merchants complained to Spain over the inspections—that is, official interference with their trade—and Philip IV disallowed further inspections: he ordered that the regulations not be enforced.³⁶ Perhaps the Spanish had learned from the case of the Marques de Gelves, Mexico's new viceroy in 1624, who had tried to enforce Spanish trade regulations and was overthrown in Mexico. Later in the eighteenth century, when the Spanish barred the importation of Chinese silks into Manila, riots occurred in Manila and the ban was lifted.

As for the residents of Manila, they made money from the Mexico-Manila trade through the *boleta* system, which allowed each citizen to ship 125 pesos' worth of goods to Mexico, though the actual amount, it has been estimated, was about eight times greater. The large merchants purchased the *boleta* rights from other citizens, and eventually predominated as shippers, though even Chinese in Manila held *boletas* and continued to use them.

Manila was truly a frontier city for the Spanish: thousands of miles distant from New Spain, and halfway around the world from Spain. And it was a drain on Spanish resources. Not until the end of the nineteenth century, when Manila turned to tobacco production, did the islands begin to provide funds for the mother country. Curiously, Manila did not become the jumping-off point for Spanish territorial expansion in Asia. Unlike the Portuguese who went to the sources of valuable commodities, the Spanish preferred that traders come to them. They eschewed taking their goods to other Asian ports. Chinese junks arrived yearly, as did traders from Macau, the Moluccas, Malacca, and India. Some years the Macaoans nearly monopolized the trade: in the 1630s Manila's imports from Macau averaged £300,000 per year.³⁷ Even when Portugal and Spain were at war from 1640 to 1685, trade continued, though it was reduced between the Portuguese and Spanish in Asia.

The Spanish Frontier City

Forms were followed in all the frontier cities—paperwork filled out, reports sent home, and customs collected, but that is only a partial story of the whole in each case. Appearances were maintained. And the "appearance" of the city seemed an acquiescence to imperial directives. The city looked like it represented imperial authority, even as the locals often did as they pleased. As early as 1573 King Philip II sent detailed directives for the creation of Spanish cities, known as the "Royal Ordinances Concerning the Laying out of New Towns." These ordinances provided a blueprint for on-the-spot officials for constructing cities, creating a large degree of conformity in the Spanish empire—officials maintained appearances—because the frontier city, and hence the empire, should look Spanish, and it did.[38]

Philip II consulted an array of experts to formulate city plans, as they took consideration of meteorology, hygiene, military needs, religious requirements, engineering, and artistry. This, indeed, was urban planning which considered the context of building cities from scratch among foreign indigenous populations. For instance, chosen sites must be on vacant land and thus not harm "Indians or natives." Although the city was built for the benefit of the Spanish, one of its purposes was to civilize the natives of the area or region. During construction, natives must be kept away; in effect, the building would be somewhat secretive. The natives should not witness the process of construction inside city walls, "so that when the Indians see them [the buildings] they will be filled with wonder and realize that the Spaniards are settling there permanently and not temporarily."[39]

The Royal Ordinances set out precise measurements for plazas, and for symmetry in roads, which were to be placed according to the "four points of the compass," to protect them from the four principle winds. Arcades and sidewalks were included, as well as an even distribution of churches, with placement of the main church so that it could be used for the defense of the city. Two hospitals were prescribed, as well as their placement—one for the contagious and one for the non-contagious. To facilitate health, the slaughterhouses, tanneries, fisheries, and other operations that produced unhealthy by-products were to be situated for the easy disposal of their refuse. The plans directed creation of healthy places, including commons for recreation, and "courtyards and stockyards . . . as large as possible to insure health and cleanliness." Also, building lots and structures were located so that residents "can enjoy the air from the south and north, which are the best." Appearance was coupled with health and function. As in the Portuguese cities, Spanish buildings, particularly houses, were to conform to one another: "Settlers are to endeavor as far as possible to make all structures uniform, for the sake of the beauty of the town."[40]

As far as the process of construction, the inhabitants were to live in tents until the city was complete. After performing the proper measurements and laying out the location of roads, plazas, and buildings, first a ditch or palisade would be constructed to protect the city from Indians. The first buildings constructed were merchant houses and shops, to facilitate the conduct of business, by which a "moderate tax" on merchandise would provide funds for erection of the public buildings.[41]

Two other items of the ordinances should be noted: first, garbage would go into the sea or on a riverbank, and the tides or current would carry away refuse. Second, town lots would be distributed by lottery as a mark of fairness to householders.[42] What is remarkable about these Royal Ordinances is that they were followed in literally thousands of places in Latin America and the Philippines—not in every detail, but in the overall layout of urban spaces, whether in town or city.[43] If New Englanders wished to make their countryside look like England with fences, pastures, old world plants, and the like, the Spanish did the same with urban environments, planting a very Spanish concept of land use in the New World and the Philippines.

As far as the actual operation of Spanish frontier towns and cities, the Spanish *cabildo* was analogous to the Portuguese *câmara*. The biggest difference between the Spanish and the Portuguese was that the Spanish created closed municipal corporations, in some ways analogous to New England towns. But Spanish municipal posts could be bought and filled for a lifetime, and even be hereditary, whereas in Portuguese and English city and town governments, posts were elected. Also, Spanish cities were subjected to frequent inspection by visiting commissioners, or by an *audencia*, a royal official who oversaw compliance with the law. There was a similar position among the Portuguese, the *relaçao*, but rather infrequently employed.

Similarly for both the *câmaras* and *cabildos*, the municipal positions were valued by individuals for their status and the opportunity to confer patronage, rather than the salaries and stipends, which were low, but individuals also benefited from the various perks of office. The *câmaras* and the *cabildos*, along with the church, provided the sinews of urban life in the Iberian frontier cities.

* * *

When we compare frontier cities from one empire to another, we note that the city was central to the Portuguese and Spanish, but not to the English and French. The French understood the importance of urban environments, and, for instance, sent instructions to its colonies to conduct ritualistic celebrations and festivals, which were reminders to the colonists that they were part of the French empire; and these public occasions were to take place in the urbanized environments—Quebec and New Orleans, for example. But outside of Quebec, urbanization itself was not an imperative receiving imperial direction, but a natural outcome of economic and political needs.[44] The English crown, too, gave little direction to colonists regarding urbanization. The crowns did step into urban affairs if severe factionalism hindered internal peace and local administration. This occurred fairly commonly in the French empire, but also periodically in the English, Spanish, and Portuguese. Administrators or groups made appeals to the mother country to settle local disputes and the mother country complied. The mother country provided the stamp of legitimacy to the local populace, and thus could end severe and disruptive factionalism among city elites. But the status of the empire, its legitimacy, had limits. Cities overthrew administrators appointed by the mother country, as occurred in Boston, New York, Charles Town, Mexico City, Acapulco, and elsewhere. And imperial authorities usually acquiesced to these fait accompli.

Commerce was the lifeblood of the frontier city. Trade was highly regulated within all the empires, yet imperial restrictions were largely disregarded when colonists could get away with it, which was frequently. Too much coast, too few cruisers to enforce regulations, and too many officials compliant with smugglers led the frontier cities to carry on commerce at their will. Without significant commerce, frontier outposts could not develop into cities. If an outpost's purpose was merely administrative and military and failed to attract population through economic activity, it remained but an outpost. On the coast of the Gulf of Mexico, St. Augustine, Pensacola, and Mobile are examples of fortified outposts that had administrative duties but never became cities in the early modern period because commerce did not sufficiently develop. If a city did develop and commerce severely fell off, as occurred in Goa and several other Portuguese cities in Asia, as well as Spanish Vera Cruz in Mexico, then the cities declined into insignificance. The frontier city had to maintain external commerce or become surrounded by a flourishing hinterland for which it could provide urban services.

The frontier cities largely controlled their own political affairs and internal regulations. Local officials and colonists understood what they had to do for the empire, and what they could get away with. I suggest that as long as a city contributed to the military demands of empire, especially when real need occurred in other parts of the empire, the mother countries were not apt to have sustained interference with self-government and disregard of trade laws. Macau, Goa, and Manila all substantially contributed to military expeditions for their empires. The same can be said of Boston, Charles Town, and even Quaker Philadelphia.[45] Colonists excelled at keeping appearances: they knew when to obey, and how to simulate obedience, so they could practice self-rule. Some trade regulations had to be followed, others could be stretched or disregarded. Imperial governments and their frontier cities generally accommodated each other's interests.

CHAPTER 2

Colonial Projects and Frontier Practices:
The First Century of New Orleans History

Daniel H. Usner, Jr.

On August 29, 2005, Matthew Broderick, the commander of the Homeland Security Operations Center in Washington, D.C., did not believe the early reports he was hearing that floodwalls had been breached in New Orleans. After all, the Army Corps of Engineers itself seemed to confirm that overtopping was the only source of rising water in Crescent City neighborhoods. Still undecided, the former U.S. Marine general saw a late Monday afternoon news report on CNN: The network broadcasted a scene from Bourbon Street, where some people were apparently partying. "The one data point that I really had, personally, visually, was the celebration in the streets of New Orleans, of people drinking beer," Broderick recalled. So with this image from the French Quarter as sufficient evidence that the city had dodged the bullet of Hurricane Katrina, the Homeland Security administrator went to bed that night confident that no walls or levees had broken.[1]

One month later, federal officials were themselves trying to dodge bullets, in the form of mounting charges about their own irresponsible and incompetent behavior. The Federal Emergency Management Agency director Michael Brown told congressmen, "My biggest mistake was not recognizing by Saturday that Louisiana was dysfunctional." Tragically, these words were all too easily believed by too many people inside as well as outside the state—sufficient proof, like the party on Bourbon Street viewed by Broderick on August 29, that the United States government owed nothing more or better to New Orleans. Reflecting on what he saw as long-term, global threads of connection, one U.S. Senator from Idaho was absolutely certain that the government of New Orleans had always been the most corrupt in our country. "Fraud is in the culture of Iraqis," Larry Craig told reporters, and "I believe that is true in Louisiana as well."[2]

Where people look when they watch New Orleans and *what* they expect to find can make a big difference, even becoming a matter of life or death for too many Hurricane Katrina victims. So, like the city's post-Katrina inhabitants and infrastructure, the history of New Orleans's image and reputation demands renewed attention. The peculiar location of New Orleans in the American imagination—as celebrated by its natives with pride and enjoyed by its visitors for profit—has long been taken for granted. Growing up there, insiders learn how unique their past is. Seduced by touristic promotion, outsiders expect to visit the most un-American city in all of America. And the Big Easy delivers! Whether playing up the "Frenchness" of the French Quarter, the "looseness" of Latin politics, or the "openness" of sensual pleasure, New Orleans performs exuberantly for the rest of the nation and for the rest of the world.

Historians know to be cautious about uniqueness, as it is a quality possessed by every person, group, place, event, or period that we might select for investigation. Yet we also understand that comparisons and connections make what we study truly worthwhile.[3] Therefore, not even a place as uncommon as New Orleans is so exceptional or exotic that it cannot contribute to a stronger knowledge about central themes and issues in American history. Recent studies have shown that the "Frenchness" or "Spanishness" of Louisiana's colonial background made less of a difference than previously thought. Particular features of the early population and of the region itself, more importantly, permitted certain forms of cultural interaction to last longer here than in other colonies that would become parts of the United States: it was a frontier city, an environment conducive to mixing, a gathering place remote from imperial minders. New Orleans, furthermore, became a nineteenth-century immigrant city not unlike New York and Boston—the most important difference being the size and influence of its African American population. Yet until recently, the exoticization and marginalization of the city's past caused historians to overlook how central it is for understanding such mainstream processes as territorial expansion and immigration. Whether looking at early advocacy for civil rights by free people of color or at the violent reaction of white supremacists to Reconstruction, no nineteenth-century city was more influential on the national scene than New Orleans. For the study of machine politics, reformism, urban sprawl, white flight, and desegregation, among other topics, the Crescent City is an essential example of major trends in twentieth-century American history.[4]

Even in the reliance on representing itself as a unique city, New Orleans is not as unusual or anomalous as we might think. By the end of the nineteenth century, many regions and cities turned to tourism as a means of profiting from cultural traditions and special attractions. While historians of the Crescent City are now explaining that much of its otherness and quaintness was self-consciously constructed over the years, attention to tourism and boosterism in other American places is showing how many different communities have exploited and distorted their pasts for the sake of self-promotion.[5] The risks and costs of this process, however, can be higher in some cases than in others. And New Orleans might be paying an inordinate price for the success of its imagined location in American fantasy and fun.

Perhaps the truly outstanding feature of New Orleans history is how its natural environment and its human population have interacted with each other over the centuries. Its location on the map turns out to be far more valuable than its location in the historical imagination. No other coastal delta in the world arguably has been inhabited by as expansive a mix of migrants as those reaching south Louisiana. Beginning with Native Americans in Late Archaic times, the influx of Frenchmen, Africans, Canadians, Acadians, Canary Islanders, Haitians, Anglo-Americans, African Americans, Irish, Germans, Croatians, Sicilians, Filipinos, Texans, Cubans, Vietnamese, and now Latinos has profoundly shaped the culture in and around New Orleans. Sustainable and unsustainable uses of the environment, creative and destructive relationships with it, all together contributed to the Crescent City's fame and shame—usually in unforeseen and unpredictable ways. But it is the incomparable interaction between the working-class culture and the bountiful wetlands of south Louisiana—for livelihood and recreation—that largely explains the city's special blend of sights, sounds, and flavors today.

Twenty-first-century New Orleans offers many essential lessons about environmental management, urban sprawl, quality of life, public policy, race relations, governmental responsibility, and, yes, even self-representation—which apply to most American cities. As Billy Sothern wrote, "The story of New Orleans following Hurricane Katrina is, even though it may be hard to accept, the story of America at the beginning of a new millennium."[6] Although Americans, especially those who call themselves New Orleanians, have wanted to see the city as different, even as exotic, now more than ever we need to realize how representative much of its history really is.

The commonplace perception of eighteenth-century New Orleans hardly makes the city seem typical. Shadowy barons, backwoodsmen, prison girls, privateers, quadroon partners, and voodoo queens have filled both popular and scholarly accounts of the region's formative years, separating its colonial past sharply from that of other parts of the United States. French and Spanish influences upon the Gulf Coast serve to explain everything from carnival to carnal sin to corruption, causing contemporary residents alternately to cherish and curse their peculiar colonial progenitors. The quaintness and remoteness of colonial Louisiana, more than incidentally, also contributed to the New Orleans allure for visitors and other outsiders seeking an un-American destination still located inside the United States. Tourists entering the World's Industrial and Cotton Centennial Exposition in 1884–1885 were informed by an official guidebook that "New Orleans . . . having been so far removed in its earlier history from the rest of the colonies, and during its occupancy by the Spanish and French—took to itself usages, customs and even a patois of its own, the story of which has furnished material for romances equaled by few other cities in this country."[7]

With a reputation so romantically appealing, how could Louisiana's colonial past ever reveal anything meaningful about early America? How could eccentric Frenchmen and Spaniards compare in importance with the English founders of Jamestown and Plymouth? Thankfully, historians now understand how the eighteenth-century Lower Mississippi Valley does not match the old images of that place and time. New research on settlement patterns, economy, Indian-colonial relations, African American slavery, gender, family life, and print culture challenges many common assumptions about the exceptionalism of the region's colonial past—in a phrase, these studies see New Orleans as a frontier city with characteristics reminiscent of the other places described in this volume. Simplistic notions about early New Orleans, however, persist in American popular and literary culture, still operating to minimize its importance in American history.

Treating early New Orleans as a frontier city in the eighteenth-century Atlantic World can break through these barriers. The tendency to treat the city's distinctive features as the legacy of its French and Spanish regimes is a trope that originated with Anglo-American observers in the early nineteenth century. Historical narratives of the city ever since then routinely open with these visitors' accounts of its odd appearance, contrasting its heterogeneous population with a homogenized mental image of the (English-speaking) Atlantic seaboard. But as part of an urban frontier, eighteenth-century New Orleans is not an anomaly but instead an especially instructive example of common patterns and processes in the Atlantic World. To find its value, however, we have to revise the model provided by Richard Wade fifty years ago.

Richard Wade's central thesis in *The Urban Frontier*, that "towns were the spearheads of the frontier," all too readily dismisses the role that non-English colonists as well as Native Americans played in the Mississippi Valley. "Planted far in advance of the line of settlement," Wade argues, the towns of Pittsburgh, Lexington, Louisville, and Cincinnati "held the West for the approaching population." Not needing any explicit definition, readers understand who is meant by "the approaching population." This assumption is reinforced throughout the early pages of the book by scattered statements about the region being "merely the haunt of Indian and animal," where "the French spun a loose web of forts and fur-trading posts." Sure, Wade acknowledges that the "story of Western urbanism" began "not where one might expect, at the foot of the Appalachians, but rather in the remoteness of the Mississippi Valley." But he then proceeds to emphasize the "slow growth," "French customs," and "curious mixture" of St. Louis's population. And where does New Orleans appear in Wade's study? Granted he focuses on the Ohio and Upper Mississippi Valleys as a coherent region unto itself. But important lessons implicit in the early development of New Orleans go completely unnoticed because it plays only a faint and distant role in Wade's analysis—as the port for goods produced by his prized network of river cities.[8]

Richard Wade nevertheless provides some invaluable insights for anyone wishing to include New Orleans in a comparative analysis of frontier cities. His towns' economic structures were shaped by their respective positions in a wider economy, what he calls the "outside world." He also observes that military garrisons and mobilizations were instrumental in stimulating commerce in these frontier cities. Policing marketplaces and the behavior of slaves, according to Wade, comprised some of the earliest town ordinances in the trans-Appalachian West. Wade finds that "wage earners were not a static class," and "in a loosely structured society, boundaries between groups were never rigid." "Urban conditions and the hiring-out custom," he also notes, "put severe strains on the structure of slavery."[9] These are helpful cues for anyone interested in the early history of New Orleans.

The exotic reputation of early New Orleans stems from the tension between desired colonial projects and the realities of frontier cities that was rather common in the Atlantic World between 1500 and 1800. As Shannon Dawdy has recently explained in *Building the Devil's Empire*, expectations for New Orleans were overly idealized because of particular circumstances around its founding. The Crescent City began as a company town meticulously planned by royal engineers under the influence of Enlightenment rationality. "It will not be as easy to execute as it was to draw it on paper," Father Pierre Charlevoix soberly wrote in January 1722 when two hundred people were camping on the banks of the Mississippi and waiting for royal engineer Adrien de Pauger to draw a construction plan for them to follow. The Jesuit had actually crossed Lake Pontchartrain from the Gulf Coast on a boat with Pauger, and although he saw only about a hundred huts and a wooden warehouse doubling as a church upon reaching "this famous town they call New Orleans," Charlevoix apparently had caught the engineer's optimism. "This wild and deserted place that canes and trees still cover almost entirely," he predicted, "will be one day, and perhaps that day is not far off, an opulent city and the metropolis of a great and rich colony."[10] In September of that same year, New Orleans was struck by a hurricane, and most of its buildings were blown down. But chief engineer Le Blond de la Tour actually expressed some relief, because all of the damaged and destroyed structures had been out of alignment with his new plan. They "would have had to be demolished" anyway, he reported.[11]

It is safe to say that residents in most colonial towns disappointed authorities in metropolitan centers, especially during the earliest years of settlement. As Ann Laura Stoler and Frederick Cooper have written about later empires, "colonial regimes were neither monolithic nor omnipotent." The production of information that we now discover in colonial archives, therefore, was determined by "competing agendas for using power, competing strategies for maintaining control, and doubts about the legitimacy of the venture" among metropolitan rulers and publics as well as among colonial bureaucrats and settlers.[12] So reports of disorderly departure from desired plans are found everywhere, but the case of New Orleans reveals how local features gave particular shape to such a perception. While Jean-Baptiste Le Moyne de Bienville was still cutting the first river cane at the selected site, this new town became an entrepôt for a highly heterogeneous array of immigrants. Canadian, French, German, and Senegalese arrivals immediately began to improvise ways of survival and adaptation in this strange world. The diversity in background and status among Europeans themselves and the relatively high number of imported slaves posed plenty of frontier challenges to official planners inside and outside New Orleans. Cost-cutting measures taken by colonial investors only exacerbated tensions between groups encountering each other for the first time. During the 1720s, for example, numerous African slaves were apprenticed to European carpenters and blacksmiths in order to facilitate construction of the town and expansion of commerce. Even those artisans who took in enslaved apprentices, however, could anticipate the deleterious effects on their later income, admitting that they "do not seek to perfect the negroes in their trades." Employment of slaves as skilled workers naturally lowered the wages of free craftsmen and heightened their resentment toward African workers.[13] The city's heavy dependence on neighboring American Indian villages for all kinds of assistance made matters even more complicated, with plenty of uncertainty accompanying the valuable foodstuffs and services provided by Acolapissas, Chaouchas, Houmas, and Chitimachas throughout the eighteenth century. The same group of Indians recruited by officials to catch runaway slaves on one occasion could just as easily fraternize with slaves on another.[14]

In addition to the composition of the town's population, environmental features of its location played an important role in shaping what I call "frontier exchange" behavior. A hundred miles of winding river and shifting silt between New Orleans and the mouth of the Mississippi River made for a treacherous "front door" to Atlantic commerce, requiring ships to travel and wait for up to six weeks. But Lake Pontchartrain and Bayou St. John behind the city offered a convenient "back door" to the Gulf of Mexico, thereby encouraging an intercoastal network of trade that would trouble colonial control. Ecological conditions of the new town and its outskirts also facilitated "back-of-town" improvisation among residents and itinerants. Wetlands and waterways protected acts of defiance and resistance, while connecting the city easily to a wider hinterland network of fluid exchange activity.[15]

Contested uses of Bayou St. John quickly became a complex and enduring theme in the history of New Orleans. Because of the access to Lake Pontchartrain afforded by this bayou, Bienville told Company officials in 1726 that "it cannot be esteemed too highly." But in order to improve navigation on Bayou St. John, "it would be necessary to clear it out, that is to say to remove from it all the tree trunks with which it is filled and even blocked in many places and to fell all the trees that hang over the banks and threaten to fall into it." One settler on the bayou was already eager to undertake this improvement—if Company equipment would be provided and additional land would be granted to him—but seasonal overflow of adjacent land would also need to be managed by the creation of man-made drainage ditches.[16] So began the vicious environmental cycle of deforestation and flood-control that would plague New Orleans into the twenty-first century, along with socioeconomic conflict between commercial and common interests.

New Orleans was inhabited by 25 percent of Louisiana's entire colonial population by the end of its first decade. "The number of little inhabitants who carry on no other business here than of trading," the Superior Council complained in 1725, undermined efforts to "find a servant or a workman to work in the fields that are in cultivation."[17] The mix of people living in bondage in and around New Orleans only made the maintenance of order and discipline more difficult. In 1726 the town by itself was home to seventy-eight African slaves, thirty American Indian slaves, and sixty European indentured servants—altogether comprising nearly 20 percent of New Orleans's core population. Contributing even further to this ethnic diversity of coerced laborers and craftsmen was the fact that the rest of the urban population included 130 soldiers stationed in New Orleans that same year. For the imperial planners of an orderly society, interaction across so many lines proved doubly threatening. If not fearing collaboration among groups with varied reasons for discontent and rebellion, they were troubled by violence between individuals whose differences in status and origin were often aggravated by excessive drinking.[18]

In late September of 1739 four soldiers deserted from their post at Bayou St. John, absconding with a sailboat and their commanding officer's trunk. Somehow they even managed to take four enslaved men and two enslaved women along with them onto Lake Pontchartrain. Lieutenant Henri de Louboey believed that this supposed confiscation of slaves by deserters had been instigated by a boatman who worked for a pitch and tar manufacturer on the north shore. Several settlers and soldiers were dispatched to pursue these fugitives, but found only their hastily abandoned boat near Pea Island. It contained two bottles of brandy, some old clothing, an army musket, and still-warm smoking pipes, together with traces of blood "indicating some quarrel that had taken place among these brigands." The next day, travelers in a pirogue from Biloxi found the remains of a man half-eaten by alligators. Louboey assumed this was one of the missing who had been killed by his companions and dumped into the sea. Nine Biloxi Indians assisted the search party along Bay St. Louis, to no avail. The deserters probably wanted to reach Spanish Pensacola, but the possibility of their being lost in coastal marshlands motivated the lieutenant "to send men acquainted with the region, who know all these windings and turnings because they have long hunted there, in order to try to find them so as to make as severe an example of them as the case deserves." Seven years later, it was learned from two runaway slaves—stowaways on a royal ship headed for Cuba who were arrested and returned to Louisiana—that a small neighborhood in Havana was inhabited by the very same soldiers and slaves who had fled New Orleans' back-of-town in 1739.[19]

Not long ago, this eighteenth-century New Orleans story would have neatly fit into an American nationalist narrative that explained the fluidity and permeability across cultural lines as simply a quaint sign of French and Spanish imperialism in a land that Providence intended for an Anglo-American empire. Such episodes might be cited to prove that the French, in contrast with the English, lacked the vigor necessary for successful colonization, thereby reinforcing notions about Louisiana's dysfunctional origins. But thanks to works on British North America from Peter Wood's *Black Majority* to Jill Lepore's *New York Burning*, our understanding of these matters has been drastically altered. Lowcountry Atlantic-seaboard towns like Charleston and Savannah obviously shared demographic, economic, and environmental circumstances with this Gulf Coastal town, and we now know that Chesapeake Bay and Mid-Atlantic ports likewise generated the kind of intercultural exchange that troubled New Orleans officials. In most Atlantic World frontier cities, a mixture of coastal and interior trade generated networks of exchange and migration that transgressed intercultural and intercolonial boundaries. Even in late seventeenth-century Massachusetts Bay Colony, the "experience of ye Indians Coming Dayly to Boston upon the occasions of Market & otherwise" warranted another in a series of attempts at legislative prohibition.[20]

New Orleans in the middle of the eighteenth century, therefore, actually resembled other Atlantic World ports, irrespective of their national affiliations. When an anonymous visitor from France described how "the inhabitants, sailors, Indians, and slaves run around freely inside as well as beyond the town," he echoed observations made, at one time or another, about Montreal, Boston, New York, Philadelphia, and Charleston. And his passing of judgment over the Crescent City's rabble likewise followed a familiar pattern: "They meet in a multitude of negro cabarets frequented by slaves who have fled their plantations either due to laziness or want, and who survive by trading stolen goods."[21] A Philadelphia grand jury, by way of comparison, complained in 1744 about an area called "Hell Town," where taverns serving "strong liquor" attracted "Apprentices, Servants and even negroes." Just upriver from the center of Philadelphia, between the Delaware River and Third Street, this was a space busy with exchange and entertainment among residents of North America's largest colonial city. For some time, workers in various conditions of temporary and permanent bondage had appropriated fairs held every May and November in Philadelphia as a customary occasion for them to take time off for excessive amusement. By 1775 these festivities were outlawed by the provincial assembly because they tended to "debauch the Morals of the People." Throughout the eighteenth century, however, taverns and bawdyhouses in Philadelphia continued to provide places where, as the *Pennsylvania Gazette* reported on August 8, 1787, "all the loose and idle characters of the city, whether whites, blacks or mulattoes . . . indulge in riotous mirth and dancing till the dawn."[22]

Particular features of New Orleans' physical environs, perhaps more so than for other colonial towns, seemed to play a notable role in enhancing frontier exchange. As that anonymous French observer added to his mid-century description, "They meet in the thick and intruding woods that border the town almost all around."[23] In a 1763 report to the Superior Council, attorney general Nicolas Chauvin de Lafrenière placed much of the blame for criminal activity, as well as for Louisiana's economic weakness, on illicit trade being promoted back-of-town by colonists who strayed from colonial plans:

> The rear of the City is infested with numbers of men without occupation. The just and severe ordinances of our Kings have always provided for the expulsion [of such people] from the Cities. These people require constant attention and deserve the utmost severity. Most of them were brought here at the cost of the King and lodged and fed on the plantations at his expense. The object was to establish cultivators on a rich and fertile soil and to provide the City through these people with the necessities of life. Living here they defeat the consummation intended, they increase the cost of living, they are the first at the markets and are consumers instead of creators.[24]

Groups of people who lived around New Orleans, this description also suggests, were as instrumental in sustaining the frontier-city conditions as were town residents themselves, ensuring that ordinary practices would continue to upset official plans throughout the eighteenth century. The black majority enslaved on nearby plantations developed important social and economic connections to the city, moving back and forth as peddlers, hired workers, and runaways.[25] Several American Indian communities situated near New Orleans were also tied to the town's market and public life. Before Europeans appeared in the Lower Mississippi Valley, Indian people had used the area that became New Orleans as a portage for seasonal gathering and traveling. Camps were built on narrow natural levees and on shell mounds, with larger settlements situated on higher ground. But after 1718, the site of New Orleans became an even busier nexus of Indian activity. Acolapissas, Houmas, Chitimachas, Tunicas and other nearby villagers regularly spent time in the colonial city selling foodstuffs and furs and even working for wages.[26] After delegates from the Biloxis and other small nations met with Governor Jean-Jacques-Blaise d'Abbadie on one June day in 1764, "they assembled near New Orleans to play ball and for diversions, attracting there numerous spectators." A space behind the city had become the grounds where Indian visitors often played stickball, otherwise known as lacrosse, which soon became the Crescent City's most popular team sport. White, black, and mixed teams of "raquette" athletes competed before large crowds throughout the nineteenth century, representing a cultural legacy of frontier exchange in New Orleans only to be forgotten later by its residents.[27]

The middle decades of the eighteenth century saw very little immigration to New Orleans, thus providing a valuable example of how marginality in the empire could also influence a frontier city's social and economic life. Interethnic patterns of exchange within the city—and between it and outlying communities—solidified into local customs through a process of creolization. Social interaction among multiple groups, in and around an urban space occupied by a slowly growing population, optimized conditions for the generation of new foodways, speechways, and other creole practices, creating that now famous cultural gumbo into which future groups of immigrants would add their own ingredients. But as Jennifer Spear has recently demonstrated, colonial elites during this same period directed instruments of law and order more aggressively against slaves and tried to racialize their own status as white.[28] Nonetheless many of these merchant-planters committed to policing slaves' behavior were themselves perceived as unruly, taking advantage of metropolitan neglect and engaging in illicit commerce. Frontier exchange practices among the various residents of New Orleans continued to destabilize colonial projects, to the chagrin of colonial officials like governor Louis Billouart de Kelérec's secretary who wrote in 1761, "The marked independence of the inhabitants has always been their greatest vice." Making imperial control even more difficult, the Superior Council of Louisiana by mid-century was occupied mainly by creole (born in the colony) planters and merchants from the New Orleans area. "The group which should be the instrument for the maintenance of the king's authority," as Thiton de Silègue reported to the minister of marine, "acts in truth just like the others. From this spirit of independence in all the classes, there come cabals, intrigues, and muttering."[29]

After France ceded Louisiana to Spain, protection of these autonomous economic and political practices motivated the colony's merchant-planter elite to lead an open rebellion in 1768. But even before that military effort would erupt and quickly fail, the very last French colonial governor was attempting to explain New Orleans' reputation for independence. In a June 7, 1764 letter to the minister of marine, Governor d'Abbadie attributed "the disorder which has been in this colony for a long time" to the colonists' passion for speculation and to the natural bounty of the land. "Immodest consumption of tafia [rum]" also contributed. Inhabitants were used to trading feverishly in both currencies and commodities, even selling merchandise bought from royal storehouses back to the King. Meanwhile, farmers were supposedly made "lazy" by "the facility with which the land renders its natural products." "Out of this kind of life," concluded this new governor, "there came an independent attitude and insubordination." In a petition just handed to him by a group of merchants, d'Abbadie saw the latest "signs of the traits of sedition and insubordination." And in the margins of this document complaining against recent changes in commercial policy, d'Abbadie responded to the petitioners' grievances point-by-point. "Everyone wants to go into trading, which is kind of speculation," he scribbled on the side of their protest against Indian trade being granted exclusively to one company. "Nobody wants to become a farmer." He then dismissed the colonists' plea of loyalty to the King by asking, "Don't people know the problems that self-interest, extravagance, and speculation on every item imaginable have caused in the colony?"[30]

Migration into and through New Orleans began to accelerate significantly under Spanish rule, and the newest groups actually added to this Atlantic World port's diversity and fluidity. After 1763, thousands of Acadians and Isleños settled upriver and downriver on the Mississippi and eventually along adjacent waterways.[31] More than twelve thousand slaves also arrived in Louisiana during the Spanish period. Mostly African in birth, they were trans-shipped to New Orleans from Jamaica, Dominica, Martinique, and other Caribbean colonies.[32] All of these newcomers found the frontier exchange economy in and around New Orleans to be beneficial during their adjustment to the Lower Mississippi Valley. Their own strategies of adaptation and resistance tended to reinforce the frontier city's pivotal role in backcountry networking. During the American Revolution, mobilization of soldiers from Cuba for Spain's campaigns against Great Britain's towns and garrisons in West Florida added substantially to illicit interactions. Creole practices carried by soldiers and slaves from Havana even began to influence New Orleans music and dance.[33] Spanish colonial law made manumission of slaves much easier than French law did, so the last third of the eighteenth century saw a dramatic growth in the size and prosperity of the city's free people of color. As an increasingly distinct social group in this urban frontier, free Blacks further diversified its already heterogeneous society.[34]

For merchants, planters, and officials committed to expanding production in Louisiana for Atlantic World commerce, the perpetuation of frontier-city exchange among its inhabitants became less and less tolerable. Efforts to impose order and discipline, therefore, became more effective as law enforcement escalated. During the last three decades of the eighteenth century, as the imperial officers tightened their grip, New Orleans was the primary locus of rising vigilance and punishment. Intercultural exchange practices consequently grew much riskier. Campaigns against runaway camps, restrictions against marketing activity, and prohibitions against slaves' movement began to alter the social landscape of the New Orleans area. A large maroon community in swamps east of town was destroyed by a military expedition in 1784, and a runaway slave named Juan St. Malo and other leaders were executed in present-day Jackson Square.[35] The influx of some twelve thousand African, Caribbean, and American slaves into Louisiana between 1804 and 1812 (in addition to nearly ten thousand white, free-black, and enslaved refugees from Haiti) further heightened anxiety over rebellion and intensified police vigilance.[36] As long as slavery existed, however, runaway-slave camps would continue to form in back-of-town wetlands, utilizing the legacy of networks from the freer, frontier-city days. And the eighteenth-century fugitive named St. Malo would be immortalized as a heroic freedom-fighter in the songs of nineteenth-century slaves and, more recently, in the poetry of Brenda Marie Osbey.[37]

By 1810 New Orleans was a city of 17,200, making it the fifth largest city in the United States and the largest in the trans-Appalachian West. (The entire Orleans Territory—what became the state of Louisiana two years later—had a population of 42,000.) Expansion of cotton and sugar agriculture and entrenchment of plantation slavery did more than anything else to transform this frontier town into a commercial center. The "front door" became far more important than the "back door" to Crescent City merchants, as more and more ships traveled up and down the Mississippi. Construction of the Carondelet Canal during the 1790s, however, did make transportation through Lake Pontchartrain and Bayou St. John easier and more profitable by bringing the bayou's water closer to town via a man-made connection and a turn-around basin. With a dual purpose of facilitating traffic along Bayou St. John and of helping drain New Orleans streets into the same bayou, it is little wonder that a French traveler noticed within a few years of its completion how "it is already so choked with mud that it can only be used by small pirogues."[38]

In light of what happened on August 29, 2005, however, it is also worth noting that the Carondelet Canal cut through a natural ridge that had protected city residents from Lake Pontchartrain. Lake water pushed by high winds or hurricanes into Bayou St. John would henceforth more easily flow toward occupied parts of town. Control over this "improved" waterway and drainage system reduced illicit trade activity among common residents and sojourners, but also introduced a new environmental hazard.[39] Political incorporation of Louisiana by the United States beginning on December 30, 1803, meanwhile, bolstered military and judiciary power over free and enslaved people still trying to maintain their own exchange network. In this regard, back-of-town New Orleanians resembled contemporaneous working people in Richmond, Virginia. A canal and basin diverting traffic around the James River falls, constructed during the late 1790s, immediately became the locus of interaction among slaves, free whites and free blacks. Public officials consequently heightened police vigilance over this area.[40]

The incorporation of New Orleans and the rest of lower Louisiana into the United States, as the newly created Orleans Territory, at first introduced new volatility and possibility for race relations inside and around the Crescent City. Peter Kastor has carefully explained for all of Orleans Territory how "White Louisianians, slaves, Indians, free people of color, and even malcontent Americans all attempted to realize their vision of a reconstituted Louisiana, in the process creating an atmosphere of uncertainty and potential violence." But as he discloses in detail, mobilization of stronger martial and legal forces by the federal government of the United States steadily hardened barriers and restrictions against the region's network of frontier exchange, while denying all people of color any means of participation in political democracy.[41]

A brief look at issues confronting the Orleans territorial government during its first year of administration reveals how quickly this process unfolded.

At first, General James Wilkinson was confident that free men of color in their own militia were more attached to the new government of the United States than were white militiamen, many of whom were still expressing their attachment to France. Fifty-five free men of color had already delivered an address to William Claiborne, soon to be governor of this new territory, offering their services "as a Corps of Volunteers agreeable to any arrangement which may be thought expedient." But Wilkinson also feared that people of color with firearms, if roused by a single incendiary, "might produce those Horrible Scenes of Bloodshed & rapine, which have been so frequently noticed in St Domingo."[42] An apprehensive response to the Haitian Revolution profoundly shaped American officials' perception of the Louisiana Purchase. For the time being, Secretary of War Henry Dearborn decided to recognize this organization of free black volunteers in New Orleans, but advised Claiborne to reduce its size "if it can be done without giving offense." Claiborne appointed two prominent white men to command the battalion of free men of color, but "a great dislike between the white Natives of Louisiana, and the free men of colour" caused persistent concern.[43]

Also troubling the territorial government early in 1804 were activities in the city's public ballrooms and on its docks. With dances held twice a week during the winter season, "a very heterogenous Mass" was gathering quite frequently. As Claiborne reported, white men paying fifty cents at the door met "Ladies of every Rank [who] attend these assemblies in great numbers. Toward the end of the Spanish regime, "a Strong guard was Stationed at the Ball room, and on the first appearance of disorder the persons concerned were committed."[44] Meanwhile, shipments of slaves from the Caribbean into Orleans Territory worried Claiborne even more deeply. "Notwithstanding all my vigilance," he reported to Mayor Jean Etienne Boré, "some improper and dangerous persons have been introduced into the Country." Inspectors were boarding ships downriver from New Orleans, but the belief among citizens "that a great, very great supply of Slaves is essential to the prosperity of Louisiana" posed serious obstacles to this vigilance.[45]

Things really heated up for United States officialdom during the summer of 1804. When a printer was handed a letter inviting free people of color to assemble "for the purpose of Memorializing Congress," white New Orleanians furiously demanded punishment of the perpetrators—free black men who had the audacity to think that incorporation into the American republic just might bring them some political rights. Thinking "that in a Country where the negro population was so great the Less noise that was made about this occurance the better," Governor Claiborne met with a few of the most influential free men of color to "express in pointed terms my disapprobation of the letter to the printer and of their contemplated meeting." Although "inquietude" among whites over this event began to subside and the governor was sure there was "nothing to fear either from the Mulatto or Negro population," he nevertheless expected that sometime in the future "the Misfortunes of St. Domingo" would occur in "this quarter of the Union." As he confessed, "Slavery Where ever it exists is a galling yoke." Slave insurrection would be hastened, however, if the United States Congress accommodated the will of most Louisiana planters and allowed continuation of the foreign slave trade.[46] In clamoring "that the Territory cannot prosper without a great increase of Negro's," as Claiborne reported directly to Jefferson, Americans joined Louisianians to demand another few years of "uninterrupted Trade to Africa," although he "frequently instanced the Horrors of St. Domingo, & reminded them of the just cause for apprehension."[47] While officials policed arriving ships in search of "Slaves that have been concerned in the insurrections of St. Domingo," the most respectable residents of New Orleans protested loudly against the impending closure of this trade. Without this source of labor, they warned that sugar, cotton, rice, and indigo could not be cultivated and that the levees needed to prevent flooding from Pointe Coupée to English Turn could not be maintained.[48]

Slavery and race on this urban frontier were being welded to economic and environmental forces in ways that would affect New Orleans for a long time to come. Besides constraining the aspirations of free people of color and guarding against the arrival of anti-slavery insurgents, Claiborne had to thwart slaves' ongoing efforts to escape enslavement. The governor was "informed that Negroes belonging to persons residing in this city and its vicinity often escape from the service of their Masters and by concealing themselves on board of Vessels (sometimes by the connivance of the Captain or Crew) pass out of the province." So he urged the navigation pilot stationed at the mouth of the Mississippi River "to prevent for the future like practices, and in all instances where you can detect such runaway Slaves arrest & secure the same at the Balize."[49] To make management even harder for territorial and city officials, by late August New Orleans faced a shortage of food supplies as farmers grew reluctant to send meat, poultry, and vegetables due to rumors of a "contagious Malady." Sure enough, yellow fever had begun to spread. The rapid growth of New Orleans was increasing the likelihood of such an epidemic, and by September seven to eight people were dying daily with "new cases . . . hourly occurring." Noting the especially high mortality rate among emigrants from the United States and Europe, Claiborne wrote to Thomas Jefferson on October 5, "Lower Louisiana is a beautiful Country, and rewards abundantly the Labour of man;—But the climate is a wretched one, and destructive to human life."[50] In the midst of losing his own wife and daughter to yellow fever, the governor also had to deal with a panic over an "Insurrection among the Negro's." "From some menacing expressions which recently fell from two Slaves; a general Spirit of Insubordination which of late has been manifested, & the circumstances of several negro's having been found travel'ing by Night with Arms in their hands," he reported directly to President Jefferson, "the impression is general among the Inhabitants of the city, that they are in eminent Danger." Claiborne strengthened patrols at night, alerted city militia into readiness, and was willing—if necessary—to "put a public Musket in the hands of every White man."[51]

Militarization of New Orleans played a powerful role in transforming its position in the Atlantic World from a frontier town into an urban center. Territorial laws expanded the police authority of white militia, and the United States Army increased its presence in and around the city. This escalation of police and military power was far from smooth, however. Local slaveowners one day might complain about negligent enforcement, as when some told Claiborne in 1806 "that the Taverns or Cabarets in the city were numerous, that Negroes and free people of colour were licensed as Tavern Keepers, and that their houses were resorted to by Slaves who passed most of their nights in dancing and drinking to their own injury and the loss of service to their Masters."[52] On another day New Orleanians might object to "Military Despotism," an accusation raised, for example, because naval officers aboard a gunboat across the river from New Orleans once interfered with what they considered a slaveowner's "cruel chastisement" of a slave woman and because French-speaking citizens traveling to and from the city in small boats were frequently threatened and detained by U.S. naval inspectors.[53] But two events in particular convinced most white New Orleanians that federal authorities were essential for their protection: the slave insurrection of 1811 that began sixty or so miles above river and the invasion by British forces in the winter of 1814–1815. Preempting both of these serious threats went a long way to reinforce the dominance of plantation slavery for the economic future of New Orleans.[54]

As frontier exchange in and around New Orleans persisted into the nineteenth century, it faced accumulating proscriptions and prohibitions against perceived disorder. "The low orders of every color . . . mix indiscriminately," one traveler disdainfully observed in 1802, "finding a market for their pilferings, and solacing their cares with tobacco and brandy. Gambling is practiced to an incredible excess. To dancing there is no end. Such a motley crew, and incongruous scene!"[55] During the 1790s and early 1800s, however, city authorities were already directing a surge of police action against back-of-town activity, especially with the establishment of a permanent city guard by 1805. Dances attended by free people of color, slaves, and whites together were outlawed. Gatherings at taverns and in public places were discouraged, commonly broken up for gambling and drinking violations. Peddlers who bought merchandise from slaves away from the public market were fined. General marketing by slaves for their own benefit was more vigilantly monitored. Movement of runaway slaves from plantations to the city, and from the city to swamps, became more difficult to practice, while slaves hiring themselves out to city residents faced tighter restrictions. Slaves employed on boats, even with the permission of their owners, were more frequently detained at the mouth of Bayou St. John. Free and enslaved men leaving New Orleans to fish on Lake Pontchartrain needed to show identification passes.[56]

It is no longer commonplace to equate "frontiers" with "open spaces," thanks to historians like Richard Wade who were challenging the Turner Thesis a half-century ago. But my own overview of eighteenth-century New Orleans, using the lens of the frontier city as suggested by this volume, can still emphasize how space matters.[57] How people interacted in and around the environment of a colonial town, as I demonstrate here, influenced society and economy in ways that departed from metropolitan plans and priorities. In this regard, New Orleans sheds a bright light on urban practices that occurred in most early American towns. Frontier-city exchange among settlers, Indians, and slaves on the periphery began as a necessary means of survival in the formative years of town-building, but persisted among some people as a form of independence and even resistance—an option for a front door and a back door. Merchants operating in colonial ports also sought advantage and autonomy through commercial activities that skirted imperial rules and regulations. The particular location of New Orleans—on a vulnerable strip of land between the Mississippi River and Lake Pontchartrain—was embraced by occupants because of easy access to networks of inland as well as coastal trade. By the time official projects proved capable of forcing the city to serve Atlantic commerce above all other interests, frontier-city practices in spaces back-of-town made an enduring imprint on the culture and image of New Orleans.[58]

Two decades ago, photographer/ethnographer Michael P. Smith coined the phrase "cultural wetlands" to characterize the diverse neighborhood cultures that he had been documenting with his camera since the 1960s. His principle objective in using these words was to compare the need to protect New Orleans' unique cultural heritage against destruction with the need to protect its surrounding biological environment against erosion. But Smith also understood the historical interplay between the city's physical environment and its human society.[59] Whether explaining the origins of Creole cuisine or second-line clubs or jazz music, an essential influence was how various people used the Crescent City's surrounding wetlands for freer social and economic exchange than was permitted by authorities. Tension between colonial projects and frontier practices occurred throughout the early Atlantic World, shaping the character of port cities as well as interior borderlands across the Americas. But how this tension played out in conflicts and collaborations back-of-town in eighteenth-century New Orleans helped create long-lasting independent space for the evolution of a particularly complex cultural mix. The rapid erosion of frontier practices in and around the city after 1800, however, would also have an enduring effect on New Orleans society and environment.

II.

Urban Space and Frontier Realities in the Eighteenth Century

CHAPTER 3

Insinuating Empire: Indians, Smugglers, and the Imperial Geography of Eighteenth-Century Montreal

Brett Rushforth

For the Sulpician priest René-Charles de Breslay, it was more than a metaphor that the Indians had their French neighbors by the throat. Breslay lived near the southwestern tip of the island of Montreal, a few hours' walk from a growing colonial town of the same name. He settled away from the French population center to minister to a small Nipissing Indian village that had risen at the confluence of the Ottawa and St. Lawrence rivers. Breslay called the village his mission, but the Nipissings called it home, suffering his presence there only after sustained pressure from their French commercial and military partners. Positioned in a small, if well-fortified, compound next to the Native town, Breslay lived as close to the Nipissings as they would allow, devoting his life to their Christianization.[1]

In the summer of 1713, his labors nearly cost him his life. As he had done many times before, Father Breslay confronted two Native men who had become drunk after buying smuggled brandy. There is no record of his words, but in writing he often complained of the social disorder created by drunken violence on the island and its harmful effects on his proselytizing. As he reproached the men for their condition, one of them snapped back at the priest, grabbing him by the neck and spitting threats into his stunned face. A sympathetic Nipissing man came to Breslay's aid, freeing him from the grasp of his attacker and shielding him from further assaults. Walking away, the men insulted the disheveled priest in their native Algonquian dialect, knowing that he would understand them perfectly.[2]

Father Breslay was not amused. Invoking French laws forbidding public drunkenness and criminalizing Indians' purchase of alcohol, Breslay demanded his attackers' imprisonment. A recent murder had been traced to Indians' alcohol consumption, raising Breslay's already substantial alarm at the growing liquor trade—a fear made personal by his own assault. An influential man in Montreal, Breslay got his wish, and the two offenders were transported into town to sober up and prepare for trial. But everyone, including Breslay, knew that the men would walk out of prison the next day and face no further consequences. Not that the alcohol trade was taken lightly by French authorities: efforts to stop liquor trafficking had consumed both church and state administrators for the better part of fifty years. The king's annual memorandum just months before advised colonial leaders that "one cannot give too much attention to preventing it." Current French law prohibited selling liquor to Natives in all but the most closely controlled settings, and it never tolerated sales in local Native towns. But Indian communities surrounding Montreal made it clear long before that they would brook no attempts to subordinate them to the French justice system, threatening to turn to the English for alcohol—and alliance—should the French clamp down too hard. So French authorities wisely chose not to prosecute their Indian neighbors.[3]

Unable to punish Indians for liquor smuggling, colonial authorities settled on pursuing their French suppliers. At Breslay's urging, Montreal's royal court identified a suspect, François Lamoureux *dit* Saint Germain, a man the priest knew well.[4] A gunsmith and minor merchant living in the heart of Montreal's commercial district, Lamoureux had a well-earned reputation as a liquor and arms smuggler. He also owned a large plot of land adjacent to Breslay's mission, which was the supposed staging ground for his smuggling operations. Within a few days the court built a strong case against him with eyewitness accounts of Lamoureux's liberal supply of brandy, beer, cider, and wine to Indian customers. A few Indians, including a Mohawk named Oronhoua who may have helped Lamoureux smuggle liquor to local villages, provided essential details that all but guaranteed Lamoureux's conviction. The judge seemed convinced of the two basic tenets of the case: that Breslay "was assaulted by drunken Indians and that the said St. Germain . . . had traded the brandy to the Indians."[5]

Leading as it did to an attack on a prominent cleric, and not being his first offense, Lamoureux's brandy smuggling could have triggered severe punishment: public flogging and a fine of up to one thousand *livres*, equivalent to almost seven years' wages for a Montreal laborer. But as the case neared its conclusion after nearly five weeks of testimony, the court abruptly ended the proceedings, remitting all evidence to the *procureur de roi*, or king's attorney, who rendered no verdict and issued no punishment. Lamoureux apparently had friends in high places, perhaps as high as the colony's governor, Philippe de Rigaud de Vaudreuil, who clashed with other colonial leaders over his own alleged liquor smuggling and who would urge caution in turning away Indian customers for fear of their defection to the English. Whatever the reason, the court's inaction ensured that Lamoureux's arrest cost him little more than a few days' time. In frustration, Breslay sailed for France to appeal directly to the aging Louis XIV, whom he had served as a young valet years before. As Breslay pursued his anti-brandy crusade, Lamoureux resumed business as usual, continuing not only the liquor trade but also unlicensed exports to French merchants in the west and smuggling to English and Iroquois traders at Albany.[6] Despite the combined efforts of church and state, the liquor trade continued apace.

Read one way, Lamoureux's trial offers a glimpse of the double measure of chaos that afflicted many frontier cities, joining the disorders of urban living to the unruliness of imperial hinterlands so distant from metropolitan order. As a site of violence, theft, smuggling, counterfeiting, illicit sex, and political corruption that seemed to penetrate all levels of society, Montreal certainly frustrated the designs of its absolutist architects. Independent Natives and defiant colonists, not wigged royals, defined the day-to-day realities there. "It is a world system," according to Richard White, "in which minor agents, allies, and even subjects at the periphery often guide the course of empires."[7] And as James Pritchard has explained, smuggling in particular "illustrates the fragility of royal absolutism in the [French] colonies," ensuring the persistent "weakness of metropolitan authority."[8]

From this perspective, the dividing lines between state and subject, colonizer and colonized, seem fairly clear. King and priest stood united for imperial order against the raw and dynamic energy of frontier traders and Indians whose venal interests ran counter to the larger agenda of projecting French religion, law, and royal glory into new lands. The drunken Indian's chokehold on Breslay could be read as a symbol of broader resistance to his mission of civilization under a Catholic monarchy. Both familiar and comprehensible, this story of frontier freedom striving against old-world absolutism has long appealed to those wishing to explain American distinctiveness. Caught up in the rhetoric of the American Revolution, late eighteenth- century political theorists set their freedom-versus-despotism morality play on the stage of the frontier fully a century before Frederick Jackson Turner unveiled his famous thesis.

Yet most recent work on frontier cities highlights the connections between colony and metropole, emphasizing continuity where others saw only rupture. Recognizing colonial cities' dependence on European goods, markets, capital, and military defense, this scholarship portrays frontier cities as imperial rather than independent spaces. "In this new story of economic linkages between empire and frontier," writes Jay Gitlin, "urban settlements become the spearheads of western settlement."[9] Striking at the wilderness and the Indians who lived there, urban frontiers proved particularly effective tools of empire and were thus critical to European expansion. In Richard Wade's now-classic treatment, cities "held the west for the approaching population."[10] In the global geography of empire, this approach contends, cities were not primarily sites of imperial weakness: they were imperial strongholds.

Rather than a dichotomy between state power and local autonomy, Lamoureux's case and its inconclusive outcome reveal that Montreal could be simultaneously independent and imperial, diverse and dynamic, but never far from European influence and state intervention. Montreal's imperial geography invited, and indeed depended upon, frontier disorders for its success. Rather than a spearhead striking a threatening blow to Native communities to allow for the advancement of European settlement, Montreal was a critical nexus where Native, colonial, and imperial cultures came together and created mutual dependencies. In the imperial geography of the French empire, Montreal mirrored and magnified its natural history as a place of convergence, drawing far-flung peoples and resources together in the service of empire. The chaos that made Montreal function so well did frustrate imperial dreams of order and subordination, but it also allowed the state to insinuate itself into the lives of the very people who challenged its authority, drawing colonists and Native peoples into conversation with an expansionist empire in profound and disorienting ways.

French investors, administrators, and priests established Montreal for three related reasons. First seen by Jacques Cartier and Samuel de Champlain as a perfect location for trade and exploration, the island quickly became the source of great religious excitement. Established in the 1640s by the Sulpician order as a mission, the site also proved an important location for solidifying military alliances. During the late seventeenth century, Montreal developed primarily as a trade center, a place of exchange where furs from the west met manufactured goods from the east. By century's end, the fur trade declined temporarily due to oversupply, but France's need for Indian military allies reached an all-time high. These three fluctuating agendas—Montreal as mission, bastion, and entrepôt—often competed for ascendancy: priests condemned the short-sighted materialism of the town's commercial activities, governors worried that priests would drive away their military allies, and merchants complained that both were destroying their profits. For all of their differences, though, each vision of Montreal needed the presence of Indians to succeed, yielding general agreement in Montreal that whatever else was done, Indians had to stay close by. Priests needed people to teach, merchants and settlers needed Indians' goods, and military strategists liked having Indians on hand to strengthen the colony's defenses. Indian peoples, then, were neither external nor even peripheral to the development of Montreal. Nor were they a necessary obstacle that the French intended to push aside. The success of the city itself, no matter whose vision of it prevailed, required Indians to be there in large numbers.

Eight times the size of Manhattan, the island of Montreal creates a choke point in the St. Lawrence River that provides both environmental and geopolitical advantages to its human inhabitants. By narrowing the river channel the island forms what is now known as the Lachine Rapids: "the most violent rapid it is possible to see," according to Jacques Cartier, who in 1535 became the first European to reach the island. Impossible to pass in a boat or canoe, the rapids made Montreal a strategic portage as Native and later French vessels landed on either side to skirt them. Montreal also guards the confluence of the Ottawa and St. Lawrence Rivers, forming a large and slow pool known as Lac des Deux Montagnes (Lake of the Two Mountains). Arcing over the northwestern section of the island, just north of the rapids, this gentle entrance into the St. Lawrence acted like a bay, providing relatively safe harbor to vessels coming down the Ottawa from the continent's northern and western interior. To the southeast the island provided access to New York and beyond via the Richelieu River, which lies just ten miles overland to the southeast and meets the St. Lawrence thirty miles downstream. The island thus stood at intersection of water routes that linked the western Great Lakes via the Ottawa River with Appalachia and the Atlantic Ocean.[11]

Iroquoian peoples recognized these advantages long before the French. When Jacques Cartier arrived in 1535, he encountered an Iroquoian town of several thousand residents called Hochelaga, surrounded for miles by "fine land with large fields covered with the corn of the country." The riverbank, village, fields, and surrounding forests were linked by a network of paths, "as well-trodden as it is possible to see." At the end of one of these paths was the town, where Cartier was welcomed and feasted with an abundance that made plain the agricultural and commercial potential of this location. By the end of his visit, he concluded that it would be an excellent site for French settlement, as "the country was the finest and most excellent one could find anywhere."[12] Seventy years later, when French colonization gained renewed momentum, Samuel de Champlain agreed, proposing as early as 1611 a French settlement on Montreal Island near the natural portage point just downstream from the rapids. By Champlain's time, Hochelaga had been abandoned by its Iroquoian residents, possibly due to disease or warfare from competition over European trade, leaving the island temporarily open for French settlement. Insufficiently funded and facing nearly constant warfare with the Iroquois, Champlain never acted on his plan, despite his hope that controlling passage through the St. Lawrence to Asia would bring vast wealth and glory to the French kingdom "inasmuch as the merchants of all Christendom would pass through."[13]

Montreal was eventually settled in 1642 by the *Societé Notre-Dame de Montréal pour la conversion des Sauvages de la Nouvelle-France*, a group of Catholic mystics who envisioned the island as a frontier mission, a dangerous but divine post that would draw Native families for spiritual and physical healing. The Society acknowledged the need for a town and farms on the island to provision the mission, and to give a critical mass of settlers for the missionaries' security, but the settlement's purpose required that Indians be drawn to Montreal rather than being pushed aside. Merchant interests supporting the enterprise also saw the advantage of attracting Indians to the island, making it a key gathering point for dispersed sources of furs and a convenient location for plying Native customers with French goods. Recognizing both spiritual and secular advantages, the Jesuit priest Barthélemy Vimont declared that the island "gives access and an admirable approach to all the Nations of this vast country . . . so that, if peace prevailed among these peoples they would land thereon from all sides."[14]

But peace did not prevail, making Montreal's centrality its greatest liability as well as its best asset. Drawing Native allies also attracted their Iroquois enemies, who needed little encouragement after several French attacks in the previous decades had grown out of France's alliance with the Iroquois' Huron enemies. One early planner expressed the sense of foreboding felt by many potential French settlers of Montreal, who feared that at any moment "all the trees of that island would change into as many Iroquois."[15] One measure of this fear was the fact that the Society had obtained the island for free from the company that controlled New France, whose associates recognized the site's potential but thought no French settlement there could survive the Iroquois threat.

French-Iroquois relations defined Montreal's early future far more than its proselytizing spirit, making it more of a bastion than a mission in its formative years. During the first decade of settlement alone, surviving records document more than one hundred clashes between New France or its allies and the Iroquois. Regular Iroquois raids in the early 1640s exploded into a massive onslaught between 1649 and 1652 that obliterated most Huron settlements and brought the entire French colony to the brink of destruction.[16] Montreal was especially exposed because of its tiny population and lack of proper defenses, and because it was the only French settlement west of the Richelieu River route taken by Iroquois raiders. The French population therefore grew very slowly. In the 1650s Montreal was home to only a handful of houses clustered at the site of the future city and a scattering of farms strewn across the island and on the banks of the St. Lawrence. By the time of the colony's first census in 1666, after nearly a quarter century of settlement, only about 650 French colonists inhabited the entire island. The town itself had only about 30 houses and just over 150 residents with no palisade or even clear boundaries to set it apart from its rural surroundings.[17]

With a combined force of colonial militia, regular troops, and Native allies, the French bludgeoned the Iroquois to the negotiating table, concluding a peace that took hold in 1667. Over the next forty years Montreal's population—both French and Native—rose dramatically as the town of Montreal took shape alongside several Indian towns that relocated to the island at this time of relative calm. The simultaneous rise of French and Indian settlements was no coincidence. They relied upon and fed one another, each a walled enclave linked in a larger island community that could not have existed without both colonial and indigenous elements.

Several Indian towns grew around the island and on its surrounding shores. The largest and most vibrant was known as Sault Saint-Louis by the French and Kahnawake by its Mohawk settlers. Located on the south shore of the St. Lawrence River just across from Montreal, this settlement began with little more than a dozen Iroquois Christians who left their villages in 1667 to avoid factional conflict over their acceptance of Christianity and their embrace of the French. If the earliest residents were drawn by their faith, the later and larger group of migrants came for the freely available land and, most importantly, the presence of a growing French town which could provide European goods and military defense. The 1660s was a decade of chastening for the Iroquois, leaving many with little but charred farmland to sustain families torn by factional conflict. Montreal promised a new beginning. And for the pro-French factions within Iroquoia it offered a path to pursue their interests without the interference of their Anglophile kin. Encouraged and provided land by the Jesuits, this small group slowly swelled to several hundred in the 1680s, and reached more than a thousand by 1700.[18]

A handful of smaller Indian villages appeared around the island at about the same time. The most diverse village was La Montagne, just northwest of the French town, settled by fragments of Huron, Iroquois, and various Algonquian-speaking nations in the late 1670s. We know very little about the nature of this town in the seventeenth century, but by Lamoureux's time there were two to three hundred residents living in ethnic clusters near a fort which contained a church and a small garrison. Sault au Récollet, situated to the northeast of the French town, was meant as a refuge for Christian Indians but ended up attracting a group of mixed religious sentiments and a range of approaches to French cultural integration that created internal tension on issues like liquor consumption. Along with the Nipissing village on Isle aux Tourtres and several smaller, seasonal villages erected during the spring and summer months, the Native population rose dramatically during the final quarter of the seventeenth century, surpassing two thousand permanent or semi-permanent residents by 1700.[19]

The colonial town of Montreal grew with its neighboring Indian towns. As the Iroquois threat subsided during the 1670s, its advantageous location drew merchants, missionaries, and enterprising craftsmen to settle there. The island's total French population reached 1,400 by 1681 and about 3,000 by 1700. During these years the town of Montreal took shape, growing from a cluster of about 30 homes in 1665 into a respectable colonial town of about 1,600 just forty years later, with a large portion of the growth occurring in the short span between 1686 and 1693. Larger than any individual Native village around the island, the town's population was still outnumbered by the combined population of Native towns surrounding it. And this was just how colonial officials wanted it. Not only did a close body of Native allies provide military security, but they also drew pelts and goods to the French that otherwise would go to their English rivals. As consumers of French goods, and traders who re-exported French goods to other Native villages, Montreal's settled Indians proved as essential to the town's commercial success as to its security.[20]

The physical form of Montreal drew upon the island's natural and Native histories as it transformed from mystical dream to practical reality. Placed at an inlet along the island's southern edge, the town took advantage of an inward flow in the river's current ideal for loading and unloading cargoes. The spot was, in fact, the site of a long-standing Indian portage road that early French maps identify as "Chemin de Lachine," or the Lachine Trail, which later developed into an important colonial road in the eighteenth century linking the city to the island's western settlements. The earliest buildings on the town site clustered along the Chemin de Lachine, which eventually became Rue Saint-Paul, home to most of the town's merchants and their warehouses. Another Native path, quite possibly one noted by Cartier leading to the base of Mount Royal, connected Montreal to the Indian town at La Montagne. Within town the "chemin des sauvages de la montagne" became Rue Saint-François-Xavier, which ran alongside the Sulpician seminary to meet Rue Saint-Paul near the port. At the intersection of these Native paths, renamed for Catholic saints and squared by imperial surveyors, stood the Place du Marché, or market square. Linking the island's northern interior to its western terminus, these paths also represented the joining of Native and colonial worlds that characterized Montreal's early history. As the last point to unload cargoes from the east and the first safe point to re-enter the river after skirting the rapids from the west, the city's commercial advantages combined with its human geography to facilitate trade between the Atlantic and the North American interior.[21]

But Montreal did not urbanize spontaneously. During the 1680s French officials mandated urban density by prohibiting private ownership of large tracts of land within the town's boundaries, which were precisely defined between 1686 and 1693 with only minor modifications thereafter. French-Iroquois relations began to deteriorate again in 1684, raising alarm at the scattered and poorly defended condition of the town. With so much of the land claimed by so few proprietors, it was also impossible to develop a critical mass of residents and services for a functioning market town. In 1688 New France's *intendant*, or chief civil and legal official, explained that building the city would provide the necessary amenities for a growing population and provide a place for them "to take cover from the attacks of the colony's enemies." One year later, a devastating attack on Montreal island by fifteen hundred Iroquois warriors only heightened the urgency of developing Montreal and its defenses, and a mostly wooden palisade was completed by the mid-1690s. By

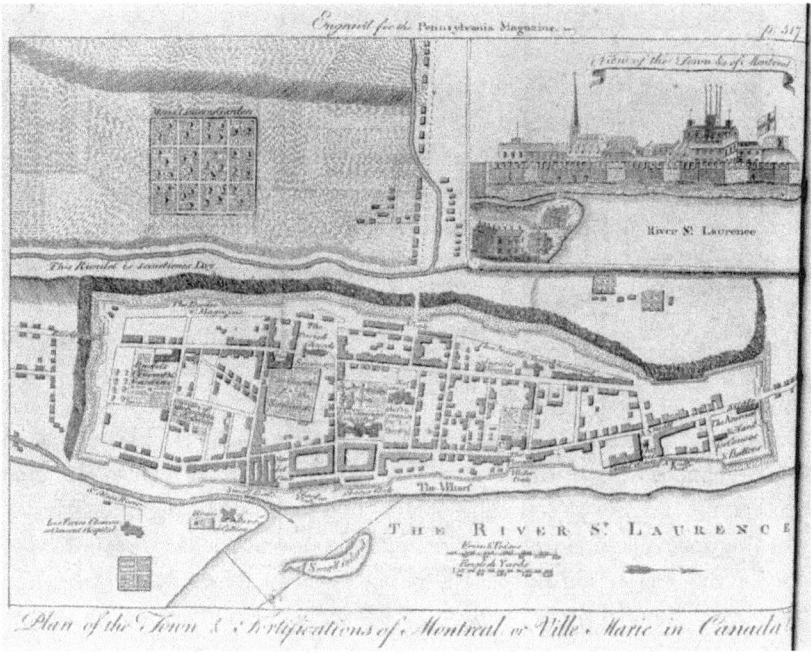

Figure 3.1. Robert Aitken, "Plan of the Town and Fortifications of Montreal, or Ville Marie in Canada," 1775. Courtesy Library of Congress.

1701, when the Iroquois met in Montreal to establish a lasting peace with New France and its Native allies, the town they entered was substantially different than the one they visited in the 1660s, having developed from a scattered mission village to an urban center on the rise. In its search for military protection and economic stability, Montreal's urbanization mirrored the town building of its Indian neighbors.[22]

By 1713 when Lamoureux and his Native partners smuggled brandy to the Nipissing village, there were about four thousand French settlers in the Montreal district and around two thousand settled Indians: one thousand at Kahnawake and another thousand at other settlements around the island. When combined with the Native peoples who came to Montreal to visit relatives, trade with French and Indian settlers, or hold diplomatic meetings with French officials, Indian populations approached parity with their French neighbors. In the broader context of the upper St. Lawrence Valley and Great Lakes, of course, Indian peoples were far more numerous.[23]

Because most Indians visited the city more often than rural French settlements, colonists living within the town interacted with Indians far more than those living in the countryside. Mohawk women came to Montreal to visit French chapels, Nipissing men brought deer meat to the market square, Oneida families visited their French friends, enslaved Apache girls carried water to the garden. One could hear a dozen or more Amerindian languages spoken around the island in 1713, especially three Algonquian tongues—Anishinaabe, Nipissing, and Abenaki—and two Iroquoian languages—Mohawk and Oneida. Beginning in 1713, hearing Mesquakie became more common as a large number of enslaved Fox Indians came to Montreal, followed by dialects spoken by a growing number of Apache and Sioux slaves who arrived in the 1720s and 1730s.[24]

François Lamoureux was both a product and a proponent of the close relationship between Indian and French frontier towns in the St. Lawrence Valley. And despite his flouting of French law, he used those relationships to link colonists and Indians alike to the French imperial state that structured their lives even as it failed to control them. By understanding his smuggling operation and the relationships that made it possible, we can see beyond the fact of Indians' presence in Montreal to the familial, geographic, and commercial dynamics that bound Indians and colonists in a web of interdependence spun by colonial forces beyond their control.

According to most surviving records, including the trial transcript, Lamoureux fit the standard profile of a petty merchant in eighteenth-century Montreal. Born and reared in Canada, Lamoureux married a slightly younger woman, fathered several children, and settled in a modest stone home on Rue Saint-Paul in the city's commercial district. Not unlike many of his neighbors, Lamoureux had a tract of land outside town which he inherited from this father. He and his tenants grew wheat and other crops there for food and occasional sale or barter. The Lamoureux family was devoutly Catholic in every outward way. His wife, Marguerite Ménard, claimed to attend mass several times a week, and the couple saw to the religious education of their young. Both Lamoureux and his wife acted as godparents for their friends' and neighbors' children.[25]

Although no one at his trial mentioned it, Lamoureux's connection to the island's Indian community went well beyond commerce. He was himself the product of French-Native intimacy, embodying the ties of kinship that were so central to his trade. His father, Pierre, was a fur trader and his mother, Marguerite Pigarouiche, was an Algonquian-speaking Indian (of an unknown nation) born in the mission village of Sillery near Quebec. Lamoureux would have learned to speak his mother's Algonquian dialect from his youth, explaining his facility with the many Algonquian tongues he mastered as an adult trader. It is likely that Lamoureux's grandfather was Étienne Pigarouich, the famed Algonquian Christian who made several prominent appearances in the Jesuits' *Relations* as a model convert turned apostate and then back again. Pigarouich offered such a moving public confession in the rough chapel at Montreal in December 1643 that many in attendance judged him equal to the priest who had given the formal sermon. The church's translators claimed Pigarouich's eloquence outshone their abilities: we "can only stammer in comparison with this man."[26]

For three generations, by Lamoureux's time, Catholicism had built a substantial community between many Indians and French. Beyond the fact of shared communion, which had a range of inconclusive meanings for Indian Catholics, Catholic ideology and the rites that emblematized it produced a network of fictive kin relationships that linked French and Native Catholics through godparenting. Lamoureux's sister, Barbe, for example, was the godmother of Louis, son of Oukiakouamigou and Marie Nikens, both Algonquians, most likely from La Montagne. Lamoureux's neighbor, a merchant named Louis Babis, acted as godfather. Lamoureux's stepmother, Barbe Le Scel, acted as godmother to the son of Michel Keskabikat and Marie-Madeleine, Algonquians (probably Nipissings) from the west end of the island. In fact, the victim and accuser in Lamoureux's trial—Father Breslay—performed nearly all of these baptisms, becoming a broker of French-Indian kinship, and who, despite standing outside these relations, exercised at least some cultural power over them. Just one month before he accused Lamoureux of smuggling, he presided over the baptism of a Nipissing girl christened Françoise. Her godmother was Lamoureux's wife. These acts may have sometimes linked the Lamoureux family with their biological Algonquian relatives, but more often they created a new kind of kinship that bound them by ritual rather than blood. At a minimum, such records demonstrate that French, métis, and Native communities maintained close contact with one another across a wide spectrum of settings never restricted to trade. And for some, these acts must have both reflected and reinforced those relationships through the culturally powerful symbols of Catholic ritual. Surviving records do not provide a direct, one-to-one correlation between Lamoureux's kinship—real or fictive—and his smuggling, but in places where such records survive these relationships produced commercial as well as familial connections.[27]

Commerce did not rely on Catholicism, however, but acted as an independent draw to Montreal's urban center. According to witnesses in Lamoureux's trial, an almost constant stream of Indian men and women flowed down Rue Saint-Paul into Lamoureux's home and warehouse. Lamoureux made no attempt to deny this element of others' testimony; to do so would have been futile. Instead, he acknowledged that "many Indians frequent his house" but protested that they were doing legitimate business there. It was a plausible defense, especially given Lamoureux's licensed profession as a gun seller which attracted a steady clientele of St. Lawrence Indians who used the weapons for hunting and defense. As a petty merchant, Lamoureux also ran a constant business of small, in-kind exchanges with individual Indian partners, a pattern several witnesses mentioned without ever suggesting it was out of the ordinary.[28]

But for the presence of the frontier city, Lamoureux would have nothing to smuggle and no pretext for trade that would cover his tracks. The city's geography, built to take advantage of Indians' historical trade routes and designed from its beginning to attract Indians, simultaneously allowed for greater Native influence and provided surveillance that was impossible when trade occurred elsewhere. Lamoureux had one home within the walled *centre ville*, or downtown, of Montreal, on Rue Saint-Paul, the city's chief commercial street built on the old Lachine Trail. French authorities had built a wall around the city to repel Iroquois attacks, but during the first half of the eighteenth century, it mostly functioned as a means of controlling traffic into and out of the city. Soldiers posted at each of the city's gates inspected goods, checked papers, and questioned anyone who seemed not to belong. But the soldiers knew that Indians did belong in the city, so they rarely interfered with their passage into and out of town. What is more, like all merchants on his street, Lamoureux may have boarded the soldiers who monitored the ports, placing him in a position to influence the degree of their scrutiny. He also lived in an especially advantageous position along the city wall, with his backyard abutting the temporary Indian villages erected each summer for trade and diplomacy. One record indicates that he may have even owned some of the land used for the encampment.[29]

Through various witnesses we learn the identity of a few of Lamoureux's regular Indian visitors. There was an Iroquois man from Kahnawake that the French dubbed "La Raquette," or Snowshoe, because they had difficulty with his Iroquois name, which different witnesses rendered as "Taouingarrou," "Toriniata," and "Caoingaront." A day laborer named Jacques Arrivé testified that he had seen Snowshoe the day before the assault as they both visited the same friend, Jean Quenet. Snowshoe was carrying two moose skins, which he then took to Lamoureux's house. Until the Iroquois trader showed up with alcohol, nothing about these events seemed out of place. Quenet's wife, Therese Hurtubise, seemed surer than Arrivé that Snowshoe had traded the skins for brandy but otherwise confirmed his account.

Another of Lamoureux's trade partners was Oronhoua, a known Mohawk smuggler from Sault-au-Récollet rumored to be one of Lamoureaux's middlemen. Oronhoua testified before the court despite French rules forbidding an Indian to testify against a French subject. During the 1710s colonial administrators debated the wisdom of this prohibition, especially since Indians themselves were in the best position to know who was smuggling alcohol into their villages. A man named Lalande suspected the involvement of Makougan (or Mak8a8an) and Sigo8ch (or Sigoouitz or Sigoouy), both Algonquian-speakers from Sault-au-Récollet. He had seen all of these men at Lamoureux's home on Rue Saint-Paul, although he admitted to having no firsthand knowledge of the alcohol trade itself.[30]

Two Indians lived permanently with Lamoureux: his slaves—Joseph and Suzanne—who did his household chores, cared for his animals, stocked his warehouse, and cooked his meals. Suzanne regularly watched Lamoureux's children, and Joseph traveled with him on trade journeys (often illegal ones) to Michilimackinac, Detroit, or Albany. Both Lamoureux and his slave Joseph were prosecuted for unlicensed and illegal trade more than once.[31] One witness in the liquor trial testified that, since Lamoureux's slave Joseph commonly carried goods around town for his master, he was able to smuggle casks of liquor in large bags designed for carrying trade cloth.[32]

We learn almost nothing from the trial record about the Nipissing drinkers. Their testimony was recorded quickly to facilitate their speedy return home. Pressure to release them came quickly. Barbe Perren testified that she received a visit the day of the arrest from a Nipissing woman she knew who was married to one of the drinkers. Angered by her husband's arrest, she walked to town to demand his release from the unjust detention, insisting that her husband "had said nothing to M. de Breslay." Women played an important diplomatic role in community relations between French and Native towns around Montreal Island. More women than men embraced Catholicism, for example, giving them greater credibility and sway with French clerical and low-level imperial officials. And informal emissaries like this one often accomplished more than formal diplomatic negotiations.[33]

The Nipissings' translator, Simon Réaume, was part of a well-connected western merchant family who spoke most of the central Algonquian languages plus the relatively similar Nipissing. Réaume's family had forged bonds with Ottawa and Illinois families through marriage, including his brother's marriage to a prominent Illinois woman that paved their family's path to trade in that region. Réaume lived across the street from Lamoureux, on the same block of Rue Saint-Paul (although he also maintained a residence in the Illinois country). Involved in the same trade and passing each other daily on the street, Réaume was a competitor in western trade with every incentive to translate the Nipissings' words to Lamoureux's condemnation.[34] But Réaume was hardly participating from a position of innocence: he had himself been tried for smuggling just five years earlier, and he appeared in liquor trafficking cases as translator and possible participant within two years of Lamoureux's trial.[35]

Lamoureux's sixteen-year-old neighbor, Marie-Anne Fafard *dite* Macouc, also testified that she had often seen and heard about Lamoureux's supplying brandy and other alcoholic beverages to Montreal's Indians. On one occasion, she told the court, she was returning to Montreal from Detroit. When they reached the island from the Ottawa River, they came ashore on Lamoureux's land, where they found nine beached canoes, "both Indian and French." On closer inspection, she found Lamoureux and several Indians lying in the canoes with their liquor, and "the Indians that were with them so drunk that they did not know where they had gotten it." Belonging to a well-known métis family from Detroit, and a cousin of the far-flung and well-connected Montours, Marie-Anne's visit to her Anishinaabe kin was as routine as Lamoureux's sleeping in a canoe with Indian traders.

Their meeting at the edge of the island hints at the impossibility of colonial officials' imperative to control illegal trade, a task that seems all the more difficult when considered with the other routine traffic to and from Lamoureux's home. Residents of every Native village around the island had some connection to this métis smuggler, either by kinship, religion, or trade. The Indians' presence, as necessary as it was to Montreal's purpose as a frontier city, frustrated some of the city's imperial ambitions. But the city was also essential to the colony's larger goal of attracting and maintaining Indian commercial and military partners. Lamoureux had what these Indian communities wanted, and to get it (or others' versions of it) they had to come to the city, building the relationships that facilitate trade on both sides of the cultural divide. Paradoxically, then, the very smugglers who evaded particular imperial controls played a prominent role in ensuring Indians' attachment to empire itself.

Just one of Lamoureux's many illegal trade voyages to the west, five years before the trial, underscores the influence of Montreal and its smugglers on the insinuation of empire into Indian communities. In 1708 Lamoureux obtained a license to go into the backcountry to hunt, but instead he used the trip to smuggle English goods to Detroit. He had bought the contraband from neighboring Indians, most likely from Kahnawake, who had traveled from Albany to Montreal with their cargo. Going directly to Detroit via Lake Erie would have been much more efficient, but Montreal offered the security of a guaranteed market and the abundance of French goods, including brandy, that the Native smugglers wanted. Colonial administrators worried about men like Lamoureux, but they also counted on them to maintain Indians' interest in coming to French places and maintaining French partnerships. From an imperial standpoint, the draw of the frontier city, even when that draw circumvented royal policy, accomplished imperial objectives as it rejected imperial authority.[36]

It was the smugglers' ability to tie Indians to the empire that made Lamoureux and his kind so difficult to prosecute. This was less because the empire was unable to punish its rogue subjects than because some imperial strategists understood smugglers' importance to France's global ambitions. Just one year after Lamoureux's trial, New France's governor and *intendant* wrote a joint letter to the king urging him to relax prohibitions on the brandy trade. "The English draw a great advantage from their brandy trade with the Indians," they explained, "which is such a great attraction to them that by this means the English attract the greatest portion of their pelts . . . [not having access to French liquor, Indians go to Albany] where they take all their beaver, which creates an open trade between them and the English." Should French merchants fail to compete in this market and thus attract Indians to Montreal, they feared that the English "will draw them all [away], to the Ruin of the Colony."[37] The battle over liquor smuggling was thus not a competition between independence and empire, but a debate over the best means of insinuating empire into a distant continent. For his supple, if self-interested, response to such challenging questions, Vaudreuil received the reward of a grateful kingdom, garnering highly coveted colonial appointments for his sons, who governed Louisiana, New France, and St. Domingue during the 1740s and 1750s. However it was accomplished, maintaining Indian alliances in New France produced tangible rewards for Vaudreuil that tied his family to the interests of the French state for generations.[38]

Father Breslay was unwilling to accept this devil's bargain. First through letters, and then during his personal visit to France, Breslay castigated New France's officials for their tolerance of liquor and other smuggling, a campaign that bore little fruit. Breslay's paternalistic chauvinism may grate on modern ears, but his invocation of French law to limit the brandy trade and its influence over Native peoples may have made his the most anti-colonial voice in the conversation. With his objections noted but ignored, Breslay was encouraged by the French crown to return to New France and continue working with the Nipissings, Abenakis, and Ottawas who lived near his mission, as long as his mission did not interfere with the security of the colony.[39]

When he returned from France in 1714, Breslay was resigned to pursuing his war against alcohol quietly from within the church. A task soon fell to him that must have strained his commitment to civility. In August 1715 Lamoureux brought his one-day-old son, François Charles, to the parish church at Sainte-Anne de Bellevue for baptism. Breslay not only baptized the child, but also acted as the boy's godfather, a highly unusual role for a parish priest. For a single ritual moment, Breslay and Lamoureux joined in recognition of their mutual commitment to a cause that transcended their personal disputes.[40] Whether they knew it or not, their lives had been similarly linked in the larger mission of the French empire as they pursued competing, but somehow complementary, visions of French imperial expansion.

It is now commonplace to view historical frontiers as complex zones of cultural interaction and innovation rather than dividing lines separating colonizer and colonized. As mixed and often independent spaces, frontiers are also generally characterized as either non-imperial or anti-imperial, inspiring a flurry of metaphors from the natural (tails wagging imperial dogs) to the technological (broken imperial machines).[41] As Lamoureux's Montreal suggests, zones of cultural accommodation could work within, and even strengthen, broader imperial strategies designed to extend imperial power. Although it stood at the farthest reaches of the French state, Montreal expanded the influence of that state not through violent exclusion or expulsion, but by inclusion and invitation. Montreal worked—for the French as much as for Indians—precisely because its walls were porous and its streets filled with those on the other side of the imaginary cultural border. Montreal worked—for the Indians as much as for the French—because it maintained intimate connections to France.

CHAPTER 4

On the Edge of the West: The Roots and Routes of Detroit's Urban Eighteenth Century

Karen Marrero

Frontiers come into existence when individuals get ahead of the political and economic policies that are meant to control them, but frontiers are also the farthest point to which an imperial power can throw its voice and expect to hear an echo of that voice come back. They can be transitional zones or lines in the sand. In what French authorities in the eighteenth century called the *pays d'en haut*, or upper country of the vast territory watered by the Great Lakes, Detroit was both place of transition and place of settlement. Prior to this time, Algonquian and Iroquois nations had lived at Detroit and traveled through the region to hunt and make war. It was coveted by British and French imperial authorities for the easy access by waterway it provided to Native nations. With the arrival of larger numbers of French and later British settlers and traders, the establishment of large numbers of Native groups, and the constant movement west and east of goods and persons, Detroit's status shifted from fort to city. In trade and imperial politics with Native groups, it sat squarely in the middle of spaces of concentrated European activity in the east and an almost exclusively Native-controlled interior to the west. Agents of government in Quebec and later New York threw their imperial voice as far as Detroit, and from there expected their local counterparts to throw it farther west. For their part, Native representatives threw their voices east with messages they expected would be heard in Montreal and New York.[1]

But the officially designated agents of state were not the only ones running relays for their empires east and west from Detroit. Those who did so most effectively were part of a highly mobile métis or creole network of mixed Native and European families that was centered at Detroit and conducted trade between Montreal and Kekionga, in what is today Fort Wayne, Indiana. Kekionga was the center of the Miami nation, and it in turn controlled traffic farther west and south.[2] By 1730, French forts at Kekionga and Ouiatenon—located near a community of Wea, a Miami subtribe—were dependencies of Detroit, and by 1757, the fort at Vincennes—located among the Piankashaw, another Miami subtribe—was also dependent on the flow of goods and people from Detroit.[3] The posts at Detroit and Michilimackinac represented the primary connecting links between the northwest and Montreal, but as the eighteenth century progressed, Detroit became the more important of these two locations. Its trading networks controlled lands of what are today northern Ohio and Indiana, southern Michigan, and the rivers flowing into Lakes Erie and Huron, as well as the system of waterways comprising the Cuyahoga, Sandusky, and the tributaries of the Miami and Scioto, Wabash, and Maumee. Centered at Detroit, merchants became wealthy dealing in furs, brandy, guns, ammunition, blankets, vermilion, and silverworks over this vast hinterland.[4]

As this chapter will demonstrate, members of the networks fashioned themselves into the standard bearers of a unique urban culture and determined economic and political affairs not only in Detroit but for the entire upper country. Their activities established Detroit as the nexus of a trading network that stretched from Montreal to the Mississippi River. Indeed, although many of them began life in New France as *coureurs de bois*, or "runners of the woods," they quickly became *coureurs de ville*, or "runners of the city," wealthy men and women who dominated the all-important fur trade throughout the eighteenth century. By the middle of the eighteenth century, this network was so important to the flow of trade, its members' activities became of increasing concern to imperial agents seeking to control resources. In Detroit, western and eastern-bound voices could be obscured, muted, or altered by the *coureurs de ville*.

In French, Detroit's name, *le détroit*, translates to "the strait." For both the French and the British, who fought over control of the vast continental interior, Detroit's natural geographic feature of being the narrowest point or strait on the waterway between New York and Montreal in the east and the Mississippi River in the west made it both a boon and a threat to state security and economic development. Detroit also figured prominently in multiple Native conceptions of territory. In 1701, at the Great Peace of Montreal convened to officially end large-scale warfare between the Iroquois on the one hand and

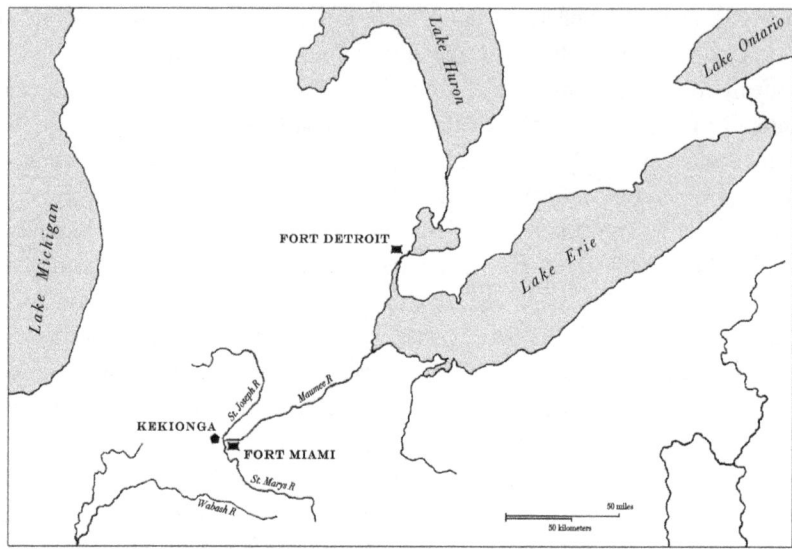

Figure 4.1. The Detroit-Kekionga corridor. Map by Craig Marrero.

the French and their allied Algonquian nations on the other, representatives of the Iroquois imperial apparatus expressed their concern over Antoine de la Mothe Cadillac's state-backed plan to build a fort at Detroit that year. There were unique challenges and anxieties around the idea of establishing a permanent physical French presence in an area that had hitherto been a place of transition. During the negotiations, the territory around Detroit was referred to as a "common bowl" because it was not an area of concentrated settlement, but a hunting territory, claimed by both Iroquois and Algonquian nations. In this transitional space, Iroquoian and Algonquian men risked encountering and making war with each other and shattering any lasting peace.[5] It was war in the previous century that had created complex and overlapping claims to the same geography involving Iroquois, Algonquian, French, and English nations.

There were also unique possibilities for economic development because French trade permits to travel to and from the *pays d'en haut* had been suspended since the last decade of the seventeenth century, when a glut of beaver furs had been discovered in the storehouses of Montreal and France. Detroit would become one of only a few state-sponsored locations where trade in furs would be allowed, which would attract a multitude of Native nations and French traders, bolster French presence in the upper country, and bring profits into French imperial coffers. The Iroquois reluctantly consented to the establishment of a fort at Detroit, despite concerns that it would lure western Algonquian nations east and bring them closer and into the orbit of the British traders at Albany, thereby cutting out the Iroquois as middlemen. But since they had suffered considerable losses in their war with the French and Algonquians previous to peace negotiations in 1701, the Iroquois were not in a position to make many demands.

The English also saw the benefits of establishing themselves at Detroit. The French preempted the English in establishing a fort, causing one English official to comment that the French intended to "secure a trade which our slothfulness and negligence hath given them the occasion of." But the English schemed to control Detroit through their allies the Iroquois, who claimed ownership of the land around Detroit.[6] Secretary of Indian Affairs Robert Livingston suggested Detroit as an ideal location at which to acquire beaver and a place that rightfully belonged to the English. He described "De Troett" as "the most pleasant and plentifull inland in America by all relation, where there is arable land for thousands of people, the only place for bever hunting, for which our Indians have fought so long." Livingston envisioned that once established at Detroit, the English could travel farther west to secure an alliance with the western Native nations, while also inviting these groups to come to Albany. Once at Albany, these nations would "see the plenty and cheapness of goods at Albany," and would be encouraged "to bring all their trade thither, and by that means augment our trade to ten tymes as much as it is now."[7] These numerous layered claims to Detroit insured its status as both a pivotal place of transition and an area of settlement in the center of competing European and Native imperial agendas and worlds.

As a designated imperial agent, Antoine de la Mothe Cadillac, Detroit's first French commandant, worked to advance the construction of a fort to simultaneously benefit the state and to further his own career and finances. The cloak of imperiality allowed him to at least temporarily divert vast resources to bolster his authority and reputation among Detroit's French and Native population. His activities did not require profound knowledge of or involvement in the intricacies of local Native cultures, and in fact were predicated on the belief that he held a position of cultural and economic superiority over Native and French fellow inhabitants. Cadillac saw his thin veneer of state-sanctioned authority crumble quickly and lead to his removal for illegal trading and gross mismanagement from Detroit within a decade. The *coureurs de ville*, on the other hand, developed networks that grew more dense and powerful over the course of the eighteenth century as they navigated at a very personal level the constantly shifting terrain of Detroit's Native-European relations. The key to exploiting Detroit's advantages lay in comprehending its position in a multitude of competing French, British, and Native imperial claims to its geography.

The *coureurs de ville* understood and capitalized on Detroit's status as a bustling locale where the constant comings and goings of Native groups, whose numbers far outstripped those of the French, occupied the majority of inhabitants' time and energy and was the driving force in maintaining a sense of community. The *coureurs de ville* hailed from polyglot communities in Europe, the Laurentian Valley, and the Great Lakes. Early French members migrated from Atlantic cities such as La Rochelle and bustling and cosmopolitan seaports of western France, where multiple religions and ethnicities existed in close quarters. Once in North America, many of these migrants established themselves in Montreal, where multi-ethnic and multilingual communities of Algonquians and Iroquoians continued to evolve, and where many different spiritual beliefs also co-existed. In the Great Lakes, nations such as the Miami had been accustomed to living in communities composed of individuals hailing from a multitude of groups that included, among many other collectives, Wea, Piankashaw, Mascouten, Odawa, Potawatomi, Mesquakie (Fox), Kickapoo, Sauk, Ojibwe, Seneca, Onondaga, Oneida, Wabanaki, Huron-Petun-Wendat, Illinois, and Ho Chunk (Winnebago).

Antoine de la Mothe Cadillac had envisioned such a Native urban space for Detroit. He built the fort at Detroit in July of 1701 at the narrowest point of the river, where any waterborne vehicle could be seen coming west from Lake Erie or east from Lake St. Clair and Lake Huron. He called it Fort Pontchartrain, in honor of the Minister of the French Navy who had backed his plan for the fort's establishment. Cadillac immediately set about encouraging mass migrations of numerous Native groups to the area. As a result, large settlements of Huron-Petun-Wendat, Odawa, and eventually Potawatomi, and smaller initial settlements of Wabanaki, Miami, Ojibwe, and Fox located on either side of the Detroit River, in close proximity to the French. Each community built its own settlement and homes and grew its own crops.

Cadillac insisted that by inviting several Native nations to settle at Detroit and conduct trade, he would control their movements, eventually convert them all to Catholicism, and impress them with the imperial range of the French colonial government. He added that the Indians would be "civilized" by building permanent dwellings in close proximity to those of the French. In their turn, by establishing a permanent presence, the French would demonstrate to the Indians that they were invested in maintaining good relations, while also preventing the British from making their way via Detroit to the upper country to trade.[8] But instead of aiding a polyglot Native community to take root at Detroit, Cadillac's efforts instead encouraged inter-tribal hostilities. These conflicts, which at times boiled over into open warfare, made it the most volatile of what historian Richard White has identified as the five zones of Indian-French interaction in the upper country.[9] Also, Cadillac's attempts to reproduce a continental French class system at Detroit, atop which he presumed to rule as a seigneur, meant he could never realize the full potential of a joint Native-European center. Cadillac's vision of a city was ultimately mired in European models, ill-equipped for the contingencies of life and trade in the upper country. The *coureurs de ville* conversely envisioned a Detroit at which they would operate unimpeded by seigneurs and the strictures of European socioeconomic policies, while using imperial resources to further develop Detroit as a commercial hub for the upper country.

Cadillac paid only lip service to the essential function of Native-French cross-cultural relations in the development of Detroit and the upper country. As an agent of empire, he misunderstood the efforts required to establish an imperial presence at Detroit. He advocated marriage between French men and Native women, but later abandoned this belief. He encouraged settlement of as many Native nations as possible in order to build up trade, but he seemed unwilling or unable to effectively understand and manage the complex and at times strained relations of these groups. He failed to understand—perhaps because he lacked any familial ties beyond his wife and children—that realizing commercial and political success would not come by making use of Detroit's geographical benefits alone. French-Native kinship networks allowed the *coureurs de ville* to concentrate power at Detroit while also extending their influence and Detroit's status outwards. Cadillac talked the metaphoric language of Native-European interaction, but his actions often contradicted his words.[10]

One such glaring disconnect occurred soon after the arrival of Cadillac's wife. When Madame Cadillac and the wife of Cadillac's second-in-command Alphonse Tonty made the decision to follow their husbands to Detroit in the fall of 1701, local Native groups were pleased at the symbolic importance of this action. French wives rarely accompanied their husbands to posts in the upper country, so their presence was evidence that the French intended to put down roots in the area.[11] Cadillac remarked in his correspondence that the arrival of his wife and Madame Tonty had caused great celebration both among local Iroquois and the Algonquian groups allied to the French. According to Cadillac, the Iroquois saw the arrival of French women of superior rank as the ultimate proof that the peace that had been negotiated in 1701 by the French was sincere.[12]

But later that year, Madame Tonty gave birth to a child that died for lack of a wet nurse. As a member of the nobility, this mother seemed unwilling or unable to nurse her own child, nor could she bring herself to request this service from a Native woman, despite the fact that the Native villages adjoining the fort at Detroit would have provided a number of wet nurses for hire. By all appearances, she sacrificed her child to the rigid concepts of gentility and class that the Cadillacs and Tontys had carried with them from Quebec and France, and in so doing, refused to build familial networks with local Native nations. Cadillac wrote of the event to authorities in Quebec as the unfortunate but inevitable result of a lack of French families at Detroit, insisting: "It is not possible that our families could live in a place inhabited by natives only. Their distress would be extreme, for they would be without any relief, as happened to Madame Tonty, who saw her infant die for want of milk, which she had not anticipated."[13] Cadillac feared that his own wife, who was about to give birth, would lose their child for the same reason, and urged his superiors to send wet nurses and French families within a year.

French authorities at Montreal and Versailles were similarly blind to the possibilities of a frontier city. The state grappled with provisioning Detroit as either a center for trade in the *pays d'en haut*, or as the spoke emanating from another hub. Three months after Detroit's formal establishment as a French post, the directors of the Compagnie de Colonie complained to Versailles of the steep expenses they were incurring in underwriting the fort. They suggested that other posts be established with the Miami on the Ouabache (Wabash) River, at the Ouisconsing (Wisconsin), and among the Sioux in order to prevent Frenchmen and Indians from going to trade with the English at Carolina and on the lower Mississippi. Detroit could then act as an entrepôt to which the Indians from all of these posts would carry furs.[14] A few years later, however, the French imperial apparatus was considering relegating Detroit to the periphery through the establishment of a fort at Niagara that would act as a center for the trade at Detroit.[15]

For the first half of the eighteenth century, angry and anxious French imperial officials expressed constant concern that Detroit was failing as a thriving settlement and that the small number of inhabitants threatened the stability of a French presence. The military advisor to the Governor General of New France believed that Detroit's establishment was the root cause of all the wars in the upper country, as this had created deep divisions within French and Native communities and had attracted a stampede of pernicious Frenchmen who conducted themselves with impunity.[16] The French colonial government's lack of faith in the profitability of Detroit led it to scrimp on its support of the fort. As early as 1710, Governor General Vaudreuil had favored withdrawing the garrison, a move he calculated would effectively lead to the abandonment of Detroit as a settlement. He offered an alternative plan for those residents who would be forced to leave once military protection was no longer available. They could be reestablished in Louisiana or on the Wabash and assist in efforts to work the recently discovered mines at the latter location.[17] Despite Vaudreuil's actions, the settlement of Detroit continued. Indeed, the *coureurs de ville* traveled to the Wabash and Louisiana not to work the mines for the French state, but to conduct business, establish partnerships, and further entrench Detroit's status as a center of trade.

Whereas colonial officials in Montreal decried Detroit's small and variable population and the seeming inability of its residents to support themselves and remain rooted according to a primarily agrarian model, the *coureurs de ville* recognized that Detroit's status as city was determined by the mobility of its Native population. In effect, Detroit held a unique status as a center of indigenous urbanity. By the mid-eighteenth century, Detroit had become "a thoroughfare between north and south for Indians" and throughout the century, bands of various Native nations "were seen there, going and coming, the year round."[18] This meant that savvy traders followed Indians to their winter hunting grounds, rather than wait at Detroit to conduct business. At other times of the year, the *coureurs de ville* occupied homes inside the walls of the French fort on a system of streets, where they conducted trade. Those among the French who wished to engage in agricultural activity received lands outside the walls of the fort.

The sheer number of Native nations turned Detroit into both a political center, where agents of government, both European and Native, met to discuss and institute policy, and a commercial center, where European and Native goods arrived to grease the wheels of diplomacy. The *coureurs de ville* understood the inter-relatedness of these two trajectories, allowing them to control the flow of merchandise by parlaying ties of family into commercial opportunities, both in Native communities and as representatives of

European imperial policy. This larger settlement composed of multiple self-sufficient and multi-ethnic communities created an emergent culture that was unique to Detroit, and a product of Cadillac's initial efforts to create a city. They were adept at capitalizing on Detroit's importance in multiple visions of urban space.

Other more enduring models of family took root at Detroit and filled the vacuum left by the state's ineffectual or illusory concepts of cross-cultural kinship, while Cadillac and Tonty were slowly losing the trust of imperial authorities and local residents, both French and Native. These other familial models of the *coureurs de ville* crossed and recreated French and Native class boundaries, often by incorporating women of elite Native kin groups. They also spanned considerable geographical distances. One such family was that of Pierre Roy and Marguerite Ouabankikoué. Roy worked for the Jesuits as an *engagé*, or indentured servant, from the age of fifteen in the upper country in the last decade of the seventeenth century. In 1703 at Detroit, he married Marguerite, who was a member of the family of, and probably sister to, the influential Miami leader Wisekaukautshe, known to the French as Piedfroid, (Cold Foot,) and leader of the powerful Atchatchakangouen or Grue, (Crane) band.[19]

Pierre was from a large family and the son of a man , also named Pierre, who had amassed land and prestige in LaPrairie, a settlement just outside of Montreal that neighbored the Mohawk settlement of Kahnawake. Like his son, the senior Pierre had begun life in New France as an indentured servant. He had immigrated to Montreal from France, and married Catherine Ducharme, a *fille du roi*. or woman sponsored by the state and sent to help populate New France.[20] Along with his significant land holdings, the senior Pierre became a pivotal player in the fur trade, together with several of his sons who became voyageurs, and with other merchants and officers based in Montreal. Through these connections, he acquired two young girl captives from the French and Native raid on Deerfield, Massachusetts in 1704.[21] Pierre and Catherine were also able to place their eldest daughter, at the age of fifteen, in the prestigious convent, the Congregation of Notre-Dame in Montreal.[22]

Pierre Roy Jr. and his Miami wife Marguerite had children at Detroit and promptly began networking with other métis families. French members of the *coureurs de ville* ranged in socioeconomic class from *engagés* and voyageurs to merchants, and in some cases, decorated officers who occupied the position of nobility in New France.[23] Native members hailed from the families of chiefs, whom Europeans sought out as the pivotal decision makers in intercultural negotiations. Pierre and Marguerite's children had merchants and members of elite Native networks as godparents. One such person was Isabelle Couc, a métis woman who had family ties among the Algonquin and the Iroquois, and who would later be known to the English she lived among as Madame Montour.[24]

In the first two decades of settlement at Detroit, two of the junior Pierre Roy's brothers came from LaPrairie to Detroit and stayed in the area for several years before continuing west. François established a trading partnership with Pierre at the Miami post of Kekionga.[25] Their brother Étienne moved through Detroit as well, and headed west and then south to Louisiana, settling on Bienville's land and acquiring capital through his marital connections to the powerful Neveu and Chauvin families there.[26] Étienne traded north to Kekionga, and his brother François ran canoes of trade goods between Kekionga and Montreal, passing through Detroit.[27] Two of Marguerite's Miami kinswomen married into prominent French families at Kekionga and Kaskaskia. Such alliances had clear benefits for trade and imperial politics, so it was not surprising that at the birth of the son of one of these women at Kaskaskia, the director of Company of the Indies stood as godfather.[28] These alliances formed a mobile network with an urbanized Detroit at its center, which stretched west to Kekionga, Ouiatenon, Vincennes, and the Illinois country and east to Montreal.

In May of 1728, Marie Magdelene, one of Pierre Roy and Marguerite Ouabankikoué's daughters, married Pierre Chesne *dit* LaButte at the Miami post at Kekionga.[29] The commandant at the Miami post, Nicolas-Joseph Noyelles de Fleurimont, signed the marriage record as one of many witnesses. The marriage took place one day after Noyelles de Fleurimont drew up papers at the Miami post to establish a partnership with Pierre and François Roy to control trade at that location.[30] Following in such quick succession, the timing of the two events illustrates the integral relationship between matters of trade and matters of family. It is easy to imagine that wedding festivities held the day after the conduct of business cemented the partnership in good feelings and intentions. The marriage was a very advantageous match for LaButte. He also had at least one brother, Charles, who had already established himself in trade at Detroit during the first decade of the eighteenth century. By virtue of his family connections, Pierre LaButte would eventually become official interpreter for the Odawa at Detroit and play a pivotal role in talks and negotiations between the Odawa leader Pontiac and British imperial agents during Pontiac's siege of the fort in 1763.

In short order, other Detroit families had married into the Chesne/LaButte and Roy network of *coureurs de ville*. Many of these members acquired trade connections to Kekionga through these marriages, including the Godefroy, Cuillerier *dit* Beaubien and Gouin families who would, as the century wore on, play greater roles in imperial efforts launched from Detroit into Miami territory. Members of the Roy and Godefroy families, for example, became Miami chiefs who wielded a great deal of political influence in French and later British efforts to maintain good relations with the Miami groups in the west. By mid-century, the lineages were tightly intertwined through marriage and godparentage and the fur trade they controlled was generating record profits for merchants and their families at Detroit.

French and British official correspondence consistently touted the unique benefits of Detroit's geography. In the late 1740s, New France's governor stressed Detroit's strategic importance: "It is to (this) post that we must cling. If there were once a thousand farmer inhabitants in that region, it would feed and defend all the others. In all the whole interior of Canada, it is the fittest site for a city where all the commerce of the lakes would center, and which . . . would overawe all the Indians of the continent. To see its position on the map is enough to perceive its usefulness."[31] Just a decade later, as the British were contemplating the limits of their newly won colony of Canada, Colonel John Bradstreet had dreams of becoming governor at Detroit and controlling the vast North American interior. In a letter to his superiors in London, he described Detroit's benefits: "This will secure the Frontier of our colonies, give us the whole of the Indian Trade in safety, effectually put a stop to the great and dangerous French plan of surrounding us with Inland Colonies and enable us to execute that Plan ourselves. . . ."[32] Detroit's location was its primary resource. Looked at through French and British eyes, it would become the launching point for an imperial apparatus that would, it was hoped again and again, organize the trade with western Indian nations, while regulating and controlling the people who operated it.

Detroit's population had grown from 270 French men and women in 1707 to 483 in 1750. By 1765, the number would increase to over 900 and was augmented by English, Irish, and Scots. In that same year, estimates of the number of local Native individuals put the number at over 2,000, meaning half of Detroit's population was Native. There were still settlements of Odawa and Huron, although the Huron had moved across the river from the French fort (in what is today Windsor, Ontario, Canada), and the Odawa had also relocated. French settlement had spread east and west outside the walls of the fort on either side. These plots had limited frontage on the water, in order for multiple landholders to have access to the river, but extended back for several miles. These ribbon farms resembled those established in the Laurentian Valley. With the large influx of new arrivals at mid-century, colonial officials thought it necessary to enlarge and further strengthen the fort. Growth outside of the walls of the fort had also greatly increased, especially due to the brisk deeding of land in the 1730s, encouraged by Governor General Beauharnois in order to make the settlement at Detroit self-sufficient in supplying its own needs for grain. Detroit possessed a sufficient number of people from various socioeconomic ranks to warrant a brisk trade in various and diverse consumer goods.[33]

Two main entrepôts, Detroit and Michilimackinac, served as interior headquarters and transshipment points for forts further west. These and other factors provided ideal circumstances for the métis family networks to consolidate their status as the richest inhabitants in Detroit. Between 1749 and 1750, a large wave of immigrants from the Laurentian Valley arrived at Detroit, settling across the river from the fort and next to the Huron-Petun community. These immigrants were mostly farmers, and they created a new French suburb with its own Jesuit-led church. Their arrival provided, at least initially, a more sedentary class of people who added a thick layer of agriculturalists to the class system that was solidifying at Detroit. With more farmers in the area, Detroit became a major supplier of agricultural produce for the western posts, which augmented its position as a center of trade.

In 1754, seven hundred canoes, a record number, came from Montreal, carrying merchandise to Detroit and returning to Montreal with furs from the interior. The largest concentration of Native Americans in the Great Lakes basin could be found at Detroit.[34] In that year the French and Indian War had broken out between the French and British in North America, and there had been a steady increase in traffic of people and goods as skirmishes broke out further west in the few years before the war. The French had increased the size of the fort in 1752 in order to accommodate this burgeoning population, building a new and larger storehouse and bakery. In order to create more space within the stockaded fort, however, it was necessary to move the wooden walls, which in turn compromised the fort's security and forced further changes for purposes of defense. The extended settlement boasted several buildings, including houses for the commandant and priest, guardhouse, barracks, church, cemetery, and king's garden.[35] The *coureurs de ville* profited by supplying the new arrivals and by absorbing them and their resources into existing family networks.[36]

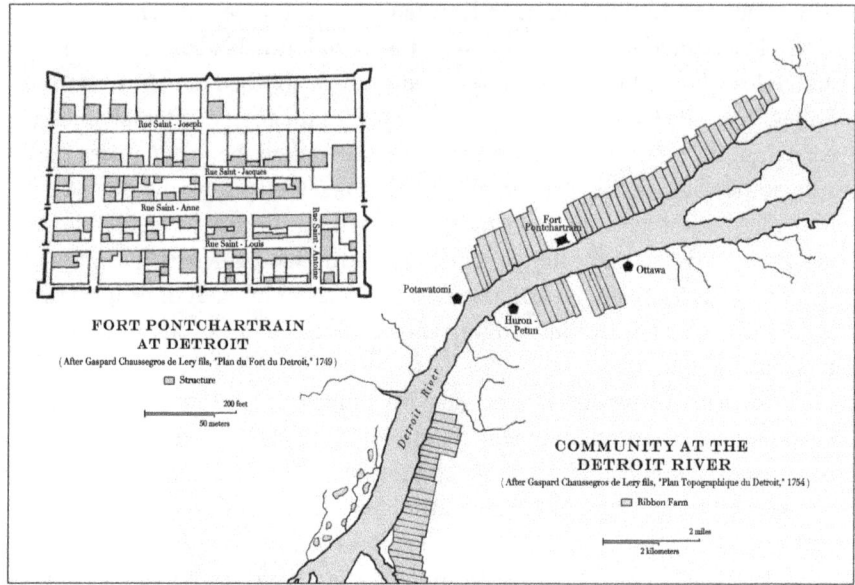

Figure 4.2. The community at the Detroit River. Map by Craig Marrero.

One of the other mechanisms by which the *coureurs de ville* families achieved outstanding wealth was through their use of slaves. Because of their western kinship connections, members of the family networks acquired and traded a large number of Native slaves from other tribes west and south of Kekionga. Indeed, the largest concentration of slaves in the upper country was at Detroit. Detroit, together with Montreal, Quebec, and Trois-Rivières, three cities that far surpassed it in terms of size and population, held almost 80 percent of the population of slaves in New France.[37] French historian Marcel Trudel also attributes this to the fact that Detroit had a permanent priest, unlike other posts in the west. The state required that slaves be baptized, which necessitated their movements through locations that provided priests for this purpose.[38] Pierre LaButte, who had married into the métis network, was the largest slaveholder at Detroit at mid-century. With the help of his slaves, LaButte cultivated over eighty-five acres of land, five times greater than the average planted by non-slaveholders.[39]

With unprecedented wealth came cultural florescence. In 1754, Simple Bocquet, the priest at Detroit, began using the words "bourgeois" and "négociant" in church records to refer to LaButte and other generous members of the *coureurs de ville*. Use of the term *négociant* signaled Detroit's firmly entrenched status as a hub controlling trade in the west. The eighteenth-century *négociant* was a wholesaler who was wealthier than the merchants and many nobles in the colony. *Négociants* worked at presenting themselves as nobility, as closely as possible, by obtaining commissions as officers in the militia. They also styled themselves as "metropolitan" and correspondingly evinced a "mode parisienne" that was meant to mimic the manners of French high society.[40] Members of the *coureurs de ville* lineages used their wealth to buy various cultural markers that displayed their power. Pierre LaButte made many contributions to the church at Detroit, at one time giving one thousand French *livres* in goods. This sum was equal to six to ten years of salary for a member of the laboring class, and one year's salary for military captains in the upper country.[41]

In 1755, Father Bocquet erected a memorial to a deceased member of his religious order. The priest had been killed by an Odawa man at Detroit half a century before, and his remains had been moved and reburied once when the original church had been rebuilt. But the second reburial in 1755 had a more pivotal significance to the community. A new and larger church had been recently built, likely funded entirely by *coureurs de ville* like Pierre LaButte, and an addition was added to house the remains of the slain priest. Father Bocquet noted in the church records that the deceased priest would have "a final resting place in keeping with his merits and with the Miracles that several persons *worthy of belief* have reported to us as having occurred through his intercession in favor of the whole parish."[42] With its own venerated and martyred priest performing miracles for leading members of the community, Detroit had developed a distinct spiritual identity that legitimized and was legitimized by its economic vitality. By the time the British had gained control of Canada, the métis family networks had fully entrenched themselves as Detroit's wealthiest citizens. They lacked the state-sanctioned credentials that accorded the officers and the fort commandant the highest position on the socioeconomic scale in New France. Their role as power brokers in social and economic relations with Native groups, however, gave them local influence and massive wealth that outstripped that of the officers.[43]

In September of 1761, Sir William Johnson, British Superintendent of Northern Indian Affairs, traveled from his home in New York to Detroit for a pivotal meeting with the Indian nations of Detroit and further west. Johnson was intent on investigating the rumors of an impending uprising of western Native groups against the British and dispelling any misgivings the western Indians had about the new British imperial dominance. Johnson sent a request via wampum belts to Detroit to convene a grand council at the fort, and from there expected the belts to be circulated west to other nations. During his stay at Detroit, troops and provisions were organized and sent west from Detroit to the posts at Michilimackinac, Kekionga and Ouiatenon, while Indians from the west came east to Detroit in such large numbers that Johnson was forced to hold the official council outside. Johnson reassured the two largest Native groups at Detroit, the Odawa and Huron-Petun, of British friendship.

Johnson called constantly upon Pierre LaButte and Jacques DesButtes *dit* St. Martin, official interpreters of the Odawa and the Huron-Petun, to speak to and hear from those local groups. Attesting to their elite status as both interpreters and leading merchants, LaButte and St. Martin were invited on several occasions to dine with Johnson, together with British officers and the commandant at Detroit. Both men were paid handsomely by Johnson for their service as interpreters. Johnson also hosted several balls for the city's well-heeled citizens that lasted through the night until seven the next morning. At one such occasion, he led Angelique Cuillerier in the first dance of the evening. Angelique was the daughter of Antoine Cuillerier *dit* Beaubien, Detroit's second largest slaveholder, wealthy merchant, and pivotal member of the extensive *coureurs de ville* family network. Johnson was so taken with her, he promised her he would write her after he returned home.[44]

While at Detroit, Johnson had discovered that wampum belts advocating war against the British had circulated to Detroit. Johnson was able to confront the Seneca messengers who had sent them and to stop the belts from traveling any further. The same trade networks that extended west from Detroit could simultaneously be the means of spreading dissension and seriously undermining the British presence there. Because of the accessibility of Detroit by water routes leading west from Fort Pitt, Montreal, and Albany, "more business was transacted in Detroit than in any other area in the five years following 1760."[45] Detroit also became the headquarters for all the British army garrisons in the upper country. Traders from Pennsylvania and New York now had an opportunity to compete with the French traders in Detroit. But while British traders waited for their Indian customers to return from their winter hunting grounds in early spring to conduct business, members of the *coureurs de ville* traveled to or with Native groups to their hunting grounds and traded on the spot. As a result, the French consistently out-produced their English counterparts. British political control could not guarantee economic control because of the pre-existing family networks and the power of the *coureurs de ville*.

Efforts by British imperial agents to control the movements of the *coureurs* proved unsuccessful. James Sterling, an Irishman who had served with the British army in the French and Indian War, would prove an exception to this general state of affairs. Sterling came to Detroit in 1761 from a successful trading venture at Niagara, bringing the financial backing of his extensive business contacts in Oswego, Schenectady, and Niagara with him. Sterling's accounts and letters provide a window into British efforts to assert economic claims to their newly won territories, while also highlighting the essential role local bourgeois *coureurs de ville* families with ties to the west continued to play in such efforts of the state.

Although Sterling had his own trade network in place that had allowed him considerable success in the east, he spent his first few years at Detroit attempting to gauge the tastes of his French and Native clientele. Sterling was well aware that his stiffest competition was with the *coureurs de ville* and their firmly established métis family networks. Despite British imperial and political control both before and after Pontiac's Rebellion, members of the networks maintained their advantage in the fur trade, which regulated the movement of virtually every other product and in which fur itself was the dominant currency. British control of local French and Native populations was tenuous at best and required the full cooperation of these groups.

Sterling had to pay dearly for the basics that French métis families already possessed, a fact that may account for the consistent tone of contempt with which he referred to the French in his letters. At one point, he fumed at having to await the arrival of clerks from Oswego, whom he planned to send to the Miami post at Kekionga to fetch goods, because, he told his suppliers: "it is rare to get a Frenchman here that can be depended on or entrusted with goods."[46] Although he could speak and write French, Sterling was forced to budget for an Indian language interpreter, paying thirty pounds a year to a Mohawk man who spoke English, French, and other Indian languages.[47] Sterling demanded an additional allowance per day for "living in exile."[48] Some of the extra monies were put toward clothing because, Sterling complained, he was "obliged to support in appearance the empty name of what the French call un gros marchand which has very much effect with the sort of cattle I have to deal with."[49] Sterling was not the only one who erroneously believed he was catering to the base tastes of the local French. On a few occasions, the wife of one of his largest trading partners back east sent down some of her own old clothes to sell at Detroit. Sterling reported back each time that most of the clothes could not be sold because they were perceived as unfashionable.

Keeping up appearances became even more costly when Sterling asked his partners back east for funds to buy a furnished house inside the fort that was located on a desirable street for trade. When purchasing the house proved too expensive, Sterling rented instead, the same house that had been previously rented by British Indian agent George Croghan. Both men thought the rental rate was exorbitant, but felt compelled to comply. The house was owned by a member of one of the *coureurs de ville* family networks living temporarily in Montreal, and was managed locally by Madame DesRuisseaux, a member of the powerful Godefroi family. It appears that although Sterling began to dress the part of the powerful merchant, his own aesthetic proclivities differed. Madame DesRuisseaux was surprised and angered when she discovered that Sterling had converted a bedroom into a storeroom and had mounted shelves on a wall, driving nails through an expensive tapestry.[50] DesRuisseaux reported the damage to the owner, who sent word that he intended to come back to Detroit to occupy the house and that Sterling should cease making any further damages.

James Sterling's fortunes and the anti-French tone of his letters shifted dramatically when he married a member of the local métis family network in 1765. This woman, Angelique Cuillerier, the niece of the last French commandant at Detroit, was the same person with whom William Johnson had become enamored during his visit four years before. In a letter to one of his trading partners, Sterling effusively described his new wife in terms of the trade advantages she and her family could provide:

> She is a very prudent woman and a fine scholar; she has been raised to trade from her infancy and is generally allowed to be the best interpreter of the different Indian languages at this place. Her family is in great esteem amongst the Indians, so much that her father was suspected to have been chosen by the Indians to command here in case they had succeeded, which only arose from his being more in favor with them than the rest of the inhabitants. He has offered me to go with goods to some of the posts in case I should have more than I can dispose of here. He is pretty rich; he has given me with his daughter to the value of near a thousand pounds in houses, money, and peltry. He has already given me possession of the houses in the fort, has paid part of the money and peltry and is to pay the remainder in one or

two years, as I may think proper to demand it. The Indians flock here daily since our marriage and lament our not having Indian goods, as they would trade nowhere else but here, if we could supply them. We shall carry on trade much better and with a great deal less expense than formerly, my wife serving as interpreter and she and I myself as clerks which I would much rather do than pay dear and be under obligations besides.[51]

Through his marriage, Sterling eliminated the costs of an interpreter, the rent on his house in the fort, the need to hire agents from the east to transport his goods west to the Miami, and the expense incurred in maintaining patronage networks. He had also gained a trade partner who was intimately knowledgeable with the local economy. Most importantly, the marriage acted as an immediate signal of Sterling's credibility to Native groups, who promised him exclusive trading privileges as soon as he could provide them with goods. Sterling had been transformed from outsider to insider by being absorbed into the métis family network, and he could therefore travel west to trade in relative safety.

The crucial means of entrance to this world was through marriage to Angelique, just as it had been for Pierre Roy through marriage to Marguerite Ouabankikoué, and for their son-in-law Pierre LaButte through marriage to their daughter Marie Magdelene Roy. Angelique, Marguerite. and Magdelene were part of the same métis network of *coureurs de ville* that stretched from Detroit across time and the eighteenth-century landscape. The women of the *coureurs de ville* freely crossed class boundaries and exhibited essential traits and practices of both European and Native groups that insured their families' economic survival at Detroit. James Sterling grew uneasy with the freedom with which his wife moved in the extended orbit of Detroit and its hinterlands. Writing to his eastern partner John Porteus on the subject of an interpreter he promised to send, Sterling assured Porteus that he could spare the man in question since "Mrs. Sterling will answer the end of an interpreter, tho' not to ride after the Indians which is now the mode here."[52] Sterling's statement reflects his view that it was not acceptable for the wife of an affluent British trader to travel to Native communities in order to conduct trade. His sentiments reflected those of the colonial British government, which became increasingly alarmed at their inability to control the French at Detroit.

It was the continued mobility of the *coureurs de ville* lineages that British imperial agents perceived as an increasing threat. In 1767, George Trumbull, the commander of Detroit, wrote to his superiors about the practice of French families selling their houses inside the fort to British newcomers. He explained that containing the French within the walls of the fort would prove beneficial in two ways: keeping them close would provide the British with a good source of intelligence about matters regarding the Indians, and, if fire broke out in the fort, it was better to sacrifice the French than the English.[53] In 1770, British commandant at Detroit James Stevenson wrote to William Johnson, expressing his concern with the local French families, whom he described as having "slip'd away to the Miamis under a pretence to trade," but who were actually, according to Stevenson "prevailing on the Indians to grant them lands [since] they propose to make a settlement there." Stevenson ordered them to quit their movements west because of his fear that "our back settlements will feel the effects of it whenever we have a war with France."[54] At this moment of mounting tension between colonists and Native groups in the west, Stevenson viewed the traditional movement of the French *coureurs de bois* along the two hundred-mile route to and from Kekionga as a threat, rather than a boon to British interests. Indeed, it was the *coureurs de ville* with links between Detroit and the Miami territories who would mobilize in the interest of their trade and families against the British at Kekionga, and Forts Ouiatenon and Vincennes during the American Revolution.

Mobility was imperative to the conduct of good trade, and the French, who had developed shared kin networks between and within Native communities that stretched west from Detroit, continued to use these connections to insure safe passage to and from Detroit. The *coureurs de ville* maintained networks that could be reinvigorated on a wide scale at any time, just as easily as they could cling closely to one family or a single post or place. Irish, Scottish, and English merchants and soldiers who married into these families found themselves part of these lineages that wove in and out of the imperial apparatus. Detroit's development was shaped by and in turn shaped these networks, providing state resources that allowed them to flourish, and, paradoxically, to subvert, handicap, and sometimes paralyze the very imperial projects that backed them in the first place. The networks allowed the *coureurs de ville* to acquire wealth and resources, and to become pivotal players in economic development.

Detroit's urbanity—the shaping of a unique local culture complete with complex economic, political and spiritual dimensions that played themselves out in matters of gender, race, and class—was set in motion before the eighteenth century. At mid-century, Detroit fully owned its status as the Montreal of the West. It had become a city dominated by the fur trade which required the free flow of resources and good relations between Europeans and Native Americans. Through their commercial activities, the *coureurs de ville* were continuously reinvigorating these good relations and benefitting from the brisk trade that resulted. The growth and diversification of the citizenry of Detroit, together with the explosion of agricultural activity, the continued settlement outside the walls of the fort, and the constant threat of colonial war that made relations with Native groups even more essential, all contributed to make the *coureurs de ville* wealthy and influential. They in turn used their wealth to bring larger numbers of luxury items and consumer goods into Detroit, as well as property in the form of slaves from places farther west.

In the early eighteenth century, the French imperial effort had been to ensure that goods and furs flowed between Montreal and certain carefully maintained and strategic posts in the *pays d'en haut*. The state wished to maintain Montreal's status as the spoke at the center of the imperial wheel that radiated westward into the vast territory controlled by Native nations. Places like Detroit were therefore meant to remain part of a provisioning hinterland that bolstered Montreal and Quebec. But, starting at the end of the second decade of the eighteenth century, the *coureurs de ville* networks actively thwarted these plans, launching their own careers as they transformed Detroit from peripheral zone to frontier city. Their commercial ventures linked Native communities and French forts across the upper country to Detroit, establishing it as the point through which all goods flowed and the place at which the value of these resources was determined. Antoine Cadillac and other imperial officials may have envisioned Detroit as a city, but they consistently undermined their own efforts. The *coureurs de ville*, however, were the ones who instituted a viable model for Detroit as an urban center.

Detroit was a center, a meeting place for political negotiation and the rituals of diplomacy, a spiritual way station through which enslaved individuals received the necessary rite of baptism that determined their viability as items of trade, and at mid-century, an agrarian breadbasket that allowed unprecedented growth in population. Its merchants and wholesalers, members of the *coureurs de ville*, provided the consumer goods and items that supplied forts and settlements further west. They acted as arbiters of urbanity by effectively exporting their methods of trade and aesthetic proclivities from Detroit.

The common thread throughout this period was the plethora of opportunities presented by movement between Detroit and its western hinterland at the Miami posts. Detroit was defined by the ease with which one could travel through it, either east or west. It was a space of concentrated activity, made important by the opportunities it presented for economic and spiritual development. It was a political hot point in imperial agendas because of the groups that moved through it and could threaten it. It was both a center and a hinterland. Its very name emphasized its status as a center of mobility: a political, economic and spiritual midpoint in European and Native imperial agendas.

CHAPTER 5

People of the Pen, People of the Sword: Pittsburgh in 1774

Carolyn Gilman

In 1775, a piece of startling news reached the Ohio Valley towns of the Delaware, Shawnee, Mingo, and Wyandot nations. The thirteen tribes of Americans had held a great council in Philadelphia and formed a confederacy to drive their Father, King George, from North America. The unbelievable part of this story was not that the Americans had rebelled against King George. It was that they were trying to cooperate.

The Indians were careful observers of the Anglo-Americans who had been pushing west of the Appalachian Mountains since the 1740s. The Natives had names for the two tribes they knew best. One tribe was generally called by an Iroquois name: *Onas*. It meant "bird quill," and it was a multilingual pun. It referred partly to the quill pens these mercantile people used as their primary tool of interaction with the Indians. The tribe of Onas seemed to solve everything by writing: account books, ledgers, and treaties, mainly. But it also referred to the name of their founder, William Penn. They called themselves Penn-sylvanians.[1]

The other tribe's name, also rendered in Iroquois, was *Ashalacoa*. It meant "Long Knife." This, too, was a pun. In a 1684 council, the Iroquois asked these people the meaning of their leader's name, which was Governor Howard. The Dutch translator improvised. Observing that "Howard" sounded much like the Dutch word for "cutlass," he translated it that way, and the name stuck. It also had a more straightforward meaning. When wanting Indian land, the Long Knives did not reach for their pens, as Pennsylvanians did; they went straight for their swords. Their preferred method of interacting with others was military conquest. They called themselves Virginians.²

In 1774, the Ohio Valley tribes had looked on aghast as the Onas and Ashalacoa had fought a very peculiar war against one another over ownership of the town of Pittsburgh. It was a war that, like many frontier conflicts, had ended up with a good many Indians losing their lives. It had confirmed the Indian diagnosis that, as one Wyandot told a Virginian emissary in 1775, "the People of Virginia were a different and distinct Nation from the other Colonies."³

The Indians were on to something. When we look at the record of what happened in Pittsburgh in 1774, it is impossible not to conclude that there were two strains of American culture represented there—cultures that were thrown into conflict by their different approaches to the issues of the frontier. The dispute between Pennsylvania and Virginia in 1774 is usually portrayed as a squabble over colonial boundaries that was settled by the extension of the Mason-Dixon line in 1780. But a closer look shows that the argument went far deeper. It was about social philosophy, the economics of the frontier, Indian relations, and the nature of the future society of the West. In fact, the Onas and Ashalacoa represented two different constructions of colonialism. It is a terrible oversimplification to imagine that American reactions to the frontier were monolithic or uniform. By looking at Pittsburgh in 1774, when the town and the fort became opposing headquarters of warring camps, we can start to tease apart the different threads of American frontier thought and behavior.

To call Pittsburgh in 1774 a "city" is to stretch the definition. It had sprung up at the intersection of several transportation routes. Not only did it lie where the Allegheny and Monongahela rivers joined to form the Ohio (historically called "the Forks"), it also was at the terminus of two major land routes across the mountains from the east. It was thus a strategic site from both military and commercial perspectives.

In 1774 Pittsburgh was only twenty years old but had already been through two wars. It had nominally bounced back and forth between the control of Virginia, France, Britain, and Pennsylvania, although it was not ceded by any Indian tribe until 1769, and then only by the Iroquois, who conveniently did not live there. It was not the first trading town to be located near the source of the Ohio. As early as 1724 the Delaware town of Kittaning had been founded where a pack-horse route from the Susquehanna Valley met the Allegheny River about forty-five miles north of Pittsburgh. By 1731 there were at least nine towns around it, including three near the Forks—Chartier's Town (Shawnee),

Shannopin's Town (Delaware), and Queen Aliquippa's town (Seneca). After 1744, three more important towns would cluster at the northernmost curve of the Ohio, just thirty miles downstream from the Forks: Kuskuskies, Sauconk, and Logstown. The last, a multitribal emporium with a population between three thousand and four thousand in 1753, became the headquarters for the trading empire of George Croghan, an irrepressible Irish rogue who ran franchise posts all the way to Pickawillany on the western border of present Ohio. Pittsburgh eventually replaced all of these towns as a commercial hub after the French and Indian War.[4]

In its short history, the town's heyday had been between 1758 and 1763, when the British Empire made a major infrastructure investment there in the form of Fort Pitt, one of three anchor posts of the British Army in the West. During its boom time as a garrison town, Pittsburgh contained (according to a census) 219 men, 75 women, and 38 children, living in 160 houses, although only 78 of these were substantial enough "to take notice of." It was fueled by coal from a mine across the Monongahela River, where residents helped themselves by loading bags full and rolling them down the steep hill. There was a sawmill on a stream called Sawmill Run across the river, and a boatyard that in 1766 supplied over sixty-five barges for a single trading company. Pack horse trains shuttled constantly across the Appalachian Mountains delivering flour, rum, and butter, but locally produced beef, bread, mutton, veal, milk, venison, beans, turkeys, and bear grease—much of it delivered by nearby Indians—rounded out the diet. There was postal service to Philadelphia by horse, and a school with twenty "Schollars." However, the town's civility should not be overstated. James Kenny, a Quaker trader, complained that "So many Roberies [are] Commited here at Nights that all [the] Noise tends to keep me from Sleep." Col. Henry Bouquet, the fort's commandant, felt that the town was a bad influence on his soldiers. "This Place is Particularly infested with a number of Inhabitants the Scum of the neighboring Provinces who have no visible means to live, except a [trading] License, & [I] think it bad Consequence for the garrison." He finally made the town off limits to his soldiers after dark.[5]

None of this lasted. First came the blow of Pontiac's War in 1763, when the nearby tribes burned the town and besieged the fort; then came the 1772 closure of the town's major employer, Fort Pitt, in a cost-cutting move by the British government. What remained in 1774 was a shadow of its former prosperity. But the fort's closure was not as fatal a blow as might be supposed, since the town had always stood on two legs—military and commercial—and now it simply fell back on trade. David McClure, a missionary describing

Pittsburgh in August of 1772, wrote, "It is the headquarters of Indian traders, & the resort of Indians of different & distant tribes, who come to exchange their peltry & furs for rum, blankets & ammunition etc.... The Village ... consists of about 40 dwelling houses made of hewed logs & stands on the bank of the Monongehala.... The inhabitants of this place are very dissipated. They seem to feel themselves beyond the arm of government, & freed from the restraining influence of religion."[6]

In what sense could Pittsburgh be called a city? Not physically: though laid out in 1765, its gridwork plan had scarcely filled in.[7] Nor was it much of a concentration of population, except seasonally; and though it still had considerable shipbuilding, warehousing, and even retail businesses, these tended to wax and wane with the times. Yet it filled many of the functional roles of a city. It was a gathering place for workers—boatmen, laborers, hunters, artisans—seeking employment in the Allegheny and Ohio valleys, and adventurers needing to be outfitted. It was a transshipment point where manufactured goods from the east and frontier products from the west (skins, livestock, food, and furs) were brought, sorted, sold, and reshipped. It was a nascent financial center where small entrepreneurs, both Indian and white, went or sent to get credit. It was a diplomatic and political center where representatives gathered to resolve disputes and forge relationships. It was, in short, a place that existed to facilitate transitions between cultural, political, and economic worlds. Its lifeblood was in the flow between those worlds.

Another symptom of urbanism was that Pittsburgh was growing increasingly at odds with the countryside around it. After 1769, when the Treaty of Fort Stanwix ostensibly extinguished the Indian title to the slice of land between the Appalachians and the Ohio, a flood of Euro-American settlers and land speculators poured in. Pittsburgh was at the intersection of two streams of migration: one from Virginia via Braddock's Road and one from eastern Pennsylvania along the Forbes Road. There is some evidence that the two groups had different ethnic compositions, with the Pennsylvanians being more diverse and Germanic, the Virginians being more homogeneous English and Celtic. But regardless of national origin, the newcomers brought values and interests quite different from those of the established residents of Pittsburgh. It was these uneasy neighbors who would come into violent conflict in 1774.[8]

There was one thing on which all Anglo-Americans around Pittsburgh agreed: they wanted to make money out of the West. They just wanted to do it in different ways.

Courtesy of Broadway, we all know that the farmer and the cowman can't be friends. If someone ever writes a rollicking musical about the Ohio Valley frontier (and they have written musicals about stranger things), then we will all be able to hum a tune about a similar legendary frontier enmity, that of traders and settlers—or as they would have said in the eighteenth century, the sutler and the settler.

The first British North Americans to arrive in the Pittsburgh region were the sutlers, who came in the 1740s, pursuing their Shawnee and Delaware customers as the Indians moved west. By the 1770s the most successful of them—men like the brothers Richard and William Butler, John and George Gibson, John Anderson, and Aeneas McKay—formed a rough-cut commercial elite in the town. The organization of the Pittsburgh fur trade was similar to the Montreal fur trade at the same time: merchant importers in Philadelphia formed annual partnerships with western traders, with the merchants providing the capital and goods, and the traders in turn hiring boatmen, clerks, and translators to run the stores in the Indian towns. Each partnership, called an "adventure," represented a separate shipment of goods and had its own books; the partnership was dissolved once the furs returned and the books were closed. A single merchant might be involved in several simultaneous adventures in different locations, and traders were continually reorganizing into new partnerships, so competitors one year might be partners the next. No one company dominated, but there was continual jostling for monopoly. The 1760s and 1770s saw a cutthroat competition between two Philadelphia merchant firms—the Quaker-Anglican partnership of Baynton, Wharton, and Morgan and a Jewish consortium including David and Moses Franks, Joseph Simon, Solomon and Andrew Levy, and Bernard and Michael Gratz.[9]

The commercial community of Pittsburgh was not all Pennsylvanian in origin, but their business ties were to Philadelphia, so their loyalties gravitated that way. But they had other loyalties as well, for these were men who existed on the Middle Ground, with one foot in the Indian community. That fact—and the power it gave them to interfere with imperial policy—earned them the opprobrium of officials such as Sir William Johnson and General Thomas Gage. The latter described them memorably as "a Sett of People . . . near as wild as the Country they go in, or the People they deal with, & by far more vicious & wicked."[10]

As a reality check on Gage's oft-quoted description, let us look at one example of a Pittsburgh trader, John Gibson. He was born in Lancaster, Pennsylvania, and was well educated by his French Huguenot mother; he spoke

English, German, and French and was steeped in the classics. At age eighteen he ran off to join the British army, which brought him to Fort Pitt. After his discharge, Gibson stayed in the west to trade. In 1763, he was descending the Ohio in a canoe with two employees when they were captured by a Delaware war party that began executing the men by burning them at the stake one by one. When the twenty-three-year-old Gibson was the only one left, an elderly woman took pity and adopted him in place of her own dead son. He lived with his Delaware mother, learning the language and assisting the tribe by writing letters, till he was freed at the end of the war. But, like many prisoners, he had formed attachments in the Indian community, and he continued to live with them. By 1765 he was importing enough dry goods, hoes, spirits, and sugar from Philadelphia to require a pack train of forty-one horses and seven drivers. He married, strategically, a Shawnee woman whose sister was the wife of a prominent Mingo named Logan. David Jones, a missionary, wrote that Gibson was "a man both of sense and learning." White Eyes, speaking for the Delaware, said, "We esteem him as one of ourselves." Like others in the tradition of Onas, Gibson had successfully straddled the cultures, and earned respect in both.[11]

The Ashalacoa arrived a decade after the first traders, in 1754. True to Long Knife tradition, they first came on a military mission: to pick a fight with the French, a task at which they were wildly successful, since they managed to set off the global conflict known as the Seven Years' War. But after 1769, a new wave of Long Knives arrived in search of land. This pre–Revolutionary War land rush was less about settlement than speculation. The main reason was the uncertainty of land titles. While the Fort Stanwix Treaty had ceded the land east and south of the Ohio, the Proclamation of 1763 was still in effect, making it technically illegal to settle west of the Appalachian Mountains. Even Pittsburgh was a squatter settlement, though the British Army needed the town so badly to serve the fort that they had reached a tortured compromise by allowing people to erect buildings there but forbidding them to sell or rent them. Starting in 1769, Pennsylvania created a land office to issue deeds in the so-called new purchase, but its authority was questioned by Virginia, as we will see. Moreover, a number of private land companies and individuals had claims, and were issuing rival deeds of unknown value. As a result, anyone who took up land there was doing it at his own risk—a state of legal limbo that attracted rootless young men and speculators, but not steady citizens.[12]

To these younger sons and aspiring immigrants, land ownership and sale was a more honorable means of achieving economic independence and self-determination than was trade. Landed estates represented a gentleman's social status, personal honor, and public reputation, as mere commercial wealth never would. In a world where the vote was tied to land ownership, it was also enfranchisement. Land meant independence from the propertied oligarchs of the East, so it was inextricable from democratic ideologies. In the heated pre-Revolutionary political atmosphere, anyone who blocked universal access to land was suspected of tyrannical tendencies.[13]

The newcomers and the established residents of Pittsburgh—the settlers and the sutlers—had opposing interests. The traders made their living in a classic extractive industry, furs. The land-hunters sought to make money exploiting a frontier resource that did not fit so well into mercantilist theory, for land could not be shipped to Europe; the money was in shipping people to it. Britain adamantly opposed this reversal of the "proper" flow of commodities, which, instead of enriching the national treasury, only threatened to extract money and labor from Britain. The land-hunters also threatened the wildlife habitat and Indian customers that were necessary to the fur trade. They brought with them a tradition of hostility toward Indians. It was not just that the Indians possessed the land they wanted. Indian-hating in America was never simple, but in this instance it was particularly tied up in social and economic grievances against fellow whites.[14] In one eloquent statement of their viewpoint, penned in 1764, Pennsylvania frontiersmen described how the British policy of appeasing the tribes, adopted after Pontiac's War, together with the diplomatic policies of the colony's Quaker leaders, came at the expense of poor whites on the frontiers. "The exorbitant Presents, and great Servility therein paid to *Indians*, have long been oppressive Grievances we have groaned under," they wrote. Not only was "Publick Money lavishly prostituted . . . to protect his Majesty's worst of Enemies . . . while at the same Time hundreds of poor distressed Families of his Majesty's Subjects . . . were left to starve neglected." They also watched "with Indignation" as Indians were "cherished and caressed as dearest Friends" while the "shocking Barbarities committed by Indians on His Majesty's Subjects are covered over and excused under the charitable Term of this being their Method of making War." To see a conspiracy in this toleration, they did not have to look farther than the merchant importers who profited from "allowing them [the Indians] a plenteous Trade of all kinds of Commodities." The westerners saw themselves caught between wealthy, eastern elitists and "imbittered Enemies," two groups in league to enrich one another at the expense of settlers.[15]

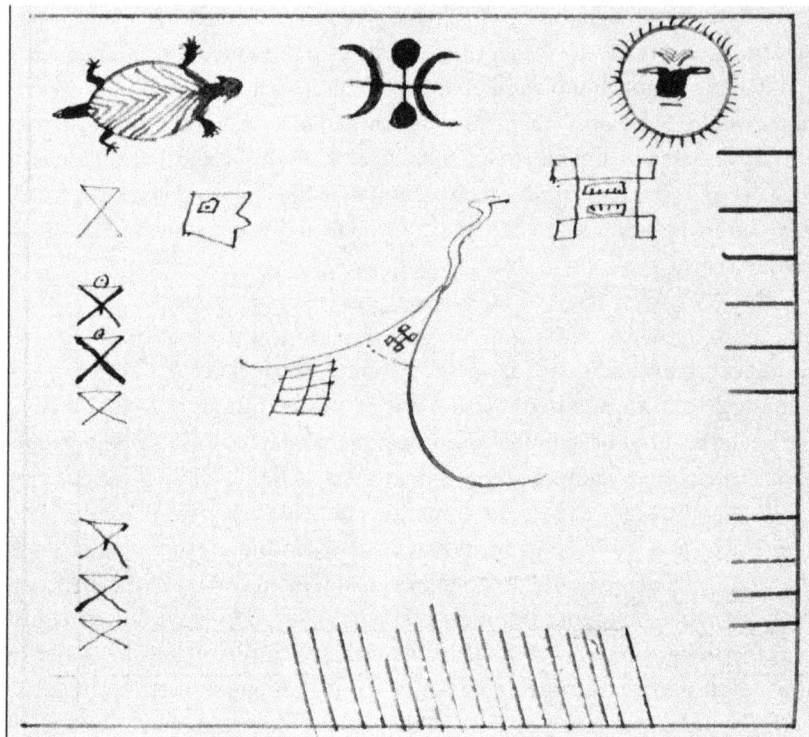

Figure 5.1. A map of Pittsburgh lies at the center of the war honors drawn by Delaware war chief Wingenund in 1775 to celebrate his role in the French and Indian and Pontiac's wars. He depicted the town as a gridwork upriver from the fort at the forks of the rivers. Courtesy Special Collections, John D. Rockefeller, Jr. Library, The Colonial Williamsburg Foundation.

In short, race hatred was a coded and socially sanctioned form of class hatred. Settlers hated Indians not just because they were savages, but because they were coddled by eastern elites.

In Pittsburgh, the corrupt alliance of wealth and savagery was embodied in the traders. They enriched the Indians beyond the means of many white frontiersmen. They supplied arms and ammunition to potential combatants. They were known to buy stolen horses from Indian raids on backcountry homes. But the issues that touched closest were ones of values. A trader's success depended on tolerance for cultural interpenetration and interdependence. By blurring the boundaries, they opened themselves to

Figure 5.2. The alliance between merchant elites and Indian tribes was the target of this anti–fur trade political cartoon. German and Irish frontiersmen are forced to carry a rich Quaker merchant and a grinning Indian on their backs through scenes of carnage. The caption begins, "The German bleeds & bears ye furs of Quaker Lords and Savage Curs." Courtesy The Colonial Williamsburg Foundation.

suspicion of being race traitors, or "white Indians." And then there was the stain of miscegenation. Missionary David McClure wrote, "The greater part of the Indian traders keep a squaw . . . as a temporary wife. Was sorry to find friend Gibson in the habit. . . . They allege the good policy of it, as necessary to a successful trade."[16] It was a custom of Indian society to which they had unapologetically adapted. But it threatened not just the cultural purity of European civilization, but the racial purity of whites, so it aroused a visceral response.

In 1774, the divided economic and social camps of Onas and Ashalacoa became mapped onto the colonial identities of Pennsylvania and Virginia, both of which claimed the Pittsburgh region. Contrary to many historians' assumptions, colony of origin was not always a good predictor as to whether a given individual would end up on the Onas or Ashalacoa side. There were Pennsylvanian Long Knives and Virginian pen people. Nor did individuals always remain in the same camp over the course of the subsequent war. It was a conflict about social boundaries masquerading as colonial ones.[17]

The state seals of Pennsylvania and Virginia, both adopted around 1776, give a sense of their contrasting self-images. The central motif of the Pennsylvania state seal shows the sources of its prosperity: a shield holding a sailing ship, a plow, and three sheaves of wheat. The shield is framed by a stalk of Indian corn and an olive branch. The olive branch, of course, represents diplomacy and peace; the corn suggests who the diplomacy was aimed at.

The Virginia state seal gets right to the point: it shows a woman warrior in helmet, brandishing a sword and spear. She stands with her foot on the throat of a fallen adversary. The motto is "Sic Semper Tyrannis" (Thus Always to Tyrants).

The reality of the two colonies was as different as their logos. Pennsylvania was founded as a community of pacifist Quakers; Virginia was founded by a joint stock company. Pennsylvania's economy was based on commerce and grain agriculture; Virginia's was based on tobacco plantations tilled by slaves. Pennsylvania had the largest city in British North America; Virginia was almost entirely rural. Pennsylvania was the most prosperous of the thirteen colonies; Virginia's economy was collapsing in an ecological catastrophe brought on by extractive agriculture, which had ruined the soil.[18]

In the 1770s, both colonies suffered from a sharp political divide between east and west. Migrants from Ireland and Scotland had fanned out to the western frontiers, giving the Appalachian valleys an underprivileged, Celtic flavor. Western settlers tended to gravitate toward Virginia. They moved there physically, in great numbers down the Shenandoah Valley, but also politically. Even though Piedmont and Appalachian Virginians were often at odds with the Anglican landed gentry of the Tidewater, both groups shared a clannish mindset and a martial tradition that the Quaker elite of Pennsylvania lacked.

The two colonies projected their own economic and historical traditions onto the West. In 1774, no one imagined that the settlement of the West would happen the way it actually did; instead, they assumed the method used in the East would be replicated. The King would grant tracts of land by charter to prominent individuals or companies that would undertake the expense, risk, and responsibility of peopling the land in an orderly fashion—providing surveys, deeds, town plans, courts, and so forth in exchange for the proceeds from land sales. Land companies from both Pennsylvania and Virginia vied for royal grants prior to the Revolution, but they did so in revealingly different ways. When Pennsylvanians campaigned for western development, they generally spoke of *colonies*. Their arguments stressed the benefit of an orderly and equitable process of settlement, in which the land company would provide civil administration until such time as the colonists were able to provide it for themselves. In their own eyes, they were going to be founding "new governments." It reflected Pennsylvania's founding by a religious community dedicated to social justice.[19]

When Virginians talked of western development, they spoke of *companies*. They stressed the enterprise, investments, and daring explorations of the company proprietors, and "the extension of Trade and the enlargement of the revenue" from opening the West to private sale and settlement. It reflected Virginia's founding as a profit-making enterprise.[20]

The two colonies' approaches to social organization on their own frontiers followed the same divergent pattern. As they expanded westward, both colonies organized newly settled territories into counties. The first thing Pennsylvania did when creating a new county was to establish a court system, and the highest officials were the magistrates. When organized in 1773, Westmoreland County (where Pittsburgh lay) had no county government or bureaucracy; all it had was a court, based in Hannastown, and a sheriff to do the court's bidding. Virginia also had courts, of course; but the most important official in its western counties was the County Lieutenant, whose main role was command of the militia. When Virginia created West Augusta County in 1774 to challenge Pennsylvania's claim to Pittsburgh, no court met for an entire year, but the county had an active militia and a Lieutenant from the outset. Pennsylvania, true to its pacifist origins, did not even have a formal militia system until 1777, when the Revolutionary War was two years old.[21]

The two colonies also had different approaches to distribution of power. This was seen most clearly in their policies toward land, the source of most wealth. The process for acquiring land in Pennsylvania was an egalitarian one, designed to discourage speculation and favor settlement by small farmers. New land claims were limited to three hundred acres. The cost of land was £5 per one hundred acres, payable at the time of purchase, to prevent large tracts from being assembled under pseudonyms with borrowed money. The procedures for getting a deed were complex and time-consuming. By contrast, Virginia's land law had been designed to perpetuate the system of landholding practiced in that state, plantation agriculture. The normal limit of a claim was four hundred acres, but provisions were made for tracts of up to one thousand acres. The cost was ten shillings per one hundred acres—a tenth of Pennsylvania's. The Virginia system was procedurally simpler, but made it easy for wealthy speculators, in collusion with county officials, to assemble large tracts into estates.[22]

The young land seekers, regardless of origin, gravitated to the Long Knife camp. A petition signed by 587 of them in May 1774 gave some of their reasons. These government-averse westerners complained that Pennsylvania's taxes were too high, its officials too intrusive, and its system gave too much power to lawyers. On the other hand, they thought Pennsylvania wasn't aggressive enough at enforcing security against the "faithless and barbarous natives."[23] On top of this, they preferred the Virginia land law. This last grievance is a little harder to understand, since on the face of it these young men of limited means should have benefited more from a system that distributed land fairly in small parcels to all, as Pennsylvania's did. Instead, they opted for a land system that favored big winners and big losers—because, of course, they all thought they would be winners. Supporting Pennsylvania meant accepting a share of wealth and power equal to their neighbor's. Supporting Virginia meant having an equal chance to strike it fabulously rich at their neighbor's expense. So they sided with the system that would eventually lead to their own impoverishment and the enrichment of elites. You might call it the casino theory of economics.

In January 1774, there arrived in Pittsburgh a swashbuckling soldier of fortune named John Connolly, who was the agent of the governor of Virginia, Lord Dunmore. Connolly issued a proclamation. Pittsburgh, he declared, was not in Westmoreland County, Pennsylvania. It was in West Augusta County, Virginia, and he was there to take charge.

Connolly summoned the able-bodied men of Pittsburgh to assemble and form a militia. Naturally, Pennsylvania's court officials showed up to intervene. Their leader was Arthur St. Clair, the county clerk—the same Arthur St. Clair who would later be governor of the Northwest Territory. He watched as eighty Virginians paraded through town shooting off their guns, then marched to the remains of Fort Pitt, where a cask of rum was opened and free booze offered to all. "This was a very effectual way of recruiting," St. Clair remarked drily. He then ordered the sheriff to arrest Connolly and told the crowd to disperse. They did, but not before taking some potshots at a peaceable Indian village across the Allegheny River, greatly alarming the women and children there.[24]

But the problem was not so easily gotten rid of. Connolly was at heart a populist demagogue who appealed to the disenfranchised by demonizing their imagined enemies. Today he might be a talk show host; he had a pitch-perfect ear for inflammatory issues. He also had the gift of blarney, for he soon talked his way out of the Westmoreland County jail. Assembling a bodyguard of twenty men to prevent his re-arrest, he left for Virginia. On March 28 he was back with an armed party, and Pittsburgh then became "the scene of anarchy and confusion."[25]

This time Connolly occupied the fort and raised a militia of "men without character and without fortune," as one resident put it. When the Pennsylvania court dared to bring Connolly to trial for disturbing the peace, he showed up at the head of 150 armed men "with colors flying and . . . their swords drawn," and proceeded to surround the courthouse. The Pennsylvania magistrates, thoroughly intimidated, allowed him to go free. Two days later he returned and arrested three of them, shipping them off to jail in Staunton, Virginia. Panic-stricken western Pennsylvanians worried that "their *property*, their *liberty*, and their *lives*, are at the mercy of a lawless desperate banditti!" "The militia here, by *Conolly's* orders, shoot down the cattle, sheep and hogs, belonging to the inhabitants, as they please; they also press horses, and take by force any part of our property they think proper, and tell us that they have authority so to do."[26]

There have been quite a few theories about what Connolly was up to, ranging from the international to the local. The Virginia Assembly suspected Lord Dunmore of sending Connolly to foment discord between the colonies to prevent them uniting in opposition to King George. This was probably true, but not the whole truth. The reason Dunmore gave—that he was defending Virginia's charter boundaries against usurpation by Pennsylvania—was also partly true. Some historians have charged that it was all about land speculation—and indeed, Connolly's invasion followed closely on the heels of a Pennsylvanian land company's victory in securing royal assent to a land grant named "Vandalia," just south of Pittsburgh. The major partners in the Vandalia Company were Pennsylvania fur traders, including John Gibson, George Croghan, and their merchant backers, Baynton, Wharton, and Morgan. Their main rival was the Virginia-based Ohio Company, whose partners were prominent war veterans. The divisions between the warring land companies thus mirrored other divisions in Pittsburgh's society.[27]

In Pittsburgh, Connolly's victims were not chosen randomly. "Conolly told us that . . . he would not suffer one *Pennsylvanian* to live on this side the [Allegheny Mountains]," reported one resident. But in the Pittsburgh context, "Pennsylvanian" largely meant "Indian trader." On June 18, Connolly issued a proclamation prohibiting trade with the Indians. It said, "Certain imprudent people continue to carry on a correspondence with, and supply the said enemies with dangerous commodities to the infinite prejudice of all his Majesty's subjects." It dawned on the Pennsylvanians that "the *Virginians* are determined to put a stop to the *Indian* trade with this Province"—which meant, in essence, putting a stop to Pittsburgh's reason for being.[28]

None of this would have been possible if Connolly had not also trumped up an Indian war. The Pennsylvanians contended from the outset that "The *Virginians* in this part of the country seem determined to make war with the *Indians*," but at first they could not imagine who would benefit from a war. Arthur St. Clair theorized that Connolly needed to concoct some "disturbances . . . that may give his manoeuvres the appearance of necessity," but it took him a long time to realize that attacks on the Indians were designed to boomerang back on the traders. An Indian war also served Dunmore's purposes. Back East, he was faced with the rebellion of the Virginia House of Burgesses over the British blockade of Boston. He needed to distract attention from Revolutionary issues and recoup his popularity. What better device than a war?[29]

The triggering event of the war, the Yellow Creek Massacre, has been endlessly dissected; but in the context of the division between the Americans, the Indians almost appear like surrogate victims.

In April 1774, a large camp of young Long Knives assembled at the mouth of the Kanawha River, intending to seek land down the Ohio; but false rumors that the Indians were on a rampage stopped them in their tracks. Eighty or ninety of them retreated to Wheeling, led by a man named Michael Cresap. There, an alarming letter arrived from John Connolly, warning the residents to protect themselves from Indian attack. One of the Long Knife mob, a twenty-one-year-old George Rogers Clark, later recalled, "A new post was planted . . . and war declared in the most solemn manner; and the same evening two scalps were brought into camp."[30]

But the scalps did not belong to enemy combatants. They belonged to two Indian employees of traders Richard and William Butler who were on their way to the Scioto with a shipment of goods. The next day the Long Knives attacked a group of Shawnee and Delaware diplomats returning from peace talks in Pittsburgh, their canoes loaded with gifts from Pittsburgh's traders. The atmosphere at Wheeling had become very volatile and ugly by now. The gang had grown to about 150 men when another set of canoes appeared on the river, led by two men who embodied everything the Long Knives abominated: John Gibson and a fellow trader, Matthew Elliott. Both were

Pennsylvanians. Both were traders. Both were married to Indian women. Soon they were waylaid.[31]

Gibson later testified, "They behaved in the most disorderly manner, threatening to kill us, and saying the damned traders were worse than the Indians and ought to be killed. In the morning Captain Michael Cresap came to the camp. . . . he advised me by no means to think of proceeding any further, as he was convinced the present party would fall on and kill every Indian they met on the river."[32]

The vigilantes could not kill Gibson without answering for it, so they selected a related target: the village of Mingo Indians at Yellow River, where Gibson's Indian wife lived with her family. Around April 30, a number of them set up an ambush across the river from the village and lured some Indians over, including Gibson's wife. She carried her infant daughter, Gibson's child, on a cradleboard. After some preliminary socializing, the Long Knives sprang their trap. They killed at least nine people outright. But the most sadistic treatment was reserved for the woman who had dared to violate racial boundaries. As they were preparing to kill Gibson's wife, she begged them to spare her child because "it was a Kin to themselves." In answer, a man shot her in the forehead, severing the strap that held the baby's cradleboard to her back. In an act of sexually charged rage, the men then mutilated her by cutting open her belly. They were preparing to dash her daughter's brains out when they thought better of it, and decided to take the child hostage instead. She was eventually returned to Gibson, who raised her.[33]

It is hard to imagine that this was a conflict about colonial boundaries.

News of the atrocity spread quickly, and set off a panic-stricken exodus of settlers fearful of Indian retribution. But the greatest immediate danger was to around a hundred Pittsburgh traders and their employees who were scattered through the Indian villages. "*God* knows what fate they have met with," one Pennsylvanian wrote. "We hope they are still alive." But the Indians' response made a sharp distinction between the Onas and Ashalacoa. "The *Indians* . . . say, that they will not kill or touch a *Pennsylvanian*," said one report. Proof came when Richard Butler and some of his employees arrived from the west in ten canoes piled high with furs, escorted by three Shawnees. They brought the news that the rest of the traders were coming overland with two hundred horses loaded with furs, all protected by a Shawnee guard.[34]

Connolly's response was revealing: he sent a troop of militia to arrest the Shawnees who had escorted Butler to safety. The traders were forewarned, and managed to smuggle the Indians across the river and out of Connolly's clutches. Arthur St. Clair expressed the collective Pennsylvanian outrage: "honour, generosity, gratitude, every manly principle, must have prompted them to be kind, and afford protection to those poor savages, who had risked their own lives to preserve the lives and property of their fellow-subjects." On almost the same day, Dunmore was writing Connolly to have his militia attack: "make as many prisoners as they can of women and children; and should you be so fortunate as to reduce those savages to sue for peace, I would not grant it to them on any terms, till they were effectually chastised for their insolence."[35]

The traders were not pacifists by any means, and they contemplated armed resistance to Connolly. But they had no support from Philadelphia, and minimal support from Pennsylvanian settlers. By July, St. Clair was convinced that "the trading people must leave *Pittsburgh*." Many did so that summer, moving up the Allegheny River to Kittaning for their own safety and the safety of their customers. Those who remained endured harassment from the Long Knives. In one incident, the Delaware businessman White Eyes, who maintained a house in the town, returned from a diplomatic mission to find his property broken into and £30 of goods stolen—enough to buy six hundred acres of land. The remnant of Pittsburgh's trading community finally erected a stockade around the town—not to protect it from the Indians, but from the Virginians in the fort. In September Lord Dunmore arrived with an army to put down his imaginary Indian uprising—for, apart from the Mingoes affected by Yellow Creek, the western Indians were still protesting that they were at peace. Nevertheless, Dunmore launched an invasion of Ohio, and finally goaded them into defending themselves.[36]

By the end of 1774, Pittsburgh had gone through a kind of ideological purge. Connolly and his extremists had driven out many of the moderates, the mediators, and the compromisers, who tended to be the more prosperous and commercially oriented frontiersmen. The Long Knives had transformed Pittsburgh from a frontier town that grew wealthy as a hub of cross-cultural connections into one that defined itself in polar opposition to the Indian country and its inhabitants. It became a place where vigilantes felt free to make death threats against visiting Indian diplomats, and where Indian property was no longer safe. That transition happened in other frontier cities, but rarely so quickly or so violently.

If we left the story there, the implication would be that America had made a fateful transition from one method of interacting with the frontier to another. But in fact, the forces of Onas made a counterstrike using their own characteristic weapon, the pen. The only reason that Dunmore's War was remembered in later years was because it produced a masterpiece of American literature that was reprinted in magazines all across Europe, quoted by Thomas Jefferson to prove the native genius of the New World, reprinted in McGuffy's Readers throughout the nineteenth century, and recited by generations of schoolchildren. That work was the speech delivered by the Mingo chief Logan, lamenting the massacre in which his family had perished. What is less well known is that the speech was originally delivered not to Dunmore, but to John Gibson, Logan's brother-in-law and just as much a victim of the Yellow Creek atrocity as Logan himself. When it was delivered to Dunmore, electrifying the gathered officers, it was not Logan speaking, but Gibson. And so Gibson's dead wife, whose name is not even recorded, achieved a belated moral victory. The immortal speech was a collaboration of two men her death had brought together in grief, a true product of the Middle Ground.[37]

Eric Hinderaker has written about Ohio Valley history as a succession of colonial models: an empire of trade, an empire of land, and an empire of liberty.[38] In one sense the events of 1774 were a transition from one imperial model to another. But the triumph of the Long Knives did not wipe out the older model. By 1775 Pittsburgh was once again hosting a great multitribal council in which diplomats from the Continental Congress in Philadelphia strove to keep the Indians neutral in the new conflict against King George. The purge of Pittsburgh could not last because it was not in the nature of a city to be a monoculture. The frontier needed such a place of intersections, where contradictions and conflicting views could play out. As long as that need existed, no side could permanently win Pittsburgh.

The subsequent history of the West continued the dialog (or dialectic) between the Onas and Ashalacoa traditions. One of the enduring contradictions of United States Indian policy was that we never chose between the two approaches. Rather, we chose both—both the pen and the sword, both treaties and military conquest, both assimilation and separatism. As a result, we have had a bewildering and often hypocritical relationship to our First Peoples. As it turns out, they have been telling us the reason for quite some time.

III.

Networks and Flows: The Frontier City in the Nineteenth and Twentieth Centuries

CHAPTER 6

Grain Kings, Rubber Dreams, and Stock Exchanges: How Transportation and Communication Changed Frontier Cities

Elliott West

It was a classic nineteenth-century frontier city. Located on a major river, it exploded from a handful of native huts to a vital center of trade by channeling to the world an abundant local resource that filled hungry needs thousands of miles away. Men on the make organized new methods of tapping the hinterland, first dominating and then exploiting the indigenous population. Local wages were high, but so were prices: staples like coffee and beans cost four times what they did in New York City. Outsiders considered this city wild and woolly, but as money poured in it took on respectable trappings—handsome public buildings (it soon was the capital of a new state), large and ostentatious private homes, and its greatest pride, a fabulous opera house with a baroque interior featuring lots of Italian marble, red velvet, and gold leaf. Before long, it boasted one of its nation's first electrical lighting systems and a bit later telephone service.

But then, trouble. The world market began to draw on other regions for the local resource, and competition drove the price disastrously downward. As so often on the frontier, the dizzying boom was followed by a painful bust.

The city might have been one of many in the Far West during the latter nineteenth-century, but it was in another country, in fact on another continent. It was Manaus, on Brazil's Negro River, just above where it joins the Amazon—nine hundred miles upstream from the Atlantic. Many thousands of wild rubber trees in the surrounding rain forest enabled the great boom. (In a variation of the metaphor of streets paved with gold, one of Manaus's thoroughfares was paved with rubber.) Its bust followed the development of rubber plantations in Asia. The opera house was the dazzling Amazonas Theater, which survives as a reminder of the years when Manaus was flush with wealth and confident of an even greater future.[1]

Manaus can remind us that frontier cities have been a global phenomenon, and have played important roles in world history since the earliest years of colonial empires. Manaus also helps us draw distinctions among frontier cities: specifically how nineteenth-century cities, in the closing phases of world frontiers, differed from frontier cities before them. This volume shows what distinguished the frontier cities of the United States from Goa, Manila, and Montreal. There are plenty of possibilities: a lot happened in the centuries between the rise of urban centers in India, the Philippines, and New France and those in California, Montana, and Oregon. The trick is to sort through those changes and to ask which had more influence than others.

For nineteenth-century America, one obvious point stands out. The United States acquired the Far West, and its far western frontier cities sprouted and grew at precisely the same time as the full blossom of the nation's transportation and communications revolutions.

American railroads were first laid out in the 1830s, but they really took off only after the easing of the 1837 depression, spreading first across the eastern United States. Then, from 1865 to 1880, the miles of trackage rose from thirty-five thousand to nearly a hundred thousand.[2] It was during those years, from 1840 to 1880, that the United States annexed or conquered the 1,200,000 square miles of the Far West, defeated its resistant Indians, organized these lands politically, and laid down their bureaucratic structures. It was then, too, that most of the West's cities appeared—or, if they had already been there, it was when these cities took on their modern shapes.

Then there was the telegraph. If we gauge communication by the obvious measures, speed and extent, the telegraph was the greatest achievement in human history.[3] It separated the man from the message. Previously, information moved only as fast as people did, with the limited exceptions of methods like semaphore and carrier pigeons. For the first time, messages moved electronically across wires, essentially at the speed of light. The scale of change was enormous: railroads moved physical objects ten to fifteen times faster than freight wagons; the telegraph moved information more than forty million times faster than a man on a galloping horse.

Samuel F. B. Morse sent Albert Vail his famous message "What hath God wrought?" in May of 1844, six months before James Polk was elected president, a year and a half before Texas was annexed, two years before the Oregon Treaty, and only four years before the Treaty of Guadalupe Hidalgo—at the precise moment of territorial expansion for a newly continental United States. The telegraph spread even more rapidly than the railroads. Morse's first line ran about forty miles from the national capital to Baltimore. By 1880 the United States alone had about two hundred thousand miles of wire strung across it, and in that year nearly thirty-two million messages crackled through the system.[4] Western cities like Phoenix, Butte, and Virginia City now were potentially in direct communication with London, Tokyo, and Calcutta.

Building an infrastructure of rails and wires and birthing the West as a distinct region, the two developments grew up together. They were historical twins, and like most twins they played off one another. The enormous distances and the varied geography of the new West stimulated new methods of railroad construction and the development of new equipment. The distances, when combined with the reality of far-scattered settlements and little direct access to markets, encouraged a partnership between the federal government and corporations to set out the networks of rails and wires across the West. And just as the challenges of the newly acquired West inspired innovations in transportation and communication, the revolution in the movement of things and information profoundly affected the emergence of the West as a distinctive region.[5] Certainly it shaped its emergent cities.

Consider San Francisco: The sleepy California port was transformed by the greatest coincidence in American history: the discovery of gold on the state's American River, roughly two hundred hours before Alta California was acquired in the Treaty of Guadalupe Hidalgo. California's first great export, gold, was a classic frontier export—an item low in volume relative to its market value. For the far-flung cities of early modern frontiers, such luxury goods as gold, silver, silk, and spices were the only feasible commerce.

Not so with California, however. Remarkably soon it began exporting a product from the other extreme, something of much greater volume, bulky and hard to handle, yet low in value per pound. California started shipping out wheat, by the thousands of bushels.[6] By the mid-1850s, after grain production in the Central Valley had satisfied the local mining towns and the local market of San Francisco, businessmen began looking outward. Wheat was shipped to Australia, Peru, Chile, Hawaii, and China, but the great boon proved to be shipments to England. In 1860, nearly half of all wheat and flour exported from California was to the British Isles, a portion that rose to eighty percent by 1867. In the following year, a bit more than one-third of all wheat exported from the United States left through San Francisco. In 1869, two hundred forty ships passed through the Golden Gate carrying wheat or flour, an average of two ships every three days; by 1882, it was five hundred fifty ships, or three every two days.

This seemingly unusual trading pattern was powered by the low cost of producing wheat in California, because from the start production there was well mechanized and accomplished on large units of land. Even more critical, however, was the revolution in movement that pushed down transportation costs. In 1869, New England shipbuilders launched the first medium clipper, or "Down Easter." It carried more than previous clipper ships and sailed faster, reducing passage from San Francisco to Liverpool from no less than four months down to as few as a hundred days. As a result, English grain production plummeted and imports increased, shifting from the relatively close-by fields of Eastern Europe to ports in India, on the Black Sea, and along the Pacific coast. Meanwhile, back in California, rapid rail construction allowed San Francisco more efficient access into the Sacramento, San Joaquin, and Salinas Valleys.

The communication revolution was just as important for California's success. The essential figure here was an under-recognized pioneer in the new economy of frontier cities, a burly, six-foot-seven-inch-tall German immigrant named Isaac Friedlander, who became known as San Francisco's "Grain King." Friedlander's genius was to realize that profits came to the mid-nineteenth-century frontier city through the coordination of information over great spaces. Shippers were not going to send vessels to some newly emerging economy without some assurance that they would find a cargo to carry; Californians were not going to keep growing wheat unless they were reasonably sure they could sell it. Friedlander developed a sophisticated system to gather estimates of local grain production and then utilized the continental telegraph and the newly completed transatlantic cable to see where commercial carriers were available around the globe. Friedlander then found the credit to bring it all together. Thus, grain grown along the San Joaquin River chugged by rail to the coast to be carried around Cape Horn on Down Easters built in New England, then delivered fourteen thousand nautical miles from San Francisco to Liverpool, where it meshed seamlessly with other shipments from India and elsewhere, satisfying the English grain market.

What distinguished San Francisco's experience as that of a frontier city was how the revolutions that were transforming the world at large were

Figure 6.1. With the help of revolutions in communication and transportation, California agriculture was born modern, as suggested in this illustration from *The Graphic*, 1883. Author's collection.

brought to bear on a place that still bore the marks that had defined frontiers for five centuries: unusually unsettled conditions and fluid possibilities, the ready availability of unexploited land and the lack of well-established legal and political systems. (As elsewhere, San Francisco was a city where displaced native peoples had been using the land in their own ways and living by their own systems for millennia—only to change with shocking speed.) In a frontier city, thoroughly modern arrangements like Friedlander's could emerge with a speed and an ease of innovation incomprehensible in more settled cities where older ways were firmly in place. In a metaphor local boosters would enjoy, San Francisco was born like Athena, springing onto the map of the United States fully formed. Through these technologies, San Francisco leapfrogged into an economy of modern production and international connectedness, becoming a hub with a speed unknown in world history.

California provided an extreme case of what could be seen elsewhere in the new American West, as suggested by an intriguing map from the 1870 census. In an effort to gauge "the *relative* power" of different areas in agricultural production, government statisticians ranked wheat-producing regions by efficiency on a scale of one to four; places producing the most bushels with the fewest workers and the least improved acreage received the highest ranking.[7] Most of the Midwest—the most productive region in terms of total output—ranked only one or two. A slice of Minnesota earned a top grade of four, and parts of Michigan and the Ohio and Mississippi valleys ranked three. Out West, where wheat production was barely under way, four areas earned a ranking of three: Montana's Yellowstone and Gallatin River Valleys, the South Platte Valley along the Colorado Front Range, the Willamette Valley of Oregon, and part of the farmland around the Great Salt Lake. California's Central Valley received the top grade as well.

And just as the Central Valley channeled its wheat through San Francisco, the other high-scoring farming areas had their own funnel cities. Bozeman, Denver, and Salt Lake City supplied large regional markets that soon would expand as rail connections improved. Portland, Oregon, was already exporting wheat, increasing dramatically when the railroad to the inland Palouse country was completed. The nation's youngest farming regions were among its most advanced, and the cities they served capitalized on their successes.

The transportation and communication advantages also enabled the growth of frontier cities in other economic zones as well. Mining centers that were plugged into the continental transportation network could quickly acquire the necessary equipment and labor, creating what were, in effect, sophisticated underground factories in an astonishingly short span of time. From its founding, Leadville, Colorado, possessed a more comprehensive industrial culture than many manufacturing centers of the East. Virginia City, Nevada, sitting over the Comstock Lode, was another obvious example. In 1861, just two years after silver was discovered there, the city had forty-six mills with more than twelve hundred stamps to process ore from the nearly fifty miles of tunnels beneath it.[8] As the mines were dug deeper, engineers devised the world's most advanced methods. In extent and size alone the operation was astounding: One pump built to suck water out of a mine ran off a flywheel forty feet in diameter and weighing 220,000 pounds.[9]

Virginia City's sprawling plant and its wormwood of mechanized tunnels was conceivable only in terms of the same combination of communication and transportation advantages that produced northern California's wheat empire. On the Sierra Nevada's eastern slope, another frontier region had suddenly opened, with the traditional lack of structure and unforeseen difficulties. Yet this frontier was different because of national infrastructure: Rails and modern shipping allowed engineers to bring in whatever they needed to exploit its suddenly revealed resources.

These connections allowed mid-nineteenth-century frontier cities to produce a far wider range of materials. The effect, once again, was to telescope their development. San Francisco quickly emerged as a manufacturing hub supplying a large portion of the Pacific coast and the interior. It produced slaughtered beef, glassware, blue jeans, and, especially, mining equipment. From south of Market Street came hoses and huge nozzles for mining, pumps and stamps, ore cleaners and amalgamating pans, retorts and boilers bound for the Comstock. Farther south along the bay were heavier industries manufacturing steel, building ships, and processing whale oil. In a remarkably short span of time San Francisco's industry was supplying a market second in size only to Chicago's.[10]

The transportation and communication revolutions set these frontier cities apart from those of the past. Like the clipper ships and the railroad, the telegraph shrank the gap between the frontier and its traditionally distinctive conditions and the rest of the world. This exchange worked both ways: as on past frontiers, new exploration and the potential for new wealth created a burst of new local knowledge. (Typically, of course, these discoveries were also grossly exaggerated and lied about.) So too could the telegraph spread what is summed up by that elusive term, the "frontier mentality." This term covers the intense excitement inspired by that burst of fresh local knowledge that found expression in an individual's compulsion to be first upon the spoor of some big chance to profit from the frontier's developing wealth.[11]

When new local knowledge spurred the frontier mentality, people went into motion. Men and women got word of some new frontier, and, like Huck Finn, they lit out for the territories. Earlier in the nineteenth century, ambitious farmers in the Carolinas heard about great farmland in Texas, and they went there. Word arrived of gold on the American River, and people rushed to California. But long before, as they descended on what Walter Prescott Webb called "The Great Frontier," others had acted out that mentality long distance.[12] Early modern frontiers opened in concert with the emergence of modern commercial life and fostered the creation of prototypes of the modern corporation. People could invest in distant booms, taking the frontier plunge alongside those who were riding or walking or sailing to some distant place. Instead of actually going there to exploit the newly available resources, they plunged vicariously by putting down their money. If these frontier investors made a profit, they succeeded not by seeking out the most valuable resources but by taking advantage of the most lucrative information. They were cultivators and prospectors, not of mining claims or fertile land, but of local knowledge.

By essentially eliminating distance, the telegraph brought the impulse and the information together instantaneously. Previously, information about frontier wealth in Macao or Goa, Jamestown or Texas, had traveled at the excruciatingly slow speed of ships and camels, horses and trains. Now it moved at light speed, at 670 million miles per hour. New local knowledge, including rumors and lies, was immediately accessible to anyone connected to the telegraphic grid. As on earlier frontiers, investors could bet on new possibilities—to take the frontier plunge without actually going there. With the telegraph, anyone along the wire could do so with virtually no lag time, as if they *were* there.

Seen in this way, the urban stock exchange becomes an emblematic site of the new western frontier, right up there with the placer claim and the homesteader's soddy. San Francisco again offers a prime example. The San Francisco Mining and Stock Exchange opened in 1862 with a handful of members paying fifty dollars each for a seat.[13] Not a dime of business was done during the first two days, but that soon changed. As more and more mining stocks were traded—thirteen hundred companies were on the exchange within a year—and as an ever-wider public became caught up in the shadow realities of rumors, speculations and lies, the result was a swirling blizzard of corporate paper. The quantity of a company's shares traded in a single day might be double the number in circulation. When news of the Big Bonanza hit in 1874, the value of Comstock paper opened at $93 million. Two weeks later it was more than $300 million, roughly one and a half times the assessed value of all San Francisco real estate. "And from whence came our orders?" a founder of the exchange later asked. He wrote:

> from San Francisco, and, literally, from the kitchen to the pulpit; from every shade in life, and from every nationality represented in San Francisco. Chinamen were large gamblers in mining stocks. Sacramento, Virginia City and Carson City were large traders; Virginia City in particular. Wherever the telegraph wire extended, our orders would roll in on us. The Eastern cities also, New York in particular... London, Paris, Berlin and Frankfort sent us orders.[14]

But if buy orders came from kitchens and pulpits, not much of the profit went to housewives and preachers. Robert Louis Stevenson, who had come to the city to court his future wife, put it well: the mining exchange was "the heart of San Francisco; a great pump we might call it, continually pumping up the savings of the lower quarters into the pockets of the millionaires...."[15] Those pockets were in the pants of the investors closest to the action and most skillful in manipulating information and riding the resulting soar and collapse of stock prices. Wealth was its raw material, wired in from across the world, but even rawer was the commodity of public hope and naïveté, gathered to yet another frontier. The prescient few could harvest it at just the right moment.

In a sense it was all invisible, the units of capital and abstract commitments riding on electricity, an economy of the ether. The material consequences, however, were enormous. Money gleaned from tens of thousands of exchanges paid for much of the development in a wide arc around San Francisco—hydraulic mining, including gargantuan water delivery systems; manufacturing; ranching; real estate; shipping; city water works; and, not least, even more railroads and telegraph lines. Thus the twin revolutions fed one another. The shrinking distances in the movement of information generated capital that was used in turn to construct economies newly possible because of the revolution in moving physical things.

The new West's connectedness had other consequences, including in its human makeup. It would have been natural to expect that easier access to the frontier would mean that the settled society of the eastern United States would reproduce itself easily—that Ohio-like neighborhoods of families would quickly appear in towns and cities in Montana, Nevada, Colorado, and California. But not so. In fact new frontier cities were, if anything, *more* out-of-line demographically with the urban East than earlier ones had been, and the reason once again was the combination of the movement revolution and persisting frontier traits.[16] Those heading west did so with ease, but they still found frontier conditions: physically crude, socially unsettled cities wanting for order and cultural amenities. That was unsurprising in itself, as social and cultural maturity is a subtle process. It takes time. But what is less obvious is how ease of movement slowed such maturity rather than speeding it up. The thinness of social and governmental basics—education, religion, reliable government and urban services—on past frontiers had discouraged families from moving west. It still did. Now, however, as families looked westward to the frontier promise, it was possible to consider pursuing that promise without going at all—that is, not going as a family unit.

There were two reasons for this demographic change. First, on these mid-nineteenth-century frontiers, entire families were less necessary to some of the work, most obviously mining, than they had been on the earlier, overwhelmingly agricultural frontiers. In the trans-Appalachian region early in the nineteenth century, for instance, adult males on their own were highly unusual and single women almost unheard of.[17] The family was the essential unit of production and support, which placed a premium as well on reproduction. For most men, heading west and living there for an extended time alone simply made no sense, and so there was nothing remotely resembling later frontier towns full of unattached men in the absence of women or children. Mechanized-agriculture frontiers also had far less need for families, and so made the gender balance of immigration dramatically more lopsided.

Second, the new transportation meant that the frontier could play a wholly different role in someone's life trajectory. In the past the assumption always had been that those moving to some distant frontier would be gone for many years, with the strong possibility that they would never return. Accounts of families taking their leave are often heartrending: Grown daughters and sons and cling to parents and grandparents, aunts and uncles, and friends, everyone weeping, wrenched by the thought that every mutual touch and sight might be the last. Now, however, it was feasible, and in fact it was often presumed, that going west would be not the start of a new life but merely a sojourn. The overwhelmingly male itinerant population included not only bachelors but also family men meaning to make money quickly and to head home or to establish a firm base before sending for wives and children. Such life-plotting would have been unthinkable without the faith that families, using new systems of movement, could voluntarily fracture and reassemble far more easily than only a couple of generations earlier.

This pattern had its international dimension. Into new western cities flooded immigrants, by far most of them men. They moved along routes smoothed by the new means of travel, drawn to work in economies born of quickened links to a wider world. They came from across the continent and from around the Atlantic and Pacific Oceans—gold- and silver-seekers from Australia, France, Peru, Germany, Sonora, and Chile, railroad workers from Ireland, Scandinavian lumbermen and fishermen, and tens of thousands of Chinese, even more heavily male than other groups, who labored in the diggings, on railroads, as domestics, and in the few businesses where they were permitted.[18] Like their native-born neighbors, a great portion of these foreigners came planning to stay a few years before heading home or bringing families to join them.

Thus the nineteenth-century frontier city held a paradox: on earlier frontiers, far more difficult to reach, settled society reproduced itself demographically almost from the start, while afterward, when people could arrive much more easily, towns and cities were often wildly out-of-whack with the demographics of immigrants' home communities. In addition, more and more women in the East were drawn to new opportunities and greater independence in places such as New York City and Boston. "The wilderness may have been the frontier for American men," David Potter has written of these years, "but the city was the frontier for American women."[19] So as western cities grew with an abundance of males, those in the East tilted in the other direction.

And while the East Coast typically is regarded as the destination for Gilded Age America's great influx of immigrants, parts of the West held a substantially higher portion of foreign-born persons. In 1870, New York had the highest percentage of immigrants of any state on the Atlantic coast (26 percent), but Montana's percentage was half again that of New York's (39 percent), Nevada's even higher (44 percent), and Idaho's double that of the Empire State (53 percent). The portion of aliens in a western town or city, furthermore, was typically substantially higher than in its state or territory as a whole. As late as 1880, thirty-one years after its boom, San Francisco still had more foreign-born persons than it had females.[20] And if we admit larger towns into the category of city, the difference in urban demography is even more striking. The percentage of aliens in a place like Idaho City, Idaho, was greater than that of any census tract in New York City.[21]

The distinctive human profiles of newer urban frontiers hold important clues to the cultural and social patterns on those frontiers. Take, for instance, the perennial question of whether the West was more violent than the settled East and, if so, why. Begin with a few commonsensical points: men are much more prone to violence than women; people are more likely to act violently toward persons of different cultures they objectify as "the other"; and violence is more likely where there is physical, economic, and sexual stress. Now consider that, in part because of their connectedness, western towns and cities were dominated by men tossed together with strangers and living lives of discomfort, of hopes dashed, and of libidos denied. Perhaps far western cities were particularly violent partly because they were so easy to get to.[22]

The revolutionary ease of movement reached deeper into the nature of frontier development as well. The two points raised so far—the early appearance of advanced economies and the flocking of so many men from so many different places—had especially doleful effects on native peoples. The environmental results of mining were bad for everybody—mountains denuded, choking clouds laced with arsenic, and hillsides washed into rivers thick with silt and poisoned with mercury. The consequences for Indians were disastrous. The boom of populations, the sudden appearance of towns and the scouring of the countryside for new strikes quickly depleted game populations, destroyed sources of plant food, and disrupted patterns of movement essential to hunting, gathering, and fishing economies. Large-scale agriculture and cattle ranching had the same deleterious effects.[23]

Nineteenth-century urban frontiers were also distinctive for how they did *not* develop: they did not facilitate local intercultural relations of the sort described by Allen Gallay, Brett Rushforth, and Daniel Usner elsewhere in this volume. Cities from Goa to Montreal to New Orleans relied on what Usner calls "back door economies," where newcomers bought or bartered with natives for subsistence needs and for marketable goods, notably furs. With the exception of the American Southwest, which entered into the new transportation and communication networks later than settlements elsewhere, such relations seem to have operated on mid-nineteenth-century urban frontiers only very briefly, if they developed at all. If these frontier cities had any back doors, they were open only a crack and then they were slammed shut. Instead, American Indians were drafted to work in the diggings and the fields or to labor as domestics, or they lived as best they could on the margins. In conditions like those Matthew Klingle described for American Indians at the end of the nineteenth century and into the twentieth, Indians in Virginia City squatted in a dump at the foot of Taylor Street, living in huts made of scrap lumber. The men earned a bit of money by splitting and carrying wood while women worked as servants for "cold grub they [could] carry home." Their competition for these menial jobs were those immigrants similarly shoved to the edges of society and the workplace, the Chinese.[24]

Finally, it is worth wondering whether the distinctive traits of nineteenth-century frontier cities have in some ways persisted and continued to shape these urban centers. The combination of older frontier-city traits and a revolutionary connectedness allowed these cities to have a remarkable flexibility to make of themselves what seemed most opportune. Today cities like Los Angeles and Seattle somehow seem freer than most to reinvent themselves. Probably the prime example, as the late Hal Rothman memorably described, is Las Vegas.[25] Jet travel, superhighways, and the instant information flow undergirding distant electronic betting permit an easy connection between the frontier mentality of plunge and grab with the perception of fabulous opportunities and anything-goes behavior. As Robert Louis Stevenson found in San Francisco, money in Las Vegas also flows from the pockets and purses of the middling masses into those of wealthy investors and the locally connected.

Such musings bring us back to Manaus, high up the Amazon, which crashed with the world rubber price in the 1920s and withered to a steamy backwater—until, that is, it was reborn. In 1966, the Brazilian government made Manaus a duty-free port, which granted the city significant economic advantages. Foreign businesses set up makeshift factories, flying in untaxed materials to be assembled with cheap local labor, and Manaus became a major electronics manufacturing center. Imported foreign goods were offered in stores and on the streets at astonishingly low prices.[26] Nine hundred miles upriver, Manaus emerged as a major international port, thanks to the next movement revolution, the airplane. Air travel again changed the calculations, as a traveler leaving Miami will spend five and a quarter hours flying to Manaus, but more than six hours to reach San Francisco.

Today Manaus is a city of nearly two million people and a major destination for bargain-hunters from around the hemisphere. Its connections and opportunities make it a strikingly modern outpost in a vast hinterland, as the writer-adventurer Joe Kane discovered in 1985. Kane was part of the first team to float the entire length of the Amazon. After weeks in the world's largest rain forest, disconnected from the networks of the twentieth century, he paddled his kayak into the port and found himself amid skyscrapers, slums, prefab factories, plush hotels, and street markets mobbed with shoppers buying

German tennis rackets, Japanese motorcycles, and Italian espresso machines. A few days later Kane shoved off for several more weeks in a watery wilderness before reaching the Atlantic.[27] Paddling out of the Amazon, Kane was passing out of an earlier mode, where frontier conditions were defined by isolation. Arriving in Manaus, he encountered the revolutionary changes begun in the mid-nineteenth-century frontier city, where distance suddenly shrank and global markets connected even remote places to international trends.

Perhaps the defining trait of the new frontiers is their ability to surprise us with startling juxtapositions. Joe Kane could have testified to that. Earlier he had stopped at a swampy village of six huts. Hauling his kayak up a bluff, he was met by a frail elderly woman, Flora, and her adolescent grandson. Physically isolated, the young man was tied to the wider world enough to develop fantasies. He dreamed of becoming a lawyer, drawing on connections he had experienced since birth. When Kane asked the boy's name, and as her grandson shrugged and played a little air guitar, Flora answered, "Elvis Presley."[28]

CHAPTER 7

Frontier Ghosts Along the Urban Pacific Slope

Matthew Klingle

On an early March morning in 1893, a small flotilla of Indian dugout canoes landed on Seattle's waterfront, filled to the gunwales with clothing trunks, furniture, tools, and passengers. Indians were hardly a novel sight around Puget Sound. The city's namesake, Seeathl, was a former Indian leader revered by natives and whites alike. Natives plied clams and fish on downtown streets, harvested crops and felled trees in the surrounding countryside, or worked as domestics for affluent white Seattleites in the streetcar suburbs. But the sudden arrival of these "red denizens" attracted a "large and curious crowd." These Indians were refugees. A gang of land-hungry white residents had razed their homes in West Seattle, across Elliott Bay, the night before. Their village, called Herring's House, had survived the four decades since Seattle's founding. Now, it was gone. As Coll Thrush argues, "every American city is built on Indian land, but few advertise it like Seattle."[1] Dispossession had preceded the sales pitch, however. Real Indians roaming the city were unwanted reminders that Seattle was a crude frontier town. Vanishing or legendary Indians were proof that it had become a cosmopolitan city. By removing Indians physically and symbolically, boosters could tell "ghost stories" of a distant and romantic past to sell a modern Seattle in the present.[2]

That same year, in another city built on Indian land and with an Indian name, two men converged to celebrate the anniversary of Columbus's first voyage to the New World. A young historian, Frederick Jackson Turner, came to Chicago to deliver an academic paper on the significance of the frontier in American history. Indians were critical to Turner's story of free land and national expansion, but once they served their purpose as foils to civilization's advance, helping to transform effete Europeans into virile Americans, they faded into stereotype or obscurity. The other man, William F. "Buffalo Bill" Cody, instead turned the frontier story into a crowd pleaser. His Rough Riders enchanted audiences twice a day opposite the gates of the Columbian Exposition with his reenactments of the wagon trains and Forty-Niners. Unlike Turner, real Indians remained vital to Buffalo Bill's story: Sitting Bull, Yellow Hand, Geronimo, and many less famous Pawnee, Sioux, and other Natives all participated in Wild West shows. Yet for all their differences, both stories "declared the frontier over" and each was an incomplete version of the other. Turner, as Richard White argues, took the conquest of nature as his premise and "considered savagery incidental." Buffalo Bill, in contrast, "made the conquest of savages central" and the triumph over nature incidental. The seeming disappearance of untamed nature and uncivilized peoples, of empty spaces and unsettled places, meant the end of the United States' frontier past.[3]

For white citizens of Seattle and other cities along America's Pacific Slope, both narratives were also an urban story. To them, the conquest of nature and the conquest of savages were an intertwined tale because, as Richard Wade has memorably described, the "towns were the spearheads of the frontier."[4] Yet these Pacific cities came of age in an era when the frontier was supposedly closing, an anxious time when multiple crises gripped Americans: agrarian radicalism, political populism, the Panic of 1893, labor unrest, urban squalor, corporate malfeasance, and political corruption. Even as many Western urbanites commemorated their colorful past in expositions and parades, they also worried what an uncertain future might bring. Frontier anxiety was more than cultural phenomenon. It also shaped and was shaped by the Progressive Era city because political chaos and social decay were real urban problems.[5] Channeling the spirit of the time, urban political and business leaders in the Far West tapped frontier angst to guide city planning and regional political economies. They took the lessons of the scholar and the showman seriously: the children of the pioneers were destined "to crowd into cities like worms" unless they redefined the contest between savagery, nature, and civilization.[6]

At the very moment that Frederick Jackson Turner mused about the closing frontier, residents of Seattle, San Francisco, and Los Angeles were fretting too. They dreaded its closing, but they also feared it might never leave. Their response was to draw explicit boundaries between city and countryside, nature and civilization, health and disease, past and present. Each city wanted to escape a messy and chaotic frontier past in order to enhance its status as a future hub for transcontinental and trans-Pacific commerce. As Elliott West has noted elsewhere in this volume, this trade relied on influence over their metropolitan borderlands—but city leaders sought to draw a firm line against the rough-and-tumble past. This geometry of metropolitan promotion had two interrelated axioms: improving the natural environment and containing or expelling uncivilized peoples. And along the Pacific coast, savagery wore more than an Indian or Hispanic face because Asian migrants and itinerant laborers were other reminders of the outmoded frontier.[7]

Metropolitan growth and frontier anxieties were not coincidental. Each informed the other as dependent variables. From the late nineteenth century through the Great Depression, political and business leaders launched massive public works projects to spur industrial growth, protect public health, expand trade, and accelerate transportation. Moving earth, building sewers, reshaping shorelines and razing slums were all designed to rub out unwanted communities and unhealthful places in the name of social and economic progress. The majesty and effectiveness of these massive public works projects and planning schemes, however, masked the internal contradictions that sustained them. Extractive industries still needed cheap and pliable labor, which meant attracting still more migrants from across the West and round the Pacific basin. Open borders for labor also meant open borders for biota. Actual or imagined pathogens tagged along when humans and other animals hopped the rails or stowed away in ships. Often, both unwanted biota and unwanted travelers were segregated in the most disrupted local landscapes, justifying still more remodeling and renewal. In their effort to transcend earlier frontier conditions, urban elites unintentionally reproduced and amplified the chaotic frontier conditions they had hoped to efface.

Perversely, but perhaps not unexpectedly, immigrant and Indian workers together with the urban poor would pay the highest price in the campaign to eradicate the urban frontier. Turner's conquest against nature and Buffalo Bill's crusade against savagery merged over time and became imbedded in place. The idea of progress so central to the frontier allegory was impossible to sustain without creating its counterpoint of decline. Dominating nature and dominating people were thus reciprocal and concomitant parts of frontier evolution. The result has been a concealed history of inequality lurking in the landscapes of America's Pacific Slope.[8]

These ghostly histories were born in the late eighteenth-century Pacific world. As a new generation of borderlands historians maintain, "older master narratives" of successive frontiers have yielded to new stories playing out on "an open-ended historical stage" of entwined "imperial, national, and cultural journeys." Decoupled from its traditional focus on the U.S.-Mexican boundary, borderlands history has gone continental and even global. It has also moved beyond its fixation on early North American history by helping scholars working on the modern era to shed their dependence upon imperial and national storylines.[9]

In this vein, almost two centuries before Americans seized the Pacific Slope and Far West, transoceanic trade and exploration had already reshaped the region. Prior to 1820, commerce between Alta California and other Pacific ports increased gradually. After Mexican independence in 1821, visits to Alta California swelled dramatically. In the two-plus decades before the Mexican-American War, more than five hundred vessels visited California ports. Although U.S. ships comprised the largest percentage, flags of at least twenty European and Pacific nations flew over California harbors. Attracted initially by the burgeoning sea otter trade, these vessels soon carried other valuable products, such as hides and tallow, with ramifications that spanned the continent.[10] In an effort to blunt American expansion into its territory farther north, the Hudson's Bay Company began to diversify its maritime and land-based fur economy. By the 1830s HBC employees shipped preserved salmon, lumber, and agricultural products out west to Hawaii and China as well as furs back east to York Factory or Montréal.[11]

It was native peoples who produced most of the resources for this worldwide trade. Yakut *promyshleniki* (Russian fur-trade contract workers), Aleut hirelings, Métis factors, Tsimshian traders, Californio *vaqueros*, and Chumash mission workers served as crew members, hunters, guides, and purveyors for Europeans and Americans, enabling the transmission of both goods and pathogens. The resulting epidemics ravaged native communities with successive waves of contact and commerce along the entire Pacific coast. Cumulative mortality rates ranged from 60 to 90 percent by the mid-nineteenth century.[12] When colonists arrived to claim the Pacific Slope as their own, they landed in places well prepared for resettlement. Preexisting networks of labor, trade, and migration had done more than precede their arrival. They had also rearranged the landscape for their benefit.[13]

America's Pacific Slope cities emerged amid these economic, epidemiological, and environmental instabilities. From Puget Sound to southern California, "high-intensity, low-frequency events," as Mike Davis terms disasters, acted as "the ordinary agents of landscape and ecological change." Earthquakes, floods, volcanoes, landslides, and natural and human-induced fires ravaged already shaky city sites.[14] Seattle eventually straddled an isthmus of steep glaciated hills ringed by mudflats, scoured by high tides, and encircled by flood-prone rivers. San Francisco emerged on the headlands of a wind-swept, arid peninsula, fronted by the tempestuous Pacific on one side and salt-encrusted mudflats on the other. Los Angeles grew up alongside ample coastal lowlands but had no decent harbor save the small bay at San Pedro, and it was bisected by the Los Angeles River, which ranged from trickle to a torrent after heavy rains.[15]

In each case, reshaping these landscapes began with indigenous labor, yet regional geographies and histories determined the extent and duration of Native participation. Californio urban society and economy would have been impossible without Indian work. Despite the corrosive effects of disease and abuse, Indians outnumbered Spanish colonists as much as six-to-one in Alta California as late as 1820. Indians in Los Angeles, Monterey, and San José toiled as domestics, day laborers, and agricultural workers.[16] During the Gold Rush years, many Forty-Niners exploited Indian labor when possible, even as most natives succumbed to disease or the brutal interracial violence that engulfed California. Those few who survived were pushed to distant reserves or were relabeled as Mexican by white Americans.[17]

The last of these cities to emerge, Seattle, relied most and longest upon Native toil. The first permanent American arrivals accommodated themselves to the longstanding practice of trade and intermarriage between Coast Salish peoples and Euro-American fur traders. Natives outnumbered colonists into the early 1870s and remained critical to Seattle's growth for much longer as they folded extractive industrial wage labor into their preexisting seasonal subsistence rounds.[18] For this reason, territorial governor Isaac Ingalls Stevens bowed to colonists' demands during treaty negotiations, agreeing to locate reservations close to industries, and placating Indians with promises of unrestricted rights to fish, hunt game, pick berries, and harvest shellfish in their "usual and accustomed places."[19]

It was a short-lived concord. A brief but bloody war in the 1850s turned neighbors into rivals. The subsequent decades only hardened enmities. By the 1880s, white property owners routinely ousted Indians from their lands, even though they continued to live in and move through Seattle as part of the region's workforce. The torching of Herring's House in West Seattle in March 1893 was only one scene in the larger drama unfolding throughout Puget Sound. Indian workers helped to build and run the wharves, sawmills, canneries, and warehouses that sustained early Seattle. Their labor helped those in power to redraw the physical landscape to sustain racial segregation while providing the necessary muscle for economic growth. But as Seattle grew, newcomers poured in. Employers did not need Indians and the Panic of 1893 drained the demand for labor of any kind, especially Indian labor, to almost empty. The refugees who arrived in Seattle that March morning were now unwanted. Indians had not disappeared from the city, but their roles had changed from vital laborers to nostalgic symbols even as many continued to work and live hidden in plain sight.[20]

Once the Panic of 1893 receded, the boom times returned thanks to the extractive industries stoking the explosive growth of the new cities of the Far West. If Richard Wade's trans-Appalachian West was born urban, the Far West was born urban *and* industrial because of the trans-Pacific world that had preceded it.[21] Gunther Barth has described the growth of San Francisco, an "instant city" filled with ravenous consumers, drawing resources from an ever-larger hinterland. The environmental consequences for the Sierra Nevada and Central Valley were dramatic. Hydraulic cannons flushed entire hillsides through sluice boxes. Downstream, acres of grasslands became fields of wheat or immense cattle pastures. Entire forests were milled into mineshaft braces and house frames.[22] In the city, Gold Rushers became squatters, filling the mudflats and estuaries with garbage, construction debris, gravel, and sand from the city's seaward shores so they could stake claims and erect buildings upon the new land. Like many nineteenth-century cities built of wood, San Francisco was a transmuted forest and often burned like one. Between 1849 and 1852, six fires consumed large sections of the city. After each blaze, as with all the others, the city move still farther onto the tidelands, unleashing more cycles of burning and building.[23] The result was a sanitary mess. Pedestrians skirted "gaping holes in the planked wharf" to avoid being "assailed by bilge-like odors" escaping open sewers.[24]

Filling tidelands to make coastal real estate was hard work that soon fell to immigrant workers. Chinese labor helped to fill in the tidelands fronting the city as well as the marshy delta northeast of San Francisco, transforming what John Muir had once described as "the most extensive and regular of all the bee-pastures of the State" into private agricultural reserves.[25] In the absence of strong federal oversight, speculators shaped tideland reclamation laws to fit their needs.[26] This was "a landscape where people worked, but did not stay," Matthew Booker has argued, part of the "wageworker's frontier" in which itinerant laborers roamed between city and hinterland in search of their livelihood.[27]

A similar dynamic unfolded in Seattle, where tidelands again seemed to

Figure 7.1. Indian camp with canoes on the Seattle waterfront at Ballast Island, c. 1891. Courtesy University of Washington, Special Collections, NA 680.

hold the opportunity for growth. Railroads would alchemize "the otherwise worthless resources of a country into gold," territorial governor Marshall Moore declared in an 1867 address, but only if residents took the initiative to spin mud into treasure.[28] As branch lines snaked out from Seattle and Tacoma to encircle timber camps, coal mines, and lumber mills, hundreds of speculators took Moore at his word and surged onto the mud to capture the prime sites for terminals and warehouses.[29] Thomas Burke, a local magistrate and later representative for the Great Northern Railroad, noted that "the craze for salt water" had induced "lunatics of high and low degree" to roost "like so many cawing crows on the mud flats" of Elliott Bay in search of quick riches.[30]

As in San Francisco, speculative building created conditions perfect for squalor and fire. The filled tidelands adjacent to Henry Yesler's sawmill, the city's first, became part of the infamous Skid Road district, also known as "the Lava Beds" for the smoldering piles of wood chips and sawdust alongside the mill. Several major fires erupted in the 1870s, culminating in the devastating 1889 inferno that inspired an updated water system and a downtown rebuilt in brick and stone. But instead of blaming haphazard growth, many white Seattleites blamed "the 'siwash' camps on the sand reef just across from Main Street"—Indian encampments—for the blazes.[31]

Blaming Indians for fires and pestilence also justified the seizure of still more tidelands for development. At the 1889 state constitutional convention, Seattle leaders backed efforts to use tidelands as inducements for industrial and railway development. Inland county representatives balked at giving railways such power, so convention delegates eventually agreed to recognize state ownership of beds and shores in navigable waters up to the line of ordinary high water. Improved land above that line would be available to develop into private property.[32] The intention was noble, but the hoped for alchemy of law and capital did not yield the intended profits. With the arrival of the Great Northern Railroad in 1893 and the promotion of various schemes to dig canals and fill tidelands, the resulting land booms delivered more acres of filled mudflats into private hands. By the time city residents voted to create a public port in 1911, Seattle officials had to fight their way through a gauntlet of privately owned mud and gravel to reach the sea.[33]

The relentless transfer of tidelands from aboriginal to white control did not fully eradicate Indians, who continued to visit and camp on their traditional hunting and fishing sites. These were age-old practices, but whites increasingly saw only acts of trespass. For their part, many Indians had nowhere else to go. A 1915 federal report found one to three thousand "landless and homeless" Indians wandering "up and down the Sound, living on the beaches and constantly evicted or ordered to move on by their white neighbors." Well-meaning reformers confused Indian destitution for backwardness and an inability to modernize.[34] In one celebrated instance, after a winter gale destroyed the shoreline shack of the late Chief Seattle's (Seeathl) nephew, Billy, and his wife, Ellen, white citizens started a relief fund. "In the old days Billy was a good provider," the *Seattle Post-Intelligencer* reported, but "the camping places along the shores of the Sound are now privately owned and no trespassers are allowed; the game has been killed; even the fish are hard to get."[35] Left unanswered was why the landscape had changed and Billy had not. Seattle needed its ports and its transcontinental railways for the Pacific trade. Indian rights were not part of that plan.

To the south, Los Angeles represented a different variation on this theme of urban enclosure in the pursuit of transoceanic and transcontinental commerce. Just as the tidelands in Seattle and San Francisco had evolved from public resource to private property, water rights and sewerage followed similar trajectories in Los Angeles. Prior to American rule, Spanish and Mexican authorities had operated under water laws that mandated equal access, communal rights, and moderation to insure orderly development. The Los Angeles *ayuntamiento*, or town council, appointed an overseer, or *zanjero*, to supervise construction of *zanjas*, or irrigation ditches, along the Los Angeles River and to adjudicate subsequent disputes. During the early years of American rule, this system held sway so long as the Californios were the majority. As American conceptions of private property and water rights took hold, the old *zanja* regime evaporated.[36]

The old water-rights regime fell before the needs of the Southern California cattle industry, first to better-financed American rancheros, then to industrial ranchers such as the San Francisco-based Miller and Lux Company.[37] Los Angeles political and business leaders wanted more than cattle lots, however. They imagined smokestacks and manufacturing jobs, too. After the railroad finally arrived, the Anglo *zanjero*, C. M. Jenkins, wrote in his 1883 report that if Los Angeles wanted "cotton, wool, paper, and dozens of other sorts of factories here," the communally held *zanja* was doing nothing but sending "our streams, more precious than Pateolian rivers . . . running to waste in unproductive sand."[38] City leaders listened and systematically dismantled the *zanja* system piece by piece, replacing it pipe by pipe with modern sewer and water lines. But municipal construction crews bypassed Chinatown and Sonora Town, located on the banks of the fast-disappearing Los Angeles River. As the growing city sucked its namesake watercourse dry, new utilities redirected wealth toward white Angelenos and their communities—and away from the city's poor and minority districts.[39]

It was not only industrialists but also their workers who shaped these new geographies of urban inequality. Turn-of-the-century Pacific cities were ports of entry for immigrant laborers as well as jobbing centers and settlement destinations. Indispensable as political pawns, necessary components of a dual labor system, Asian workers were both particularly despised and desired, and, like Indian workers, they were not dismissed but cordoned off from the larger community.[40]

The enclosure of Asian laborers in the Pacific West, like the exclusion of Indian workers, had both urban and rural dimensions. In the countryside, the passage of alien land laws made immigrant land ownership impossible, and extralegal violence against Chinese, Japanese, and other immigrants served as an additional means of subordination. Most had no recourse but to flee to the city, but housing covenants, school discrimination, and franchise restrictions proved equally oppressive.[41] In many cases, public officials justified urban enclosure to prevent social and public-health problems. Yet they tolerated tremendous porosity in other social boundaries to facilitate free trade. Trade and labor overcame nativist sentiments, even after the 1882 Chinese Exclusion Act, because a vibrant and vigorous transnational exchange of illegal and legal immigrants, goods, and commodities connected China with its expatriates across the Americas.[42]

No industry demonstrated this complex reciprocity within Pacific Slope cities much as fishing. By 1854, Chinese migrants established fishing camps on the eastern shore of San Francisco Bay, before moving south to Monterey, San Pedro, and San Diego in the 1860s. The completion of the transcontinental railroads dispersed still more Chinese onto the seas. In the salmon canneries of Alaska and British Columbia, most Chinese were industrial laborers, prized by operators for their skill at cutting and processing fish—and reviled by white workers for the same reason. Seattle soon became a central jobbing center for Chinese labor contractors hiring out to Alaskan and British Columbian canneries after mining debris wiped out the salmon runs of the San Francisco Bay Area. Yet the perceived distinctiveness of Chinese fishermen along the entire coast led to an easy way to assign blame for shrinking fisheries: an 1880 law in California prohibited all aliens from fishing public waters. Eventually struck down by the U.S. Circuit Court as unconstitutional, the act found favor with both Progressive conservationists and anti-immigrant activists who were often one and the same.[43]

Barred from the fin fisheries, the Chinese turned to other species favored by East Asian consumers, processing shellfish for United States and Canadian Chinatowns or markets in Canton or Hong Kong. Drying or curing sea urchins, abalone, and squid was difficult work. The resulting odors, concentrating along urban shorelines, repelled white Americans and underscored the perception of Chinese as unhygienic and inassimilable.[44] At the same time, the mounting environmental damage to San Francisco Bay helped to harden racial divisions. As native shellfish and fin fisheries declined, entrepreneurs transplanted Atlantic oysters, leading to another short-lived boom, until the sensitive bivalves succumbed to a noxious cocktail of pollutants: human waste, oil refinery spills, smelter runoff, and slaughterhouse offal. By the early twentieth century, harvests plummeted. Active only in restricting access instead of stopping pollution, state regulators now required expensive licenses, established catch quotas, and restricted certain gear. None of these efforts succeeded and the oyster fishery collapsed. By the 1920s "oyster pirates," including many Chinese and other Asian immigrants, were catching and eating contaminated shellfish in secret while oyster growers were forced out of business.[45]

Nativist conservation policies also shaped reactions to the massive transformation of Seattle's watersheds and subsequent fights over diminished fishing. A series of massive floods catalyzed a new consensus to build a network of canals, waterways, and levees around Puget Sound. Beginning in 1914, city and state engineers removed oxbows and meanders along the lower Duwamish River, the city's largest, replacing it with the straight Duwamish Waterway. The nation's entry into World War I turned the Duwamish into the Northwest's industrial arsenal, home to shipyards, marine shops, and a young aviation company named Boeing.[46]

Remaking the Duwamish for global trade also led to the ultimate demise of Seattle's local commercial fishery. Dominated largely by immigrants and Indians of limited capital unable to relocate, the fishery was already in trouble. Decades of habitat destruction and pollution had already depleted nearby salmon runs; retooling the city's watershed added to the decline by changing fish migration routes or obliterating spawning grounds. State authorities were reluctant to oppose development now that Seattle was challenging San Francisco's commercial dominance. Instead, officials turned to artificial propagation to make more fish, opening hatcheries across the state.[47] Following the war, Seattle sport anglers allied with industrialists and shippers to complain that "aliens not only . . . completely monopolize our fishery," as a 1919 report concluded, but they also "destroy it while monopolizing it." After several contentious public hearings, the state fish commission closed Elliott Bay and the Duwamish River to commercial fishing.[48] Throughout the 1920s, most charged with illegal fishing had Italian, Greek, Slavic, or Japanese surnames. Some others were likely Indians trying to find a living off reservation.[49]

Civic and business leaders celebrated their triumph in remaking urban space to serve commerce, yet they also faced again the contradictions of promoting Pacific trade while enclosing or excluding immigrant and Indian labor. In the first years of the twentieth century, following the forcible acquisition of Hawaii and the Philippines, plus the completion of the Panama Canal, urban boosters along the Pacific Slope saw an opportunity to tout their cities as gateways to the new transoceanic frontier. World's fairs were one popular device. Modeled on the 1893 Columbian Exposition, the 1894 Midwinter

International Exposition in San Francisco, complete with a sanitized rendition of the Forty-Niners' mining camps, testified to the city's rising economic and cultural ambitions. More than a decade later, Portland opened the 1905 Lewis and Clark Exposition, Seattle held the 1909 Alaska-Yukon-Pacific Exposition, or AYPE, and San Diego and San Francisco, in 1915, staged rival expositions.[50]

Unlike other world's fairs, these celebrations emphasized future commercial imperialism over historical commemoration. Anticipating the Panama Canal's completion, San Franciscans built a five-acre working model of the waterway, complete with lighthouses, locks, and dams at the 1915 fair. Seattle built replicas of Alaskan mines and staged exhibits of Asian arts for their exposition, while San Diegans blended Mission-style architecture lit by modern electric lights. At all of these fairs, nature had a prominent role. According to *The World's Work*, "Nature's own great exposition," held "the mind in thrall" at Seattle's fair by opening the "world's wondrous treasure box" for exploitation.[51]

Exposition promoters further hyped each city's natural advantages by linking social and economic progress to racial advancement. "The red man of the Pacific Coast is present everywhere," reported the *Seattle Times*: the "glares and grins" of the "dun-colored totem poles" dotting the fairgrounds, the instructional and scientific exhibits crowding the Smithsonian Institution and U.S. Government Buildings, the Wild West Shows staged by Arapaho, Cheyenne, and Lakota performers, and the Eskimo and Igorrote Villages of the amusement quarter peopled with Tlingit and Inuit from Alaska and Igorots from the Philippines.[52] Actual Indians still worked and lived in Seattle, but they and other savages were denigrated as anachronistic relics. When an Igorot named Ka-lang-ad supposedly "escaped" from the village, the *Seattle Times* editorialized, "the time is past when tattooed and painted savages" roamed the woods.[53] Yet the savage past still had work to do in the present at these fairs by reminding visitors why history mattered now. A young Herbert Hoover, visiting London in 1912 to promote San Francisco's upcoming Panama-Pacific International Exposition, explained how "in these days of stifling struggle our people" needed to "have a heritage of race" as well as material prosperity.[54]

Fusing the conquest of nature to the conquest of savagery at these world's fairs seemed to pay off for urban boosters, if measured by foreign commerce. Transpacific trade increased three times faster than transatlantic trade after 1913, doubling from 6 to 12 percent of the nation's total foreign commerce.[55]

The opening of the Panama Canal was one clear reason why; effective promotion of the urban Pacific Slope was another. This was a success surely by any measure, but lost in the celebration was how the legacies of history now began exacting costs on each city's immediate environment and their poorest, most marginal citizens.

Here is where urban frontier anxiety turned back on itself. Frederick Jackson Turner may have cast aspersions on cities, but he did not ignore them entirely, referring to the "complexity of city life" and the rise of America's "manufacturing civilization" throughout his signature essay.[56] What he left unexamined was how urban Americans might survive the vanishing frontier. The responses were as varied as their proponents. Some advocated returning to Jeffersonian agrarianism principles through homesteading and irrigated agriculture. Others urged Americans to take up outdoor sports or nature education. Still others agitated for opening new frontiers overseas through colonization or trade. No matter the proposed solution, all relied upon the continued "frontier dialectic," pitting savagery and nature against Western civilization and modernity.[57] And all cast the struggle as mortal combat. As novelist Frank Norris explained in 1902, if the "blood-instincts" of the Old World were lost without the frontier, they might find new outlets through trade. "Competition and conquest are words easily interchangeable," he wrote, and "we cannot speak of it but in terms borrowed from the glossary of the warrior."[58]

This was Progressivism as primitivism and modernism combined. Seen this way, Richard Wade's martial "spearheads" imagery takes on new relevance.[59] By elaborating the border as the measure of national sovereignty, North American governments wanted to do more than extend their commercial reach. They wanted to restrict Asian migration as well as regulate Asian trade.[60] Pacific Slope cities were literally on the front line of this foreign campaign and they were often the first to face the collateral damage at home. City leaders wrestled with the contradictions of expanding trade while restricting immigration, encouraging industrial growth while preventing environmental destruction, and promoting employment while discouraging vagrancy and social disorder. It was easy for some frontier worriers to tell city-weary Americans to light out for the wilderness. It was harder for those running the metropolis to detach frontier anxieties from urban life because the end of the frontier foreshadowed the end of progress itself.

Some Progressive thinkers offered a way out. Herbert Croly, in his influential 1909 book *The Promise of American Life*, blamed the frontier age, in part, for the "morally and socially undesirable distribution of wealth." He called for newly empowered civic institutions "responsible for a morally and socially desirable distribution of wealth." Croly pinned his hopes on cities in particular as "the most fruitful field for economically and socially constructive experimentation." Urban leaders enjoyed the "unique chance" to protect their communities by using their expertise and resources "for the amelioration of the sanitary, if not the fundamental economic and social, condition of the poorer people."[61] Even those Progressives unwilling to jettison what they saw as the vibrant individualism and energetic entrepreneurialism of the frontier past accepted Croly's advice. Writing in 1910, Theodore Roosevelt lauded the "pioneers that pushed the frontiers of civilization westward" but acknowledged that the "general welfare" now demanded "a greater variety of good qualities than were needed on the frontier."[62]

Progressives like Croly had reason to hope cities might promote progress in a post-frontier America. By the dawn of the twentieth century, American cities had accrued significant powers to acquire water and power, condemn private property, regulate industry and commerce, pursue infrastructure improvements, and regulate citizens' behavior and movement in the name of public health. (For example, many Progressives, including Theodore Roosevelt, endorsed Los Angeles' seizure of the Owens River as its own.) In particular, public health officials and municipal engineers were, to paraphrase James Scott, the eyes and hands of an assertive metropolitan state.[63] They were border guards who worried that porous borders had led to social and environmental instability. In response, these latter-day praetorians tried to reassert environmental and civic boundaries politically or, failing that, they tried to change their cities physically. They would erase what remained of the frontier in their city even as they eulogized their cities' romantic origins.

In San Francisco, natural disaster provided the pretext for establishing a new order. The April 18, 1906, earthquake liquefied the filled tidelands, destroying several commercial and shipping districts. The resulting fires consumed what the temblor had not flattened, driving as many as 250,000 people from their homes. The refugees lived in makeshift tent camps until the following summer, but these were anything but homogeneous communities. Even in temporary quarters, middle-class and native-born whites segregated themselves from working-class immigrants, who, in turn, separated themselves from the even more lowly Chinese. Facing another round of recrimination and discrimination from white assistance groups, many Chinese decamped to Oakland or other Chinatowns, relying upon the segregated social networks of support spanning the Pacific Rim.[64]

Once rebuilding commenced, San Francisco's ruling caste of real estate developers, city officials, newspaper publishers and their elected advocate, Mayor James D. Phelan, tried again to oust the Chinese, hoping to shove them to faraway Hunter's Point, an industrial district of slaughterhouses and tenements south of downtown. Some white citizens had already taken matters into their own hands, looting Chinatown in late April as the embers still cooled. But the Chinese community's transnational connections trumped local sentiment. Leaders formed the Sub-committee for the Permanent Location of Chinatown, and mobilized the Chinese legation and members of the Chinese Six Companies to apply pressure. The Chinese Consul-General informed federal authorities that trade might be redirected to other Pacific ports instead of San Francisco unless the Chinese were permitted to stay, and San Francisco Chinese merchants spoke openly about the appeal of Portland, Tacoma, or Seattle. These tactics worked. The nativists relented and within two years, Chinatown's population returned to its pre-quake level.[65]

The victory of Chinatown did not end white persecution, however. In 1907, an outbreak of bubonic plague, the second in four years, provided city officials with another excuse for expelling the Chinese. "The disease must be built out of existence," the head of the anti-plague campaign proclaimed, and then went on to explain why: whole neighborhoods of non-white and poor residents were unsanitary and needed to be eliminated. White San Franciscans, like their counterparts across the country, had long seen immigration and poverty as avenues for disease. For decades, sanitarians had conducted numerous campaigns to eradicate typhoid, tuberculosis, and other infectious diseases often blamed on immigrants and social deviants.[66]

Since the plague originated in Asia, it was easy to blame the Chinese for new outbreaks. During an earlier plague scare in 1900, Chinese leaders successfully defended their community against charges that cultural practices caused and exacerbated disease. Now, seven years later, in the wake of disaster, they were less successful. Teams of sanitarians streamed into Chinatown and other immigrant neighborhoods. Whole blocks were fumigated with sulfur dioxide gas and washed with bichloride of mercury solution. Professional rat catchers earned $2.50 daily, plus bounties to eradicate the vermin. Hundreds of thousands of rodents were trapped, shot, or poisoned. City storm drains washed dead rats into the bay, where they floated in enormous rafts circling the sewer outfalls.[67]

The campaign to eradicate the plague initiated a wholesale reconfiguration of urban space as private spaces of domestic consumption became conflated with public spaces of civic production. As in other American cities at the time, fears over poor sanitation found new scientific credence with the growing acceptance of germ theory. Chickens, pigs, cows, and horses that had lived in the city alongside immigrant and working-class residents were now exiled to the countryside. Like earlier episodes in New York and other Eastern cities, San Francisco's working poor tried and failed to resist. The city Board of Supervisors also passed new ordinances requiring that all wooden frame buildings have concrete, gravel, or packed earth floors or foundations to repel vermin. By 1909 more than six million square feet of San Francisco had been paved over with asphalt or concrete. It had also become a less rustic and more expensive place to live and work.[68]

Hatred for Asians, foreign pathogens, and invasive biota infiltrating the United States soon aroused authorities all along the Pacific Coast. Scientists, physicians, and municipal officials, drawing from Frederic Clements's incipient theories on plant ecology as well as pseudoscientific eugenics, framed aliens as invaders intent on colonizing the New World and crowding out native species, including white Americans. They needed to be quarantined, removed, or bred out of existence if white native-born Americans were to survive.[69] An America under siege and in decline horrified Frederick Jackson Turner in particular. In the twilight of his career at Harvard, he repeatedly lamented how the closed frontier heralded rising population and diminished resources. The safety valve no longer functioned, and Turner morphed into a crass Malthusian. In a gesture worthy of today's most zealous environmentalists, he suggested in a 1923 note that a "friendly comet" or a "chemist's bomb" might put an end to the quandary.[70]

Far West city leaders did not have comets to hurl or bombs to explode, but they did have laws and technology on their side. They used both to avert Turner's post-frontier apocalypse by temporarily destroying their cities in order to save them. New borders were quickly drawn and erected between clean and dirty, white and non-white, affluent and poor, and domesticated and dangerous nature. The earlier fluidity of life in the frontier city was being intentionally concealed or erased. Professional sanitarians and white-dominated labor unions alike adopted surveillance techniques to track immigrants at work and at home. They also led boycotts of Chinese-made articles in the name of protecting health and workers' rights. Immigrants disembarking at Angel Island in San Francisco Bay faced increasingly strict examination and quarantine regimens before being allowed, if at all, to set foot on the mainland. Local Chinese political and business leaders vigorously fought some measures, but as Nayan Shah argues, occasionally they also joined in the effort to sanitize Chinatown, eliminating remnants of an older Chinese bachelor society, rooting out opium dens, and closing residential hotels. Attacking recent immigrants was an effective means for some landed Chinese immigrants also to prove their loyalty and worth to city officials and white antagonists in the business community.[71]

In Los Angeles, the proximity to the Mexican border heightened clashes over immigration, disease, and civic improvement. Even as civic leaders romanticized the city's Hispanic heritage to attract tourists and investors, they simultaneously struggled to whitewash its Mexican history. The undoing of the *zanja* system was one step; new zoning laws were the next. Impoverished ethnic enclaves in East Los Angeles, created decades earlier by municipal policy and civic neglect, now faced extreme social and environmental pressures. Across the city, residents of all classes protested noxious meatpacking and rendering plants that processed Central Valley cattle, refineries cracking petroleum siphoned from Southern California beaches, and crematoria collecting and burning human corpses. In response, reformers pushed through citywide laws curbing and redistributing pollution. Zoning created healthier and cleaner neighborhoods on the city's largely white and affluent west side while pushing polluters into the east side's dirtier, industrial neighborhoods populated by minorities and the poor.[72]

Changes in the metropolitan landscape of pollution and residence also intersected with changes in the regional geography of labor migration and immigration. The rapid growth of Southern California's agricultural sector in the late nineteenth and early twentieth centuries, driven by massive federal and state reclamation projects and investment by agricultural and railroad conglomerates, relied upon a pliable supply of labor to pick citrus, lettuce, strawberries, and other crops.[73] Japanese, Chinese, Filipino, and Korean immigrants were both laborers and producers, but Mexicans and Mexican Americans now made up the bulk of the itinerant workforce. Pushed by the economic and political disruptions of the Mexican Revolution and pulled by labor contractors and enticements of higher wages, they dominated the orange groves and industrial floors of metropolitan Los Angeles, made possible, in part, by the appropriation of Owens Valley water. Mexican workers shuttled between city and suburb, countryside and metropolis, Mexico and the United States by rail, streetcar, bus, and automobile. But within greater Los

Angeles, the transformation of the Southland's landscapes, coupled with patterns of chain migration, channeled new arrivals into preexisting enclaves.[74]

The enclaves in town were subjected to the same assaults as in other Pacific Slope cities. When bubonic plague struck Los Angeles in 1924, local authorities immediately quarantined the "Mexican district" adjacent to the Los Angeles River. Police officers cordoned the neighborhood, home to 1,800 to 2,500 people, and then expanded their exclusion zone as the plague spread. Abatement crews fumigated homes and buildings with hydrocyanic gas and carbon monoxide. They also set rattraps and spread out poison over a broadening war zone. As one newspaper article later reported, officials "had to destroy a large part of Los Angeles"—more specifically, the Mexican part. Wrecking crews cut a devastating swath in the name of urban renewal and public health. Approximately twenty-five hundred buildings were demolished or burned. As buildings were swept aside, phalanxes of sanitarians marched block-by-block, fumigating buildings, killing rats, and collecting the bodies for autopsies.[75]

Much of the campaign was kept quiet for fear of negative publicity, less out of concern for displaced Mexicans, African Americans, Japanese, and other minorities than for the city's reputation as a tourist destination and investment magnet. Blurring biotic and human others, city boosters and public health officials often portrayed Mexicans as rats, debating how to prevent measures that "would scatter" the problem or provoke an angry "stampede." As one University of California zoologist wrote later, Mexicans tended to "huddle together," thereby "spreading various epidemics throughout our population."[76] These observers were not entirely wrong. Crowded living conditions and insufficient sanitary infrastructure did provide fertile ground for infectious disease. What they failed to recognize was how the city's planning and political economy had created this landscape of poverty and misery.

Urban renewal had not whitened the barrios in Los Angeles; instead, it had concentrated and excluded them. Attention soon turned toward limiting the number of Mexicans coming in the first place. Well-intentioned white reformers, often working with leaders in the Mexican American community, came to see Mexican immigration itself as a health threat, both to the body politic of Los Angeles and the bodies of white Los Angelenos.[77] When the U.S. Army Corps of Engineers later straitjacketed the Los Angeles River in a concrete aqueduct, it was no accident that the hydraulic reengineering of the river coincided with further marginalization of Mexican communities living and working along the hardening banks.[78]

Figure 7.2. Disinfecting crew at work, 1500 East 4th Street, Los Angeles, during the 1924 plague outbreak. Courtesy The Bancroft Library, University of California, Berkeley.

But perhaps the best analog to Turner's apocalyptic comet was the reengineering of Seattle's landscape, where city engineers almost completely reshaped the entire city in a few short years. As the city spread across steep glaciated hills and filled-in tide flats, minority neighborhoods clustered in low-lying and neglected places became the target of the same reforms as elsewhere. Typhoid, typhus, and other diseases were commonplace in these enclaves, although Seattle was spared outbreaks of plague. It was also spared the disasters like the one that rocked San Francisco, but in the minds of some city leaders, the Klondike Gold Rush of 1897–1898 was the demographic equivalent of an earthquake. R. H. Thomson, the city engineer during the Progressive Era decades, recalled streets so full of hoboes, would-be miners, vagrants, and pimps "that you can hardly walk through them." The population ballooned from 3,553 in 1880 to 237,194 in 1910, one of the fastest municipal growth rates in the Far West.[79] Many of the poorest settled or squatted on recently filled tidal flats. "From the street car windows and railway coaches," the *Seattle Post-Intelligencer* reported in 1899, "glimpses are caught of Shacktown, but the daily lives of the cosmopolitan inhabitants, their tales of adventure, of grinding sorrow, of domestic unhappiness are not revealed."[80]

Seattle reformers wanted to tackle poor sanitation and immorality simultaneously. Thomson had concluded that the city faced three interlocked environmental problems: insufficient and contaminated water supplies, poor drainage, and rugged topography, each of which also yielded significant social consequences. The solution to all three lay in reestablishing proper boundaries between water and land. Beginning in 1892, Thomson oversaw sewer construction, tideland filling, and the acquisition of the Cedar River as the city's proprietary supply, completing the hydraulic landscape by building a gravity-driven pipeline to Seattle ten years later.[81] With water in hand and sanitation plans in place, Thomson then turned his attention to leveling the city's hills, which he blamed for many "offensive" and "impassable grades," some exceeding 10 percent.[82]

The first regrade, completed in 1898 along First Avenue at the foot of Denny Hill, relied on steam shovels and horse-drawn carts. When property values in the now-flattened neighborhood subsequently soared in an already hyper-inflated market, other businesses and residences embraced Thomson's "struggles to up build this city."[83] With water from the Cedar River, contractors also turned to mining technologies, unleashing hydraulic cannons against the hills and running sluices to carry the tailings to the waterfront.[84] City residents and observers alike championed regrading as "the product of Western conditions" that required "pioneering engineering methods."[85] They championed the sheer power necessary to reverse eons of geology while wiping away some of Seattle's most blighted neighborhoods in the name of civic reform.

And the regrades were as impressive as they were destructive. On the first Denny Hill regrade, engineers and contractors sent nearly 5.5 million cubic yards of dirt and rock into Elliott Bay, displacing scores of squatters' shacks along the shoreline to make room for development. The Jackson Street regrade cut through part of Seattle's Asian and African American neighborhoods, enabling city inspectors to condemn whole blocks of homes and apartment buildings in the name of progress. According to *Engineering News*, remaking the physical landscape required altering the social fabric, too. Jackson Street, once a "dirty, filthy region that had naturally become the immoral center of Seattle," was cleansed and uplifted thanks to what one city engineer called "a natural world-making force" for "municipal improvement."[86]

Yet like a meteor strike, regrading left more ruin than renewal in its wake, justifying still more regrading despite growing opposition to the practice. In the former Jackson and Dearborn Street regrade districts, home to the some of the city's poorest neighborhoods, water percolated into the exposed slopes and triggered wave after wave of destructive landslides. Eventually even the state Supreme Court unanimously concluded in *Wong Kee Jun v. Seattle*, the last of the so-called "Jackson Street regrade cases," that the city engineers were to blame.[87] Yet despite legal challenges and wrecked homes, by the 1920s, property owners across the city were clamoring again for new regrade projects to remove "a very cheap and undesirable residence section" on what was left of Denny Hill and to eliminate Profanity Hill in the center of Seattle's Skid Row, where the earlier Jackson and Dearborn regrades had yielded a slide-prone area filled with "dilapidated" abodes. Engineers again assaulted Denny Hill regrade, but the Great Depression turned off the money and the hoses for good before engineers could complete the remaining projects.[88]

The consequences of this earthmoving as usual fell largely on the city's minorities and working poor. Displaced from their neighborhoods and unable to find affordable housing, many built shacks and houseboats along the polluted Duwamish Waterway and Elliott Bay waterfront. There were also exiles from Seattle's impoverished rural environs, where sawmills, mines, and farms had never fully recovered from the short but severe depression after World War I. The famed sociologist Roderick D. McKenzie, then a young professor at the University of Washington, explained this social chaos in ecological terms, explaining how waves of "foreign races and other undesirable invaders" continued to sweep over Seattle. As a result, the city had not yet reached its "climax stage" where the "dominant type" of ecological community could "withstand the intrusions of other forms of invasion."[89] Thanks to these emigrants and immigrants, Seattle still displayed "many marks of the frontier" even as it was "rapidly entering upon a metropolitan area, the future of which lies in the Pacific."[90]

The Great Depression forestalled Seattle's metropolitan future as still more waves of displaced laborers washed over the city. In late 1931, hundreds of unemployed erected a Hooverville on vacant land owned by the Port of Seattle, just south of Downtown. One observer called the encampment "a junkyard for human junk" and "a scrap-heap of cast-off men."[91] City officials tried to remove Hooverville by fire and truncheon, but the residents of this "hobo city" fought back, burrowing into the ground and constructing roofs of tin or steel. Eventually, the city relented and allowed squatters to stay, but refused to provide water or electricity to the thousand-plus men who lived there. Even this level of charity angered some Seattleites, who called upon city officials to redouble their efforts. "We recognize the fact . . . that it is unlawful to shoot or drown them," Mary Gamble Young of the North End Improvement

Club wrote to the city council about a squatter camp in the Interbay district, "but—we want you to do something about it."[92] The nation's entry into World War II provided the pretext for action. In April 1942, the new Seattle Housing Authority torched the shanties and evicted the inhabitants.[93]

Wartime mobilization seemingly closed the chapter on the frontier past along the urban Pacific Slope. On the filled tidelands of San Francisco Bay and Puget Sound, shipyard workers displaced drifters to assemble destroyers and Liberty Ships. On the banks of the straightened Duwamish River and entombed Los Angeles River, airplane plants churned out a bomber or fighter plane a day. Still, past practices endured. Japanese and Japanese American civilians were evacuated and sent inland to relocation camps in the name of national security. Thousands of African Americans who came west and Mexicans who came north for work were funneled into the now-segregated landscapes of the metropolitan Far West. Meanwhile, public health officials again grappled with containing migrants and the diseases they carried. By the war's end, boosters in all three cities believed they had escaped history and eluded the calamity of Turner's closed frontier. What they failed to realize was how their faith in progress had helped to propel the inequities of the past into an unfolding future.

The frontier is, after all, a metaphor, one that contains within it legacies of inequality and violence as often as the hope of renewal and innovation. In the case of the *fin de siècle* urban Far West, frontier rhetoric both justified and ignored particular changes within social and environmental networks linking city and hinterland. Those relationships were rarely equivalent in cause or consequence. In the longer history of the region, Pacific Slope cities illustrate how frontier anxieties lived on when civic and business leaders sought to reinvent their communities in response to unsettling changes. Given the state of scientific knowledge and political economy at the time, their triumphs were undeniable: improved public health, affordable utilities, innovative urban planning, and an elevated quality of life for many residents.

Yet these accomplishments were neither universally enjoyed nor democratically distributed. The legacies of dispossession and destruction became doppelgangers that haunted buoyant boosters of Western urban progress. These malevolent spirits, hard to exorcise and difficult to vanquish, never fully disappeared. Cities continued to reorganize their extractive and commercial hinterlands and reshaped their immediate environs in turn. With each round of remodeling, present tradeoffs piled on top of past consequences, the costs passed on to those people and places least able to oppose the penalties. As

Paul Sabin concludes in his assessment of American expansion into the Pacific, "this past of the American West is truly unbroken and it remains so today."[94] And part of that past is metropolitan, too.

The histories recounted in this essay come largely from the turn of the twentieth century, but perhaps the most tantalizing and complex stories may come from reflecting back across even broader scales of time and space. As urban centers organized their hinterlands beginning in the late nineteenth century, the broader ecology of resources and energy production they marshaled influenced where and how urbanites built their homes, workplaces, and public spaces.[95] This was never a simple case of geographical determinism, however. Migration and immigration have also shaped metropolitan environmental and social dynamics. As Dorothy Fujita-Rony reminds us, we must also examine the American West from the perspective of Asian immigrants, "a perspective shaped by both land and water."[96] For salmon cannery workers from Quezon City, mill workers from Osaka, fishermen from Canton, or miners from Thessaloniki, the foreign cities of San Francisco, Seattle, and Los Angeles were not distant locales but second homes.[97]

Pacific Slope cities also became second homes to floral and faunal immigrants as well as points for overseas embarkation. Migrant laborers brought unwanted or even dangerous animals, food, microbes, and plants with them to North America. The dispersal of these weedy species along railway tracks and local waterways speak to the complex and cross-informing pathways of environmental history. The social and ecological consequences of military occupation, transoceanic trade, and tourism also link the histories of Seattle, Los Angeles, and San Francisco to Hawaii, Alaska, the Philippines, and Indochina.[98] Biologically and socially, Pacific Slope cities truly were the "spearheads" of American global expansion.

Wade's imagery is a reminder of why metaphors matter, even an exhausted trope like the frontier, but also why careful historical context remains essential. The frontier as an idea came of age, lived, and died in the span of a few short decades at the turn of the twentieth century even though we have debated its significance ever since. Yet metaphors can and do encapsulate histories that persist with us. The two frontiers of Turner and Buffalo Bill, the conquest of nature and the conquest of savagery, endure in today's culture. They inhabit places as well as stories, processes as well as locations, borderlands as well as nations, no matter how much we try to remove or forget them.[99]

Present-day cities bear the traces. In Seattle, gleaming skyscrapers frame snowcapped peaks, trendy condominiums rise over the eponymous Denny Regrade neighborhood, container ships unload goods from China, and Boeing jets arcing toward Japan and Korea trace contrails in the skies. Boosters call this twenty-first-century "metronatural" Seattle a metropolis set in nature and made beautiful by man; yet a shadow city, a metrotoxic Seattle, stands here, too.[100]

These spectral cities lurk along the entire coast. At the San Francisco International Airport, city, state, and federal officials screen tourists and immigrants from East Asia for pandemic flu or other infectious diseases, while merchants in Chinatown shutter their shops after every Asiatic disease scare. The Centers for Disease Control and Prevention quarantine station at San Francisco International Airport is one node in a security system stretching from Anchorage to San Diego.[101] Nevertheless, interlopers slip through: Asian longhorned beetles, Eurasian water milfoil, and human contraband. Several times every year, longshoremen at San Pedro or Long Beach open ship containers filled with dead and dying stowaways from around the globe. Most elude capture to join the denizens of illegal immigrants that sustain the Southland's economy.[102]

And along the filled Elliott Bay waterfront and the straightened Duwamish Waterway, signs sprout from the mud, warning not to eat contaminated crabs, clams, oysters, or fish, especially after a heavy rain flushes pollutants into the former estuary. The signs are in seven languages: English, Spanish, Chinese, Vietnamese, Laotian, Khmer, Russian, and Tagalog. Tours along the concrete-encased Los Angeles River, the crumbling seawall at Hunter's Point in San Francisco, the dusty alleys of Barrio Logan in San Diego, and the stagnant reaches of Portland's Columbia Slough reveal similar places scarred by pollution and segregation. These are places where the past dwells.[103]

Much has changed since a band of Indians fled their burning homes in early Seattle, but much remains familiar to their living descendants today. In 2009, members of the Duwamish Tribe opened their new tribal longhouse and cultural center in West Seattle, a few hundred yards away from where Herring's House once stood. Speaking to a packed crowd, tribal chairwoman Cecile Hansen noted how the tribe had "completed one phase of getting our own home." The other phase remained elusive: the Duwamish were embroiled in a decade-long court battle with federal authorities to prove they were not extinct, facing opposition from both Bureau of Indian Affairs officials and rival Puget Sound tribes who feared the Duwamish would lay claim to scarce salmon and shellfish grounds.[104]

If early frontier cities stand for stories of national triumph, America's more recent Pacific Slope cities are cautionary tales of overreach, unexpected consequences, and costs deferred to future generations. To paraphrase Richard Wade's conclusion to *The Urban Frontier*, any history that omits this dimension of urban life relates only part of the story of the westward expansion.[105]

Otherwise, all we are telling are ghost stories.

IV.

Renderings: Visualizing and Reading the Frontier City

CHAPTER 8

Locating the Frontier City in Time and Space: Documenting a Passing Phenomenon

Timothy R. Mahoney

In his book *The Urban Frontier* Richard Wade described frontier cities as the "spearheads of the frontier." Like all classic descriptions, it is succinct, evocative, and elusive. The literal sharpness of the metaphor—the "spearhead," piercing ahead of the wave of settlement—suggests that frontier cities have a precise location and function, serving as intermediary between the core system behind it and the frontier out in front of it.[1]

Yet, on the other hand, the fact that a spear is thrown suggests volatility—of speed, of location—that has long complicated historians' efforts to define and understand the phenomenon. After all, cities and towns, unlike spears, do not move through the air. No town or city ever really "moved" with a frontier, though of course many individuals, traders, speculators, boosters, workers and occasionally even buildings did.[2] A city is dynamic but also geographically stationary; the frontier is dynamic and geographically in motion. The frontier city—defined by its interaction with a moving entity—was a volatile and unstable place. To some it may seem that the concept of "frontier city" is, by its very nature, paradoxical. After all, relatively few urban places on the frontier had the time to develop into frontier cites—or frontier urban places with city or metropolitan characteristics—before the frontier was on the move. Most frontier towns were fleeting and transitory places that, by the nineteenth century, sprouted up out of nowhere and either quickly developed into something else or stagnated, declined, or even disappeared. Those towns that survived and did develop into "frontier cites," often became recognizably "urban" only after the frontier had moved on, and they began losing the very frontier qualities that interaction with the frontier had given them. Thus even the most developed frontier cities were "frontier cities" for only a very short time before they matured into central places or entrepôts in a more settled urban system. The frontier city, therefore, is at best a moving target that is notoriously hard to identify and study.

This is not to say that there are no frontier cities. As the essays in this volume attest, there were frontier cities, places that had urban characteristics on the frontier. Yet, given the fact that the "frontier" and "city" only coexisted in relatively few places, one wonders how useful this seemingly paradoxical concept, defined literally as an urban place on the frontier, remains. Or do we need to expand the definition of the "frontier city" to include towns and cities that remained close enough to the receding frontier to continue to provide a range of frontier-oriented services and functions and thus retained some of their "frontier" quality. The literature suggests that historians have taken the second course of analysis. Grasping and then resolving the paradox of the frontier city involves exploring in depth the dynamic nature, over time, of the interactions between the frontier town or city and the frontier. By examining the changing nature of the interactions between the two across an ever-changing zone of encounter that lay between them, one can recognize patterns that suggest a broader definition of a frontier city.

Even though they operate within a dynamic context, most cities establish a specific function and predictable interactions with other towns and cities within the system. In contrast, the frontier city operates on or near the edge of a system. Beyond that edge was somewhere out there, a territory that was still not quite integrated into the hub's activities. It was tentative, unsettled, and, particularly across a "hard" or a "closed border," difficult, dangerous, or provocative to cross. Some have called this zone a "near frontier" to describe an area across the hinterland that was still not quite integrated into the frontier city's activities. Others have used the "borderlands" or even "the middle ground" to evoke this sense of insecure, undependable, and contested zones of encounter. The English word *liminal* has it root in Latin notions of boundary, and that just beyond the *limen*, or threshold. The Romans merely ran a road out through an area and drew a map to show that it was their territory. They called it part of the Empire even while admitting it was not yet really theirs, economically, socially, or politically. From the perspective of the center, such in-between places, border zones, and borderlands were analogous to the urban "zone in transition" or "zone of emergence," to use two intra-city terms from the Chicago School of sociology. In varying degrees, almost every urban place that played a role in some phase of the transformation of such a zone from frontier to a settled region warrants the term "frontier" town or city.

Situated near such a zone, the frontier city's basic function as an intermediary between the center of the system and its expanding frontier was affixed to a fluid and unstable frontier. As a result it stood generally alone and unconnected to stable structures. Its functions and interactions were, for the most part, unsettled, ad hoc, and discursive, making the town economy one-dimensional, fragile, unstable, and volatile. The result of such instability was that relatively few urban places on the frontier actually developed into urban places one could call towns or cities. Most were proto-urban places that have been described as camps, outposts, stepping-off places, entry points, outfitting points, transfer points, relay points, or simply nodal points. In any case, the range of adjectives applied to the word "point" suggests the variety and lack of clarity about what exactly happened at such places on the map.[3]

Many, indeed in some areas, most, frontier settlements failed to survive. "Towns in mining districts are like mushrooms," an observer in Denver remarked in 1860. "Houses spring up today and tomorrow a rich new discovery is made and away go the mines, traders, merchants, and all and perhaps the town is never heard of again."[4] In each of these places, residents had to fight aggressively to develop to the next stage of urban growth, or they would find themselves struggling and their city would become stalled in a secondary or tertiary place in the urban system, no longer able to provide services and goods to expanding settlements. In something like "up or out," frontier cities either achieved and maintained dominance, lost their "frontier" character, or, as in many cases, simply withered away or disappeared.

Those that did survive became commercial outposts, supply depots, small trading communities, transshipment centers, meeting grounds, or termini. Even so, few of these places warranted the designation of a town, much less a city. Carl Abbott notes, for example, that few such "tenuous forts[s] or tiny trading post[s]" could be "counted as a town," for they lacked any of the "characteristics of a town," which he details as having the intention of permanence, a private real estate market, a seat of government, and a diverse local economy sustaining commercial relations between people on the frontier and the core of the system.[5] As places where frontier adventurers gathered and rested, rather than founded and settled, such places lacked a sense of permanence. Since developing a deeper function with more intensive interactions often took time, by the time a frontier outpost became a town or city that warranted the designation of "frontier city," the frontier on which it was located may have moved away.

Even so, if a frontier city is defined, like any urban place, both by its internal structure and dynamics on the ground where it is located, as well by its function in and interactions with regional, national, and even global systems in which it plays a role, then it is apparent that the "frontierness" or frontier nature of a place, could linger long after the frontier had receded. A frontier city was defined by the nature of its interactions with the frontier and the impact those interactions had on its structure. Its frontier quality, ethos, or milieu, rooted in its frontier interactions and experiences, could continue to imprint itself on the city's economy, society, politics, and culture, as well as in its relationship or interactions with other urban places and its surrounding hinterlands, for many years. The people of the town and the frontier traded and interacted directly, and operated within each other's space.

The presence of the "frontier" and the feeling that it was adjacent or near pervaded life in a frontier city. Its proximity created an air of tentativeness, anxiety, unsettledness, as well as a stirring and exciting town life. It was a place that essentially existed in the future. The residents of almost all such towns believed that their city was the "city of the future," giving it an unreal "future city" atmosphere, as David Hamer argues.[6] In spite of whatever security was established or settled arrangements put in place, such frontier towns still had a tentative, reckless, hectic quality. Their residents understood that the space out by the frontier was not yet under control; they were in an outpost, on the edge, at the periphery, of controlled and safe and systemically integrated areas.

Thus, while the definition of any "frontier city" is fleeting and transitory, a city could remain a frontier city, even as it evolved and the frontier receded, taking with it the frontier conditions that had shaped the city, so long as it maintained some direct interaction with the frontier. A frontier city was a town that served as a stepping-off place, or a supply depot to the frontier without the use of intermediary merchants at smaller places established between the frontier city and the frontier. D. W. Meinig suggests that the emergence of the depot or the "commercial outpost . . . would likely channel subsequent developments," especially given the considerable investments needed to reach distant outposts.[7]

Frontier cities engaged in increasingly regular trade with the center because the ability of its merchants to supply those across the frontier with goods exceeded local supplies or production capacity, and because it had also outgrown the capacity of its surrounding hinterland. Compelled, as a result, to import goods and services, frontier cities welcomed the trade, as self-sufficiency meant isolation, and direct arrangements for imports meant connection. Hence, in the interest of flexibility, a more useful definition of a frontier city might be any town or city in which all, most, or at least some of its people—as merchants, public officials, traders, workers, and travelers—operated in a framework in which they still had direct access to the frontier.

Over time, the key factors that shaped the nature of interactions across this zone of encounter between the frontier city and the frontier across North America were the movement of the frontier itself, the political and social values, goals, and policy that shaped the interactions between the frontier city and the frontier, and contemporary business and banking methods and communication and transport technology. Of these, the business methods and communication and transport technology contributed most to the volatility of the frontier city and its changing interactions with the frontier and the system, as the specific cases in the essays by Elliott West, Alan Gallay, and Matthew Klingle in this volume demonstrate. In this essay, I plan to reflect on these and other cases, to lay out some general principles to define the frontier cities' evolution.

The impact of the changing business methods and the technology of transport and communication on both the internal development of the frontier city, and its interaction with the metropole, was most apparent during three critical phases of early urban development on the frontier: 1) the establishment of an isolated outpost; 2) the emergence of a "commercial outpost"; and 3) the development into a central place or regional entrepôt with an organized hinterland. Put roughly, each of the stages represents: 1) an incomplete early form of frontier city or town; 2) the "classic" frontier city or town, and 3) the waning of a town or city's frontier stage.

When, for example, a frontier settlement or town lay far out, beyond any reasonable access to the center of the system, its economy was isolated and separated from the larger economy of the regional or national system. When "interior" outposts or towns had limited access from the coastal plain, rivers (or, later on, from the railroads), residents, for the most part, were on their own and had to rely on a combination of self-sufficiency, a rudimentary barter system of exchange with each other as well as with an occasional merchant who settled there. These settlements maintained an uneasy dependence on interactions with Native Americans, relieved only occasionally by interactions with "the outside."

The outposts, missions, or forts, spread across the British, French, or Spanish empires in North America in the seventeenth and eighteenth centuries operated as such relatively isolated "frontier outposts," connected by discursive, irregular, slow-motion, intermittent networks of trade and exchange that were unable to generate the dynamism and feedbacks of a system. Politically, as Abbott notes, they engaged in the "punches, and counter punches . . . of imperial feints," and hence could not advance economically with any regularity. Connected only discursively and intermittently to the metropole, the outposts of the French and Spanish Empires remained isolated for decades.[8]

In later generations, the technological advances shrank the years spent in this uncertain first phase. While interior places like Lexington, Worcester, or Springfield, Massachusetts, Lancaster, Pennsylvania, or Augusta, Maine depended on single traders with connections to Boston, New York, or London, bringing a stock of goods on perhaps an annual basis, those in Lexington and Louisville, Kentucky, Cincinnati, Ohio, and St. Louis, Missouri relied on the occasional overland freight or keel boat until the arrival of the steamboat in the 1810s.[9] Steamboats increased the volume and frequency of trade and the motivations to make large shipments by flat boat to New Orleans to sell surpluses in the southern market. On the upper Mississippi river in the 1820s and 1830s, riverside settlements such as Keokuk and Dubuque, Iowa, or Alton, Quincy, and Galena, Illinois experienced such isolation only for a season or two before the steamboat made each a point of commercial exchange. But interior places such as Springfield, New Salem, and Rockford, Illinois, or Iowa City and Des Moines, Iowa, would not be drawn into the system for years.[10]

In general, this frontier outpost stage was relatively short-lived for any frontier place on the coast, or major navigable river, or with the equivalent of direct access to the railroad depending on the scale of commitment and activity coming from the entrepôt. On the coast of North America, British settlements like Boston, Philadelphia, or even Charleston were outposts for only a few years. So too, places established on the westward-moving frontier of the United States experienced this outpost stage—with its classic marker of self-sufficient production and barter trade to support an occasional shipment from the outside—for less than a decade.

Further west, the invention of steamboats and then railroads combined with the telegraph to shorten this stage dramatically. Indeed, by the time one reached the Far West, towns that were established as outposts—as opposed to trading posts or forts—were plugged so quickly into the larger economic and urban system that few residents saw any need to produce goods and services to maintain self sufficiency. Usually within the first season, while the town or city itself remained a work in progress, one could acquire most of one's needs from the first merchants who, in return, would buy wheat, lumber, or minerals to ship to the market. Over time, from the seventeenth century to the early twentieth, as a result, this stage became shorter and shorter, as access improved and thus "outposts" just appeared, pretty fully supplied, without having had to rely on self-sufficient farming and craft production at all.

A far more critical phase of development that was much more affected by technological developments in communication and transport occurred when this initial outpost initiated more regular and sustained contact with the metropole. Attracting more investment, such a city became a true economic outpost: in D. W. Meinig's characterization, a "fixed point of commercial exchange." The arrival of a permanent merchant class "triggered the local market" and thus "plugged the local economy into the regional market."[11] Wherever this happened—on the Upper Mississippi River at Alton in 1815, Quincy about 1825, Galena in 1827, and Rock Island, not until 1835, on the Upper Missouri at Kansas City about 1850, St. Joseph about 1843, Omaha in 1854, or further west at Denver in 1858—commercial outposts transformed themselves into central places or regional entrepôts with widespread trading contacts.[12] As these connections became ever more permanent, "frontier cities" gradually lost their frontier function and identity.

Exorbitant prices were a classic marker of the frontier commercial outpost. A nascent frontier economy was initially supported by capital brought by settlers and merchants. This support could last for a season, several years, or in some cases, a decade or more. Whatever specie merchants received, they quickly transmitted it to the metropole to settle credit obligations. Because it took so long for orders to be received and for goods to be shipped from the metropole, merchants were compelled to order most of their inventory early so it would arrive before the start of the season. This forced them to tie up much of their capital in their inventories. As a result, they carried a heavy debt load which precluded further expansion of business.

The depth of investment from the metropolis combined with the increased flow of trade and people to that point from both the metropolis and the hinterland, to establish a classic frontier city as a commercial outpost.

Seventeenth-century Boston was a good example of a settlement that quickly became a commercial outpost. In spite of the effort of town officials to limit the number of local merchants who had the right to trade, other merchants began to establish connections with London and British merchants. Such contacts, secured often by family and social connections or by previous business contacts or references, began to assure a steadier supply of goods and enabled merchants to stock shelves with some degree of regularity. When goods flooded the town, prices dropped and profit margins declined, eventually compelling many merchants to seek efficiencies through functional (wholesale or retail) or product specialization, or supplying more remote settlements.[13] Alan Gallay has found a similar dynamic in the development of the frontier economies of Goa, Macau, and Manila, each of which enhanced its role in the international trade system by supplying other frontier cities across Asia.

Though some Boston merchants were initially able to set up outposts immediately west of Boston and up the Connecticut River, high costs, depleted supplies, and intense competition precluded any great success. For a while Boston traders had outposts scattered across western and central Massachusetts and up along the Maine coast. When resources there declined, others went further west and north, including one merchant who set up a monopoly on the Connecticut River at Springfield. But Indian hostility and resistance from Dutch, Swedish, and especially French traders against English intrusion constrained their success.[14]

A similar shift away from a frontier configuration in a town's mercantile sector was readily apparent in the transformation of trade in late colonial New York City. In the mid-seventeenth century, the New York market, like that of most frontier venues, was dominated by unspecialized merchants or "general importers" who ran general stores which they supplied directly from England and from which they sold goods into the frontier districts of the upper Hudson River valley. Like all such merchants, they struggled to find sufficient capital to maintain an inventory suitable to the local or regional market. As the volume of trade increased, however, wholesalers appeared, along with commission agents, who advised the supplier back in England what to send, and then aggressively disposed of the goods in the market place. Merchants began to sink their capital into processing raw materials for market, or using some local or regional resources to manufacture products that could become a substitute for imports.[15]

In Cooperstown, New York, and countless other places, merchants established reliable supplies of goods for nearby farmers, who in turn focused increasingly on production for market. Operating in the framework of a settled system of commerce, any market town like Cooperstown would face considerable competition from nearby towns. Indeed, Cooperstown was one town among many imbedded in a regional network of towns centered at Albany and then at Schenectady, both of which would grow dramatically after the construction and opening of the Erie Canal in the 1825.[16]

Farther west, in what would become Galena, Illinois, local lead deposits motivated the first trade with St. Louis as early as the late eighteenth century. In 1816, George Davenport set up a temporary post at Galena to trade with the Indians, and over the next several years at least ten other traders clustered around the site. But it was the arrival of Moses Meeker, a Cincinnati merchant who brought a full load of goods and maintained commercial connections back home, who established himself as the first permanent merchant, establishing Galena's wider ties.[17]

By 1825, two steamboats regularly plied the waters of the Upper Mississippi between St. Louis and Galena. By the time the city was platted and named in 1827, it was a classic frontier urban outpost, whose merchants traded goods across a wide area of northern Illinois, southern and central Wisconsin, and along the Upper Mississippi river valley. The next advantage came at a midpoint, when Antoine Le Claire, a mixed-race interpreter and river trader, established a town plat on the west bank of the Mississippi river in 1832. Within a few years his success in establishing a ferry at that point, gaining the county seat, and opening up direct trade with St. Louis enabled the town—Davenport—to become a commercial depot along the river. Davenport served both as the midpoint of the St. Louis and Galena system, and depot of eastern Iowa.[18]

Though Leclaire's initial advantage allowed him to gain a near-monopoly control of local trade, he was shrewd enough to recognize that competition and diversity, as well as reinvestment in the fledging city, would grow the place and enhance his wealth. So while he invested in a hotel, built a new wharf, and platted off more land, he sold land to newcomers on liberal terms and supported and encouraged their efforts. As Davenport merchants extended their efforts farther west to develop connections with newly established interior towns, such as Iowa City, Ottumwa, and Des Moines, and began to act more and more as specialized wholesale merchants, they ushered in a post-frontier stage of development in which boosters were less concerned with the town's access to the frontier than its place within the burgeoning regional urban system.[19]

So it continued, in Nebraska City, in Denver, in Leadville, as railroad depots and mineral strikes determined the paths of settlement and market structure.[20] Within months of the silver rush, Leadville—with the help of investors in St. Louis, Chicago, Davenport, Iowa, and New York—became a classic frontier city, complete with industrial-scale smelters to process the silver. Soon, however, economies of scale and transport cost efficiencies drew the smelters down to Denver, diversifying and sustaining that city's economy for decades.[21]

Despite being the classic image of a frontier city, as a "commercial outpost," this stage was relatively short-lived for most locales. As mercantile competition increased amid a building volume of trade and further improvements in transportation, the merchandising sector consolidated, turning profits which could be reinvested in expansion. By shortening the time it took to communicate with, ship something to, or receive something from a frontier city, the cause and effect feedback between the core and frontier city accelerated. This allowed quicker, cheaper, larger-scale, and less risky economic activity. More importantly, such accelerated feedback triggered specialization, division of labor, and a drive to achieve economies of scale. Each of these increased returns and triggered further development, as Elliot West has shown in regard to San Francisco and Matt Klingle in regard to Seattle in other essays in this volume.

Town merchants, desirous of developing trade, extended credit to farmers and then were often compelled, given the lack of specie, to accept produce for payment. In some ways, merchants had no choice, as they needed something in remittance for the credit extended that they could use to settle their rising debts back East. In an era of slow communication and shipping, orders for goods for a coming season from frontier merchants had to be out several months to a year ahead and shipped weeks or months ahead to arrive at the beginning of the season. Thus almost all a merchant's capital went into his stock of goods, the returns on which were at most a guess, based on previous activity. If, as they did in the interior East and later in the early West, merchants went on "buying trips" to New York or Philadelphia, they could be gone for months, leaving the business at home unattended.

From the other direction, entrepôt wholesale merchants sought ways to get goods in their customers' stores more quickly. Increasingly frustrated by the wait for news or buyers from a frontier outpost, they began to ship ahead of the orders—gambling, of course, on the hope that all their goods would be sold. As the volume of shipping increased, merchants sought to achieve economies of scale that would reduce per-unit costs and garner a larger market share. If they miscalculated, of course, an excess of goods could flood a frontier market and badly destabilize it. This occurred a number of times in San Francisco in the years after the Gold Rush. One merchant charged in December 1853 that eastern merchants, three months away by the quickest route, hedged their bets by shipping as many goods as possible without regard to anticipated demand. As a result, they had "crushed us with goods against fearfully ruinous prices, against a slowly increasing population, against good judgement and a constantly failing market." He pleaded with them to "cease shipments, not partially but altogether for four months." The risk of delay or, worse, the destruction of an entire shipment by some mishap would threaten a merchant with ruin, so he paid high insurance rates.[22] Among many notable examples of such disasters, for example, the steamboat Bertrand, which sank in the Missouri River above Omaha on April 1, 1865, was carrying 250 tons of dry goods for several merchants in Virginia City and Missoula, Montana, to be shipped via Fort Benton. The goods that sunk with the ship constituted the full annual stock of one merchant and large portions of the annual stock of others.[23]

Thus many merchants became produce shippers as well as wholesalers or retailers of commercial goods as a matter of expediency, to try to reduce their debt through the sale of raw materials or investment in processing manufacturing. By creating a steady market for agricultural goods, such merchants established their town or city as a central place, and drew more settlers to the immediate hinterland and more people to town. As they shifted their attention away from supplying the receding frontier to trying to achieve a specific regional economic function as an entrepôt within the regional urban system, the "frontier town" or "frontier city" quality of the place declined.

The railroad, of course, changed all this. As Lewis Atherton notes, "no longer did the [Western] merchant buy the bulk of his supplies for the year at one time; no longer was it necessary for him to visit the seaboard; no longer did he risk the loss of his goods. The railroad brought the goods he now could order as he needed; it brought traveling salesman to him, so it was possible for him to spend his time at home attending to his business; and the greater safety of the railroad relieved him of the worries he had faced in the days of river transportation."[24]

Increasingly, with these efficiencies and savings, more capital accumulated, so the advantages of the entrepôt could be translated to distant outposts, and to "warehousing cities," serving both ends of the spectrum.[25] Skipping entire stages of development, these "instant cities" seemingly appeared out of nothing, turning access to goods into city-boosting capital.[26]

However, these arrangements placed frontier urban economies under a heavy debt burden to the entrepôt and made them more prone to volatile boom and bust cycles.

Thus the key transition that undermined the "frontier" element of the frontier town was a deepening interaction with a "prospective hinterland," where settlers or producers began to provide a viable exportable product that merchants could exchange for goods and then sell into the national market.[27] Carl Abbott, for example, notes that the "urban history as frontier history deals with . . . the evolution of raw outposts into permanent communities with diversified economies—in short the full incorporation of" a region "into the system of modern capitalism."[28] Early in its development, the frontier city lacked any system of towns and cities across its hinterland through which it could deal with the frontier itself. Its merchants were primarily general retailers who helped assemble shipments to the frontier. The appearance of specialized wholesale merchants clearly indicated an increasing effort to achieve efficiencies through larger scale operations in order to sell goods across the hinterland. Thus the evolution of an organized trading system—which could be defined as the beginnings of a distinctive region—marked the waning of the town's classic frontier stage.

In most cases, as Eugene Moehring notes, western frontier cities, "forged growth by promoting the growth of urban networks" and establishing a relationship with its hinterland.[29] One way to define the frontier city is a city that was surrounded by a contested zone of encounter, or tentative catchment area, rather than an organized hinterland. Settled and established towns and cities have hinterlands, frontier cities and towns do not: by filling in this area with an urban system of trade and exchange consisting of secondary central places and supply depots that traded with and were dependent on the city, merchants transformed this contested realm into an urban hinterland. As they did, these secondary towns and cities—all closer to the frontier—began to act as supply depots for those heading to the frontier, co-opting frontier city merchants and eroding the city's frontier identity.

Cities could still retain some of that identity by keeping open some channels of interaction with the frontier. Often they did this by undertaking or investing in large-scale, heavily funded ventures into the frontier that smaller places could not support. If such commercial contacts with the frontier endured, its frontier function—or at least a remnant of it—could linger on as a niche within the local and regional economy for some time, even while the interactions with the hinterland developing between the city and the frontier deepened. Thus it could retain some frontier qualities long after the physical proximity of the frontier has passed.

San Francisco, for example, quickly scaled the ranks to become an economic powerhouse for the entire region. Within a few years, places like Benecia, Sacramento, Marysville, and Stockton became distribution outposts to San Francisco's emerging transshipment center. And within a year or two of the Gold Rush, Sacramento merchants shifted their trade from selling to miners passing through town to selling more and more wholesale merchandise to city-based businesses and mining-camp entrepreneurs. By supplying merchants in smaller towns or mining camps across the mining hinterland, they established Sacramento as a regional wholesaling entrepôt for an emergent hinterland. San Francisco merchants also connected with merchants at Portland to draw Oregon in as a hinterland that supplied wheat and lumber, which was then shipped into the interior via Sacramento.[30]

As William Cronon notes, Chicago likewise had a fairly brief frontier period, serving as a jumping-off point and supply depot for settlers moving into northern and central Illinois and southern Wisconsin through the early 1840s. The completion of the Illinois and Michigan Canal, the establishment of a fleet of boats that traded up and down Lake Michigan, the rapid construction of railroads to the northwest, west, and south, and the development of efficiencies in handling and shipping produce and processing lumber and hogs in the late 1840s and 1850s drew vast amounts of wheat, lumber, and livestock from an ever-growing hinterland into Chicago. In return, local merchants across a vast region shifted their connections from St. Louis or Cincinnati, drawn into Chicago's trading orbit.[31]

Meanwhile, Chicago's manufacturing base, at least in the early years, developed directly out of the vast resource base that its trading advantage gained them access to. The capital accrued from trade was invested in the processing of flour, livestock, and lumber. The easy access to raw materials provided by a focus on transportation allowed for economies of scale to kick in and for entrepôt producers to out-produce those in the hinterland. This intense centralization then triggered further clustering effects, or external economies, that continued to draw manufacturing, and thus population, from ever farther away, toward the entrepôt. Such intense centralization—that brought in wheat from as far away as the Dakotas, livestock from Texas, and lumber from the northwest and upper peninsula of Michigan—was rather quickly undermined by the basic economic reality that it is cheaper to process goods closer to their point of production or their location.[32] Thus as competitors in gateway cities, portals, depots, or entrepôts to the west and north drew processing toward them, Chicago took advantage of its proximity to domestic markets, workers, and capital and shifted to heavy manufacturing and service industries. Thus, in some ways, Chicago was never much of a "frontier city." Its hinterland developed and expanded and became the basis of its growth and development too quickly to enable it to maintain close contacts with any frontier. Even so, as late as the 1870s, its merchants were active in the Rocky Mountain west, across the north country and the Montana frontier.

St. Louis demonstrates the lingering power of a once-successful frontier city across a vast trading area of the Plains. Though outflanked by Chicago railroad interests, St. Louis remained a considerable economic force throughout the century, competing head-to-head with Chicago and New York interests. Some of its merchants continued to directly supply frontier outposts in the Upper Missouri River valley and the Rockies into the late 1870s and early 1880s.[33] St. Louis capitalists invested deeply in Leadville, Colorado, and for a while the St. Louis and Chicago boosters fought it out on Harrison Avenue (its Main Street named after a St. Louis investor) during the 1878–1885 boom. Eventually, investors from Iowa and Chicago drew smelting operations down to Denver and east to Omaha, and they were in turn supplanted by New Yorkers such as the Guggenheims and the Dows after 1900.[34] Even so, St. Louis entrepreneurs maintained niche connections across Nebraska, Colorado, and the Dakotas long after Chicago had taken control of both. For example, even though Lincoln, Nebraska, was, by the 1890s, a secondary regional wholesaling satellite of Chicago, a number of entrepreneurs maintained direct St. Louis connections via railroads built southeast, into Missouri. Thus St. Louis's "frontier" identity lingered well into the 1880s since it retained a key role in steamboating to the northern Great Plains and continued to trade by railroad with towns across the Rockies and in the Southwest.[35]

Likewise, Seattle emerged in the 1890s as the terminus of the Great Northern Railway and thus an extension of capital and trade from Chicago and Minneapolis. It also took much of the northward ocean traffic from San Francisco to Portland. The Klondike gold rush of 1897–1898, the Nome gold rush in 1899–1900, and the establishment of Anchorage in 1915 transformed Seattle into the gateway to Alaska. As such it maintained elements of its "frontier city" ethos well into the twentieth century, with elements remaining today, as Matthew Klingle has explained elsewhere in this volume.

Each of these frontier cites varied dramatically in its experiences and history, according to its geographical location, access to natural resources, the presence of competing towns or cities, and especially the resources and technology of communication and transportation available to them. As Carl Abbott has noted, "more than anything else, cities are vast devices for exchanging information, and changing technologies of transportation and communication have keyed the differences among different urban areas."[36] Over time and space, frontier cities that emerged as termini or entrepôts in North America became more quickly integrated into the contemporary urban and economic system and thus were much more dynamic and volatile.

Elements of the frontier milieu lingered in each place for years after the city had technically ceased being a frontier city. The cities maintained aggressive transshipping sectors and many warehouses, focused on extractive manufacturing, and invested broadly in their hinterlands, with a lot of speculation and exaggeration still in the air. This speculative environment brought young men, very diverse ethnically and racially. Their demographic was united more in their avarice, and their quests as speculators, investors, confidence men, dreamers, and entrepreneurs.

Investors relied on the other groups of newcomers: miners, sailors, fishermen, cowboys, steamboatmen, longshoremen, hunters, trappers, and cattlemen, as well as cutthroats, gamblers, card sharks, blackguards, ruffians, desperadoes, vigilantes, sporting men, and dudes. Frontier cites were quite masculine spaces where men competed, jostled, and jousted to establish a position, a reputation, and defend their honor. Gamblers, saloon keepers, and prostitutes openly flouted the law. This floating population would differ from subsequent streams of immigrants who came to more developed frontier cities by their association with the "frontier ethos" and their desire to be part of the ragged edge, politically, economically, and socially. Their presence becomes an essential marker of frontier status because these folks knew what they sought and where to find it—and how to quickly abandon one place for another as the currents of development shifted. Through their own networks of information, they seemed to show up at just the right time hoping to strike it rich.

This was the experience in Jamestown, Virginia, in the 1610s, in Cincinnati in the 1800s, in Keokuk in the 1830s and 1840s, in Dodge City and Leadville in the 1870s, in Seattle in the 1880s, in Anchorage in the 1910s and 1920s, and various interior frontier places throughout the twentieth century.[37] As late as the 1970s and 1980s, in Gillette, Wyoming, Alexandra Fuller notes, that "the inconvenient biology of human bodies creating logistical and law enforcement problems for the communities that host the oil-field workers—food and porta-potties, beds and trailers, drugs and sex"—in yet another boomtown.[38]

Eventually, as prospects declined, the boosters of these frontier cities would move on, as would the majority of workers, vagrants, and adventurers. The "bachelor community" aspect of such places would be balanced by an increased number of women.[39] So too, the skewed class structure would even out with a small elite, a midsized middle class, and, in many places (especially in the West), a large working-class presence. In time, manufacturing, which at first was extractive, either atrophied or shifted toward the production of capital goods. Steadily, the frontier milieu declined and disappeared—though not completely, allowing remaining boosters to cash in on its last "frontier asset"[40] or two, cultivating a public culture of museums, historic sites, annual festivals, parades, amusement parks, and companies that sustained the images and myths of the city's "Frontier Days."

Such festivals are held in numerous western towns and cities, including Prescott, Arizona; Cheyenne, Wyoming; Virginia City, Nevada; and Calgary, Alberta. Ironically, the brevity of these annual events, and the mobility of their participants who pass through town—often traveling on a festival circuit like merchants, miners, and workers have done throughout the city's history—evoke the fleeting and volatile nature of the original frontier city they commemorate. Yet the recurrence of these events year after year as long-standing traditions in the city's booster ethos, also reminds one, that the classic frontier city was less an urban "spearhead" on the frontier than a city behind the frontier that maintained connections to it, even after it had established regular systemic interactions with other towns and cities across its hinterland and the national urban system.

By nature, the frontier city is a volatile, unstable, and thus, to some, it seems a paradoxical urban place. Lacking sufficient systemic support, it could exist one moment and literally be gone the next. Most frontier cities have been moving targets, either developing into more mature urban places before one can grasp their character, or stagnating, or even disappearing. As a result, the frontier city remains, in many if not most cases, elusive. And yet, the impact of the presence or proximity of a frontier—defined generally as a zone of encounter across which intercultural and international relations remained in flux—often marked itself so deeply on the early economic, social, political, and cultural character of frontier urban places that developed into a regional entrepôts, that they could continue as frontier cites so long as they maintained some direct contact with the moving frontier.

CHAPTER 9

Mapping the Urban Frontier and Losing Frontier Cities

Peter J. Kastor

Estwick Evans worried about New Orleans. A New Hampshire native who engaged in a lengthy passage through the northern and western borderlands in 1818, Evans expressed those fears in a detailed narrative of his travels. When it came to New Orleans, the quintessential frontier city, Evans asked "will not our citizens . . . more readily imbibe, and more freely communicate the corrupt practices of this place? But, if by the praiseworthy conduct of our citizens residing in New-Orleans, immorality shall be checked, and good principles introduced, then, indeed, it will prove a purchase, not only for our country, but for mankind."[1]

What do we make of this passage? At first glance, Evans's worries seem to be the typical ranting of so many New Englanders who saw in the frontiers of North America the corruption that emerged when civilized Anglo-Americans came in contact with the decivilizing trifecta of Catholic religious culture, French and Spanish political culture, and multiracial contact culture. But remove "New Orleans" from the picture and this could well read like Thomas Jefferson's tirade in *Notes on the State of Virginia* that "the mobs of great cities add just so much to the support of pure government, as sores do to the strength of the human body. It is the manners and spirit of a people which preserve a republic in vigour. A degeneracy in these is a canker which soon eats to the heart of its laws and constitution."[2]

That similarity is more than coincidental and, in the end, not nearly so problematic as it may appear. It seems impossible to tease from Evans the threads of his commentary on frontiers from his commentary on cities. Yet the confluence of the two goes a long way toward explaining not only how Evans described New Orleans, but more generally how American print and visual culture went about constructing the cities of North America's frontiers.

With that in mind, I would like to explore how frontier cities entered the American imagination through a series of travel narratives and maps published during the early American republic. To that end, this essay employs many of the same sources as the other participants in this volume, but for different purposes. Much of the best work in political, cultural, and social history has sought to extract the lived reality of North American frontiers from a set of deeply problematic texts. This work has sought to separate the wheat from the chaff, extracting a limited amount of believable information and discarding the large amount of extraneous or inaccurate material. I don't envy the challenge of scholars who must disentangle a historical narrative about people who left few written records of their own from the cultural baggage that Europeans and Euro-Americans carried with them to the frontiers of North America. Indeed, my goal is to treat those problems as opportunities. I want to situate all the downsides of printed sources—the skewed perceptions, the misunderstood moments, the self-serving racial stereotyping—at the center of a discussion that will examine not only the cultural attitudes that informed how people described frontier cities, but the generic conventions that informed how printed and visual texts further determined that description.

I emphasize this focus on travel narratives and maps from the early republic because scholars in a broad range of fields have long announced the important role that images of the West would play in American culture, but they have usually opted for other objects to explain the representation of frontier cities. They have long emphasized the importance of self-defined artists, especially novelists and landscape painters. Likewise, scholars have tended to gravitate toward the antebellum era, in large part because that was exactly when those novelists and landscape artists turned their attention to the West. The late colonial era and the early republic tell a very different story. Maps and travel narratives would play the dominant role in visualizing frontier cities. Meanwhile, the people who produced those objects never considered themselves artists. Instead, it was a disconnected cohort of mapmakers, travelers, explorers, publishers, and part-time writers who shaped how Americans conceived of the West in general and frontier cities in particular.[3]

Equally important, mass-producing the maps that were such an important part of describing frontier cities was extraordinarily difficult in the

United States, and this technical matter also separates the early republic from the antebellum era. Although the United States enjoyed a robust capacity to mass-produce the printed word, it had only a limited capacity to mass-produce maps, or for that matter any other visual images.

As a result, I am less concerned with the realities of intercultural contact that are so often at the center of the scholarship about frontiers than I am with the ways printed texts struggled to establish typologies for frontier cities.[4] I want to discuss the ways that published accounts of frontier cities were pulled in different, often opposing, directions that reflected a broader debate about how to understand frontier cities. At one moment these were places on a frontier, at least as frontiers were understood by Euro-American observers in the late eighteenth and early nineteenth centuries. The texts that described these places deployed the familiar terminology of frontiers: the line between civilization and savagery, the absence of cultural sophistication, the chronic underdevelopment. At the same time, these were cities, and as such seemed to exist outside frontiers. Frontier cities were imagined with closer connections to distant metropoles than to their immediate surroundings. Accordingly, these printed and visual texts deployed another vocabulary no less contrived and predetermined than the language they used to describe frontiers. Cities could embody sophistication, development, and above all civilization, but they could also be locations of corruption and decline.

Within this ambiguity, these texts engaged in a battle about whether frontier cities could redeem or endanger the republic. That debate often turned on the degree to which these places fit within models of frontiers or of cities. To some observers, frontier cities represented the worst decivilizing elements of the frontier. For others, the frontier provided the means to redeem the city. That was certainly the case for Thomas Jefferson, who advocated the creation of towns on frontiers not simply as a way to stimulate regional development, but also with the expectation that frontier settlers could prevent the corruption he associated with eastern cities. Finally, cities might provide the means to redeem frontiers. Estwick Evans certainly hoped so, believing that a city could civilize a region endangered by a host of frontier evils.

The growth of frontier cities therefore proceeded on a trajectory adjacent but not identical to the growth of white settlement more generally. The United States developed a particular language for celebrating the settlers who built farms on distant frontiers. Cities were something different. For some, the city was the necessary safeguard for the settler, preventing geographic and cultural isolation. For others, the farmer was the necessary safeguard against the city, guaranteeing that the frontier would be the home of white freeholders rather than the corrupt denizens of an urban landscape.

But understanding these issues of content only works with appropriate attention to issues of form. The representation of frontier cities within texts emerged not just at a particular moment in frontier history, but also within a particular moment in publishing history. The capacity to describe frontier cities in published form responded directly to the generic conventions and technological limitations of American publishing in the early republic.

The breadth of this published record would explode the confines of any paper. After all, describing frontier settlement became part of the publishing tradition in the Atlantic World from the moment Europeans first encountered the Americas. So for purposes of precision—and brevity—I have chosen to focus on texts produced within the United States during the half-century following independence. I make some reference to work of Europeans, especially those texts that influenced Americans or circulated widely within the United States. But this remains fundamentally an American story, discussing how the representation of frontier cities informed the ways that Americans described themselves.

In chronological terms, I begin this discussion with the last quarter of the eighteenth century, when Americans struggled to describe frontier cities in the face of considerable technical limitations. I then shift to the early nineteenth century, when American publishing acquired far greater capacity for western description, a technical development that coincided with international and domestic changes that transformed the boundaries and politics of North American frontiers. Finally, I close by considering the far-reaching changes of the antebellum era that transformed not only the reality of frontier life, but also the representational tools available to Americans.

At the heart of this discussion is not only the meaning of frontier cities, but more generally the definition of frontiers. *Describing* frontier cities in print and visual culture fits within a broader project of *claiming* North American territory. Perhaps so, but that story of conquest too easily overshadows the complex and contingent ways in which Americans struggled to locate—in every sense of the term—the cities of North American frontiers.

Understanding how Americans described frontier cities begins not with the people who actually created those descriptions, but rather with the publishing industry that circulated the information. As much as any subject, the media proved no less important than the message. An image (or, rather, a set of images) of frontier cities emerged through a highly specific set of print and visual traditions, technological limitations, economic pursuits, and policymaking imperatives. The limited capacity of American publishing initially meant that the visual and, to a lesser degree, the written representation of frontier cities would be dominated by Europeans. Within these confines, however, a set of generic conventions emerged within the United States, concerned primarily with arguing about whether the development of an urban frontier would help or harm the republic.

Describing frontiers in print—especially in visual form—proved extraordinarily difficult. The United States possessed a printing industry that amazed observers on both sides of the Atlantic. Yet much of that production was limited to political pamphlets, newspapers, religious tracts, and laws.[5] And those printers rarely turned their attention to book-length studies of the West or of frontier cities. Meanwhile, the United States had only a small cadre of engravers and publishers trained in the highly exacting work of cartographic publication.[6]

As a result, Americans eagerly consumed geographic information, but most of the published representation of North American frontiers remained the work of Europeans, whether they were travelers, authors, or cartographers. Those books and maps established many of the objectives and measures of accuracy that shaped how Americans would go about describing frontier cities. After centuries in which European maps and travel narratives were most notable for the outlandishness of their claims or the inaccuracy of their details, during the eighteenth century a variety of factors—Enlightenment science, commercial interests, and the growth of travel literature as a popular genre—reshaped how Europeans represented North America. While the Spanish continued to treat geographic information as state secrets, French, British, and German publishers produced a growing number of books and maps that described frontier cities throughout the Americas. These objects continued a tradition of making expansive territorial claims for European empires, but they did so with growing technical expertise. This hardly means that Europeans had a clear picture of the North American West. To the contrary, the European image of North America was still shaped as much by ignorance as it was by knowledge. But the technical capacity to create a published representation of that landscape had grown considerably.[7]

In addition to maps, European publishers also produced other forms of illustration—local vistas, street scenes, historic events—that the United States simply could not match. Indeed, when it came to representing frontier cities, the United States produced almost none of these objects during the early republic. Instead, Americans would represent frontier cities in visual form almost exclusively through maps, and a small number of them.

Americans were quick to acknowledge this state of affairs. When policymakers sought to determine national boundaries or to set western policy, they looked to European sources. And as Americans began to publish their own accounts of frontier cities, they began by drawing on information first published in Europe.[8]

In sharp contrast to these European developments, representing frontier cities in the United States became the province of a small number of Americans, their work reflecting specific strengths in regional publishing. Rather than break new aesthetic ground, this cohort sought to emulate Europeans even as they sought to displace them. The editors, mapmakers, printers, and booksellers (occasionally one and the same) who proved so crucial to shaping the written and visual image of frontiers were primarily located in the cities of the Northeast. Philadelphia—which possessed both a robust publishing community and a cohort of cartographic engravers—produced the most important maps of the West. Meanwhile, of all places it was New England, particularly Boston, that produced some of the most important and abundant written descriptions of frontier cities. Although the regional culture of New England was perhaps the farthest removed from frontier concerns, New England publishers were the largest producers of educational materials, and many of the first representations of frontier cities were in reference books and school texts as well as the early travel narratives that rolled off New England presses.[9]

The impact of Philadelphia and New England is all the more striking in comparison to Virginia. After all, the Old Dominion played a far greater role in populating and governing the West, producing not only many of the settlers who descended on the trans-Appalachian West during the early republic, but also most of the officials who assumed leadership in the territorial system. Yet for all this influence, the limited publishing capacity of Virginia and the near-absence of cartographic publishing guaranteed that Virginia would play almost no role in creating a published representation of frontier cities.

Yet this hardly means that Philadelphia and New England lacked a frame of reference for representing frontier cities. To the contrary, if frontiers were unfamiliar places to the publishing community, cities were not. The cities that produced books and maps, Philadelphia and Boston, were themselves the subjects of books and maps, as were other cities like Baltimore and Charleston. Printers had long reproduced books and maps that reinforced the central, conflicting tropes of urban description. Cities were at once centers of civilization and of corruption. American travelers took these tropes with them when they visited frontier cities, often reproducing them in their published accounts. But so, too, did authors and editors in Philadelphia or Boston. They brought those assumptions and experiences with them as they produced the first books and maps to describe frontier cities.

Within these highly specific technical and aesthetic confines, Americans struggled to represent the cities of North American frontiers. They did so primarily though a small number of books and maps. There was more at work here than some vague sense of cultural nationalism, a vital point in understanding the process of landscape representation in the early republic. A small number of Americans were arguing that the nation needed its own literary and artistic production in order to establish itself as an independent nation. But the people making those claims were—not surprisingly—men and women who defined themselves as writers and artists. The men who sought to represent western cities saw things differently. In an abstract sense, Americans were indeed attempting to *claim* North America through the creation of a domestic publishing industry that would describe the United States on the Americans' terms. But in the print shops and bookstores of the United States, or on the desks and drafting tables of American writers and cartographers, the goals were more pragmatic. American printers hoped to displace their European competitors through direct market competition. The federal government was eager to see a domestic industry of landscape description that would help sustain American territorial pretensions.[10]

These were the technical and economic circumstances that shaped what the United States could produce. But as that cultural production got under way, just what sort of frontier cities emerged from these highly specific institutional and political circumstances? There was no simple answer, for Americans were divided in their conclusions about the cities in particular just as they were divided about frontiers in general.

In their efforts to create a printed and visual record of frontier cities, Americans seemed to approach the task with all the ethnic chauvinism and cultural baggage they could muster. But the portraits that emerged were always more than mere expressions of national, racial, or ethnic supremacy. To the contrary, the apparent uniformity of these describers (white, Anglo-American, generally well educated) collapsed as other factors shaped their work. The men who described frontier cities generally fell into the following five groups: boosters, geographers, cartographers, explorers, and travelers.

Their descriptions of frontier cities emerged through this intersection of regional diversity, authorial objective, and generic conventions.

The boosters were among the most prolific describers of frontier cities, and for obvious reasons. Land speculators, aspiring town builders, and would-be local politicos all saw tremendous benefits in portraying every emerging hamlet as the Athens of the West. This had certainly been the case in European empires throughout the Western Hemisphere, and it was a tradition that Americans joined with a vengeance. The boosters were particularly eager to promote places like Pittsburgh, Chillicothe, Lexington, and Nashville. They were less concerned with the trans-Mississippi West or the Great Lakes, let alone the Far West beyond, and for obvious reasons. First, many of the boosters were financially invested in converting new settlements into vibrant cities, and few of them were connected to any projects west of the Mississippi. Second, the boosters sought to celebrate the capacity of the United States to replace savagery with civilization, and they were hardly willing to acknowledge that Europeans could achieve the same goal.

The Americans were not the first to do so, and they would not be the last. Boosterism—and its close relative, hucksterism—would be a mainstay in western history. Meanwhile, European imperial projects in other parts of the world generated a similar paper trail, characterized by similarly exaggerated enthusiasm.[11]

The boosters proclaimed that these places were, indeed, cities. But what made them cities? Demography alone did not do the job. Instead, it was the combination of population density, economic development, a built environment of technical sophistication, and a cosmopolitan culture that created a frontier city. The surrounding landscape was always fertile, the region was always ripe for further development and profitable investment. Perhaps most important, these were fundamentally civil and civilized settlements. Unlike the rural farms and villages that characterized (and in some ways still characterize) frontiers, these new frontier cities were important civilizing forces. They were the homes of schools, banks, courts, and other institutions of civilized society. Yet if these cities formed a civilizing bulwark against the uncivilizing landscape that surrounded them, as *new* cities far removed from the emerging metropoles of the Atlantic seaboard, frontier cities would be civil and virtuous. They could be the centers of commerce, development, and social connections. They could promote the independence of individual farmers while offsetting the potential isolation that so many observers characterized with the frontier.

Consider the case of Zadok Cramer, a printer and bookseller in Pittsburgh. Cramer regularly published a book called *The Navigator*. Part travel guide, part showpiece of western development, and always revenue-producer for Cramer, *The Navigator* invoked the boosters' techniques for celebrating frontier cities as part of a larger effort to attract settlers to the West. In the 1802 edition, for example, Cramer wrote that "the local situation of this town is so very commanding, that it has been called the Key to the Western Country." He was referring directly to Pittsburgh's relationship to the surrounding rivers, but he was also imagining a future as a regional metropole. He described "near 400 dwelling houses, many of them large and elegantly built with brick; and about 2000 inhabitants."[12] He may have favored Pittsburgh, but he had similar compliments for Cincinnati, Louisville, and other emerging river cities of the Ohio Valley. That attitude was particularly clear in Cramer's comment on Marietta. The first major settlement established by the early boosters and speculators of the Northwest Territory, Marietta was soon overshadowed by the other frontier cities of the Ohio Valley. To Cramer, however, this was a story of growth. "The progress of this town and the adjacent settlement was, for several years much impeded by Indian wars; but now bids fair to become a place of considerable importance.... The inhabitants of Marietta are among the first who have exported the produce of the Ohio country, in vessels of their own building."[13]

Cramer produced new guides in the years that followed, in the process chronicling the emergence, growth, and in some cases the decline of aspiring frontier cities. Regardless of the fate of any one city, however, Cramer's message was the same. The construction of frontier cities marked an unstoppable, civilizing development of the trans-Appalachian frontier.[14]

Cramer's work also exemplified the degree to which describing frontier cities during the late eighteenth century was primarily achieved through words rather than pictures. Most immigrant guides, including Cramer's, generally eschewed illustration. What visual material they did include usually consisted of local river surveys.[15] Although Cramer published in the nineteenth century, his work was very much that of the eighteenth century, when the United States possessed only limited capacity for illustrated publishing. This remained the case for Cramer in no small part because he operated from Pittsburgh. Living in a frontier city that possessed only the most basic publishing capacity, Cramer was incapable of visualizing frontier cities. Nor was Pittsburgh unique. Throughout the earlier republic, frontier cities could not describe themselves.

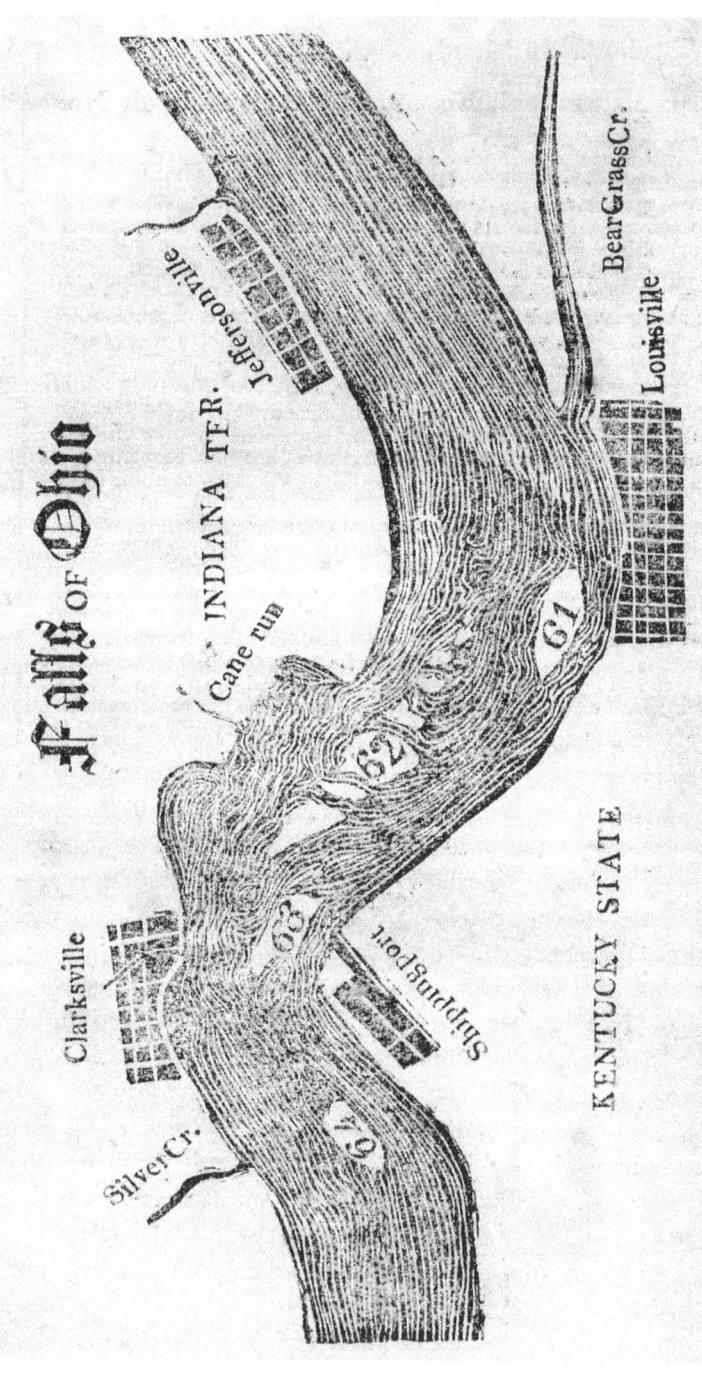

Figure 9.1. Map of the Ohio River and towns. Zadok Cramer, *The Navigator: Containing Directions for Navigating the Monongahela, Allegheny, Ohio, and Mississippi Rivers* (Pittsburgh: printed and published by Cramer, Spear, & Eichbaum, 1814), 124. Courtesy St. Louis Mercantile Library Association of the University of Missouri–St. Louis.

If the boosters were going to describe frontier cities, they would need to do so through the publishing capacity in cities that, appropriately rather than ironically, definitely were not on frontiers. One of the first men to conclude there might be real value to a visual representation of frontier cities was John Filson. An avid speculator in and relentless booster of Kentucky, his 1784 *Discovery, Settlement and Present State of Kentucke* became a landmark in American natural history and environmental writing.[16] It was also a landmark in cartographic publishing, for Filson separately commissioned an engraver named Henry Pursell to produce a map. Pursell's work was quite literally a road map for the kind of settlers that Filson hoped to attract with his book. It showed routes that connected the emerging settlements of Kentucky to the population centers of neighboring states, especially Virginia. Filson's account of emerging civil communities took visual form in the towns of Lexington and Louisville, which appear as diversified settlements connected to the larger world by roads heading in all directions.[17]

The map that Filson commissioned did more than describe Kentucky. It constituted one of the first attempts within the United States to create a mass-produced visual representation situating frontier cities within a broader West. But Filson used these new technical capacities to advance an old idea in boosterism. He described frontier cities as the font of energy, prosperity, and civilization.

Throughout these years, published local maps that went beyond the general representation of Cramer or Filson were still few and far between. This remained the case in the United States even as the trade in urban maps produced in Europe continued. In the process, those European maps implicitly announced which cities mattered. By 1776, for example, emerging frontier cities like New Orleans and Montreal were already the subject of numerous well-distributed published maps. Consider Jacques Nicolas Bellin's 1764 map of New Orleans (figure 9.3). Only a few years earlier, the Crescent City had been a struggling settlement, the center of a colony that both France and Spain considered strategically valuable but economically unsuccessful.[18] In Bellin's visual description, however, New Orleans was a solid, well-planned community.

Maps produced into the nineteenth century announced the growth of places like New Orleans or Montreal which might be located in intercultural contact zones but which, from the perspective of urban design, looked little different from cities that were located far way from anything that would be called a "frontier."[19] The genre itself contributed to this process. The standard conventions of urban maps had a tendency to make any settlement appear

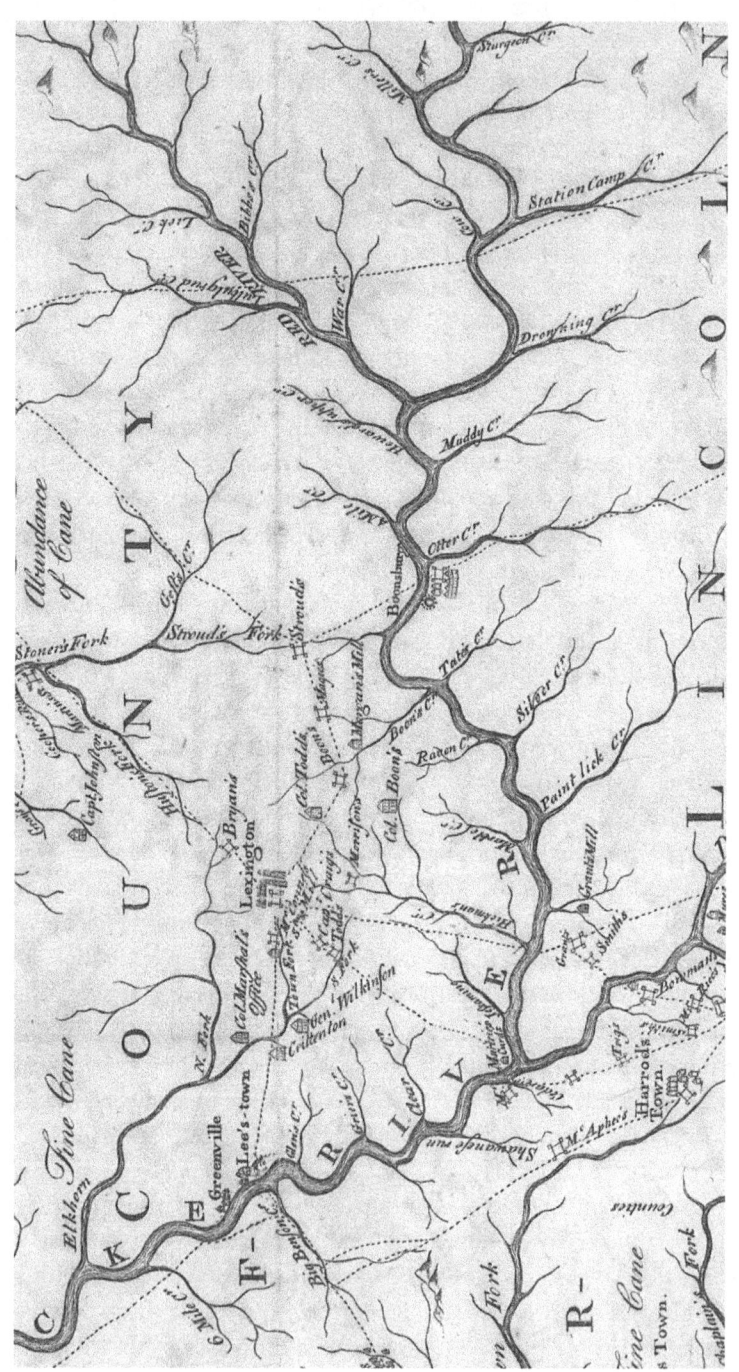

Figure 9.2. Map of Lexington and surrounding area. From John Filson, *This Map of Kentucke* . . . (Philadelphia: H. D. Pursell, 1784). Geography and Map Division, Library of Congress

Figure 9.3. Jacques Nicolas Bellin, *Plan de la Nouvelle Orleans* (Paris, 1764). Geography and Map Division, Library of Congress.

larger, more complex, and more thoroughly planned than an actual visit might suggest.

Americans struggled against the limitations of their own publishing capacities to produce similar descriptions of their own frontier cities, or any cities for that matter. Political circumstances and publishing developments overlapped to make this sort of representation both timely and possible. During the 1790s and early 1800s the federal government sought to consolidate its hold over frontier cities like Vincennes, Detroit, and Natchez. In 1803, the Louisiana Purchase extended federal boundaries to encompass the two most important frontier cities of the Mississippi Valley: New Orleans and St. Louis. Meanwhile, a new cohort of engravers trained in the cartographer's art and a new cadre of geographic publishers combined to produce a slew of maps and books that sought to describe the United States even as the nation underwent geographic transformation. This development in publishing actually lagged well behind territorial expansion. It was only in the 1810s and 1820s that Americans began to represent these cities on a greater scale and with greater precision.[20]

For example, it was over a half-century after Bellin's map of New Orleans, and almost a decade after the United States acquired New Orleans through the Louisiana Purchase, before Americans produced a major map of New Orleans. In 1817, New York and New Orleans printers, Charles Del Veccio

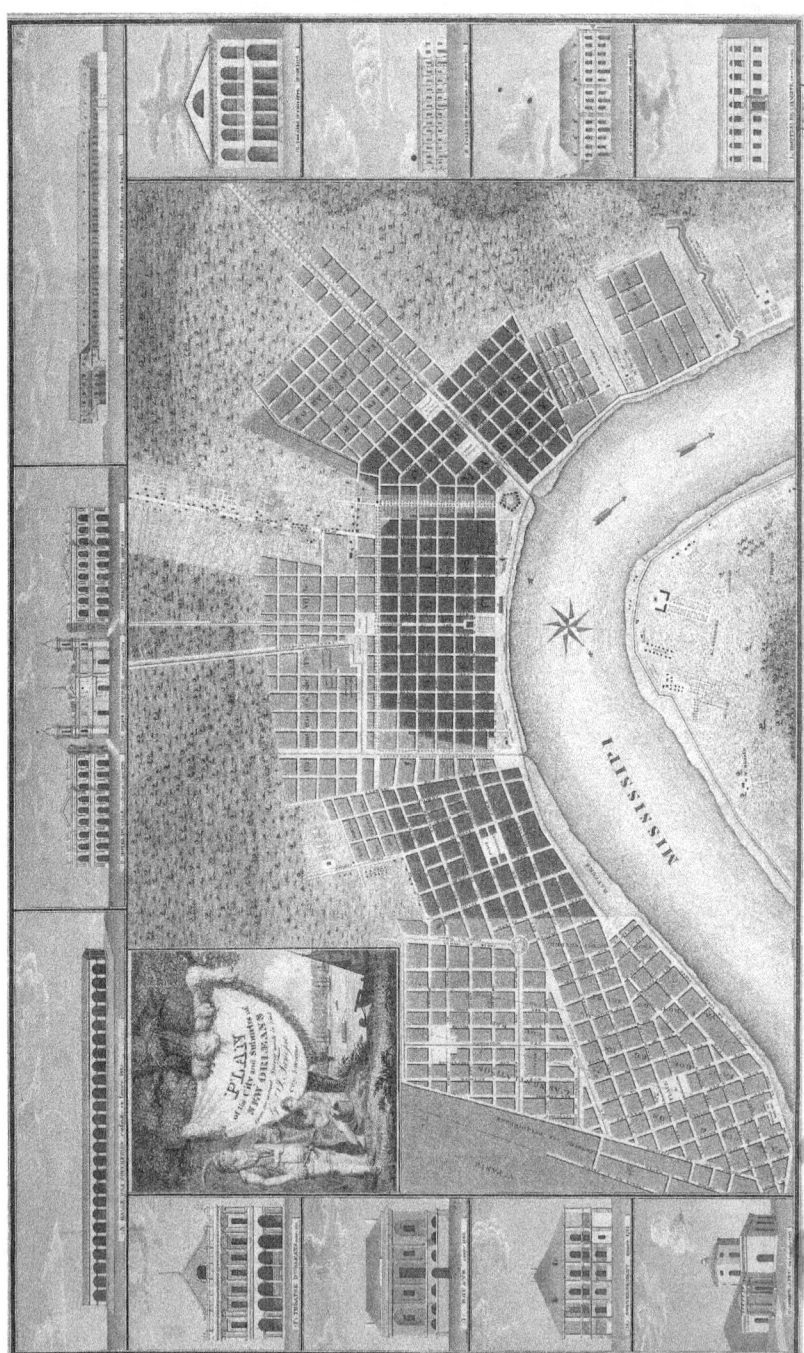

Figure 9.4. I. Tanesse and William Rollinson, *Plan of the City and Suburbs of New Orleans: from an actual survey made in 1815* (New York and New Orleans: Charles Del Vecchio, P. Maspero, 1817). Geography and Map Division, Library of Congress.

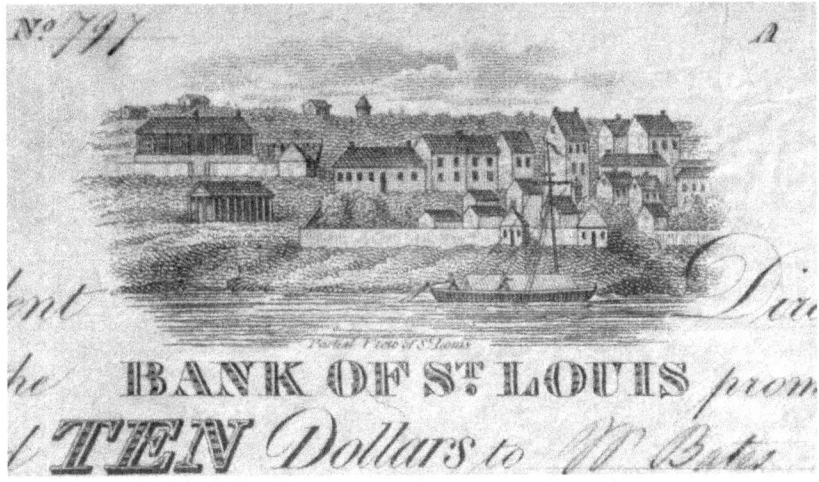

Figure 9.5. Bank of St. Louis, $10 denomination (detail), March 1817. Eric P. Newman Numismatic Education Society.

and P. Maspero, respectively, produced what would eventually become one of the most widely circulating maps of early New Orleans (figure 9.4). *Plan of the City and Suburbs of New Orleans* did more than portray New Orleans as a growing city. The map quite literally surrounded the city with a set of sophisticated institutions: government buildings, theaters, and a publicly funded school.

St. Louis underwent a similar staggered introduction in print and visual culture. St. Louis was the subject of written description, but it would be years before the struggling frontier outpost generated the published maps that would announce it as a city.

One of the first examples came from 1817, and it took the form not of a map or a book illustration but rather something as seemingly simple as a ten-dollar bill. Issued by the Bank of St. Louis, the currency note included a small representation of the waterfront development. St. Louis emerges as the site of diversified construction—large and small buildings, French-designed homes and neoclassical structures—and a busy waterfront. That this was on a bank note was no small affair, for all frontier cities hoped to establish their credentials as cities by demonstrating a strong financial infrastructure. Even the medium of the bank note—an engraving on paper—stood as a reminder of the importance of the physical medium of representing cities. After decades in which the paucity of engravers made frontier cities incapable of

Figure 9.6. The St. Louis waterfront. From E. Dupré, *Atlas of the City and County of St. Louis, by Congressional Townships* . . . (St. Louis: E. Dupré, 1838), frontispiece. St. Louis Imprints Collection, St. Louis Mercantile Library Association at the University of Missouri–St. Louis.

representing themselves visually, something as simple as a banknote was an announcement that frontier cities could describe themselves in both words and pictures.

The first widely circulating maps of St. Louis only appeared in the 1820s. By 1838, St. Louis was finally producing the visual record to announce itself as a city. An atlas published that year showed local plots and listed landowners. It also included an illustration of the city's waterfront, portraying the sort of bustling development, transportation, and commerce that came to define the image the city hoped to create for itself in the nineteenth century.

The growth in American publishing was equally dramatic in its representation of the cities of the trans-Appalachian West, and with much the same point. Maps of cities like Cincinnati, Louisville, and Lexington portrayed this sort of development in words and pictures. These maps showed well-planned cities growing quickly from their humble origins. But to what degree were these still cities on frontiers? The very creation of these visual representations suggested that these places were *not* the locations of give-and-take, of intercultural contact, or of ill-defined rules and power. In other words, these representations claimed that in becoming cities, these places had lost all the characteristics that historians now use to define a place as a frontier.[21]

Although these maps certainly had an implicitly celebratory quality to them, it is important to distinguish them from the more explicitly booserish quality of work like John Filson's. Filson certainly hoped to generate profits from their books, but that was only one facet of his efforts to profit from western development. Filson was a speculator first and writer second. In sharp contrast, the new generation of American cartographic publishers were, first and foremost, publishers. That their work dovetailed with that of the boosters created no problem for them, but they nonetheless belonged to a different cohort with different concerns.

Yet the work of publishers was hardly uniform in supporting the boosters' claims. To the contrary, the expanding publishing capacity of the United States would play a crucial role in supporting the claims of another group that described frontier cities in far more ambivalent terms.

Even as boosters told a story of how places ceased to be frontiers, other describers and other texts told a different story altogether. Rather than redeem the republic, frontier cities might destroy civilization. Jedidiah Morse, the leading American geographer, established a pattern for describing frontier cities that his professional colleagues quickly emulated. Morse's title as "geographer" can be deceiving. Morse and others like him were concerned not just with cartography and geographic measurement. Rather, many of them produced schoolbooks and general reference works that situated geography at the center of a broader educational project. They addressed topography and ecology, but above all they hoped to describe the political and demographic jurisdictions of the world.

Morse himself relied on boosterish western promoters like Filson, but he drew very different conclusions. Morse worried that weak civic institutions would decivilize western settlers. Yet if Morse implicitly celebrated cities (he had plenty of good things to say about Boston, Philadelphia, and New York), unlike Filson, he doubted the capacity of frontier cities to preserve a civilized culture.

Morse considered the western reserve of the United States "not only the most extensive, but by far the richest, and most valuable part of our country." It had "the finest land in the world . . . [and] there is nothing in other parts of the globe, which resembles the prodigious chain of lakes in this part of the world." But that very potential had the seeds of obvious problems for Morse. For now the West "remains in it original state, and lies buried in the midst of its own spontaneous luxuriousness." For Morse, luxury was never a good thing. The great question for Morse—as indeed it was for Jefferson and Filson—was whether the West could develop an appropriate culture.[22]

Morse and Jefferson may seem confusing. They should, because their own work on frontier cities contained inherent and revealing contradictions. Jefferson sought to celebrate frontier towns as an example of western settlement, but his criticism of eastern cities threatened to undermine any celebration of their frontier counterparts. Conversely, Morse idealized the cities and towns of the Northeast, yet he was unable to apply that celebratory outlook to the towns and cities emerging in the West. The two men also could not have been more different politically. A New England Federalist, Morse was dismayed at Jefferson's presidential victory in the election of 1800. Historians have tended to treat Morse accordingly, focusing primarily on his periodic political machinations and emphasizing his differences with the likes of Jefferson. But when it came to discussing frontier cities, both Morse and Jefferson contributed to a print culture that saw real dangers in urban development.

Understanding Morse and Jefferson is so important because they are not only emblematic of broader debates in politics and culture, but because they were particularly important in shaping the image of frontier cities. As a public figure, Jefferson repeatedly sought to shape the West. As a private individual, Morse's publishing career established many of the standards for how writers and editors described the nation. Both men imported—and often conflated—their ideas about the West and about urban life into their efforts to make sense of frontier cities.

And it was the comments of men like Morse and Jefferson that got to the core of how Americans struggled to make sense of frontier cities through print and visual culture. Any attempt to represent those cities was never entirely an attempt to describe the frontier. The broader debate about cities inevitably affected, and occasionally threatened to consume, the discussion of frontiers. And in that reality lies the profound challenge for studies of frontier cities. The subject remains primarily the concern of frontier historians, but urban historians are the specialists who have most thoroughly theorized how Americans conceived of the city through culture. Once again, the realities of American publishing proved crucial. Neither Morse nor Jefferson actually lived in cities, but most American editors and publishers did.

Boosters and critics, publishers and cartographers, these Americans had all engaged in a debate about frontier cities that they often did not even know was occurring, but which nonetheless went on within the texts they produced. This debate among Americans had been under way for almost a generation before the critics received additional support in the reports from a diverse set of individual travelers: men and occasionally women who passed through the frontier regions that most geographers chose to avoid.

These travelers had their own concerns about frontier cities, yet if they shared the same tone of anxiety that marked some geographies, that tone emerged from very different roots.[23] As a result, while Morse's fears about the West might be rooted in the particular culture of the Northeast, this concern about the way that frontiers could decivilize even the most virtuous soul was common currency in western landscape description during the eighteenth century. The usual culprit was the general condition of frontier life. Weak institutions of civil society could not check the natural, baser human instincts. Meanwhile, Indians presented a seductive alternative with the promise of a carefree existence. White commentators concluded the same impulse could overcome white settlers. The West would quite literally take civilized Americans and transform them into uncivilized savages.[24]

Meanwhile, other detractors focused much of their scorn on the intercultural contact and interracial unions that abounded in the frontier cities of the French and Spanish empires. Texts produced in the United States mirrored the general attitude among whites, especially those in the East, who were committed to racial supremacy and racial separation. Many of those American texts also drew directly on claims first made by Europeans. For example, Estwick Evans's concerns about New Orleans in 1819 bore considerable similarity to the comments of Jacques Pitot, a Frenchman who in 1802 published an account of his own travels through the North American frontiers. He described "a public ball, where those who have a bit of discretion prefer not to appear, organized by the free people of color, is each week the gathering place for the scum of such people and of those slaves who, eluding their owner's surveillance, go there to bring their plunder."[25]

While Pitot's outrage might resonate with Anglo-Americans, Pitot operated from highly specific concerns. He blamed the corruption of the local urban population (whether Francophone white, Afro-Louisianian, or Native American) on a lax Spanish administration, as a part of a broader critique of Spanish imperial policy. Americans had their own reasons to decry the corruption of frontier cities like New Orleans, St. Louis, Montreal, and Santa Fe. Celebrations of rural independence in the United States had always used urban Europe as the foil. Meanwhile, Americans expressed their own anxieties about their own cities, fearing that the possibilities of the New World might be overwhelmed by the same urban decay that was consuming the Old World.

The result was a powerful critique of frontier cities that was constantly doing battle with the unchecked optimism of the boosters, speculators, and men like Jefferson who imagined the frontier might redeem the city. Nor were these comments limited to Europeans and New Englanders. Some of the first Americans to reach New Orleans and St. Louis, many of them committed expansionists or loyal Jeffersonians, shared Pitot's conclusions. They, too, believed that frontier cities suffered from their proximity to the frontier. To this they added that all European imperial systems were fundamentally corrupt, and that corruption took root in the cities the Europeans had created on the frontiers of their American colonies.[26]

Even as the promoters, geographers, travelers, and cartographers struggled to find some way of conceptualizing frontier cities, the people whose work is most often associated with describing the frontier were strikingly absent from this discussion. Throughout the early republic, the federal government dispatched a variety of public officials to explore, survey, and report on the West. Most of those explorers produced major written works as well as maps. Missing from most of their discussion was any substantive discussion of the frontier cities that were of so much concern to other describers. This became the case in part for the obvious reason that these expeditions usually began where major white settlements ended. Yet other factors came into play. First and foremost was the assumption that it was not the task of the explorers to describe themselves or their world. Instead, most of them carried explicit instructions to focus their efforts on describing the unfamiliar, the exotic, the unknown. In fact, most of their expedition accounts began at the moment they *left* frontier cities to begin exploring points farther west. So while private travelers assumed that readers wanted to know about the European and Euro-American settlements in the West, federal explorers usually ignored them altogether.[27]

Of course, cities *were* exotic places, a fact which helps make sense of the particular cultural space in which people situated frontier cities. After all, the majority of people in North America at the turn of the nineteenth century lived in rural—not urban—settings. Similarly, travelers in the late eighteenth and early nineteenth centuries always commented on the cosmopolitan exoticism of the cities of the Atlantic World. But for American explorers, frontier cities functioned *within their published texts* as the gateway from the familiar to the exotic. All the more striking is the fact that many of the men who led these expeditions had extended careers in federal employment that usually situated them in frontier cities.

Yet this hardly means explorers avoided frontier cities altogether. But their books and maps described places of dense population that few Euro-Americans would consider cities. Instead, the published texts of western exploration provided detailed accounts of the Indian metropoles of the North American West. The Lewis and Clark Expedition famously spent the winters of 1804–1805 and 1805–1806 in the center of large village groupings: the Mandan one year and the Clatsop the next. The 1819–1820 Yellowstone Expedition of Stephen Harriman Long resulted in a published narrative that offered its own accounts of dense Indian settlement among the Mandan. Meanwhile, the Freeman-Custis Expedition of 1806 concluded in a showdown with the Spanish among the Caddo villages of the Red River valley.[28]

The explorers did not use the word "city" to describe the centers of Indian population in the Far West, in large part because they did not think the word was appropriate to what they saw. Nonetheless, their words described places of dense population, complex social organization, and elaborate trade. Meanwhile, their maps quite literally put Indian settlement on the map, situating Indians by the thousands on the printed representation of the North American landscape. The mere existence of those maps was something of a revolution unto itself. All of them were produced in Philadelphia. During the 1810s and 1820s, when American explorers published their accounts, Philadelphia's cartographic community was mass-producing stand-alone maps and multi-page atlases, displaying both technical skill and business savvy that had been almost entirely absent two decades before.

It took text and visual materials together to make these claims. The maps of the various western explorers located Indian cities on the landscape, but in a manner that was never so distinctive as the cities created by white settlers. It was left for the detailed text to describe the large populations, the complex social structures, the vigorous trade, and the permanent dwellings that made these Indian villages into places that whites might not call cities, but which they nonetheless acknowledged as metropoles of the frontier.

Scholars of mapmaking have long recognized that maps, like those by the American explorers, did more than *describe* the land. They were vital to the numerous European and Euro-American projects to *claim* the land as the property of individuals, companies, nations, or empires. Maps made these territorial claims in regional and continental terms, but they could also do so in local urban terms, albeit in varied, complex, and subtle ways. For example, maps could situate Indian settlements within national boundaries, but hardly as a way to announce Indian autonomy. The maps of American explorers did so as part of a broader effort to announce federal sovereignty in the West. Maps could also erase Indian frontier cities while proclaiming the growth of their Anglo-American counterparts, as Filson had done for Kentucky. These efforts constituted a direct counterpart to the 1838 atlas of St. Louis (figure 9.6). In the same way that the atlas sought to describe individual claims to property, other maps situated whole frontier cities within broader claims of ownership.

Dupré's 1838 atlas marks an appropriate conclusion to this story, for it reinforces the ways in which cultural production, demographic change, and urban development overlapped to shape how Americans conceived of frontier cities. A series of profound demographic and cultural changes occurred on the frontiers of North America during the 1820s and '30s. Early frontier settlements (St. Louis, Natchez, or Chicago) became more densely populated cities. Meanwhile, some of the earliest frontier cities were located in places that were no longer frontiers. New Orleans, Louisville, or Cincinnati may have undergone incremental change, but Louisiana, Kentucky, and Ohio no longer fit the criteria for "frontiers." In addition to these changes for existing frontier cities, it was during the antebellum era that a host of new frontier cities came into being.

Yet no less important were the representational changes that corresponded with—but were never entirely caused by—these developments in demography and settlement. The profound changes in print and visual culture in that antebellum era kept pace with the profound changes at work on frontiers, combining to alter how Americans understood frontier cities in the decades that followed.

Understanding that process begins by considering two Americans who proved crucial to describing the frontiers of North America. After a half-century of situating frontier cities within a larger continental geography, Jedidiah Morse finally traveled to a frontier in 1820 on an extended tour with the nominal focus of reporting to a missionary society on the condition of Indians along the U.S.-Canadian border. He visited places like Detroit and Mackinac.[29] Earlier that year, Henry Rowe Schoolcraft had passed through the same region on one of a series of western travels that resulted in major published narratives.[30] Schoolcraft wrote that "Detroit occupies an eligible situation on the west banks of the strait that connects Lake Erie with Lake St. Clair.... The town consists of about two hundred and fifty houses, including public buildings,* and has a population of fourteen hundred and fifteen inhabitants, exclusive of the garrison.† It enjoys the advantages of a regular plan, spacious streets, and a handsome elevation of about forty feet above the river, of which it commands the finest views." Schoolcraft explained that the old French style of architecture had given way to the norms of New York, adding that "an air of taste and neatness is thus thrown over the town, which superadded to its elevated situation, the appearances of an active and growing commerce, the bustle of mechanical business, its moral institutions,* and the local beauty of the site, strikes us with a feeling of surprise which is the more gratifying as it was not anticipated." The asterisks pointed to written lists of public and private institutions similar to the buildings that appeared so proudly in the maps of frontier cities.[31]

In sharp contrast to Morse who had little to say about Detroit and Mackinaw, Schoolcraft considered Detroit a model for development. Of course, development had a particular meaning for Schoolcraft. He described the capital of the Michigan Territory as a budding metropolis, with a well-planned town replacing the older frontier exchange outpost. Schoolcraft later became an Indian agent and married a woman of Ojibwa and Irish-American ancestry. He considered himself fundamentally sympathetic to Indians. Nonetheless, Detroit's possibilities as a city hinged on its capacity to replace Indian dominance with white planning.

Despite their differences, Morse and Schoolcraft had participated in a similar process of cultural production. Geographers, cartographic publishers, and the authors of immigrant guides did more than announce the existence of frontier cities. These men chronicled their development, creating a publication history of growth and conquest that was often more apparent than real. Equally important, this story emerged in large part from the economic needs of publishers. The dynamic changes in political geography during the late eighteenth and early nineteenth centuries proved crucial to the rate and profits of publication. The regular exchange of territorial claims (either through treaty or warfare), the forced removal of Indians, and the information from western explorers provided publishers with the ideal marketing rationale to explain why Americans should regularly purchase new editions of atlases they might already own. Frontier cities were part of this story as well. Some quite literally grew before a viewer's eyes. For example, the typeface that publishers used to show emerging frontier cities of the Ohio River Valley went from small fonts often overshadowed by neighboring Indians to large fonts that commanded the landscape.

Morse and Schoolcraft completed their visits to Detroit on the eve of changes in American cultural production and publication that held the potential to transform the representation of frontier cities. Schoolcraft himself—unlike so many other Americans who described frontier cities—now occupies his own space alongside other contemporary literary figures such as James Fenimore Cooper, Nathaniel Hawthorne, and Washington Irving. All of these men sought to develop a national literary scene while promoting various forms of cultural nationalism. But we lump the men who had represented frontier cities into this cohort at our own peril. While many of them were, in fact, public officials committed to federal policy, few saw themselves as literary figures and few expressed any commitment to cultural nationalism.[32]

Not only were Americans producing more books than ever before, but in the 1820s and 1830s the American publishing industry began to produce maps that rivaled those of their European competitors. Once again, this was hardly an act of cultural nationalism, but rather a shift of technical capacity within a highly competitive market. Equally important, Americans produced illustrations that were both detailed and cost effective. These travel narratives, maps, and illustrations continued to describe frontier cities throughout the nineteenth century. Yet at the very moment of their fulfillment, these generic forms faced new competition from texts that would eventually displace them in an effort to locate frontier cities within the American imagination. Novels, landscape paintings, lithographic surveys, and other forms of published representation increasingly assumed the cultural space occupied by travel narratives and maps.[33]

Indeed, frontier cities were among the first subjects of this cultural production. When John Caspar Wild, the Swiss-born artist who became a pioneer in lithography, came to the United States, he chose American cities as one of his first subjects. His list of subjects included not only places like New York, Philadelphia, and Boston, but also Cincinnati and St. Louis, old frontier cities which, by the 1830s, quite literally looked very much the same as their eastern counterparts.[34]

But frontier cities were represented, imagined, and interpreted very differently in the antebellum era than they had been during the early republic. The cities themselves had changed. By the mid-nineteenth century, many of the old frontier cities—dominated by the interaction among Frenchmen,

Spaniards, Indians, and people of mixed-race ancestry—had undergone a demographic transformation when Anglo-Americans became the majority. Meanwhile the towns that Anglo-Americans had built from scratch demonstrated that the United States could build its own frontier cities. Yet no less important were the media that described these places. The book-publishing industry and the penny press delivered an effusion of narratives, in sharp contrast to the first accounts published only a generation before. Meanwhile, engraved and lithographic urban scenes increased not only the *quantity* of visual representation, but forever transformed the *quality* of visual representation. Maps, of course, remained profoundly important in the ways Americans understood the West, but they mattered less for the representation of frontier cities. Urban street scenes of the type that Wild produced responded to very different generic conventions than maps. They told different stories. Most importantly, by removing frontier cities from the frontiers that surrounded those cities in maps, these new forms of representation could increasingly separate frontier cities from frontiers.

That process of broad cultural change was well under way when Alexis de Tocqueville visited the United States. Too often, however, Tocqueville receives primacy of place as the quintessential describer of North America. In the intervening decades separating that Frenchman from an earlier generation of French travelers, Americans had created their own corpus to describe the cities of North American frontiers. In their own efforts to lay claim to North America, those describers had sought to resolve the place of cities on the frontier. In the end, that proved an awkward pursuit, one that revealed how Americans represented not just frontiers, but their country at large.

CHAPTER 10

Private Libraries and Global Worlds: Books and Print Culture in Colonial St. Louis

John Neal Hoover

When I think about the best cultural indicators of any frontier city, my mind goes immediately to the work of John Francis McDermott, an interdisciplinary scholar of the history of the book before such terms were coined. In a scholarly career stretching from the 1930s to the 1980s, McDermott investigated the cultural and intellectual history of his beloved St. Louis. From his very first book, *Private Libraries in Creole St. Louis,* McDermott tracked the distribution of books and their appearance in early communities of the Midwest in a way destined to debunk long-held notions of what the frontier meant to people of the past and the present, and how a frontier city served as connection point between the presumed wilderness and the very centers of erudite culture.[1]

McDermott was a painstaking sleuth, constantly rediscovering lost manuscripts from early territorial governors, documents of explorers, and records of merchants. His bibliographical dedication to the work of John James Audubon, Washington Irving, Seth Eastman, and George Caleb Bingham often left his findings on St. Louis founders Pierre Laclede and Auguste Chouteau for other scholars to explicate. But McDermott remained cognizant of the special place of such bibliographical studies in St. Louis, seeking to reconstruct the local libraries and learn how the frontier manifested itself in such a mixed-up culture stew as was present in a frontier city.[2] Time after time, McDermott returned to the theme of private libraries in frontier St. Louis, cataloging the books owned by early American St. Louisans such as William Clark, Jedediah

Smith, John Mullanphy, Frederick Bates, and W. Price Hunt, and seeing such books as implicitly civilizing determinants of frontier participants.[3]

To this day the grand Turnerian thesis of culture moving inexorably from east to west in an unbroken continuity still infects much thinking subliminally among current writers and popular history, and ignores the multicultural timelines in the history of the European colonies of North America, if not the world over. Yet McDermott's research presaged the insights on frontier cities we have found here. He proved conclusively that St. Louis was never backward or isolated. We might further suggest that frontier cities did not develop either culturally or socially according to central-place theory. The inhabitants of such western places did not stand idly by waiting for a critical mass of easterners to arrive in order to establish cultural institutions; rather, they gathered ideas, collected books and maps, and kept in touch with correspondents from a variety of places and people in the East, in Canada, in Europe, and in Indian country.

His methodology remains a good one. In order to compare Montreal in the last days of the seventeenth century to, say, Boston in the same period, McDermott would have started to dig in probate records and archives to prove that there were as many as ten books in the French settlements of the St. Lawrence Valley for every one tome belonging to the few Puritan divines in frontier Boston in the early 1670s.[4]

Some twenty-five years ago, at the annual meeting of the Bibliographical Society of America, I was asked by a colleague from the Library of Congress, knowing of my connection with an early St. Louis library, just what some of the major bibliographical studies might be on our city. I instantly remarked that one of the best still was John Francis McDermott's *Private Libraries in Creole St. Louis*, even then long out of print. Perhaps it was the exotic title with the word *Creole* in the title—a term with a long history of shifting and often contested meanings—or the delight at the prospect that the bibliography of an entire city might perhaps be based on cookbooks of spicy recipes of one type or another, but regardless, my friend started laughing uncontrollably as he walked away, shaking his head at such a strange bibliographical concept.

Yet, like the concept of frontier cities themselves, those who can get beyond their initial surprise can learn a tremendous amount from early libraries and bibliographic projects like McDermott's. We can see the tastes, culture, and aspirations of early cities in Europe and North America refracted in McDermott's work, his scouring of St. Louis's early probate records, circuit court records, surviving letters, contemporary travel and biographical sketches, and early newspaper reviews and notices in order to bring life back into the documents of those who came here from Spain, France, and the United States and who strode across the eighteenth century and early nineteenth with such importance and style.

And yet such methods and such records in comprehensive depth *still* remain virtually an untapped resource in studying the comparative bibliographies of various early regions in colonial North America, either affiliated with New England, New France and Louisiana, or New Spain and Mexico.

McDermott fretted over the paradox of early travelers—especially those from the young United States, before the Louisiana Purchase—who commented on St. Louis's isolation, as if on "the confines of the Wilderness."[5] Given St. Louis's position from its very beginnings as a commercial center and an administrative capital, such a view was always mistaken; the city's relatively small size obscured its importance as a center for far-flung commercial transactions across two thirds of a continent. Yet early nineteenth-century American writers such as Timothy Flint, Edmund Flagg, and especially Washington Irving promulgated the idea of St. Louis's backwoods isolation. Those wishing to promote the supposed "civilizing" effect of Anglo-American political and cultural institutions in the so-called old French country of the Mississippi River valley ignored the existing cultural refinements of French colonial cities like St. Louis and New Orleans as they remade them on their own terms.

The key to understanding the paradox of these early French outposts, and all frontier cities, is the nature of their residents—world citizens by any meaningful measure. When Pierre Laclede from Béarn by way of New Orleans, Charles Gratiot from Lausanne by way of London and Montréal, Jean Pierre Cabanné, Jacques de St. Vrain, Dr. Antoine Saugrain, and Louis Cortambert from all corners of the French-speaking world came to St. Louis, they brought a constant influx of new ideas. Visiting travelers, whether critical or not in their later reflections, also demonstrated St. Louis's cosmopolitan, *un*confined nature, simply by their increasing numbers and the books they eventually produced. Basil Hall, André Michaux, Georges-Henri-Victor Collot, and François Marie Perrin du Lac all commented on St. Louis as a commercial center, and all such centers tended to create global attitudes through trade—a signature sign of frontier cities, with connections just as evident in New Orleans, Montreal, New York, Boston, and Detroit. These writers visited cities whose residents knew and read their works. The evidence remains in the early editions of their books preserved in St. Louis collections, evidence that their ideas were considered and embraced.[6]

McDermott, in examining the probate records of St. Louis between 1764 and 1800, considered book ownership as an indicator of how an eighteenth-century French frontier city eschewed isolation and decline. Of approximately six hundred white citizens in St. Louis in this period, almost seventy heads of households owned nearly three thousand books, exclusive of duplicates, collectively.[7] As Helmut Lehmann-Haupt long ago concluded, non-Anglophone colonial libraries were often private, family repositories, imported from European booksellers, and French St. Louis certainly bears this out, with huge numbers of books possessed outside of any public or quasi-public or subscription library until the 1820s. This remains hard to imagine for bibliographers who have focused on studies of the book in this period along the Atlantic seaboard.

In eighteenth-century St. Louis, there were virtually no institutions of public education and no public libraries, yet thousands of books were owned across virtually all settled families. Such private libraries included titles of scientific as well as literary holdings and historical and religious volumes. The founding family, that of Pierre Laclede and his Chouteau descendants, obviously possessed pronounced interests in trade and commerce, politics, and property. Auguste Chouteau himself, the patriarch and friend to so many subsequent leaders of the frontier capital, was a great freethinker—a quarter of his books were on the Index. From Ovid to Ariosto, from Defoe to Fielding, from Descartes to Diderot, the citizens of the early, tiny outpost of St. Louis were well read and informed, ready to create a city which left its mark on the world stage.

Remarkably, many of these books were passed down and survive, regionally, in private hands and in public research collections to this day. The early St. Louis merchant families who founded the city were avid readers of a wide array of classics; sets of Voltaire from the very age of the *philosophes* with local ownership marks are represented in local libraries. Often the property lists of books of the founding citizens of this city ran into hundreds of titles. Such Old World–style collections were formed and kept within one's study, one's own library, rather than communally held in public institutions, as was more common in Anglophone communities.[8]

A brief glance at some of McDermott's bibliographic discoveries reveals both the breadth of reading matter circulating in early St. Louis and the literary self-consciousness these first inhabitants possessed as urban pioneers. The earliest private library of record in eighteenth-century St. Louis was formed by a Laurent Trudeau. At his death in 1774, his books were not itemized, but in the same year Louis St. Ange de Bellerive's estate listed the French military code and Charlevoix's history of the Spanish colonies, appropriate books for the commandant of the area's Fort Chartres in the French Illinois country.[9]

Pierre Laclede's library perfectly reflected this well-educated businessman— commerce, finance, taxation, marine law, history, military affairs, travels, and literature spread across an astonishing three hundred titles in 1778, including some of the first sets of the classics west of the Mississippi, as well as John Locke, Bacon, Rousseau, and Descartes.[10]

At the time of his death, the merchant Silvestre Labbadie in 1794 was one of the wealthiest men in St. Louis. In his library was one of Jefferson's favorite books in the French edition, and thus crucial subsequently to Lewis and Clark's Corps of Discovery: Jonathan Carver's *Travels in the Interior of North America*.[11]

Cleric Pierre Didier, a Benedictine monk forced to flee revolutionary Paris, died in St. Louis in 1799. He and merchant Gabriel Cerré, who died in 1802, left behind the largest libraries up to their time in St. Louis. In these hoards, books on philosophy and religion vied with Cervantes, Cook's *Voyages*, and numerous other historical and political titles.

Antoine Saugrain, descended from booksellers and publishers in Paris, became the surgeon of the military hospital at St. Louis. His library remained in his descendants' hands well into the twentieth century and was quite extensive, reflecting an interest in medicine, chemistry, and botany, to be sure, but also history, politics, and physics.[12]

The Chouteau family provided the best glimpse of book ownership in early St. Louis. Auguste Chouteau left perhaps the largest of the early French libraries in St. Louis, and his is reflective of his extensive knowledge of world affairs and the growing presence in his city (a city which he, as the story goes, helped create at the young age of fourteen) of American influence at the time of his death in 1829.[13] His own important manuscript book on the founding of St. Louis has been preserved in the Mercantile Library since his son, Gabriel, presented it in 1857.[14] Some of the most important works on New France existed on Chouteau's shelves: Lafitau's seminal treatise on the Iroquois; La Hontan's *Travels*; Hennepin, and scores of early works on North America, fortified with modern law, science, and the classics. It is clearly evident that the long historical rendition or prelude to Chouteau's *Narrative* was based in part on extensive reading of grand historical texts present in the Chouteau library. Chouteau, in collecting histories of Europe and North American exploration and settlement, created a material and literary context into which he might place himself and his city, both worthy of belonging to a broader master narrative of urbanity and progress.

Thus, from its beginnings St. Louis had citizens with the means and the inclination to read and collect books for their, or their family's, private use. However public libraries in any sense of the modern meaning were not established until the early nineteenth century in the bustling frontier city.

As the town grew larger, the need was finally felt for the creation of such a public library. By 1808, with the Americans firmly in control administratively after the Louisiana Purchase, St. Louis was one of the first printing centers west of the Mississippi, along with New Orleans and a few other places. Local newspapers such as the bilingual *Missouri Gazette*,[15] pamphlets, books of civil ordinances and other laws, even early creative literary efforts, were being produced here, not exclusively imported. Textbooks were needed for schools, and as the strategic importance of St. Louis was rediscovered in the nineteenth century, there was a need for some form of preservation and free access to this information. The first locally printed play, poem, arithmetic, primer, city directory, and history were produced at the beginning of the 1820s. How nice to have been a buyer at St. Louis's first bookseller, the Essex Book Shop![16]

The private French libraries gave way to the early American subscription libraries across the entire Illinois country of the French settlers. Individuals would become library patrons and members for a fee; proprietary shares would be sold for the purpose of acquiring a collection of useful books for general consumption. This is the heritage maintained by the members of today's St. Louis Mercantile Library. The first attempt at creating this sort of public collection from donations from the earlier private collections came and went in 1811. Other abortive efforts occurred in 1818 with the creation of such institutions as a "Reading Room and Punch House," and the St. Louis Debating Society's St. Louis Library Company.[17]

But St. Louis received its first lasting public library in 1824, when the Mayor and several other citizens founded the St. Louis Library Association. This institution, the first large collection of public books for the citizens of St. Louis, was in existence until 1839, when it finally closed its doors, transferring its valuable collections of books on all subjects to the library of the St. Louis Lyceum.[18]

The bibliographical importance of the Lyceum experiment to St. Louis was enormous, even if it was, again, not a sustainable model. In the span of a generation it passed a portion of the collection of the earliest library company, that of the St. Louis Library Association, along with its own extensive book collection, its archives, catalog, and business records, and that of smaller literary societies and donations to it from the earliest families, in 1851, to the St. Louis Mercantile Library Association, which had the backing and management of the thriving merchant community and dedicated philanthropists wishing to preserve their cultural legacy in such a public institution. This is also an intriguing cultural circumstance. The Mercantile Library, traditionally dating its founding to 1846, is one of the oldest libraries anywhere in the trans-Mississippi, but few writers except McDermott have realized the unbroken heritage of St. Louis's public libraries, through specific mergers, dating from 1824. Given that heritage, the Mercantile could have claimed that earlier date of founding, making frontier St. Louis's first library one of the oldest in continuing existence, virtually as old as such institutions as the Boston Athenaeum and those libraries of Providence, Cincinnati, and New York.[19]

Michael Winship has found that, in the early 1850s, books published in New York were routinely accessioned by the St. Louis Mercantile Library Association within weeks of their publication.[20] Already a transportation center by then, St. Louis's distribution networks could get books deep into the rural reaches of its economic or trading territories within the period of an additional few days. By examining library records in St. Louis and comparing dates to original newspaper notices and later references such as the *Bibliography of American Literature*, it can be shown that the Mercantile Library in St. Louis often acquired books published in Boston, New York, or Philadelphia—Emerson, Thoreau, Lowell, Parkman, Stowe, Whittier, Whitman, Melville, immediately on publication, in some cases the very same day that the Harvard College Library accessioned these books.[21] Such data radically changes our notion of intellectual frontiers in this era.

The continued vitality of the St. Louis Mercantile Library as a bridge to earlier cultural days along the frontier, side-by-side with more contemporary book centers, has ensured that a significant number of the earliest books read by the first citizens of St. Louis have survived in the original editions. In 1851, the Mercantile Library bought approximately two-thousand of the non-duplicated titles from the St. Louis Lyceum for roughly fifty cents per volume (or a bit over one thousand dollars). The records created when these books were accessioned provide a glimpse of not only the earliest private libraries of

St. Louis but also a composite of all the early St. Louis public book collections that had survived.

The Mercantile has preserved the earliest library catalogs, circulation records, and membership rolls of its predecessors, the Lyceum and the old Library Association. Numerous eighteenth-century French works in history, the classics, fiction, science, travel, and biography exist side-by-side in the catalog with their English counterparts, testifying to a moment when two separate frontier literary stories were linked within one library collection,[22] and through that, representing the mind or composite intellect of a frontier city.

Many of the books that were bought by the Mercantile Library itself (especially worn books or much early fiction) were not added to the permanent collection. But over eleven hundred titles, with accession numbers between #8000 and #9100, were included from those years. Of that span, 153 books (or 15 percent) were published in the eighteenth century in Amsterdam, Paris, London, Philadelphia, or Boston and are present. Many of these have ownership marks of some of the earliest French citizens, as noted above, demonstrating how books circulated across all boundaries as St. Louis grew from a village to a metropolis.[23]

Eighteenth-century books are fascinating barometers for the North American frontier city. These books were international best sellers in their day. Just as the first merchants of St. Louis were connected economically to other urban centers in both North America and Europe, so were they connected through their books to a broader world of literary production, scientific thinking, and map making. The very presence of such books in early libraries disproves notions that eighteenth- and nineteenth-century frontier cities were confined, isolated, or restrained, thus confirming the implications of McDermott's bibliographical studies.

Charles Peterson reversed the measure in *Colonial St. Louis: Building a Creole Capital* by tracing the depth and variety of historical sources about St. Louis surviving worldwide.[24] This was, in short, a two-way street. Others in very distant places were also thinking about St. Louis, and this frontier place was inscribed in maps and documents being produced in Spain, in France, and elsewhere. The immediacy of this shared print culture seems to prove that frontier cities such as St. Louis did not simply attain "culture" as they matured, increased in size, or became part of a regional economy; rather, as McDermott meant to suggest with his provocative and startling title, this frontier place—from its very inception—had access to the latest thoughts of

Rousseau and Voltaire. St. Louis was an urban place in Indian country. That was no contradiction. It was never a wilderness.

These books are still being rediscovered, and with them their very special associations. Only recently a two-centuries-old root cellar was excavated by amazed archaeologists in the old French town of Florissant, in northern St. Louis County. I was asked to take a look at the cache of books that was found in a long-forgotten foundation, open to the elements but preserved by loving hands in this region when the city was young.

I have reflected on the existence of early libraries and the evolution of a specific early library, the Mercantile, which through books in "frontier" days created a memory, a version of one city's past. There were simultaneous developments and thus interesting sidebars for researchers to investigate in this field of cultural history. Rather than following a geographical progression from east to west, early libraries and their sources of supply arose simultaneously. The Vincennes Library Company in Indiana (1806); the Albion, Illinois, Public Library (1818); John Mason Peck's books in southern Illinois, a legendary collection of the 1820s; the Edwardsville Public Library of 1819, of which the catalog survives and many of the first books are now preserved at Southern Illinois University at Edwardsville; early books sold by Joseph Philipson in 1807 in St. Louis; the Kaskaskia library of Father Gibault (1790); private libraries from Ste. Genevieve before 1810; Bartholomew Tardiveau's extensive collection of books in New Madrid before 1801; the first presses in early Kentucky, and Joseph Charless's printing of books and newspapers in St. Louis after 1807—the details may overwhelm, but all together, the evidence of these early libraries which seemingly arose overnight in Missouri and Illinois demand renewed research if we wish to gain a full picture of frontier cities, and intellectual underpinnings of the life in all the cultures of early America.[25]

Taking McDermott's work one step further, we might pay more attention to the circulation of books and letters in these French-speaking frontier cities, questioning how distribution worked in languages other than English. We might also probe the divide between private and public in the cultural realm. Such inquiries might provide another opportunity for decentering our traditional national narratives. And we should remember that the inhabitants of a frontier city such as St. Louis also produced letters, maps, and various kinds of texts that were shaped not only by what they read, but also by what they experienced in cross-cultural encounters with the native peoples of the area. Historians need to read these texts as the products of multiple epistemologies.

Founders of St. Louis and the developers of the trans-Mississippi West more generally found inspiration and knowledge in books; their eyes pored avidly over the lines of text with curiosity, interest, and ambition, when the volumes and the city and region were both quite young. Many of these books remain to us today—a decidedly strong and rewarding link to the lost world of these frontier cities.

EPILOGUE

Frontier Cities and the Return of Globalization

Jay Gitlin, Barbara Berglund, and Adam Arenson

From Goa to Montreal, from Manaus to Los Angeles, the essays in this volume have covered a lot of ground, geographically, chronologically, and thematically. But we do find that the same characteristics emerge in so many frontier cities, as their local stories and negotiations are set into larger global and hemispheric contexts of unequal power relations and imperial ambitions. The growth of these cities was more likely to be driven by trade and local circumstances than any mythic line of settlement. And the legacy of frontier experiences has shaped these cities long after that initial frontier encounter has ended.

The essays in this volume explore an aspect of the past we think has been under studied. Frontier cities, as we understand them, were carriers of culture, in some cases explicitly shaped by imperial guidelines and points of exchange, there to facilitate and harness various forms of interaction among residents and exploit local resources which might connect to distant markets. These places, as urban expressions of settler colonialism and tools of empire and nation-building, often exerted transformative power. At the same time, frontier cities relied on Native neighbors as well as people pushed into these new spaces by migrant and immigrant labor flows to be their customers and producers, laborers and tourists. Frontier cities thereby encouraged various forms of inclusion as well as exclusion—economic, social, and cultural—in shared physical spaces shaped, to varying degrees, by all participants. As we have said, we think the study of these neglected frontier cities can connect various fields, reanimate western history, and provide a surprisingly relevant point of comparison with modern American cities.

Epilogue

The stories in this volume's chapters do not exhaust the paths and legacies experienced in frontier cities. As we discussed how to close this volume, we reflected on the powerful and very different frontier city stories of the three cities where we make our institutional homes: New Haven, Connecticut; Tampa, Florida; and El Paso, Texas. Each offers yet another aspect of the frontier city—and suggests more avenues for frontier city research. It is our sense, in short, that the "frontier city" as a conceptual framework encourages us to notice aspects of the past, missing pieces of the urban puzzle, that have gone unnoticed. Moreover, we think that the change of perspective that the very notion of the frontier city suggests pushes us to reorient our narratives in ways utterly relevant to contemporary global and transnational conditions. We offer the following three brief pieces as examples of that reorientation.

* * *

Everything about New Haven seems to conjure up the term *colonial*. New Haven's first historians and chroniclers, writing in the 1830s, looked back in time to find the origins of the city's steady habits and growth.[1] What they stressed was the city's college-educated founding duo, the merchant Theophilus Eaton and the Reverend John Davenport, representing the city's twin pillars of prosperity and piety. They also highlighted the city's nine-square grid plan, a landmark in the history of American town planning and the very essence of rational order imposed upon the land.[2] New Haven, its past, present, and future, seemed to embody the best of the Anglo-American tradition. When industrialization and immigration transformed the city toward the end of the nineteenth century, Yankee old-timers would look back upon the city's colonial past as a golden age.

Yet that word *colonial* implied a limited frame through which to view the past. In the case of New Haven, it tends to fix our gaze on those iconic well-ordered nine squares. Substitute the word *frontier*, and other aspects of the city's history appear. Indeed, during the first Anglo-Dutch War of 1652–1654, New Haveners described themselves in the records in 1653 as a "fronteere plantation," "more exposed to enemies and dangers th[a]n before."[3]

Virtually unknown today is the Quinnipiac Indian reservation that existed on the town's east shore from its founding in 1638 until 1773. Quinnipiac leader Momauguin originally reserved some twelve hundred acres on the east shore in 1638. At the time of the final sale in 1773, when the Quinnipiac community moved to Farmington, Connecticut, only thirty acres remained.

Not until 1900 would a historian, Charles H. Townshend, remind his local audience—in a publication with a very limited print run—that the city had included a reservation for almost a century and a half.[4] Enlarge the "colonial" frame with the concept of the frontier city and suddenly names on the land—Wigwam Point, Indian Neck, Montowese, Menunkatuck—provoke new questions about the city's history. The town's founders in 1638 were well aware of the opportunity that two epidemics in 1633 and 1634 and the Pequot War to the east provided for settlers looking to secure a foothold along the coast. This was no mere coincidence.[5]

Looking with new eyes on the city's past, we find Native people in a variety of places. In 1748, young scholar Samson Occom prepared to become Yale's first indigenous student, but eyestrain forced a change of plans. When a Wampanoag man, Moses Paul, was convicted by a jury of killing a white man in a tavern in nearby Bethany, Connecticut, late in the year 1771, Occom returned to New Haven at the request of Paul—who felt that racial bias had shaped the verdict—to preach an execution sermon. Joanna Brooks, the editor of Occom's collected writings, has noted how Occom's sermon, "using sin as a leveler of racial and class distinctions," indicted all those present ('Indians, English, and Negroes') . . . as sinners in need of redemption." The sermon, published in October of 1772, went through nineteen editions and established Occom's reputation as a leading preacher and author.[6] As Brooks notes, "Occom's writings comprise the most extensive Native-authored commentary on colonialism to survive the colonial era."[7]

Samson Occom's sister, Lucy Occom Tantaquidgeon, stayed in Uncasville, Connecticut. Lucy Occom Tantaquidgeon, her daughter, and her granddaughter deeded a plot of land on Mohegan Hill to the tribe "for the building of a community church."[8] That church became and remained the center of Mohegan life. In 1978, Gladys Tantaquidgeon was still giving visitors (including our Yale-based editor) a tour of the museum she had co-founded in 1931. Due in part to her work preserving her community's history and traditional knowledge, the Mohegans received federal acknowledgment in 1994. That same year, Yale awarded her an honorary doctorate. She died in 2005 at the age of 106.[9]

For several years now, the Native American Cultural Center at Yale and our growing body of Native students have honored graduating Native seniors with a wonderful reception at Mohegan Sun, the tribe's casino and luxury hotel. Mohegan leaders have been extremely welcoming and Native elders from around the state have taken pride in our students and have looked after them during their years at Yale away from their own families and communities. At ceremonies at Yale, we have once again heard the words of thanks—*táput ni*—in a local Native language that Yale students might have heard in New Haven in the eighteenth century. As it has become increasingly obvious in the last two decades that Connecticut is a place on the map of Indian country, part of what Samson Occom called "this Indian world," it becomes even more appropriate to re-envision New Haven's past as a frontier city.

Viewing New Haven as a frontier city produces an enhanced and altered historical narrative. Clearly, New Haven remained a frontier city for at least a century and a half after its founding. New Haveners in the late eighteenth century and early nineteenth centuries retained an interest in western lands in Ohio and Mississippi,[10] pursued trade in the West Indies, and exploited resources in the South Atlantic.[11] While later generations might look back and venerate the genteel virtues of a mature colonial culture, their ancestors long maintained what Elliott West describes in this volume as a "frontier mentality." In 2007, New Haven—responding to the transnational flow of people across ineffective borders—decided to offer municipal services and an Elm City Residence Card to protect an estimated ten-thousand-plus undocumented immigrants from Mexico, Ecuador, and elsewhere (many of them of overwhelmingly indigenous Central American backgrounds).[12] In issuing this first municipal identification card in the United States, we may fairly say that New Haven, balancing local realities and national regulations, continues to "see like a city."

* * *

Like New Haven, Tampa is not typically thought of as frontier city. In fact, since the early twentieth century its identity as a place has been constructed around the public display of a mythic history that shuns frontier pioneers in favor of pirates. Tampa's pirate-oriented past is given its fullest expression at the annual Gasparilla Festival, begun in 1904 as a side event to larger promotional extravaganzas. In recent years, Gasparilla has evolved into a Mardi Gras–like celebration during which the mayor surrenders the keys of the city to an invading flotilla of rogue pirates. That Gasparilla commemorates the murky legend of the Spanish pirate Jose Gaspar, who is said to have patrolled the West Coast of Florida in the late eighteenth and early nineteenth centuries—but who has eluded all efforts at historical documentation—is not enough to dull the city's enthusiasm for this ritual event. By 1974, when

Tampa was awarded a National Football League franchise, Tampans had so thoroughly associated pirates with their city that calling their team "the Buccaneers" was a natural choice.[13]

Yet despite its love affair with mythic pirates, Tampa is a city that emerged and has continued to develop in the context of varied and shifting frontier conditions and processes. From the early sixteenth to the early nineteenth century, Florida underwent repeated colonial incursions from Spain, France, and Britain, making the region as a whole an unstable, multivalent frontier of encounter for Europeans, Indians, and African-descended people. If there were a real, historical Jose Gaspar, this was the world that produced him and in which he lived most of his life. Tampa's founding as an urban place came at the end of this long period of rivalries between European states and begins with the United States' acquisition of Florida in 1819 and the establishment of Fort Brooke on Tampa Bay in 1824. In the Gasparilla legend, Jose Gaspar is said to have jumped from his ship to his death rather than be captured by conquering Americans.

Fort Brooke was one of a number of forts built in Florida in the early nineteenth century to mark new imperial realities and to mediate the multicultural landscape—just like those in other frontier regions of North America. Fort Brooke's mission was two-pronged: to distribute the supplies and services guaranteed to the Seminole Indians following the first Seminole War and to protect white migrants and their interests, which generally meant subduing and controlling nearby African American and Seminole communities. Not only did Seminole communities often provide safe haven for runaway slaves, but the Seminoles also refused to remain contained on reservations in Florida's interior or to relinquish their land and move west when it became a desirable commodity. Interaction with the Seminoles—whether in tense daily exchanges, periods of relative harmony, or outright warfare—configured every phase of the first decades of Tampa's development.[14]

From its founding, Fort Brooke and the civilian community that grew up around it functioned as a point of connection, a place that, although designed to symbolize and effect U.S. domination, also brought Seminoles and whites together. On casual visits to the fort, Indians sometimes stayed overnight, camping at a spring about a mile away. The first Fourth of July celebration at Fort Brooke in 1824 brought Indians together with officers and men stationed there for shared oratory, food, and drink. As young men, the Seminole leaders and warriors, Osceola and John Horse, were regular visitors to the fort where they befriended, traded with, and drilled with soldiers there. Later the press tended to suggest that the two gained American military training and insights with nefarious intent. But the reality of young Seminoles, socializing and training with American troops, suggests other interpretations and possibilities.[15]

The civilian settlement adjacent to the fort was finally chartered as the town of Tampa in 1855. Conflict with the Seminoles, devastating hurricanes, and deadly disease routinely derailed periods of hopeful growth. At the time of the 1880 census, the population stood at a mere 720 inhabitants with challenging travel isolating it from the north until the arrival of the railroad in 1884. From the start, however, despite its small size and fragility, the frontier settlement had nascent urban characteristics: it functioned as a trading center; its population was dense relative to the areas around it; and it had amenities such as hotels, bars, a theater, gambling saloons, and eventually a church, a school, and other commercial establishments. For a southern frontier settlement, it was also atypically multicultural and cosmopolitan—with U.S. whites from both northern and southern states; free and enslaved blacks; Cubans and other Caribbean migrants; and the Seminoles, whose incorporation of African-descended people made them a racially blended group. One of its important early entrepreneurs, who moved to the town from Key West in 1839 was Odet Philippe, a mulatto originally from Haiti. With connections and encouragement from the community's white leaders, Philippe bought lots and other property and opened a billiard hall, a ten-pin alley, and an oyster shop. He also operated the settlement's first cigar-making facility.[16]

The problem with the Jose Gaspar legend and Gasparilla is not so much that it is based on myth or that it is historically inaccurate. The real problem is that it promotes a version of Tampa history that makes invisible its frontier past and the history of nascent urbanity and encounter—some of it painful and violent, all of it fascinating—that characterized it. Jose Gaspar, after all, chose to jump off the boat to his death rather than interact with the American conquerors. It also leads to a tendency to see Tampa's history in isolated pieces rather than as part of a more interconnected story. Recognizing Tampa as a frontier city, and taking its frontier past seriously, allows for connections to be drawn between what often seem like compartmentalized and anomalous parts of its history: its origins in a remote military fort, in a newly acquired U.S. territory, central to the Seminole Wars; its rise in the late nineteenth century as an industrial frontier based on cigars and immigrant labor; and its recent allure for migrants eager to begin new lives in the Sunshine State—land of schemes and dreams—a truly volatile frontier of global credit markets and labor flows.

Seen through a frontier city lens, Tampa's past and present can be conceptualized in new, more holistic ways, marked by the ongoing qualities characteristic of urban frontier places: intense multicultural interaction, multiple flows of migrants and immigrants, economic concentration and risk, and transnational connections. Even Jose Gaspar, a mythic figure traversing the interstices of Atlantic World empires, becomes much more interesting when seen in this light. And the presence of the multimillion-dollar Seminole Hard Rock Casinos in Orlando and Hollywood—owned and operated by the Seminole tribe—takes on new cultural and economic significance when placed in this larger historical context.

* * *

The frontiers in El Paso, Texas, have remained an omnipresent fact of the city's history. Situated at a break in the mountains where the river now known to Americans as the Rio Grande turns north, El Paso was always a gathering place for the indigenous peoples of the region. And El Paso has prospered not just because of its local geography, but also because of its status as a place in between: at first, as between the Aztecs' cities in central Mexico and the cities of the Pueblos, in what we now call northern New Mexico. In 1598, Juan de Oñate passed through the El Paso region, along a path that Spanish authorities would call the Camino Real del Interior, the inland route for the king's conquerors and colonizers. He named the city for the Spanish, and held a ceremony of Thanksgiving, grateful to have founds the river's water and green pastures after the long trek across the Chihuahuan Desert.[17]

Yet the Pueblo peoples of northern New Mexico were not happy to see Oñate and his successors. Close to one hundred years of contact with Europeans who styled themselves as new regional authorities had made them guarded, suspicious of the claims of benevolence from men who called themselves *conquistadores*. Oñate enforced his rule over the Pueblo by committing horrific acts against the populace—imprisoning women and children, and cutting off the right foot of every man he could catch as a punishment for their resistance. A few generations later, Oñate's successor Antonio de Otermín would face the massive Pueblo Revolt of 1680, as the Native leader Popé gathered traditional enemies to stand against the Spanish order. Otermín abandoned northern New Mexico and retreated with one group of Pueblo Indians, the Tigua, back to El Paso. There, the Spanish authorities balanced new investments in the local settlement with their desire to reconquer the Pueblo of northern New Mexico, which the Spanish finally did again in 1695.[18]

This first El Paso was south of the river, on the wide floodplain of the Rio Grande. But that city ceased to be El Paso in 1848, when, with the Treaty of Guadalupe Hidalgo, the United States acquired more than 525,000 square miles north of the river, turning it into a national border. Oñate's settlement among the Tigua, called Ysleta after the Spanish name for these Indians—the Ysleta del Sur Pueblo, both distinguishing them and linking them to the Ysleta Pueblo of northern New Mexico—would have remained in Mexico, except for the fact that the flood seasons of 1829 and 1831 had shifted the river south of their mission settlement, leaving it just to the east of the new United States city of El Paso.[19] A generation later, the city on the south side of the river was renamed to honor Benito Juárez, the hero of the successful struggle for Mexico to throw off the rule of French-sponsored Emperor Maximilian.[20]

In its one hundred and fifty years on a permanent frontier, El Paso has been a city shaped by American traders reaching El Paso via the Santa Fe Trail and the Camino Real; by the easterners posted at Fort Bliss to guard the city for the United States, the Confederacy, and then the United States again; by the transformation brought by the Southern Pacific transcontinental railroad in 1883; and by the experience of immigrants—Syrian and Chinese, Eastern European and Mexican—who sought to profit from the deep and ongoing cross-border relationship with Ciudad Juárez.[21] Together, these two cities have struggled with what it means to be a borderland metropolis, inextricably linked by immigration, trade, and family ties but often separated by opposing national policies.

The earliest frontier city history of El Paso has been resurrected in the city's public art and architecture in the past half-century. When a group enamored of the *conquistadores* proposed placing a much larger than life-size statue of Oñate at the center of the city in 1989, Tigua, Chicano, and other activists protested the efforts to glorify a murderer and torturer. Though the outcry did not end city support for the statue, it did succeed in getting it moved out of downtown, the name changed to merely *The Equestrian*. The controversy also stymied the creation of more statues to dubious heroes of El Paso's past.[22]

Even more profoundly, the Tigua Indians have reasserted their history since attainment of federal recognition in 1968, reshaping their built environment through construction of a new tribal museum, a casino, and even gas stations and health center in the style of the Pueblo architecture of northern

New Mexico, reemphasizing their ancestral ties to another region.[23] Today, it is an easy drive from *The Equestrian* statue to the Tiguas' new adobe-like buildings, all within the United States but all within view of the massive Mexican flag just over the border. The palimpsest of cultural, political, and economic agendas continues to shape El Paso as a frontier city.

* * *

In New Haven, Tampa, and El Paso, frontiers remain zones of interpenetration, to paraphrase another touchstone book, Howard Lamar and Leonard Thompson's *The Frontier in History*.[24] Frontiers can be places of gaps, differences, and competitions, but frontier cities are also arenas for juxtapositions, connections, and opportunities. Frontier cities were unique places to examine and exploit political, cultural, and economic differences, and to exchange and learn from each other's distinctive reservoirs of knowledge.

In our age of re-globalization, the everyday reality of frontier cities has become the renewed experience of the whole world, at a much greater pace. Natives, newcomers, immigrants, and migrants had much in common in the past; that is obviously even more the case today. In the global village of modern life, juxtapositions tend to be less dramatic.

Recovering the history and legacy of frontier cities is an important task all across North America. We hope the stories of these frontier cities will encourage a renewed dialogue that connects the past to the present.

NOTES

Introduction

1. Coeur qui Brule to Delassus, 1800, Box 3, Chouteau Collections, Missouri Historical Society, St. Louis.

2. We cannot know if Coeur qui Brule spoke French, and it is very likely that he dictated the letter. But it is quite possible that he spoke some French; for just one example of Indians (especially slaves and former slaves) "who talked excellent French," see Patricia Cleary, *The World, the Flesh, and the Devil: A History of Colonial St. Louis* (Columbia, MO: University of Missouri Press, 2011), 282. The letter does indicate that Coeur qui Brule understood what the French wanted to hear. While he probably wanted his visit to have diplomatic and commercial ramifications, the particular choice of words would seem to indicate the genuine curiosity of a tourist.

3. Coeur qui Brule to Delassus, 1800, Box 3, Chouteau Collections, Missouri Historical Society, St. Louis. For the Missouri Indians story, see Jay Gitlin, *The Bourgeois Frontier: French Towns, French Traders, and American Expansion* (New Haven: Yale University Press, 2010), 18; J. Frederick Fausz, *Founding St. Louis: First City of the New West* (Charleston, SC: History Press, 2011), 118–120.

4. Gitlin, *The Bourgeois Frontier*; Fausz, *Founding St. Louis*; and Patricia Cleary, *The World, the Flesh, and the Devil: A History of Colonial St. Louis* (Columbia: University of Missouri Press, 2011), 42–48. In her book on early St. Louis, Cleary describes the place as a "global village . . . at once isolated—distant from European seats of power—and part of vast continental and trans-Atlantic networks of trade and migration" (37). Her characterization fits nicely into our formulation of frontier cities.

5. Richard C. Wade, *The Urban Frontier: Pioneer Life in Early Pittsburgh, Cincinnati, Lexington, Louisville, and St. Louis* (Cambridge: Harvard University Press, 1959), 1. Wade's book is a classic source but, a half-century on, is showing its age. Wade went on to tell Euro-American stories of solving "Indian problems" and "civilizing" in ways that current histories would question. For a sense of these differences, see Adam Arenson, "The Double Life of St. Louis: Narratives of Origins and Maturity in Wade's *Urban Frontier*," *Indiana Magazine of History* 105:3, Richard Wade Special Issue (September 2009), 246–261, and Barbara Berglund, *Making San Francisco American: Cultural Frontiers in the Urban West, 1846–1906* (Lawrence: University Press of Kansas, 2007), 221.

6. While Truett and Hämäläinen have outlined complementary trends in borderlands studies emphasizing "spatial mobility, situational identity, local contingency, and the ambiguities of power" we insist on calling these frontier cities, rather than borderlands cities. Pekka Hämäläinen and Samuel Truett, "On Borderlands," *Journal of American History* 98:2 (September 2011), 338. The geographic distance of frontier cities from imperial centers and global markets is what helped define them, not merely their place along the seam of various patterns of control. Moreover, far from being "local and regional" (Hämäläinen and Truett, 349), frontier cities describe places we think are most often local and global. They are most interesting when they are the sites of this juxtaposition.

We don't agree that frontiers are, by definition, places or zones that include a teleology driven by European newcomers—as we insist throughout, *frontier* is a word redeemable from the Turnerian viewpoint. Full global integration removes the frontier nature of these places, but the interplay of their city logic and their frontier logic determines how, at different timescales, in different ways, and to different ends, frontier cities continue to be their own centers. They provide a narrative that recasts both national and imperial developments. Frontier cities, in this way, provide a link to later transnational conditions. Cities never close.

7. See especially William Cronon, George A. Miles, and Jay Gitlin, eds., *Under an Open Sky: Rethinking America's Western Past* (New York: W. W. Norton, 1992); Patricia Nelson Limerick, *The Legacy of Conquest: The Unbroken Past of the American West* (New York: W. W. Norton, 1987); Howard Lamar and Leonard Thompson, eds., *Frontier in History: North America and South Africa Compared* (New Haven: Yale University Press, 1981); and Jeremy Adelman and Stephen Aron, "From Borderlands to Borders: Empires, Nation-States, and the Peoples in Between in North America," *American Historical Review* 104:3 (June 1999), 814–841.

8. For the imperial inclinations of the early United States see, for example, Amy Kaplan, "'Left Alone with America': The Absence of Empire in the Study of American Culture," in *Cultures of United States Imperialism*, ed. Amy Kaplan and Donald Pease (Durham: Duke University Press, 1993) and Carroll Smith-Rosenberg, *This Violent Empire: The Birth of an American National Identity* (Chapel Hill: University of North Carolina Press, 2010).

9. Raymond Williams, *The Country and the City* (London: Chatto & Windus, 1973). See also Dolores Hayden, *Building Suburbia: Green Fields and Urban Growth, 1820–2000* (New York: Pantheon Books, 2003); Carl Abbott, *How Cities Won the West: Four Centuries of Urban Change in Western North America* (Albuquerque: University of New Mexico Press, 2008); Sam B. Warner, Jr., *The Urban Wilderness: A History of the American City* (Berkeley: University of California Press, 1995); Lewis Mumford, *The City in History: Its Origins, Its Transformations, and Its Prospects* (New York: Harcourt, Brace and World, 1961).

10. Robert S. Lopez, "The Crossroads Within the Wall," in *The Historian and the City*, ed. Oscar Handlin and John Burchard (Cambridge: MIT Press, 1963), 27–28.

11. Henri Lefebvre, *The Production of Space*, trans. Donald Nicholson Smith (Oxford, UK: Blackwell, 1991); Gyan Prakash and Kevins Kruse, eds., *The Spaces of the Modern City: Imaginaries, Politics, and Everyday Life* (Princeton: Princeton University Press, 2008).

12. This is reflected in recent figures presented at the meeting of the Urban History Association in 2010. Of the ten most cited scholars in the *Journal of Urban History*, books on the twentieth century dominated, with only two works that focused on an earlier period. And of the books reviewed in that publication since 2005, the temporal breakdown is illuminating. The journal reviewed 181 books in the "1870 to the present" category while the period spanning from the ancient world to 1870 warranted the review of only 52 books. Clay McShane presented these figures at the Urban History Association meeting's roundtable session, "The American Urban History Canon," October 21, 2010.

13. As the Australian historian Penelope Edmonds has recently argued, the "pervasive trend of privileging city planning and infrastructure over culture and identities, of focusing on colonial cities without attention to the dispossessed and displaced Indigenous peoples on whose land these cities were built, as well as the wider issues of settler colonialism and race, represents a methodological schism between the disciplines of history and urban studies." Penelope Edmonds, *Urbanizing Frontiers: Indigenous Peoples and Settlers in 19th-Century Pacific Rim Cities* (Vancouver: University of British Columbia Press, 2010), 8. See also Gitlin, *The Bourgeois Frontier*, 187–190; Adam Arenson,

The Great Heart of the Republic: St. Louis and the Cultural Civil War (Cambridge: Harvard University Press, 2011), chapter 1.

14. Coll Thrush, *Native Seattle: Histories from the Crossing-Over Place* (Seattle: University of Washington Press, 2007); Philip J. Deloria, *Indians in Unexpected Places* (Lawrence: University Press of Kansas, 2006).

15. Melvin M. Webber, among others, shaped our thinking about "community without propinquity" and the "non-place urban realm." See Melvin M. Webber et al., *Explorations into Urban Structure* (Philadelphia: University of Pennsylvania Press, 1964); Joel Garreau, *Edge City: Life on the New Frontier* (New York: Doubleday, 1991); Robert Fishman, *Bourgeois Utopias: The Rise and Fall of Suburbia* (New York: Basic Books, 1987); and Robert Bruegmann, *Sprawl: A Compact History* (Chicago: University of Chicago Press, 2005). Historians have been slow to apply such insights to cities and communities in the past. For one example, however, see John Mack Faragher, *Sugar Creek: Life on the Illinois Prairie* (New Haven: Yale University Press, 1986).

For recent investigations of Seattle and its Native environs, see Matthew Klingle, *Emerald City: An Environmental History of Seattle* (New Haven: Yale University Press, 2007) and Thrush, *Native Seattle*.

16. Berglund, *Making San Francisco American*.

17. For studies without an urban angle, see Theodore Binnema, *Common and Contested Ground: A Human and Environmental History of the Northwestern Plains* (Norman: University of Oklahoma Press, 2001); Alfred W. Crosby, *Ecological Imperialism: The Biological Expansion of Europe, 900-1900* (New York: Cambridge University Press, 1986); Alfred W. Crosby, *The Columbian Exchange: Biological and Cultural Consequences of 1492* (Westport, CT: Greenwood, 1972); Kathleen DuVal, *The Native Ground: Indians and Colonists in the Heart of the Continent* (Philadelphia: University of Pennsylvania Press, 2006); Andrew C. Isenberg, *The Destruction of the Bison: An Environmental History, 1750-1920* (New York: Cambridge University Press, 2000); Richard White, *The Middle Ground: Indians, Empires, and Republics in the Great Lakes Region, 1650-1815* (Cambridge: Cambridge University Press, 1991).

18. For key studies of these other continents, Frederick Cooper and Ann Laura Stoler, eds., *Tensions of Empire: Colonial Cultures in a Bourgeois World* (Berkeley: University of California Press, 1997); Anne McClintock, *Imperial Leather: Race, Gender, and Sexuality in the Colonial Conquest* (New York: Routledge, 1995); Mary Louise Pratt, *Imperial Eyes: Travel Writing and Transculturation* (New York: Routledge, 1992); Catherine Hall, *Civilising Subjects: Metropole and Colony in the English Imagination, 1830-1867* (Chicago: University of Chicago Press, 2002); Timothy Mitchell, *Colonising Egypt* (Berkeley: University of California Press, 1988); Paul A. Kramer, *The Blood of Government: Race, Empire, the United States, and the Philippines* (Chapel Hill: University of North Carolina Press, 2006); Vicente L. Rafael, *White Love and Other Events in Filipino History* (Durham: Duke University Press, 2000).

For some recent attempts at applying these insights to North America, see Ann Laura Stoler, ed., *Haunted by Empire: Geographies of Intimacy in North American History* (Durham: Duke University Press, 2006); Adele Perry, *On the Edge of Empire: Gender, Race, and the Making of British Columbia, 1849-1871* (Toronto: University of Toronto Press, 2001); Berglund, *Making San Francisco American*; and Alexandra Minna Stern, *Eugenic Nation: Faults and Frontiers of Better Breeding in North America* (Berkeley: University of California Press, 2005).

There is a substantial literature on cities in colonial Latin America. It is impossible to avoid cities when studying the American empires of Portugal and Spain, whose policymakers understood urban planning as a critical tool of authority and an expression of culture. Well-ordered cities provided a level of legibility in distant colonies. Indigenous peoples were incorporated into both empires and were clearly visible in their cities. Not surprisingly, historians of Latin America have produced studies of colonial cities that take both empire and indigeneity very seriously. See, for example, Dora P. Crouch, Daniel J. Garr, and Axel I. Mundigo, *Spanish City Planning in North America* (Cambridge: MIT Press, 1982); Alejandro de la Fuente, *Havana and the Atlantic in the Sixteenth Century* (Chapel Hill: University of North Carolina Press, 2008); Jay Kinsbruner, *The Colonial Spanish-American City: Urban Life in the Age of Atlantic Capitalism* (Austin: University of Texas Press, 2005); Jane E. Mangan, *Trading Roles: Gender, Ethnicity, and the Urban Economy in Colonial Potosí* (Durham: Duke University Press, 2005); María Emma Mannarelli, *Private Passions and Public Sins: Men and Women in Seventeenth-Century Lima* (Albuquerque: University of New Mexico Press, 2007).

19. Howard Roberts Lamar and Leonard Monteath Thompson, *The Frontier in History: North America and Southern Africa Compared* (New Haven: Yale University Press, 1981); John C. Weaver, *The Great Land Rush and the Making of the Modern World, 1650–1900* (Montreal: McGill-Queen's University Press, 2003); Robin W. Winks, *The Myth of the American Frontier: Its Relevance to America, Canada and Australia*, Sir George Watson Lecture, 1971 (Leicester, England: Leicester University Press, 1971); Paul Sabin, "Home and Abroad: The Two 'Wests' of Twentieth-Century United States History," *Pacific Historical Review* 66:3 (August 1997), 305–335; Adam Arenson, "Anglo-Saxonism in the Yukon: The Klondike Nugget and American-British Relations in the 'Two Wests,' 1898–1901," *Pacific Historical Review* 76:3 (August 2007), 373–403.

20. Here we are thinking of, for example, William Cronon, *Nature's Metropolis: Chicago and the Great West* (New York: W. W. Norton, 1991); John Mack Faragher, *Sugar Creek: Life on the Illinois Prairie* (New Haven: Yale University Press, 1988); Jeffrey S. Adler, *Yankee Merchants and the Making of the Urban West: The Rise and Fall of Antebellum St. Louis* (New York: Cambridge University Press, 1991); John M. Findlay, *Magic Lands: Western Cityscapes and American Culture after 1940* (Berkeley: University of California, 1992); Berglund, *Making San Francisco American*; Carl Abbott, *How Cities Won the West*; Eugene P. Moehring, *Urbanism and Empire in the Far West, 1840–1890* (Reno: University of Nevada Press, 2004); Gunther Barth, *Instant Cities: Urbanization and the Rise of San Francisco and Denver* (New York: Oxford University Press, 1975); Mike Davis, *City of Quartz: Excavating the Future in Los Angeles* (New York: Verso, 1992); Matthew Klingle, *Emerald City*; Thrush, *Native Seattle*.

21. Contrast Patricia Nelson Limerick, *Legacy of Conquest: The Unbroken Past of the American West* (New York: Knopf, 1987); Andrew Isenberg, *The Destruction of the Bison: An Environmental History, 1750–1920* (New York: Cambridge University Press, 2000); Walter T. K. Nugent, *Into the West: The Story of Its People* (New York: Knopf, 1999); William Cronon, *Nature's Metropolis: Chicago and the Great West* (New York: W. W. Norton, 1991); James Brooks, *Captives and Cousins: Slavery, Kinship, and Community in the Southwest Borderlands* (Chapel Hill: University of North Carolina Press for the Omohundro Institute of Early American History and Culture, 2002); Stephanie E. Smallwood, *Saltwater Slavery: A Middle Passage from Africa to American Diaspora* (Cambridge: Harvard University Press, 2007); Kathleen DuVal, *The Native Ground*; Stuart B. Schwartz, *All Can Be Saved: Religious Tolerance and Salvation in the Iberian Atlantic World* (New Haven: Yale University Press, 2009); Daniel Richter, *Before the Revolution: America's Ancient Pasts* (Cambridge: Harvard University Press, 2011); and Ira Berlin, *Generations of Captivity: A History of African-American Slaves* (Cambridge: Harvard University Press, 2004).

See also the critiques in Robert Johnston, "Beyond 'The West': Regionalism, Liberalism, and the Evasion of Politics in the New Western History," *Rethinking History* 2 (Summer 1998), 239–277;

and Stephen Aron, "Lessons in Conquest: Towards a Greater Western History," *Pacific Historical Review* 63 (1994), 125–147, which have bearing on the scope of analysis.

22. Arenson, comment, and Samuel Truett, "Global Crossings, Local Tales: Seeing the World in Borderlands and Transnational History" (paper presented at "The South African Influence on Landscapes of the American West," Western History Association annual meeting, Incline Village-Lake Tahoe, October 15, 2010). For classic works of western history that were global in their outlook, see Howard R. Lamar, *Dakota Territory, 1861–1889: A Study of Frontier Politics* (New Haven: Yale University Press, 1956); Howard R. Lamar, *The Far Southwest, 1846–1912: A Territorial History* (New Haven: Yale University Press, 1966); Harold A. Innis, *The Fur Trade in Canada: An Introduction to Canadian Economic History* (New Haven: Yale University Press, 1930); Hubert H. Bancroft, *The Works of Hubert Howe Bancroft*, 39 vols. (San Francisco: A. L. Bancroft & Co., 1882–1890).

Chapter 1

1. This summons is reproduced as Document 1 in the Appendix to C. R. Boxer, *Portuguese Society in the Tropics: The Municipal Councils of Goa, Macao, Bahia, and Luanda, 1510–1800* (Madison: University of Wisconsin Press, 1965), 153–154.

2. Useful documents on Portuguese interactions with many of the islands of Southeast Asia can be found in Ronald Bishop Smith, ed., *The First Age of the Portuguese Embassies, Navigations and Peregrinations to the Kingdoms and Islands of Southeast Asia (1509–1521)* (Bethesda: Decatur Press, 1968). On the Portuguese in East Africa, and their connections to India and other points east, see Michael N. Pearson, *Port Cities and Intruders: The Swahili Coast, India, and Portugal in the Early Modern Era* (Baltimore: Johns Hopkins University Press, 1998). For an introduction and overview of European activities in Asia, see J. H. Parry, *The Age of Reconnaissance* (Cleveland: World Publishing Company, 1953). Photographic images of many of the wonderful artifacts obtained by the Portuguese through trade with Asia, Africa, India, and elsewhere in this period are reproduced and discussed in Jay A. Levenson, ed., *Encompassing the Globe: Portugal and the World in the 16th and 17th Centuries* (Washington, D.C.: Smithsonian Institution, 2007).

3. The most thorough analysis of Portuguese trade in China from the mid-seventeenth to mid-eighteenth centuries is George Bryan Souza, *The Survival of Empire: Portuguese Trade and Society in China and the South China Sea, 1630–1754* (Cambridge: Cambridge University Press, 1986).

4. On the movement of silver to China, see Dennis Flynn and Arturo Giráldez, "Silk for Silver: Trade via Manila and Macao in the 17th Century," *Philippine Studies* 44 (1996), 52–68; Dennis Owen Flynn, *World Silver and Monetary History in the 16th and 17th Centuries* (Aldershot, England: Ashgate, 1996); Dennis O. Flynn and Arturo Giráldez, "Born Again: Globalization's Sixteenth Century Origins," *Pacific Economic Review* 13:3 (2008), 359–387; Kenneth Pomeranz, *The Great Divergence: China, Europe, and the Making of the Modern World* (Princeton: Princeton University Press, 2000).

5. On Potosí, see Jane Mangan, *Trading Roles: Gender, Ethnicity, and the Urban Economy in Colonial Potosí* (Durham: Duke University Press, 2005); P. J. Blackwell, *Miners of the Red Mountain: Indian Labor in Potosí, 1545–1650* (Albuquerque: University of New Mexico Press, 1984).

6. Flynn and Giráldez, "Silk for Silver," 62–64.

7. Sofia Sanabrais, "The Biombo or Folding Screen: Examining the Impact of Japan on Artistic Production and the Globalization of Taste in Seventeenth-Century New Spain" (Ph.D. diss., New York University, 2005).

8. Luís Filipe Barreto, *Ploughing the Sea: The Portuguese and Asia, c. 1480–c. 1630* (Lisbon:

Comissão para as Comemorações dos Descobrimentos Portugueses, 2000), 52. For a detailed discussion of Portuguese trade with Asia in this period, especially of Portuguese investment and returns among both crown *and* private interests, see James C. Boyajian, *Portuguese Trade in Asia under the Hapsburgs, 1580–1640* (Baltimore: Johns Hopkins University Press, 1993). But also see A. R. Disney, *Twilight of the Pepper Empire: Portuguese Trade in Southwest India in the Early Seventeenth Century* (Cambridge: Harvard University Press, 1978).

9. Leslie España Bauzon, "Deficit Government: Mexico and the Philippine *Situado* (1606–1804)" (Ph.D. diss., Duke University, 1970).

10. For Goa's relationship with other Portuguese settlements, particularly in the Bay of Bengal, see Sanjay Subrahmanyam, *Improvising Empire: Portuguese Trade and Settlement in the Bay of Bengal, 1500–1700* (Delhi: Oxford University Press, 1990). For an overview of Goa's trade, and of secondary sources analyzing that trade, see M. N. Pearson, "Goa-Based Seaborne Trade, 17th–18th Centuries," in *Goa Through the Ages*, vol. 2, *An Economic History*, ed. Teotonio R. de Souza (New Delhi: Goa University, 1990), 146–175.

11. On Goa, see M. N. Pearson, "Looking Outward: Colonial Goa in the Sixteenth Century," in *The Rise and Growth of the Colonial Port Cities in Asia*, ed. Dilip K. Basu (Berkeley: University of California Press, 1985), 8–11 and "Goa During the First Century of Portuguese Rule," *Itinerario* 8:1 (1984), 36–57. A. Da Silva Rego analyzes Portuguese administration of its Asian empire, with a particularly thoughtful discussion of Goa, in *Portuguese Colonization in the Sixteenth Century: A Study of the Royal Ordinances* (Regimentos) (Johannesburg: Witwatersrand University Press, 1959).

12. Kenneth J. Banks, *Chasing Empire Across the Sea: Communications and the State in the French Atlantic, 1713–1764* (Montreal and Kingston: McGill-Queen's University Press, 2002). Banks shows the usefulness of the city to imperial intentions, but the city is not central to the building or maintenance of empire. An excellent overview of the city for the Spanish can be found in Richard L. Kagan, *Urban Images of the Hispanic World, 1493–1793* (New Haven: Yale University Press, 2000).

13. Gary B. Nash, *First City: Philadelphia and the Forging of Historical Memory* (Philadelphia: University of Pennsylvania Press, 2001); John W. Reps, "$C^2 + L^2 = S^2$?: Another Look at the Origins of Savannah's Town Plan," in *Forty Years of Diversity: Essays on Colonial Georgia*, ed. Harvey H. Jackson and Phinizy Spalding (Athens: University of Georgia Press, 1984), 101–151.

14. Walter Rossa, *Cidades Indo-Portuguesas: Contribuições para o estudo do urbanismo português no Hindustão Ocidental*, trans. Richard Trewinnard (Lisbon: Comissão Nacional para as Comemorações dos Descobrimentos Portugueses, 1997), 50–51.

15. Afonso de Albuquerque to King Manuel, April 1512, in *Albuquerque: Caesar of the East*, ed., trans., and annot. T. F. Earle and John Villiers (Warminster, England: Aris & Phillips, Ltd., 1990), 147. Timothy J. Coates shows the success of the intermarriage policy in seventeenth-century Goa, where both "Portuguese men and women found marriage to Goans and other South Asians more desirable than to each other." Coates explains this largely in economic terms. See his book, *Convicts and Orphans: Forced and State-Sponsored Colonizers in the Portuguese Empire, 1550–1775* (Stanford: Stanford University Press, 2001), 159–161.

16. Rossa, *Cidades*, 41.

17. For the operation of the *câmara* in Goa, see Boxer, *Portuguese Society*, 12–41, 141–149.

18. For the administration of Portuguese India in its intended form and in practice, which compares administrative effectiveness in different Indian settlements, see M. N. Pearson, *The Portuguese in India* (Cambridge: Cambridge University Press, 1987). Much interesting discussion of cultural interaction and transition in Goa can be found in Shihan de Silva Jayasuriya, *The Portuguese in the East: A Cultural History of a Maritime Trading Empire* (London: Tauris Academic Studies, 2008).

19. Rossa, *Cidades*, 94.

20. For Macau I draw upon Boxer, *Portuguese Society*, 42–71; Souza, *Survival of Empire*; B. V. Pires, "Origins and Early History of Macau," in *Macau: City of Commerce and Culture*, ed. R. D. Cremer (Hong Kong: UEA Press, 1987), 7–21; R. D. Cremer, "From Portugal to Japan: Macau's Place in the History of World Trade," in Cremer, *Macau*, 23–38; Barreto, *Ploughing the Sea*; Clive Willis, ed., *China and Macau: Portuguese Encounters with the World in the Age of Discoveries* (Aldershot, England: Ashgate, 2002); Malyn Newitt, *A History of Portuguese Overseas Expansion, 1400–1668* (London: Routledge, 2005).

21. Boxer, *Portuguese Society*, 43.

22. The document is reproduced along with other useful documents on Macau in Willis, *China and Macau*, 84–86. On Bocarro, see Garcia de Orta, "Antonio Bocarro and the 'Livro do Estado da Índia Oriental,'" in *Portuguese Conquest and Commerce in Southeast Asia, 1500–1750*, ed. C. R. Boxer (London: Variorum Reprints, 1985), chapter 10.

23. Boxer, *Portuguese Society*, 56–57.

24. A good starting point for contextualizing Portuguese activities in Nagasaki with the rest of Asia is Newitt, *History of Portuguese Overseas Expansion*. See also C. R. Boxer, *The Christian Century in Japan, 1549–1650* (Cambridge: Cambridge University Press, 1951); Catarina Madeira Santos, *Portugal auf den Schiffsrouten der Welt*, trans. Jonathan Weightman (Lisbon: Comissão Nacional para as Comemorações dos Descobrimentos Portugeses, 1997), 37–40. Much valuable material on the Spanish and Portuguese in Japan can be found in Antonio de Morga, *Sucesos de las Islas Filipinas* (Mexico: Geronymo Balli, 1609). For an English translation, see E. H. Blair and J. A. Robertson, trans. and eds., *History of the Philippine Islands . . . by Dr. Antonio de Morga*, 2 vols. (Cleveland: Arthur H. Clark Company, 1907), especially the end of volume 1. Sanjay Subrahmanyam reminds us that Japanese trade was important to Portuguese development in Asia, but that it "represented no more than *one* of several new directions taken by the Portuguese enterprise in this period." *Improvising Empire*, 141–142.

25. M. N. Pearson, "Spain and Spanish Trade in Southeast Asia," in *European Entry into the Pacific: Spain, and the Acapulco-Manila Galleons*, ed. Dennis O. Flynn, Aruturo Giraldez, and James Sobredo (Aldershot, England: Ashgate, 2001), 118–120.

26. For the early development of Manila, see Robert R. Reed, "The Foundation and Morphology of Hispanic Manila: Colonial Images and Philippine Realities," in Basu, *Rise and Growth*, 197–205. Much of the primary source material is available in Emma H. Blair and James A. Robertson, eds., *The Philippine Islands, 1493–1598*, 5 vols. (Cleveland: Arthur H. Clark Company, 1903–1909). See also John L. Pheland, *The Hispanization of the Philippines: Spanish Aims and Filipino Responses, 1565–1700* (Madison: University of Wisconsin Press, 1959); Daniel F. Doepper, "The Development of Philippine Cities Before 1900," *Journal of Asian Studies* 31 (1972), 769–792. The best discussion of Spain's movement of the capital from one place to the next, finally settling on Manila, can be found in Robert R. Reed, *Colonial Manila: The Context of Hispanic Urbanism and Process of Morphogenesis* (Berkeley: University of California Press, 1978), 17–26. Indispensible for study of Manila is de Morga's history published in 1609. An experienced Spanish official, his work includes not only his observations from living in the Philippines, but draws on (and reproduces excerpts from) documents no longer extant. Blair and Robertson, *History of the Philippine Islands* (especially the end of volume 1). For the history of early Manila, and of the Manila Galleon, still useful is William Lytle Schurz, *The Manila Galleon* (New York: E. P. Dutton, 1939).

27. Boyajian, *Portuguese Trade*, 232–234, 236.

28. Reed, *Colonial Manila*, 53; M. T. Paske-Smith, "The Japanese Trade and Residence in the

Philippines: Before and During the Spanish Occupation," in Flynn et al., *European Entry*, 139–164; Pearson, "Spain and Spanish Trade," 125–126.

29. Reed, *Colonial Manila*, 54–55, provides two valuable maps of Manila that include the location of the ethnic enclaves outside the city.

30. For the Chinese community in Manila, see Lucille Chia, "The Butcher, the Baker, and the Carpenter: Chinese Sojourners in the Spanish Philippines and Their Impact on Southern Fujian (Sixteenth-Eighteenth Centuries)," *Journal of the Economic and Social History of the Orient* 49:4 (2006), 509–534, especially 509–523; Berthold Laufer, "The Relations of the Chinese to the Philippine Islands," in Flynn et al., *European Entry*, 55–92; Pearson, "Spain and Spanish Trade," 117–138; Benito Legardo, Jr., "Two and a Half Centuries of the Galleon Trade," in Flynn et al., *European Entry*, 337–365.

31. Katherine Bjork, "The Link That Kept the Philippines Spanish: Mexican Merchant Interests and the Manila Trade, 1571–1815," *Journal of World History* 9:1 (Spring 1998), 42. For varying aspects of the Manila trade, see the essays published in Flynn et al., *European Entry*.

32. Bjork, "Link That Kept," 42–46.

33. The best study of the Philippine trade in the context of its relationship to both Mexico and Spain is Bauzon, "Deficit Government." See also Bjork, "Link That Kept," 25–50; C. R. Boxer, "*Plata es Sangre*: Sidelights on the Drain of Spanish-American Silver in the Far East, 1550–1770," in Flynn et al., *European Entry*, 165–186.

34. Bjork, "Link That Kept," 33–37; Bauzon, "Deficit Government."

35. Luke Clossey, "Merchants, Migrants, Missionaries, and Globalization in the Early-Modern Pacific," *Journal of Global History* (2006), 49–51.

36. William J. McCarthy, "Between Policy and Prerogative: Malfeasance in the Inspection of the Manila Galleons at Acapulco," *Colonial Latin American Historical Review* 2:2 (Spring 1993), 167.

37. Pearson, "Spain and Spanish Trade," 123; Hang-Sheng Chuan, "The Chinese Silk Trade with Spanish America from the late Ming to the Mid-Ch'ing Period," in Flynn et al., *European Entry*, 241–259; Clossey, "Merchants, Migrants," 41–58.

38. "Royal Ordinances Concerning the Laying Out of Towns," trans. Zeliz Nuttall, *Hispanic American Historical Review* 5:2 (May 1922), 249–254.

39. Ibid., quotations from 250, 254.

40. Ibid., quotations from 250, 253.

41. Ibid., quotation from 252.

42. Ibid.

43. Kagan, *Urban Images*.

44. Banks, *Chasing Empire*; Kenneth J. Banks, "A Little Versailles in the Wilderness: Quebec, and the Aesthetics of Royal Power, 1670–1760" (paper presented at The Center for Historical Research, Ohio State University, May 16, 2008).

45. For Philadelphia, see Nathan Ross Kozuskanich, "'For the Security and Protection of the Community': The Frontier and the Makings of Pennsylvanian Constitutionalism" (Ph.D. diss., Ohio State University, 2005); for Boston, see Richard R. Johnson, *Adjustment to Empire: The New England Colonies, 1675–1715* (New Brunswick: Rutgers University Press, 1981); for Charles Town, see Alan Gallay, *The Indian Slave Trade: The Rise of the English Empire in the American South, 1670–1715* (New Haven: Yale University Press, 2002).

Chapter 2

1. Christopher Cooper and Robert Block, *Disaster: Hurricane Katrina and the Failure of Homeland Security* (New York: Times Books, 2006), 151, 237.

2. Bill Walsh, "Idaho Senator Says Fraud Part of La. Culture," *Times-Picayune*, October 15, 2006, A-18.

3. John Lewis Gaddis, *The Landscape of History: How Historians Map the Past* (New York: Oxford University Press, 2002), 14.

4. For a sample, see Arnold R. Hirsch, "New Orleans: Sunbelt in the Swamp," *Sunbelt Cities: Politics and Growth Since World War II*, ed. Richard M. Bernard and Bradley R. Rice (Austin: University of Texas Press, 1983), 100–137; Kim Lacy Rogers, *Righteous Lives: Narratives of the New Orleans Civil Rights Movement* (New York: New York University Press, 1993); Pamela Tyler, *Silk Stockings and Ballot Boxes: Women and Politics in New Orleans, 1920–1963* (Athens: University of Georgia Press, 1996); Alecia P. Long, *The Great Southern Babylon: Sex, Race, and Respectability in New Orleans, 1865–1920* (Baton Rouge: Louisiana State University Press, 2004); Kent Germany, *New Orleans after the Promises: Poverty, Citizenship, and the Search for the Great Society* (Athens: University of Georgia Press, 2007).

5. Anthony J. Stanonis, *Creating the Big Easy: New Orleans and the Emergence of Modern Tourism, 1918–1945* (Athens: University of Georgia Press, 2006); J. Mark Souther, *New Orleans on Parade: Tourism and the Transformation of the Crescent City* (Baton Rouge: Louisiana State University Press, 2006); Kevin Fox Gotham, *Authentic New Orleans: Tourism, Culture, and Race in the Big Easy* (New York: New York University Press, 2007). For comparable studies of other American cities and regions, see Dona Brown, *Inventing New England: Regional Tourism in the Nineteenth Century* (Washington, DC: Smithsonian Institution Press, 1995); Simon J. Bronner, *Popularizing Pennsylvania: Henry W. Shoemaker and the Progressive Uses of Folklore and History* (University Park: Pennsylvania State University Press, 1996); Thomas S. Bremer, *Blessed with Tourists: The Borderlands of Religion and Tourism in San Antonio* (Chapel Hill: University of North Carolina Press, 2004); Stephanie E. Yuhl, *A Golden Haze of Memory: The Making of Historic Charleston* (Chapel Hill: University of North Carolina Press, 2005); and Steven Conn, *Metropolitan Philadelphia: Living with the Presence of the Past* (Philadelphia: University of Pennsylvania Press, 2006).

6. Billy Sothern, *Down in New Orleans: Reflections from a Drowned City* (Berkeley: University of California Press, 2007), xx. To sample how the storm and its aftermath are already influencing scholarship about the city's past, present, and future relationship with the rest of the nation, see the special issue of the *Journal of American History* 94 (December 2007), 693–876, "Through the Eye of Katrina: The Past as Prologue," ed. Lawrence N. Powell and Clarence L. Mohr.

7. *Historical Sketch Book and Guide to New Orleans and Environs Edited and Compiled by Several Leading Writers of the New Orleans Press* (New Orleans, 1885), Introduction (n.p.). For closer analysis of how the otherness of colonial Louisiana was deliberately written into nationalist and regionalist narratives over the nineteenth century, see Daniel H. Usner, Jr., "Between Creoles and Yankees: The Discursive Representation of Colonial Louisiana in American History," in *French Colonial Louisiana and the Atlantic World*, ed. Bradley G. Bond (Baton Rouge: Louisiana State University Press, 2005), 1–21. I explain how twentieth-century historians handled this representation in Usner, "The Significance of the Gulf South in Early American History," in *Coastal Encounters: The Transformation of the Gulf South in the Eighteenth Century*, ed. Richmond F. Brown (Lincoln: University of Nebraska Press, 2007), 13–30.

8. For a breakthrough analysis of how Richard Wade helped perpetuate the Anglo-American narrative's appropriation of St. Louis's early history, see Adam Arenson, "The Double Life of St. Louis: Narratives of Origins and Maturity in Wade's *Urban Frontier*," *Indiana Magazine of History* 105 (September 2009), 246–261.

9. Richard C. Wade, *Urban Frontier: The Rise of Western Cities, 1790–1830* (Cambridge: Harvard University Press, 1959), 1–7, 42, 66–67, 79–89, 119, 126.

10. Pierre-François-Xavier de Charlevoix, *Journal d'un voyage fait par ordre du roi dans l'Amérique septentrionale* (Paris: Nyon fils, 1744), 3:429–430, 438–439.

11. Shannon Lee Dawdy, *Building the Devil's Empire: French Colonial New Orleans* (Chicago: University of Chicago Press, 2008). For a valuable discussion of urban refounding after disaster, see Adam Arenson, *The Great Heart of the Republic: St. Louis and the Cultural Civil War* (Cambridge: Harvard University Press, 2011), 20–27.

12. Ann Laura Stoler and Frederick Cooper, "Between Metropole and Colony: Rethinking a Research Agenda," in *Tensions of Empire: Colonial Cultures in a Bourgeois World*, ed. Cooper and Stoler (Berkeley: University of California Press, 1997), 3–6, 17–18.

13. Dunbar Rowland and A. G. Sanders, eds. and trans., *Mississippi Provincial Archives: French Dominion* (Jackson: Mississippi Department of Archives and History, 1929), 2:599, 623–624, 654. For an overview of these frontier relationships in early New Orleans, see Daniel H. Usner, Jr., *Indians, Settlers, and Slaves in a Frontier Exchange Economy: The Lower Mississippi Valley Before 1783* (Chapel Hill: University of North Carolina Press, 1992), 31–63.

14. Daniel H. Usner, Jr., "American Indians in Colonial New Orleans," in *Powhatan's Mantle: Indians in the Colonial Southeast*, ed. Gregory A. Waselkov, Peter H. Wood, and Tom Hatley, rev. ed. (Lincoln: University of Nebraska Press, 2006), 163–186.

15. Christopher Morris, "Impenetrable but Easy: The French Transformation of the Lower Mississippi Valley and the Founding of New Orleans," *Transforming New Orleans and Its Environs: Centuries of Change*, ed. Craig E. Colten (Pittsburgh: University of Pittsburgh Press, 2000), 22–42; Dawdy, *Building the Devil's Empire*. To learn how the physical geography of Boston also influenced both the market activity among workers and the response from officials and merchants, see Phyllis Whitman Hunter, *Purchasing Identity in the Atlantic World: Massachusetts Merchants, 1670–1780* (Ithaca: Cornell University Press, 2001), 25–27, 101–105.

16. *Mississippi Provincial Archives: French Dominion*, 3:516.

17. Heloise H. Cruzat, trans., "Louisiana in 1724: Banet's Report to the Company of the Indies, Dated Paris, December 20, 1724," *Louisiana Historical Quarterly* 12 (1929), 125; *Mississippi Provincial Archives: French Dominion*, 2:418–419.

18. Usner, *Indians, Settlers, and Slaves*, 46–59; Shannon Lee Dawdy, "The Burden of Louis Congo and the Evolution of Savagery in Colonial Louisiana," in *Discipline and the Other Body: Correction, Corporeality, Colonialism*, ed. Steven Pierce and Anupama Rao (Durham: Duke University Press, 2006), 61–89.

19. *Mississippi Provincial Archives: French Dominion*, 1:405–406; "Records of the Superior Council," *Louisiana Historical Quarterly* 19 (April 1936), 479, 503–504.

20. Jean M. O'Brien, *Dispossession by Degrees: Indian Land and Identity in Natick, Massachusetts, 1650–1790* (New York: Cambridge University Press, 1997), 69. Important studies that reinforce this comparison in various ways include Peter H. Wood, *Black Majority: Negroes in Colonial South Carolina from 1670 through the Stono Rebellion* (New York: Alfred A. Knopf, 1975); Timothy Breen and Stephen Innes, *"Myne Owne Ground": Race and Freedom on Virginia's Eastern Shore, 1640–1676* (New York: Oxford University Press, 1980); Billy G. Smith, *The "Lower Sort": Philadelphia's Laboring*

People, 1750–1800 (Ithaca: Cornell University Press, 1990); John Mack Faragher, *Daniel Boone: The Life and Legend of an American Pioneer* (New York: Henry Holt and Company, 1992); Betty Wood, *Women's Work, Men's Work: The Informal Slave Economies of Lowcountry Georgia* (Athens: University of Georgia Press, 1995); Philip D. Morgan, *Slave Counterpart: Black Culture in the Eighteenth-Century Chesapeake and Lowcountry* (Chapel Hill: University of North Carolina Press, 1998); Timothy James Locker, *Lines in the Sand: Race and Class in Lowcountry Georgia, 1790–1860* (Athens: University of Georgia Press, 2001); Jane T. Merritt, *At the Crossroads: Indians and Empires on a Mid-Atlantic Frontier, 1700–1763* (Chapel Hill: University of North Carolina Press, 2003); April Lee Hatfield, *Atlantic Virginia: Intercolonial Relations in the Seventeenth Century* (Philadelphia: University of Pennsylvania Press, 2004); Jill Lepore, *New York Burning: Liberty, Slavery, and Conspiracy in Eighteenth-Century Manhattan* (New York: Alfred A. Knopf, 2005); James E. McWilliams, *Building the Bay Colony: Local Economy and Culture in Early Massachusetts* (Charlottesville: University of Virginia Press, 2007).

21. "Report on Louisiana," n.d. [ca. 1750]. Louisiana Miscellany Collection, Library of Congress, Manuscripts, f. 1493, quoted in Samuel Wilson, *The Vieux Carré, New Orleans: Its Plan, Its Growth, Its Architecture* (New Orleans: Marcou O'Leary and Associates, 1968), 37.

22. Smith, *The "Lower Sort,"* 21–26; Steven Rosswurm, *Arms, Country, and Class: The Philadelphia Militia and "Lower Sort" during the American Revolution, 1775–1783* (New Brunswick, NJ: Rutgers University Press, 1987), 35–37; Clare A. Lyons, *Sex among the Rabble: An Intimate History of Gender and Power in the Age of Revolution, Philadelphia, 1730–1830* (Chapel Hill: University of North Carolina Press, 2006), 193–195.

23. "Report on Louisiana," quoted in Wilson, *Vieux Carré*, 37.

24. Henry P. Dart, ed., "Cabarets of New Orleans in the French Colonial Period," *Louisiana Historical Quarterly* 19 (July 1936), 581.

25. Gwendolyn Midlo Hall, *Africans in Colonial Louisiana: The Development of Afro-Creole Culture in the Eighteenth Century* (Baton Rouge: Louisiana State University Press, 1992); Thomas N. Ingersoll, *Mammon and Manon: The First Slave Society in the Deep South, 1718–1819* (Knoxville: University of Tennessee Press, 1998).

26. Usner, "American Indians in Colonial New Orleans."

27. Carl A. Brasseaux, trans., ed., and annot., *A Comparative View of French Louisiana, 1699 and 1762: The Journals of Pierre Le Moyne d'Iberville and Jean-Jacques-Blaise d'Abbadie* (Lafayette: Center for Louisiana Studies, 1979), 118. For more information about the presence and influence of American Indians in the city during the nineteenth century, see Daniel H. Usner, Jr., *American Indians in the Lower Mississippi Valley: Social and Economic Histories* (Lincoln: University of Nebraska Press, 1998), 111–137.

28. Jennifer M. Spear, *Race, Sex, and Social Order in Early New Orleans* (Baltimore: Johns Hopkins University Press, 2009).

29. Marc de Villiers du Terrage, *The Last Years of French Louisiana*, trans. Hosea Phillips and ed. Carl A. Brasseaux and Glen R. Conrad (Lafayette: Center for Louisiana Studies, 1982), 101–102. For comparable sources of tension between officials and merchants in eighteenth-century New York, see Cathy Matson, *Merchants and Empire: Trading in Colonial New York* (Baltimore: Johns Hopkins University Press, 1998), and Thomas M. Truxis, *Defying Empire: Trading with the Enemy in Colonial New York* (New Haven: Yale University Press, 2008). Also see Wim Klooster, "Inter-Imperial Smuggling in the Americas, 1600–1800," in *Soundings in Atlantic History: Latent Structures and Intellectual Currents, 1500–1830* (Cambridge: Harvard University Press, 2009), 141–180, for analysis of the fuller context.

30. Villiers du Terrage, *Last Years of French Louisiana*, 215–217. For details about the Louisiana Rebellion of 1768, see John Preston Moore, *Revolt in Louisiana: The Spanish Occupation, 1766–1770* (Baton Rouge: Louisiana State University Press, 1976; Carl A. Brasseaux, *Denis-Nicolas Foucault and the New Orleans Rebellion of 1768* (Ruston: Louisiana Tech University Press, 1987); and Dawdy, *Building the Devil's Empire*, 219–246.

31. Carl A. Brasseaux, *The Founding of New Acadia: The Beginnings of Acadian Life in Louisiana, 1765–1803* (Baton Rouge: Louisiana State University Press, 1987); Gilbert C. Din, *The Canary Islanders of Louisiana* (Baton Rouge: Louisiana State University Press, 1988).

32. Thomas N. Ingersoll, "The Slave Trade and the Ethnic Diversity of Louisiana's Slave Community," *Louisiana History* 37 (Spring 1996), 133–161; Jean-Pierre Leglaunec, "Slave Migrations in Spanish and Early American Louisiana: New Sources and New Estimates," *Louisiana History* 46 (Spring 2005), 185–209.

33. For this early Cuban influence on New Orleans, see Ned Sublette, *The World That Made New Orleans: From Spanish Silver to Congo Square* (Chicago: Lawrence Hill Books, 2008). Highlighting political and economic channels during the Spanish era, Sublette underscores Kongo influence on slave community and culture in Louisiana via Cuba. In 1787, for example, 41 of 108 ships leaving New Orleans went to Havana. In 1798, 63 of 102 left for Havana.

34. Kimberly S. Hanger, *Bounded Lives, Bounded Places: Free Black Society in Colonial New Orleans, 1769–1803* (Durham: Duke University Press, 1997); Spear, *Race, Sex, and Social Order*.

35. Hall, *Africans in Colonial Louisiana*, 317–374; Gilbert C. Din and John E. Harkins, *The New Orleans Cabildo: Colonial Louisiana's First City Government, 1769–1803* (Baton Rouge: Louisiana State University Press, 1996).

36. Paul F. Lachance, "The Politics of Fear: French Louisianians and the Slave Trade, 1786–1809," *Plantation Society* 1 (June 1979), 162–197; Leglaunec, "Slave Migrations;" Peter J. Kastor, *The Nation's Crucible: The Louisiana Purchase and the Creation of America* (New Haven: Yale University Press, 2004), 115–120, 127–131; Nathalie Dessens, *From Saint-Domingue to New Orleans: Migration and Influences* (Gainesville: University Press of Florida, 2007).

37. George Washington Cable, "Creole Slave Songs," *Century Magazine* 31 (April 1886), 814–815; Brenda Marie Osbey, *All Saints: New and Selected Poems* (Baton Rouge: Louisiana State University Press, 1997), 108–114. For discussion of a later maroon-camp leader, see Bryan Wagner, "Disarmed and Dangerous: The Strange Career of Bras-Coupé," *Representations* 92 (Fall 2005), 117–151.

38. Charles César Robin, *Voyage to Louisiana, 1803–1805* (New Orleans: Pelican Press, 1966), 30–31.

39. Edna B. Freiberg, *Bayou St. John in Colonial Louisiana, 1699–1803* (New Orleans: Harvey Press, 1980, 298–321; Ari Kelman, *A River and Its City: The Nature of Landscape in New Orleans* (Berkeley: University of California Press, 2003), 19–86; John Magill, "On Perilous Ground," *Louisiana Cultural Vistas* 16 (Winter 2005–2006), 32–43.

40. James Sidbury, *Ploughshares into Swords: Race, Rebellion, and Identity in Gabriel's Virginia, 1730–1810* (New York: Cambridge University Press, 1997), 151–183.

41. Kastor, *Nation's Crucible*, 56.

42. Clarence E. Carter, ed., *The Territorial Papers of the United States* (Washington, DC: Government Printing Office, 1940), 9:159–160, 174–175.

43. Dunbar Rowland, ed., *The Letter Books of William C. C. Claiborne, 1801–1816* (Jackson: Mississippi State Library and Archives, 1917), 2:54–55, 217–218. For a close analysis of Claiborne's decision making over this issue, see Erin M. Greenwald, "To Strike a Balance: New Orleans' Free Colored Community and the Diplomacy of William Charles Cole Claiborne," in *Nexus of Empire:*

Negotiating Loyalty and Identity in the Revolutionary Borderlands, 1760s-1820s, eds. Gene Allen Smith and Sylvia L. Hilton (Gainesville: University Press of Florida, 2010), 113–139.

44. *Letter Books of William C. C. Claiborne*, 1:354.
45. *Letter Books of William C. C. Claiborne*, 2:113–114, 134.
46. *Letter Books of William C. C. Claiborne*, 2:244–246.
47. *Territorial Papers*, 9:222.
48. *Territorial Papers*, 9:265–266.
49. *Letter Books of William C. C. Claiborne*, 2:256–257.
50. *Letter Books of William C. C. Claiborne*, 2:310–311; *Territorial Papers*, 9:280–309.
51. *Territorial Papers*, 9:298.
52. *Letter Books of William C. C. Claiborne*, 3:357.
53. *Letter Books of William C. C. Claiborne*, 4:129–130, 229.
54. Adam Rothman, *Slave Country: American Expansion and the Origins of the Deep South* (Cambridge: Harvard University Press, 2005), 73–162; Daniel Rasmussen, *American Uprising: The Untold Story of America's Largest Slave Revolt* (New York: HarperCollins Publishers, 2011).
55. Berquin-Duvallon, *Travels in Louisiana and the Floridas, in the Year 1802, Giving a Correct Picture of Those Countries*, trans. John Davis (New York, 1806), 53–54.
56. January 22, January 29, 1796, October 6, 1797, January 21, 1803, Records and Deliberations of the Cabildo, New Orleans Public Library; May 19, August 8, December 3, 1804, April 4, May 18, 1805, August 6, 1806, March 18, 1807, October 3, 1810, November 2, 1812, August 14, 1813, Proceedings of the Counseil de Ville, New Orleans Public Library; *Letter Books of William C. C. Claiborne*, 1:380, 393.
57. For some insightful commentary on what he calls "a longstanding geographical turn in early American history," see Trevor Burnard's July 2008 essay on Common-Place, "A Passion for Places," www.common-place.org/vol-08/no-04/burnard.
58. The imaginative performance of an improvisational past is perhaps the most important expression of New Orleans' unique identity, continuing into the twenty-first century. See Michael P. Smith, "New Orleans' Carnival Culture from the Underside," *Plantation Society in the Americas: An Interdisciplinary Journal of Tropical and Subtropical History and Culture* 3 (1990), 11–32; Joseph Roach, *Cities of the Dead: Circum-Atlantic Performance* (New York: Columbia University Press, 1996); and Roger D. Abrahams, with Nick Spitzer, John F. Szwed, and Robert Farris Thompson, *Blues for New Orleans: Mardi Gras and America's Creole Soul* (Philadelphia: University of Pennsylvania Press, 2006).
59. Smith, *"New Orleans' Carnival Culture from the Underside,"* 12, 32.

Chapter 3

1. Breslay founded both a French parish and an Indian mission at the west end of Montreal. The latter was actually a fortified compound with a chapel and a residence adjacent to the Nipissing village on Isle-aux-Tourtres, separated by a narrow channel from the main island. See E. A. Chard, "Breslay, René-Charles de," *Dictionary of Canadian Biography*, vol. 2 (Toronto: University of Toronto Press, 1969).
2. "Procès contre François Lamoureux dit Saint-Germain, armurier, accusé de vente d'eau de vie des sauvages," Sept. 7, 1713, Bibliothèque et Archives nationales du Quebec, Montreal (BANQ-M), TL4, S1, D1483. The trial record comprises more than seventy manuscript pages, including transcripts of all interrogations, depositions, and judicial orders.

3. "Procès contre François Lamoureux;" and, for the murder, "Procès contre Claude Dudevoir, aubergiste, le nommé Bineau et Jacques Milot, accusés d'avoir vendu de l'eau de vie aux sauvages et provoquer ainsi le meurtre de l'un des sauvages," June 13, 1713, BANQ-M, TL4, S1, D1457. For the king's memorandum, see "Extrait du memoire du roi a Vaudreuil et Bégon," 1713, Archives nationales d'outre-mer (ANOM), Colonies, C11A vol. 34, 32–32v, 32 (quote) ("on ne peut avoir trop d'attention d'empecher"). For New France's long and contentious battle over the liquor trade, see Peter Mancall, *Deadly Medicine: Indians and Alcohol in Early America* (Ithaca: Cornell University Press, 1995), 137–154; W. J. Eccles, *The Canadian Frontier, 1534–1760* (Albuquerque, 1969), 57, 112, 146; and Jan Grabowski, "The Common Ground: Settled Natives and French in Montreal, 1667–1760" (Ph.D. diss., Université de Montréal, 1993), especially 193–245. For Natives' refusal to submit to French justice, see Grabowski, "French Criminal Justice and Indians in Montreal, 1670–1760," *Ethnohistory* 3 (Summer 1996), 405–429.

4. For marriages and baptisms, see Programme de recherche en démographie historique, *Repertoire des actes de baptême, marriage, et sepulture (RAB)*, CD-Rom (Quebec: PRDH, 1997). Breslay had performed the marriages of Lamoureux's stepsister (*RAB*: 47672) and cousin (*RAB*: 47831), and baptized Lamoureux's niece (*RAB*: 42329), and just three years before the trial, had baptized and then buried Lamoureux's illegitimate child (*RAB*: 15304).

5. "Breslay a eté insulté par des Sauvages yvres et que le nomeé St. Germain habitant du d. Lieu a traitté l'eau de vie aux sauvages." "Procès contre François Lamoureux."

6. "Procès contre François Lamoureux." For Lamoureux's smuggling, see "Procès contre René Godefroy, sieur de Linctot, commandant du fort Saint-Louis, François Lamoureux dit Saint-Germain, arquebusier, et Charles Lemaire dit Saint-Germain dit Lirlande, accuse de faire de la traite avec les sauvages," July 15–25, 1716, BANQ-M, TL4, S1, D1960; and "Procès contre François Lamoureux dit St-Germain, arquebusier et marchand, accusé de vente de boisson aux sauvages," July 8–24, 1726, BANQ-M, TL4, S1, D3289. For Breslay sailing for France, see letter of Nov. 15, 1713, ANOM, Colonies, C11A vol. 34, 25.

7. Richard White, *The Middle Ground: Indians, Empires, and Republics in the Great Lakes Region, 1650–1815* (Cambridge: Cambridge University Press, 1991), xi.

8. James Pritchard, *In Search of Empire: The French in the Americas, 1670–1730* (Cambridge: Cambridge University Press, 2004), 255–256. The most prominent exception to this rule is Francis Parkman, who caricatured New France as hopelessly mired in the swamp of absolutist Catholicism. Recent French-language literature tends to balance understanding of the state, colonists, and Indians more successfully. See especially Gilles Havard, *Empire et métissage: Indiens et Français dans le Pays d'en Haut* (Quebec: Septentrion, 2003); and Havard and Cécile Vidal, *Histoire de l'Amérique française* (Paris: Flammarion, 2008). For a survey of recent historiography on this topic, see Christopher Hodson and Brett Rushforth, "Absolutely Atlantic: Colonialism and the Early Modern French State in Recent Literature," *History Compass* 8 (2010), 101–117.

9. Jay Gitlin, "On the Boundaries of Empire," in *Under an Open Sky: Rethinking America's Western Past*, ed. William Cronon, George Miles, and Jay Gitlin (New York: W. W. Norton, 1992), 72.

10. Richard Wade, *The Urban Frontier: The Rise of Western Cities, 1790–1830* (Cambridge: Harvard University Press, 1959), 1.

11. Jacques Cartier, *The Voyages of Jacques Cartier*, ed. Ramsay Cook (Toronto: University of Toronto Press, 1993), 65.

12. Cartier, *Voyages*, 61.

13. Marcel Trudel, *The Beginnings of New France, 1524–1663*, trans. Patricia Claxton (Toronto: McClelland and Stewart, 1973), 187; Samuel de Champlain, *The Works of Samuel de Champlain*,

trans. John Squair (Toronto: University of Toronto Press, 1971), 2:331 (quote). For the best overall history of early Montreal, see Louise Dechêne, *Habitants and Merchants in Seventeenth-Century Montreal*, trans. Liana Vardi (Montreal: McGill-Queens University Press, 1992).

14. Quoted in W. J. Eccles, *The Canadian Frontier, 1534–1760* (Lincoln: University of Nebraska Press, 1969), 40.

15. "Tous les arbres de cet Isle se devraient changer en autant d'Iroquois." François Dollier de Casson, *Histoire de Montréal, 1640–1672* (Montreal: Eusebe Senécal, 1871), 18.

16. José António Brandão, *Your Fyre Shall Burn No More: Iroquois Policy toward New France and Its Native Allies to 1701* (Lincoln: University of Nebraska Press, 1997), Table D.1.

17. Dechêne, *Habitants and Merchants*, 16–17, Table A; and Mario Lalancette and Alan M. Stewart, "De la ville-comptoir à la ville fortifiée: Évolution de la forme urbaine de Montréal au dix-septième siècle," in *Habitants et marchands; Twenty Years Later: Reading the History of Seventeenth- and Eighteenth-Century Canada*, ed. Sylvie Dépatie, Catherine Desbarats, Danielle Gauvreau, Mario Lalancette, and Thomas Wien (Montreal: McGill-Queens University Press, 1998), 259.

18. Gretchen Lynn Green, "A New People in an Age of War: The Kahnawake Iroquois, 1667–1760" (Ph.D. diss., College of William and Mary, 1991); Louis Lavallée, *La Prairie en Nouvelle-France, 1647–1760* (Montreal: McGill-Queens University Press, 1992), 51–61; Evan Haefeli and Kevin Sweeney, *Captors and Captives: The 1704 French and Indian Raid on Deerfield* (Amherst: University of Massachusetts Press, 2003), 55–77; Allan Greer, *Mohawk Saint: Catherine Tekakwitha and the Jesuits* (New York: Oxford University Press, 2005), 89–110; and Daniel K. Richter, "Iroquois versus Iroquois: Jesuit Missions and Christianity in Village Politics, 1642–1686," *Ethnohistory* 32 (Winter 1985), 1–16.

19. Ibid.

20. Dechêne, *Habitants and Merchants*, Table A; and Lalancette and Stewart, "De la ville-comptoir à la ville fortifiée," 259.

21. "Villemarie dans l'isle de Montréal," Nov. 13, 1685, ANOM, Archives du dépôt des fortifications des colonies FR ANOM 03DFC466C; and "Plan de la Ville de Montréal levé en l'année 1704," Nov. 15, 1704, ANOM, Archives du dépôt des fortifications des colonies, FR ANOM 03DFC468A.

22. Lalancette and Stewart, "De la ville-comptoir à la ville fortifiée," 274; for the 1689 attack, known as the "Lachine Massacre," see Eccles, *Canadian Frontier*, 120.

23. Grabowski, "Common Ground;" and Dechêne, *Habitants and Merchants*, Table A.

24. Brett Rushforth, *Bonds of Alliance: Indigenous and Atlantic Slaveries in New France* (Chapel Hill: University of North Carolina Press for the Omohundro Institute of Early American History and Culture, 2012).

25. Information about Lamoureux was gleaned from trial records in the BANQ-M; as well as *RAB*.

26. For Lamoureux's mother, see Marriage, Sept. 22, 1693, Notre-Dame de Montreal; Marriage Contract for François Lamoureux *dit* Saint-Germain and Marguerite Ménard, July 26, 1712, Montreal; and Cyprien Tanguay, *Dictionnaire genealogique des familles Canadiennes depuis la fondation de la colonie jusqu'a nos jours* (Baltimore: Genealogical Publishing Company, 1967), 1:342. Étienne Pigarouich's wife was also named Marguerite and is known to have children near the age of Lamoureux's mother. See Baptism of March 3, 1643, Sillery. For Pigarouich's life and confession, see Elsie McLeod Jury, "Pigarouich, Étienne," *Dictionary of Canadian Biography*, vol. 1 (Toronto: University of Toronto Press, 1967); and Reuben Gold Thwaites, ed., *The Jesuit Relations and Allied Documents* (Cleveland: Burrows Brothers, 1898), 25:249–257 (quote, 257).

27. Baptism of Aug. 12, 1700, Notre-Dame de Montréal; Baptism of Feb. 28, 1705, Sainte-Anne

de Bellevue; Baptism of Apr. 26, 1705, Sainte-Anne de Bellevue; and Baptism of Aug. 15, 1713, Sainte-Anne de Bellevue. Bellevue was the name of Lamoureux's seigneury, where Breslay served on-and-off as the parish priest in addition to his missionary duties. For Catholicism and kinship in a similar setting, see Susan Sleeper-Smith, "Women, Kin, and Catholicism: New Perspectives on the Fur Trade," *Ethnohistory* 47 (Spring 2000), 423–452.

28. "Procès contre François Lamoureux" 1713.

29. Adhémar database, Centre Canadian d'Architecture, Montréal; and Archives de la Province, *Aveu et dénombrement de Montréal* [1731] (Quebec, 1943), 7, 130.

30. For the debate about Indian witnesses in liquor cases, see Vaudreuil et Bégon to the minister, Nov. 15, 1713, ANOM, Colonies, C11A, vol. 34, 26v–27.

31. See, for example, "Procès contre Nicolas Sarrazin, avironnier, Pierre Sarrazin et Joseph, esclave panis de François Lamoureux, accusés d'avoir préparé un voyage de traite dans l'Outaouais, sans permis," Feb. 18, 1712, BANQ-M, TL4, S1, D1328; "Procès en appel de François Lamoureux dit Saint-Germain . . . contre une sentence les accusant de traite illégal," Oct. 29, 1714, BANQ-M, TL4, S1, D1638; and "Procès contre François Lamoureux dit Saint-Germain, arquebusier et marchand, accusé de vente de boisson aux sauvages," July 8, 1726, BANQ-M, TL4, S1, D3289.

32. "Procès contre François Lamoureux," 1726.

33. On women and Catholicism, see Greer, *Mohawk Saint*; and Green, "The Kahnawake Iroquois."

34. Adhémar database, Centre Canadian d'Architecture, Montreal.

35. "Procès contre Simon Réaume, voyageur, accusé d'avoir introduit illégalement des paquets de castors en ville et de les avoir vendus à M. Pascaud," Aug. 4, 1708, BANQ-M, TL4, S1, D1124; and "Procès contre Louise Leblanc, épouse de Paul Bouchard, accusée d'avoir vendu de l'eau de vie à un sauvage," Aug. 7, 1710, BANQ-M, TL4, S1, D1248.

36. Clairambault d'Aigremont to the minister, Nov. 14, 1708, ANOM, Colonies, C11A vol. 29, 59v–60.

37. "[L]es Anglois tirent un grand avantage du commerce qu'ils font avec les Sauvages de leur eau de vie ce qui est une si grand attrait pour eux que par ce moyen les anglois attirent les plus grande partie de leurs pelleteries . . ." (235) [Not having access to French liquor, Indians go to Orange] "ou ils portent tous leur castor, ce qui forme un commerce ouvert entre leur et les anglois, enfin ces Sauvages ne resistent point à l'attrait de l'eau de vie les anglois se les attireront tous, d'ou la Ruine de la Colonie" (235v). Vaudreuil and Bégon to the minister, Sept. 20, 1714, ANOM, Colonies, C11A, vol. 34, 235–235v.

38. Yves Zoltvany, *Philippe de Rigaud de Vaudreuil* (Toronto: McClelland and Stewart, 1974).

39. Chard, "Breslay."

40. Baptism, Aug. 23, 1715, Sainte-Anne de Bellevue.

41. Andrew R. L. Cayton and Fredrika J. Teuta, "Introduction: On the Connection of Frontiers," in *Contact Points: American Frontiers from the Mohawk Valley to the Mississippi, 1750–1830* (Chapel Hill: University of North Carolina Press for the Omohundro Institute of Early American History and Culture, 1998), 1–15; Gregory Evans Dowd, "Wag the Imperial Dog: Indians and Overseas Empires in North America, 1650–1776," in *A Companion to American Indian History*, ed. Philip J. Deloria and Neal Salisbury (Oxford: Blackwell Publishers, 2004), 46–67; and White, *Middle Ground*, ix–xvi.

Chapter 4

1. Richard White notes that Detroit "officially faced east toward the Iroquois and the English whom it was intended to confine" in *The Middle Ground: Indians, Empires, and Republics in the Great Lakes Region, 1650–1815* (Cambridge: Cambridge University Press, 1991), 150. In *Facing East from Indian Country: A Native History of Early America* (Cambridge: Harvard University Press, 2001), Daniel Richter places Europeans arriving from the Atlantic on the periphery of a vast, complex, and vibrant world inhabited by hundreds of Native nations. This author concurs with Richter that such a view allows us to "to turn familiar tales inside out" by identifying with Native historical agents and to "alternate between the general and the personal" (9) in writing histories. The present chapter speaks to eighteenth-century European efforts to expand their imperial and economic agendas farther and farther west in order to reach Native nations. But, as this chapter also shows, high-ranking imperial agents who developed policy were not the ones traveling through Indian country, and they were therefore often uninformed as to the nuances and channels of Native-European interaction and mutual influence. Lines of communication moved east, west, south and north, depending on the era and on the familial networks that were the means for cross-cultural conversation.

2. Jacqueline Peterson published a groundbreaking study of elite métis lineages in "Prelude to Red River: A Social Portrait of the Great Lakes Métis," *Ethnohistory* 25:1 (Winter 1978), 41–67. Although Peterson mentions the Detroit métis in her study, her main focus is on the upper Great Lakes in the late eighteenth and early nineteenth centuries. Her description of the lifeways of the métis is applicable in some ways to those who operated at Detroit in an earlier period, but there are subtle differences in culture that can be ascribed to Detroit's central importance in imperial networks in the *pays d'en haut*.

3. White, *Middle Ground*, 123.

4. Elmore Barce, *The Land of the Miamis: An Account of the Struggle to Secure Possession of the North-West from the End of the Revolution until 1812* (Fowler, IN: Benton Review Shop, 1922), 10.

5. Gilles Havard, *The Great Peace of Montreal of 1701: French-Native Diplomacy in the Seventeenth Century*, trans. Phyllis Aronoff and Howard Scott (Montreal and Kingston: McGill-Queen's University Press, 2001), 145, 148–49.

6. The English counseled the Iroquois that they should reassert their former claims of conquest of the area around Detroit acquired during the Beaver Wars. Iroquois sachems, however, felt they could not keep the French out of Detroit. On July 19, 1701, twenty of their sachems deeded title to the King of an area they claimed by right of conquest—a tract eight hundred miles long and four hundred miles wide that included Detroit. Although the Iroquois considered themselves to have only temporarily placed the land under the protection of the King, the English would use the deed to push their claims to Detroit for decades. For French fears that the Iroquois would favor their English allies, see William N. Fenton, *The Great Law and the Longhouse: A Political History of the Iroquois Confederacy* (Norman: University of Oklahoma Press, 1998), 346. For English advice to the Iroquois that they reassert their claim to Detroit by right of conquest and for the Iroquois confession that they could not prevent settlement at Detroit, see Fenton, 356. For English claims to Detroit through the Iroquois deed, see Fenton, 389, and Francis Jennings, *The Invasion of America: Indians, Colonialism, and the Cant of Conquest* (New York: W. W. Norton and Company, 1975), 125.

7. *Documents Relative to the Colonial History of the State of New York*, ed. E. B. O'Callaghan (Albany: Weed, Parsons, and Company, Printers, 1854), 4:650.

8. "Project d'un nouvel etablissement au détroit des lacs Erie et Huron, Extrait du mémoire du Roi au sieur chevalier de Callières, Gouverneur, et au sieur de Champigny, Intendant de la Nouvelle France, Versailles, 27 mai, 1699," in Charles J. Balesi, *The Time of the French in the Heart of North America 1673–1818* (Chicago: Alliance Française Chicago, 1991), 134–135.

9. White, *The Middle Ground*, 146.

10. For Cadillac's change in opinion about Native-European marriages, see White, *The Middle Ground*, 70. For Cadillac's lack of knowledge of the intricacies of relations of Native groups at Detroit, see White, *The Middle Ground*, 83.

11. Gilles Havard, *Empire et métissages: Indiens et Français dans le Pays d'en Haut 1660–1715* (Paris: Presses de l'Université Paris-Sorbonne, 2003), 628.

12. "Mémoire de Lamothe Cadillac au Ministre donnant la description du Détroit," Québec, September 25, 1702, BAC, Série C11E, Correspondence générale, vol. 14, Folio 119.

13. The entire French passage reads: "il n'est pas possible que nos familles peussent demeurer dans un lieu qui ne seroit habité que par des sauvages,; leur misere seroit extreme; puis quelles seroient sans aucun secours, comme il en arrive au Madame Tonty qui aveu mourir son enfant pour avoir manqué de lait, a quoi elle ne s'attendoit pas. Je crains que la même chose n'arrive a ma femme qui étoit sur le point d'accoucher quand je suis parti, celle n'est pas extraordinaire, suivre que ces dames seroient nourrir leurs enfans, ainsi il n'ya suis a balancer de les faire decendre des l'année prochaine, si on ne permet pas a quelques familles d'aller s'y établir, affin quelles se puissent soulager dans ces facheuses conjonctures." "Mémoire de Lamothe Cadillac au Ministre donnant la description du Détroit," Folio 120. English translation used here appears as M. La Motte Cadillac, "Description of Detroit," *Michigan Pioneer and Historical Society Collections* (Lansing, MI: Robert Smith Printing Co., 1904), 139. For the comment that women of surrounding Native villages could have served as wet nurses, see Timothy Kent, *Ft. Ponchartrain at Detroit: A Guide to the Daily Lives of Fur Trade and Military Personnel, Settlers, and Missionaries at French Posts* (Ossineke, MI: Silver Fox Enterprises), 1:43.

14. "Copie de la lettre des directeurs de la Compagnie de la Colonie au ministre Pontchartrain," November 4, 1701, Bibliothèque et Archives Canada (BAC), Série C11A, vol. 19, Folios 36 and 36v.

15. "Rapport de Clairambault d'Aigremont au ministre concernant sa mission d'inspection," November 14, 1708, BAC, Série C11A, vol. 29, Folio 32.

16. "Lettre de Louvigny au ministre," Québec, October 30, 1715, Série C11A, Folio 229v.

17. "Lettre de Vaudreuil au ministre," Québec, November 3, 1710, BAC, Série C11A.

18. Peter Dooyentate Clarke, *Origin and Traditional History of the Wyandotts, and Sketches of Other Indian Tribes of North America* (Toronto: Hunter, Rose and Co., 1870), 37.

19. For Pierre Roy as an *engagé*, see Yvon Lacroix, *Les Origines de la Prairie, 1667–1697* (Montréal: Éditions Bellarmin, 1981), 134. For the marriage of Pierre Roy and Marguerite Ouabankikoué, see Rev. Fr. Christian Denissen, *Genealogy of the French Families of the Detroit River Region 1701–1936*, rev. ed. (Detroit: Detroit Society for Genealogical Research, 1987), 2:1108, and René Jetté, *Dictionnaire généalogique des familles du Québec* (Montréal: Presses de l'Université de Montréal, 1983), 1022.

20. For a biography of Pierre Roy, Sr., see Michel Langlois, *Dictionnaire Biographique des Ancêtres Québécois 1608–1700* (Sillery, QC: Éditions du Mitan, 2001), 4:310–311. For Catherine Ducharme as a "fille du roi" (daughter of the King), see Yves Landry, *Orphelines en France, pionnières au Canada: Les Filles du roi au septième siècle; suivi d'un Répertoire biographique des Filles du roi* (Montréal: Leméac Éditeur Inc., 1992), 308.

21. Pierre Roy, Sr., and his wife Catherine Ducharme acquired eight-year-old Elizabeth Corse;

Corse's eight-year-old cousin Martha French married Pierre and Catherine's son Jacques at the age of sixteen; see Evan Haefeli and Kevin Sweeney, *Captors and Captives: The 1704 French and Indian Raid on Deerfield* (Amherst and Boston: University of Massachusetts Press, 2003), 245–247.

22. Andrée Désilets, "Roy, Marguerite, *dite* de la Conception," *Dictionary of Canadian Biography Online* , vol. 3, http://www.biographi.ca/009004-119.01-e.php?id_nbr=1638, April 30, 2012.

23. According to historian Louise Dechêne, the fur trade drew men from up and down the French socioeconomic hierarchy; see *Habitants and Merchants in Seventeenth Century Montreal*, trans. Liana Vardi (Montreal and Kingston: McGill-Queen's University Press, 1992), 120–121.

24. For more on Madame Montour and the pivotal role she played in Native-European relations, see Alison Duncan Hirsch, "Indian, *Métis*, and Euro-American Women on Multiple Frontiers," in *Friends and Enemies in Penn's Woods: Indians, Colonists, and the Racial Construction of Pennsylvania*, ed. William A. Pencak and Daniel K. Richter (University Park: Pennsylvania State University Press, 2004), 63–84.

25. "Contract of François and Pierre Roy to conduct trade at the Miamis," May 12, 1719, Burton Historical Collection, Detroit Public Library. The agreement enabled considerable traffic in goods and people into the Miami village for years following; see Ls-A. Proulx, *Rapport de L'Archiviste de la Province de Québec pour 1921–1922* (Québec, Imprimeur de Sa Majesté le Roi, 1922), 196–213 for a list of permits granted to François and Pierre.

26. *Mississippi Valley Mélange: A Collection of Notes and Documents for the Genealogy and History of the Province of Louisiana and the Territory of Orleans*, ed. Winston de Ville, vol. 2 (Ville Platte, LA: privately printed, 1995).

27. John D. Barnhart and Dorothy L. Riker, *Indiana to 1816: The Colonial Period* (Indianapolis: Indiana Historical Bureau, 1971), 19.

28. *Mississippi Valley Mélange*, vol. 1, 14. The Roy family continued to operate and gain power throughout the entire eighteenth century and into the nineteenth. For a more detailed discussion of how these kin connections increased the influence of that family network in the arena of European-Native relations, see Karen Marrero, "'She Is Capable of Doing a Great Deal of Mischief': A Miami Woman's Threat to Empire in the Eighteenth-Century Ohio Valley," *Journal of Colonialism and Colonial History* 6.3 (Winter 2005), http://muse.jhu.edu/journals/journal_of_colonialism_and_colonial_history/toc/cch6.3.html. For further genealogical information on the Roy family, see Sammye Leonard Darling, "Takamwa of the Miami Tribe," *Michigan's Habitant Heritage* 25:4 (October 2004), 179–184; Suzanne Boivin Sommerville, "André Roy *dit* Pacanne: Documentation for Another Son of Pierre Roy and Marguerite OuabanKiKoué," *Michigan's Habitant Heritage* 29:4 (October 2008), 153–160; and Suzanne Boivin Sommerville, "André Roy *dit* Pacanne, Son of Pierre Roy and Marguerite OuabanKiKoué, and his Brother, François Roy, Voyageur and Interpreter," *Michigan's Habitant Heritage* 30:1 (January 2009), 23–29.

29. Registre de Ste. Anne Detroit, vol. 1, no. 1252, Reel 1, Burton Historical Collection, Detroit Public Library, 204.

30. Original document #2583 from the microfilm copy of the notarial records of Jean-Baptiste Adhémar, Archives Nationales du Québec à Montréal. For a description of the trade agreement, see S. Dale Standen, "'Personnes sans caractère': Private Merchants, Post Commanders and the Regulation of the Western Fur Trade, 1720–1745," in *De France en Nouvelle-France: Société Fondatrice et Société Nouvelle*, ed. Hubert Watelet and Cornelius J. Jaenen (Ottawa: Presses de l'Université d'Ottawa, 1994), 274.

31. The French passage reads: "C'est à ce dernier endroit qu'il faut aujourdhui le plus attacher. S'il y avoit une fois dans ce canton mille habitans cultivateurs, il nourriroit et défendroit tous les

autres. C'est de tout l'interieur du Canada l'endroit le plus propre à établir une ville ou se reuniroit tout le commerce des lacs, et qui munie d'une bonne garnison et entourée d'un bon nombre d'habitations seroit a portée d'en imposer à presque tous les sauvages du continent. Il suffit d'en voir la position sur la carte pour en sentir l'utilité. . . ." Roland Michel, Comte de la Galissoniere, in *Anglo-French Boundary Disputes in the West 1749–1763, French Series*, vol. 2, *Collections of the Illinois Historical Library*, ed. Theodore Calvin Pease (Springfield: Illinois State Historical Library, 1936), 27:16–17.

32. Colonel John Bradstreet, February 1762, in Peter Marshall, "Imperial Policy and the Government of Detroit: Projects and Problems 1760–1774," *Journal of Imperial and Commonwealth History* 2:2 (January 1974), 157.

33. For population figures of 1707, see Almon Ernest Parkins, *The Historical Geography of Detroit* (Lansing: Michigan Historical Commission, 1918), 55. For 1765 population, see Brian Leigh Dunnigan, *Frontier Metropolis: Picturing Early Detroit, 1701–1838* (Detroit: Wayne State University Press, 2001), 50. For an estimate of Native population, see Dunnigan, 36. For comments of Beauharnois, see Parkins, 71. For the self-sufficiency of Detroit because of the influx of 1749–1750, see Dunnigan, 35. Dunnigan comments that at the mid-century point, "Detroit was finally on a firm footing and was about to become one of the breadbaskets of French military operations in the West." Dunnigan, 35

34. *Historical Atlas of Canada: From the Beginning to 1800*, vol. 1, ed. R. Cole Harris (Toronto: University of Toronto Press, 1987), plate 41.

35. Dunnigan, 46.

36. For a discussion of this second state-sponsored wave of immigration to Detroit, see Lina Gouger, "Les convoys de colons de 1749–1750: Impulsion gouvernementale decisive pour le développement de la region de Windsor," in *Le Passage du Détroit: Trois cents ans de presence Francophone* (Passages: Three Centuries of Francophone Presence at Le Détroit), ed. Marcel Bénéteau, Working Papers in the Humanities (Windsor, Ontario: Humanities Research Group, 2003), 11:47–57.

37. Marcel Trudel, *Dictionnaire des esclaves et de leurs propriétaires au Canada français* (LaSalle, QC: Éditions Hurtubise HMH, 1990), xx.

38. Marcel Trudel, *L'esclavage au Canada Français: Histoire et Conditions de L'esclavage* (Québec: Presses l'Université Laval, 1960), 97

39. Brett Rushforth, "Savage Bonds: Indian Slavery and Alliance in New France" (Ph.D. diss., University of California Davis, 2003), 216.

40. Gilles Havard and Cécile Vidal, *Histoire de l'Amérique française* (Paris: Éditions Flammarion, 2003), 371.

41. Rushforth, 216.

42. George Paré, *The Catholic Church in Detroit 1701–1888* (Detroit: Gabriel Richard Press, 1951), 155.

43. As has been previously mentioned in this chapter, the ranks of the *coureurs de ville* contained men who hailed from many different classes in New France, including officers. In the first few decades of the eighteenth century, commandants and officers at the western posts participated in the fur trade despite attempts by colonial authorities to censure and control this activity. In relations with local Native groups, the commandant was supposed to occupy a position of impartiality as arbiter. Commandants such as Cadillac and his successor Tonty failed to maintain this objective position when they partnered with some but not other local French families and Native groups. But the *coureurs de ville* possessed enough economic clout that they could bring about the removal of commandants, as was the case in 1727 when this group's petitions to imperial authorities for the

ouster of Alphonse de Tonty were finally successful. As the century wore on, colonial authorities in Quebec sought to severely restrict participation of the officers in the trade. Interestingly, at about the same time, the *coureurs de ville* began to organize their own regiments commanded by bourgeois officers. For the participation of officers in the fur trade at the western posts, see Standen, "'Personnes sans caractère.'" For a discussion of the class system in New France, see Allan Greer, *The People of New France* (Toronto: University of Toronto Press, 1997), and particularly in Montreal, which, like Detroit, was dominated by the trade in furs and with Native groups; see Louise Dechêne, *Habitants and Merchants*.

44. Johnson kept a diary of his activities at Detroit that was published as an appendix in William L. Stone, *The Life and Times of Sir William Johnson, Bart.* (Albany: J. Munsell, 1865), 2:456–464.

45. Walter S. Dunn, Jr., *Frontier Profit and Loss: The British Army and the Fur Traders, 1760–1764* (Westport, CT: Greenwood Press, 1998), 109.

46. James Sterling to Mr. James Syme, Detroit, June 8, 1762, James Sterling Letterbook, William L. Clements Library, University of Michigan.

47. Sterling to Syme, June 8, 1762.

48. James Sterling to Captain Walter Rutherford, Detroit, November 22, 1762, James Sterling Letterbook.

49. Sterling to Syme, June 8, 1762.

50. James Sterling to George Croghan, Esq., Detroit, January 31, 1762, James Sterling Letterbook.

51. James Sterling to John Duncan, Detroit, February 26, 1765, James Sterling Letterbook.

52. James Sterling to John Porteus, Detroit, September 4, 1765, James Sterling Letterbook.

53. George Trumbull to Thomas Gage, Detroit, April 16, 1767, Thomas Gage Papers, American Series, William L. Clements Library, University of Michigan.

54. Captain James Stevenson to Sir William Johnson, Bart., Detroit, December 18, 1770, Chicago Historical Society.

Chapter 5

1. John Heckewelder, *Account of the History, Manners, and Customs of the Indian Nations*, ed. William C. Reichel (1876; reprint, Whitefish, MT: Kessinger Publishing, 2006), 142; C. A. Weslager, *The Delaware Indians: A History* (New Brunswick: Rutgers University Press, 1972), 166. The Delaware translation of *Onas* was *Miquon*. See also Randolph C. Downes, *Council Fires on the Upper Ohio: A Narrative of Indian Affairs in the Upper Ohio Valley until 1795* (Pittsburgh: University of Pittsburgh Press, 1940), 18; James H. Merrell, *Into the American Woods: Negotiators on the Pennsylvania Frontier* (New York and London: W. W. Norton, 1999), 172.

2. "Ashalacoa" is the spelling given by James Smith, *A Treatise, on the Mode and Manner of Indian War* (Paris, KY: Joel R. Lyle, 1812; reprint, Chicago: Barnard & Miller, 1948), 42. For the derivation, and other spellings in languages as far away as Mandan, see Arthur Woodward, "The 'Long Knives,'" *Indian Notes* 5:1 (January 1928), 64–79. The Delaware translation was *Mechanschican* (see Heckewelder, *Account*, 142–143) and the Ojibway was *Kitchimokomans*; see Arent S. DePeyster, "Speech to the Western Indians," *Wisconsin Historical Collections* 18 (Madison: Wisconsin Historical Society, 1908), 380. See also Downes, *Council Fires*, 91.

3. Reuben Gold Thwaites and Louise Phelps Kellogg, eds., *The Revolution on the Upper Ohio, 1775–1777*, Draper Series, vol. 2 (Madison: Wisconsin Historical Society, 1908), 52.

4. For the towns, see Michael N. McConnell, *A Country Between: The Upper Ohio Valley and*

Its Peoples, 1724-1774 (Lincoln and London: University of Nebraska Press, 1992), 22, 25; William M. Darlington, *Christopher Gist's Journals, with Historical, Geographical, and Ethnological Notes* (Pittsburgh: J. R. Weldin & Co., 1893), 33–34, map opp. 80; Helen Hornbeck Tanner, ed., *Atlas of Great Lakes Indian History* (Norman: University of Oklahoma Press, 1987), 41. On the prewar fur trade, see Eric Hinderaker, *Elusive Empires: Constructing Colonialism in the Ohio Valley, 1673-1800* (Cambridge: Cambridge University Press, 1997), 21–45; Richard White, *The Middle Ground: Indians, Empires, and Republics in the Great Lakes Region, 1650-1815* (Cambridge: Cambridge University Press, 1991), 186–222; McConnell, *A Country Between*, 37–112; John A. Garraty and Mark C. Carnes, eds., *American National Biography* (New York and Oxford: Oxford University Press), 5:752–754.

5. David Dixon, *Fort Pitt Museum: Pennsylvania Trail of History Guide* (Mechanicsburg, PA: Stackpole Books, 2004), 27; James Kenny, "Journal of James Kenny, 1761–1763," ed. John W. Jordan, *Pennsylvania Magazine of History and Biography* 37:145 (January 1913), 1–47; 37:146 (April 1913), 152–201. The particulars mentioned by Kenny are on pages 6 (coal mine, sawmill), 17 (robberies), 28 (buildings), 29 (school), 39, 43 (diet), 162 (postal service). The boatyard is from Max Savelle, *George Morgan: Colony Builder* (New York: Columbia University Press, 1932), 26.

6. David McClure, *Diary of David McClure, Doctor of Divinity, 1748-1820*, ed. Franklin B. Dexter (New York: Knickerbocker Press, 1899), 45, 53.

7. Thomas Hutchins, *A Topographical Description of Virginia, Pennsylvania, Maryland, and North Carolina*, ed. Frederick Charles Hicks (London: Printed for the author, 1778; reprint, Cleveland: Burrows Brothers Co., 1904), 77. Trader John Campbell is credited with laying out the town, as he later did for Louisville. Ensign Hutchins himself may have helped, since he was stationed at Fort Pitt at the time. See Thwaites and Kellogg, *Revolution on the Upper Ohio*, 231.

8. R. Eugene Harper, *The Transformation of Western Pennsylvania 1770-1800* (Pittsburgh: University of Pittsburgh Press, 1991), 4–7.

9. There is no modern history of the Pittsburgh fur trade. Information can be found in William Vincent Byars, *B. and M. Gratz: Merchants in Philadelphia 1754-1798* (Jefferson City, MO: Hugh Stephens Printing Co., 1916); Savelle, *George Morgan*; and Kenny, "Journal." See also Clarence Walworth Alvord and Clarence Edwin Carter, eds., *The New Regime 1765-1767*, Illinois State Historical Library, *Collections*, vol. 11, British Series, vol. 2 (Springfield: Illinois State Historical Library, 1916), and *Trade and Politics 1767-1769*, Illinois State Historical Library, *Collections*, vol. 16, British Series, vol. 3 (Springfield: Illinois State Historical Library, 1921).

10. Alvord and Carter, *New Regime*, 510.

11. John B. Gibson, "General John Gibson," *Western Pennsylvania Historical Magazine* 5:4 (October 1922), 299–305 (second quote, 305); David Jones, *A Journal of Two Visits Made to Some Nations of Indians on the West Side of the River Ohio, in the Years 1772 and 1773* (New York: Reprinted for Joseph Sabin, 1865), 63 (first quote); Allen Johnson and Dumas Malone, eds., *Dictionary of American Biography* (New York: Charles Scribner's Sons, 1931), 7:253; William Wesley Woollen, *Biographical and Historical Sketches of Early Indiana* (Indianapolis: Hammond & Co., 1883), 11; Reuben Gold Thwaites and Louise Phelps Kellogg, eds., *Documentary History of Dunmore's War, 1774*, Draper Series, vol. 1 (Madison: Wisconsin Historical Society, 1905), 11; Consul W. Butterfield, *The Washington-Crawford Letters* (Cincinnati: Robert Clarke & Co., 1877), 69. The information on Gibson's wife comes from Charles A. Hanna, *The Wilderness Trail, or The Ventures and Adventures of the Pennsylvania Traders on the Allegheny Path* (New York: G. P. Putnam's Sons, 1911), 1:381.

12. Thomas Sergeant, *View of the Land Laws of Pennsylvania* (Philadelphia: James Kay, Jr., and Pittsburgh: John I. Kay, 1838), 61; Thomas Perkins Abernethy, *Western Lands and the American*

Revolution (New York: Russell and Russell, 1959), 91–93. For the Pittsburgh compromise, see Kenny, "Journal," 28, 152.

13. A good description of the mentality is Andrew R. L. Cayton, "Land, Power, and Reputation: The Cultural Dimension of Politics in the Ohio Country," *William and Mary Quarterly*, 3d ser., 47 (April 1990), 266–286.

14. Peter Silver, *Our Savage Neighbors: How Indian War Transformed Early America* (New York and London: W. W. Norton, 2008).

15. Matthew Smith and James Gibson, *A Declaration and Remonstrance of the Distressed and Bleeding Frontier Inhabitants of the Province of Pennsylvania* (Philadelphia: William Bradford, 1764).

16. McClure, *Diary of David McClure*, 53.

17. The vacillations of William Crawford and George Croghan are good examples. Crawford, a Virginian, started out on the Pennsylvanian side, probably because he identified with the social class of the Pennsylvanians, and only later switched over. Croghan, a Pennsylvanian, switched sides so many times he lost the trust of everyone. John Gibson, the Pennsylvania trader, ended up commanding the Thirteenth Virginia regiment in the Revolution. Many other examples could be given.

18. On Pennsylvania, see Hinderaker, *Elusive Empires*; on Virginia, see David Hackett Fischer and James C. Kelly, *Bound Away: Virginia and the Westward Movement* (Charlottesville: University of Virginia Press, 2000).

19. See Sir William Franklin's scheme in Alvord and Carter, *The New Regime*, 248–257, and Samuel Wharton's in *The Papers of Benjamin Franklin*, ed. Leonard W. Labaree and Whitfield J. Bell (New Haven and London: Yale University Press, 1959–), 31:525–548, especially 539.

20. Clarence W. Alvord and Clarence E. Carter, eds., *The Critical Period 1763–1765*, Illinois State Historical Library, *Collections*, vol. 10, British Series, vol. 1 (Springfield: Illinois State Historical Library, 1915), 24; see also the petitions of George Mercer and George Mason in Kenneth P. Bailey, *The Ohio Company of Virginia and the Westward Movement 1748–1792* (Glendale, CA: Arthur H. Clark Co., 1939), 314–327.

21. Abernethy, *Western Lands*, 93, 136; Bruce J. Egli, "The First Battalion, Westmoreland County Militia," *Westmoreland History* 2:2 (Summer 1996), 17.

22. Harper, *Transformation of Western Pennsylvania*, 8–10; Robert A. Jockers, "Speculators and Squatters: The Frontier Beginnings of Moon Township," *Western Pennsylvania History* 87:2 (Summer 2004), 20, 22–27; Stephen Aron, *How the West Was Lost: The Transformation of Kentucky from Daniel Boone to Henry Clay* (Baltimore and London: Johns Hopkins University Press, 1996), 65–81.

23. Peter Force and M. St. Clair Clarke, eds., *American Archives*, 4th ser. (Washington, DC: M. St. Clair Clarke and Peter Force, 1837), 1:275–276.

24. Force and Clarke, *American Archives*, 1:267 (quote), 484. The whole conflict would later be replayed in territorial Ohio, and St. Clair would assume the same role. See Cayton, "Land, Power, and Reputation."

25. Force and Clarke, *American Archives*, 1:269.

26. Force and Clarke, *American Archives*, 1:262 (first quote), 264, 271 (second quote), 272 (third quote), 469 (last quote).

27. Abernethy, *Western Lands*, 54.

28. Force and Clarke, *American Archives*, 1:470 (first quote), 475 (second quote), 549 (third quote).

29. Force and Clarke, *American Archives*, 1:287 (last quote), 469 (first quote).

30. James Alton James, ed., *George Rogers Clark Papers 1771–1781*, Illinois State Historical Library, *Collections*, vol. 8, Virginia Series, vol. 3 (Springfield: Illinois State Historical Library, 1912), 7.

31. Force and Clarke, *American Archives*, 1:468, 484; Augustine Prevost, "Turmoil at Pittsburgh: Diary of Augustine Prevost, 1774," ed. Nicholas B. Wainwright, *Pennsylvania Magazine of History and Biography* 85:2 (April 1961), 147.

32. Thomas Jefferson, *Notes on the State of Virginia* (New York, Evanston, and London: Harper Torchbooks, 1964), 212–213.

33. Butterfield, *Washington-Crawford Letters*, 87; Jefferson, *Notes*, 216, 221, 228; Thwaites and Kellogg, *Dunmore's War*, 10, 16; Prevost, "Diary," 149.

34. Force and Clarke, *American Archives*, 1:429, 469 (first quote), 473 (second quote).

35. Force and Clarke, *American Archives*, 1:429, 473 (last quote), 474 (first quote), 483, 484.

36. Force and Clarke, *American Archives*, 1:287, 463, 547, 549 (quote).

37. Anthony F. C. Wallace, *Jefferson and the Indians: The Tragic Fate of the First Americans* (Cambridge and London: Harvard University Press, 1999), 1–4; Jefferson, *Notes*, 212–213, 225–226.

38. Hinderaker, *Elusive Empires*.

Chapter 6

1. E. Bradford Burns, *A History of Brazil* (New York: Columbia University Press, 1980), 330–339; Collin M. MacLachlan, *A History of Modern Brazil: The Past Against the Future* (Wilmington, Del.: SR Books, 2003), 62–64.

2. U.S. Bureau of the Census, *Historical Statistics of the United States, Colonial Times to 1970*, Bicentennial ed., pt. 2 (Washington, D.C.: GPO, 1975), 731. Here are a few especially useful works from the enormous literature on the construction of the national rail system: Winthrop M. Daniels, *American Railroads: Four Phases of Their History* (Princeton: Princeton University Press, 1932); James E. Vance, Jr., *The North American Railroad: Its Origin, Evolution and Geography* (Baltimore: Johns Hopkins University Press, 1995); Maury Klein, *Union Pacific* (Garden City, N.Y.: Doubleday, 1987); George Rogers Taylor, *The American Railroad Network, 1861–1890* (Cambridge: Harvard University Press, 1956); John F. Stover, *American Railroads* (Chicago: University of Chicago Press, 1961); David Hayward Bain, *Empire Express: Building the First Transcontinental Railroad* (New York: Viking, 1999); John F. Stover, *Iron Road to the West: American Railroads of the 1850s* (New York: Columbia University Press, 1978).

3. For general works on the telegraph, see Alvin F. Harlow, *Old Wires and New Waves: The History of the Telegraph, Telephone, and Wireless* (New York: D. Appleton-Century Company, 1936); Lewis Coe, *The Telegraph: A History of Morse's Invention and Its Predecessors in the United States* (Jefferson, N.C.: McFarland, 1993); Robert Luther Thompson, *Wiring a Continent: A History of the Telegraph Industry in the United States, 1832–1866* (Princeton: Princeton University Press, 1947).

4. Armin E. Shuman, "Report on the Statistics of Telegraphs and Telephones in the United States," in *Report on the Agencies of Transportation in the United States, Including the Statistics of Railroads, Steam Navigation, Canals, Telegraphs and Telephones, Tenth Census, 1880* (Washington, D.C.: GPO, 1881), 4:784–785.

5. A recent splendid work on early nineteenth-century American history makes a similar point and makes it more broadly, arguing that the transportation and communications revolution were key to bringing the evolving young republic into focus as a true nation: Daniel Walker Howe, *What Hath God Wrought?: The Transformation of America, 1815–1848* (New York: Oxford University Press, 2007).

6. On the California wheat trade during these years, see Rodman W. Paul, "The Wheat Trade

Between California and the United Kingdom," *Mississippi Valley Historical Review*, 45:3 (December 1958), 391–412.

7. U.S. Bureau of the Census, *Ninth Census, The Statistics of the Wealth and Industry of the United States* (Washington, D.C.: GPO, 1872), 3:80–81, 367.

8. Two classic older accounts of the Comstock Lode and its astonishing physical plant are Dan De Quille, *History of the Big Bonanza: An Authentic Account of the Discovery, History, and Working of the World Renowned Comstock Silver Lode of Nevada* (Hartford, Conn.: American Publishing Company; San Francisco, Calif.: A. L. Bancroft and Co., 1876); and Eliot Lord, *Comstock Mining and Miners* (Washington, D.C.: GPO, 1883). A newer account is Ronald M. James, *The Roar and the Silence: A History of Virginia City and the Comstock Lode* (Reno and Las Vegas: University of Nevada Press, 1998).

9. James, *Roar and the Silence*, 58.

10. Richard Walker, "Industry Builds the City: The Suburbanization of Manufacturing in the San Francisco Bay Area, 1850–1940," *Journal of Historical Geography* 27:1 (2001), 37–38.

11. For three interesting case studies of the role of such a mentality in immigration westward, see Dianne Newell, "The Importance of Information and Misinformation in the Making of the Klondike Gold Rush," *Journal of Canadian Studies*, 21:4 (1986–87), 95–111; Cole Harris, "Industry and the Good Life Around Idaho Peak," *Canadian Historical Review*, 66:3 (September 1985), 315–343; and S. M. Glover and M. C. Towner, "Long-distance Dispersal to the Mining Frontier in late 19th Century Colorado," *Behaviour* 146:4-5 (2009), 677–700.

12. Walter Prescott Webb, *The Great Frontier* (Boston: Houghton Mifflin, 1952).

13. Jos[eph] L. King, *History of the San Francisco Stock Exchange Board* (1910; reprint, New York: Arno Press, 1975), 9–10.

14. Ibid., 78.

15. Robert Louis Stevenson, "Old and New Pacific Capitals: San Francisco," 1883, in *The Works of Robert Louis Stevenson* (New York: Charles Scribner's Sons, 1892), 2:435.

16. The demographic profile of western urban centers was most out-of-line with those of the East in mining camps. For two recent studies on some of the implications on California's mining frontier, see Susan Lee Johnson, *Roaring Camp: The Social World of the California Gold Rush* (New York: W. W. Norton, 2000) and Brian Roberts, *American Alchemy: The California Gold Rush and Middle-Class Culture* (Chapel Hill: University of North Carolina Press, 2000).

17. For a demographic study of the trans-Appalachian region illustrating this pattern, see James E. Davis, *Frontier America, 1800–1840: A Comparative Demographic Analysis of the Settlement Process* (Glendale, Calif.: Clark, 1977).

18. Besides Johnson, *Roaring Camp*, see also Adele Perry, *On the Edge of Empire: Gender, Race, and the Making of British Columbia, 1849–1871* (Toronto: University of Toronto Press, 2001).

19. Don E. Fehrenbacher, ed., *History and American Society: Essays of David M. Potter* (New York: Oxford University Press, 1973), 284.

20. U.S. Bureau of the Census, *Ninth Census, The Statistics of the Population of the United States* (Washington, D.C.: GPO, 1872), 1:299; U.S. Bureau of the Census, *Report on the Social Statistics of Cities*, comp. George E. Waring, Jr. (Washington, D.C.: GPO, 1887), 800.

21. For demographic studies of mining towns, where these patterns were most exaggerated, see Elliott West, "Five Idaho Mining Towns: A Computer Profile," *Pacific Northwest Quarterly*, 73:3 (July 1982), 108–120; Ralph Mann, *After the Gold Rush: Society in Grass Valley and Nevada City, California, 1849–1870* (Stanford: Stanford University Press, 1982).

22. This is the thesis of David T. Courtwright, *Violent Land: Single Men and Social Disorder from the Frontier to the Inner City* (Cambridge: Harvard University Press, 1996).

23. On consequences for Indians in California, see Johnson, *Roaring Camp*; Andrew C. Isenberg, *Mining California: An Ecological History* (New York: Hill and Wang, 2005); and Rodman W. Paul and Elliott West, *Mining Frontiers of the Far West, 1848–1880* (Albuquerque: University of New Mexico Press, 2001).

24. *Virginia City, Nevada, Territorial Enterprise*, June 14, July 30, 1872; *Virginia City, Nevada, Virginia Evening Chronicle*, January 5, 1875, Russell M. Magnaghi Collection, Bancroft Library, University of California, Berkeley.

25. Hal Rothman, *Devil's Bargains: Tourism in the Twentieth-Century American West* (Lawrence: University Press of Kansas, 1998), especially chapter 12, and *Neon Metropolis: How Las Vegas Started the Twenty-first Century* (New York: Routledge, 2002).

26. "A Rumble in the Jungle," *Containerisation International* 35:8 (2002), 30–33.

27. Joe Kane, *Running the Amazon* (New York: Alfred A. Knopf, 1989), 246–249.

28. Ibid., 190.

Chapter 7

Portions of this essay were adapted and excerpted from Matthew Klingle, *Emerald City: An Environmental History of Seattle* (New Haven: Yale University Press, 2007). I am grateful for permission to reprint that material here. Thanks to Jay Taylor, Connie Y. Chiang, Adam Arenson, Barbara Berglund, and Jay Gitlin, plus the participants of the 2008 "Frontier Cities" conference in St. Louis and the Southern Maine American History Reading Group, for their help and suggestions. Thanks also to the Bowdoin College Faculty Development Committee for a Fletcher Family Fund Grant to cover image reproduction and permissions fees.

1. *Seattle Times*, March 7, 1893, as quoted in Coll Thrush, *Native Seattle: Histories from the Crossing-Over Place* (Seattle: University of Washington Press, 2007), 82–83, quotation at 3.

2. Thrush, *Native Seattle*, 3–16.

3. Richard White, "Frederick Jackson Turner and Buffalo Bill," in *The Frontier in American History*, ed. James Grossman (Berkeley: University of California Press, 1994), 7–11.

4. Richard C. Wade, *The Urban Frontier: Pioneer Life in Early Pittsburgh, Cincinnati, Lexington, Louisville, and St. Louis* (Cambridge: Harvard University Press, 1959; Chicago: University of Chicago Press, 1972), 1.

5. For frontier anxiety at the end of the nineteenth century, see David M. Wrobel, *The End of American Exceptionalism: Frontier Anxiety from the Old West to the New Deal* (Lawrence: University Press of Kansas, 1993), 27–68. For urban chaos, see Paul S. Boyer, *Urban Masses and Moral Order in America, 1820–1920* (Cambridge: Harvard University Press, 1978).

6. White, "Frederick Jackson Turner and Buffalo Bill," 10. For examples of other celebratory expositions tinged with frontier angst, specifically the 1894 Midwinter International Exposition in San Francisco, see Barbara Berglund, *Making San Francisco American: Cultural Frontiers in the Urban West, 1846–1906* (Lawrence: University Press of Kansas, 2007), 171–217.

7. A few definitions are in order. The word *urban*, rarely used before the nineteenth century, describes primarily a city or town and its immediate environs. In contrast, an older word, *metropolitan*, denotes complex connections between a city and its colonies. It is more expansive, evocative of networks and associations, not discrete locations, pushpins on a map, or static frontiers. *Metropolitan* speaks more specifically to how cities are zones of contact, conflict, or accommodation wherein consequences reverberate inside and beyond town limits. In using *metropolitan*, I borrow

from William Cronon's work on Chicago, which in turn rests on the idea of "metropolitanism" as developed in Canadian history: *Nature's Metropolis: Chicago and the Great West* (New York: W. W. Norton & Co., 1991). For useful overviews of the concept by one of its proponents, see J. M. S. Careless, "Frontierism, Metropolitanism, and Canadian History," *Canadian Historical Review* 35 (March 1954), 1–21; and *Frontier and Metropolis: Regions, Cities, and Identities in Canada before 1914* (Toronto: University of Toronto Press, 1989). For an American attempt at metropolitanism prior to Cronon, see Charles Gates, "The Role of Cities in the Westward Movement," *Mississippi Valley Historical Review* 37 (September 1950), 277–278; and "The Concept of the Metropolis in the American Western Movement," *Mississippi Valley Historical Review* 49 (September 1962), 299–300. For recent efforts by urban historians to use "metropolitan" in the post–World War II era, see Andrew Needham and Allen Dietrich-Ward, "Beyond the Metropolis: Metropolitan Growth and Regional Transformation in Postwar America," *Journal of Urban History* 35 (November 2009), 943–969.

8. For one assessment of Turner as a ghost (or a disinterred corpse), see Richard White, "Reply from an Empty Grave," *Columbia: The Magazine of Northwest History* 9 (Fall 1995), 4–6.

9. The best recent survey of borderlands historiography is the introduction to a recent edition of the *Journal of American History* devoted to the topic. See Pekka Hämäläinen and Samuel Truett, "On Borderlands," *Journal of American History* 98 (September 2011), 338–361 (quotation at 360–361). See also Jeremy Adelman and Stephen Aaron, "From Borderlands to Borders: Empires, Nation-States, and the Peoples in Between in North American History," *American Historical Review* 104 (June 1999), 813–841.

10. David Igler, "Diseased Goods: Global Exchanges in the Eastern Pacific Basin, 1770–1850," *American Historical Review* 109 (June 2004), 705–707.

11. Robin Fisher, *Contact and Conflict: Indian-European Relations in British Columbia, 1774–1890* (Vancouver: University of British Columbia Press, 1977), 1–48; and Richard Somerset Mackie, *Trading Beyond the Mountains: The British Fur Trade on the Pacific, 1793–1843* (Vancouver: University of British Columbia Press, 1997).

12. Igler, "Diseased Goods," 707–719.

13. David A. Chang, "Borderlands in a World at Sea: Concow Indians, Native Hawaiians, and South Chinese in Indigenous, Global, and National Spaces," *Journal of American History* 98 (September 2011), 384–385. I take the term *resettlement* from Cole Harris, *The Resettlement of British Columbia: Essays on Colonialism and Geographical Change* (Vancouver: University of British Columbia Press, 1997).

14. Mike Davis, *Ecology of Fear: Los Angeles and the Imagination of Disaster* (New York: Metropolitan Books, 1998), 10–20. It is important to note that the Pacific Northwest is also prone to cataclysmic earthquakes, volcanic eruptions, and other "high-intensity" events even if they have not occurred as often or dramatically since American rule. See Coll Thrush with Ruth S. Ludwin, "Finding Fault: Indigenous Seismology, Colonial Science, and the Rediscovery of Earthquakes and Tsunamis in Cascadia," *American Indian Culture & Research Journal* 31 (Fall-Winter 2007), 1–24.

15. D. W. Meinig, *The Shaping of America*, vol. 3, *Transcontinental America, 1850–1915* (New Haven: Yale University Press, 1998), 38, 44–45; Matthew Klingle, *Emerald City: An Environmental History of Seattle* (New Haven: Yale University Press, 2007), 14–17, 46–49.

16. Steven W. Hackel, "Land, Labor, and Production: The Colonial Economy of Spanish and Mexican California," in *Contested Eden*, 111–146; Hackel, *Children of Coyote, Missionaries of Saint Francis: Indian-Spanish Relations in Colonial California, 1769–1850* (Chapel Hill: University of North Carolina Press for the Omohundro Institute of Early American History and Culture, 2005), 272–320. I use the terms *Native* and *Indian* interchangeably when referring to indigenous peoples

in aggregate to reflect the historical complexity behind these labels, preferring to use *Indian* in the context of relations with or comments by non-Indians whenever possible.

17. Matthew Morse Booker, "Real Estate and Refuge: An Environmental History of San Francisco's Tidal Wetlands, 1846–1972" (Ph.D. diss., Stanford University, 2005), 32–44; Albert Hurtado, *Indian Survival on the California Frontier* (New Haven: Yale University Press, 1988), 100–218; Stephen J. Pitti, *The Devil in Silicon Valley: Northern California, Race, and Mexican Americans* (Princeton: Princeton University Press, 2002), 1–50; Susan Lee Johnson, *Roaring Camp: The Social World of the California Gold Rush* (New York: W. W. Norton & Co., 1999), 25–234.

18. Alexandra Harmon, *Indians in the Making: Ethnic Relations and Indian Identities around Puget Sound* (Berkeley: University of California Press, 1999), 13–71.

19. For treaty negotiations, see Harmon, *Indians in the Making*, 72–86, 103–217. For Indian labor migration, see John Lutz, "Work, Sex, and Death on the Great Thoroughfare: Annual Migrations of 'Canadian Indians' to the American Pacific Northwest," in *Parallel Destinies: Canadian-American Relations West of the Rockies*, ed. John M. Findlay and Ken S. Coates (Seattle: Center for the Study of the Pacific Northwest in association with University of Washington Press; Montreal: McGill-Queen's University Press, 2002), 80–103; Paige Raibmon, *Authentic Indians: Episodes of Encounter from the Late-Nineteenth-Century Northwest Coast* (Durham: Duke University Press, 2005), 74–97. For Indians and Seattle's economy, see Thrush, *Native Seattle*, 47–49, 72–161. Seattle's case fits a larger pattern of city building and indigenous dispossession in the Anglo-American history of settler colonialism. For comparison, see Adele Perry, *On the Edge of Empire: Gender, Race, and the Making of British Columbia, 1849–1871* (Toronto: University of Toronto Press, 2001); and Catherine Hall, *Civilising Subjects: Colony and Metropole in the English Imagination, 1830–1867* (Chicago: University of Chicago Press, 2002).

20. Thrush, *Native Seattle*, 83–86.

21. David Igler, "The Industrial Far West: Region and Nation in the Late Nineteenth Century," *Pacific Historical Review* 69 (May 2000), 159–192.

22. Gunther Barth, *Instant Cities: Urbanization and the Rise of San Francisco and Denver* (New York: Oxford University Press, 1975); Andrew Isenberg, *Mining California: An Ecological History* (New York: Hill and Wang, 2005), 73–98; Thomas C. Cox, *Mills and Markets: A History of the Pacific Coast Lumber Industry to 1900* (Seattle: University of Washington Press, 1974), 46–137. Actual statistics, which included lumber from Puget Sound, the Columbia River, and California, were 75,523,000 million board feet (MBF) in 1860 and 147,631,000 MBF in 1867. See Cox, *Mills and Markets*, 303.

23. Booker, "Real Estate and Refuge," 72–79; Joanna Leslie Dyl, "Urban Disaster: An Environmental History of San Francisco after the 1906 Earthquake" (Ph.D. diss., Princeton University, 2006), 53–58. For fires and urban development, see Christine Meisner Rosen, *The Limits of Power: Great Fires and the Process of City Growth in America* (New York: Cambridge University Press, 1986).

24. C. A. Murdock, *A Backward Glance at Eighty: Recollections and Comment: Massachusetts 1841, Humboldt Bay 1854, San Francisco 1864* (San Francisco: P. Elder, 1921), 107, as quoted in Booker, "Real Estate and Refuge," 71.

25. John Muir, "The Bee Pastures," in *The Mountains of California* (New York: Century Company, 1894), 340–342, quoted in Booker, "Real Estate and Refuge," 105–106.

26. Booker, "Real Estate and Refuge," 124–125. According to Sucheng Chang, the profits reaped by delta tideland speculators were immense: after paying $1 to $4 per acre for swampland and spending another $6 to $12 to drain it, the Tide Land Reclamation Company sold it for $20 to $100

per acre. See *This Bittersweet Soil: The Chinese in California Agriculture, 1860–1910* (Berkeley: University of California Press, 1987), 185.

27. Booker, "Real Estate and Refuge," 148. Booker also quotes from sociologist Paul Taylor's interview with an unnamed observer of California agriculture during the Great Depression who said "we are not husbandsmen. We are not farmers. We are producing a product to sell." See Paul Taylor and Dorothea Lange, *American Exodus: A Record of Human Erosion* (New York: Reynal & Hitchcock, 1939), 147. For the "wageworkers' frontier," see Carlos A. Schwantes, "The Concept of a Wageworkers' Frontier: A Framework for Future Research," *Western Historical Quarterly* 18 (January 1987), 39–55.

28. Marshall Moore, "Address," December 9, 1867, in Charles M. Gates, *Messages of the Governors of the Territory of Washington to the Legislative Assembly, 1854–1889* (Seattle: University of Washington Press, 1940), 139, 142.

29. *Seattle Post-Intelligencer*, January 3, 14, February 19, December 30, 1888; January 10, 1889.

30. Thomas Burke to Carrie L. Allen, May 1, 1888, box 20, Thomas Burke Papers, Special Collections Division, University of Washington Libraries.

31. *Daily Intelligencer* (Seattle), July 27, 1879; Thomas Prosch, "A Chronological History of Seattle from 1850 to 1897," typescript (Seattle, 1901), 259–260, Special Collections Division, University of Washington Libraries. For Indians and fires, see Thrush, *Native Seattle*, 63–64. For the 1889 fire, see Clarence B. Bagley, *History of Seattle from the Earliest Settlement to the Present Time* (Chicago: S. J. Clarke Publishing, 1916), 419–428.

32. *Seattle Post-Intelligencer*, August 19, 23, 1889; Jacob Furth to William F. Prosser, April 16, 1890, box 2, Harbor Line Commission, Survey Notes, Correspondence, and Reports, Washington State Department of Natural Resources, Washington State Archives. For tideland laws, see Wilfred J. Airey, "A History of the Constitution and Government of Washington Territory" (Ph.D. diss., University of Washington, 1945), 497–521; and *Laws, Rules and Regulations Governing the Appraisement and Sale of Tidelands of the State of Washington* (Olympia, 1893), box 1, Harbor Line Commission Reports, Washington State Department of Natural Resources, Washington State Archives.

33. Padraic Burke, *A History of the Port of Seattle* (Seattle: Port of Seattle, 1976); and Richard C. Berner, *Seattle 1900–1920: From Boomtown, Urban Turbulence, to Restoration* (Seattle: Charles Press, 1991), 141–152.

34. Samuel A. Eliot, *Report Upon the Conditions and Needs of the Indians of the Northwest Coast* (Washington, DC: GPO, 1915), 17, 21. For Indian policy at the time, see Frances Paul Prucha, *The Great Father: The United States Government and the American Indian* (Lincoln: University of Nebraska Press, 1984), 2:657–686; Harmon, *Indians in the Making*, 131–159; and Thrush, *Native Seattle*, 85–91.

35. *Seattle Post-Intelligencer*, January 6, 7, May 11, 1910. For a similar analysis, see Thrush, "City of the Changers: Indigenous People and the Transformation of Seattle's Watersheds," *Pacific Historical Review* 75 (February 2006), 89–111.

36. David S. Torres-Rouff, "Water Use, Ethnic Conflict, and Infrastructure in Nineteenth-Century Los Angeles," *Pacific Historical Review* 75 (February 2006), 119–126.

37. For land claims conflicts in the Los Angeles area, see Karen Clay and Werner Troesken, "Ranchos and the Politics of Land Claims" in *Land of Sunshine: An Environmental History of Metropolitan Los Angeles*, ed. William Deverell and Greg Hise (Pittsburgh: University of Pittsburgh Press, 2005), 52–66. For cattle and gold mining, see Isenberg, *Mining California*, 101–130; Igler, *Industrial Cowboys: Miller & Lux and the Transformation of the Far West, 1850–1920* (Berkeley: University of California Press, 2001), 19–59.

38. City of Los Angeles, "Zanjero's Report, 1883," *Los Angeles Municipal Reports, 1879–1896*, 115, quoted in Torres-Rouff, "Water Use," 127.

39. Torres-Rouff, "Water Use," 127–140. For the Los Angeles River in this era, see Blake Gumprecht, *The Los Angeles River: Its Life, Death, and Possible Rebirth* (Baltimore: Johns Hopkins University Press, 1999), 9–130.

40. The classic study in this vein is Alexander Saxton, *The Indispensable Enemy: Labor and the Anti-Chinese Movement in California* (Berkeley: University of California Press, 1971). For an overview of the dual labor system, see Richard White, *"It's Your Misfortune and None of My Own": A New History of the American West* (Norman: University of Oklahoma Press, 1991), 282–288.

41. For racial covenants and residential discrimination, see Quintard Taylor, *The Forging of a Black Community: Seattle's Central District from 1870 through the Civil Rights Era* (Seattle: University of Washington Press, 1994), 79–158; Judy Yung, *Unbound Feet: A Social History of Chinese Women in San Francisco* (Berkeley: University of California Press, 1995); and Scott Kurashige, *The Shifting Grounds of Race: Black and Japanese Americans in the Making of Multiethnic Los Angeles* (Princeton: Princeton University Press, 2008), 13–90. For Seattle covenants in particular, see "Segregated Seattle: A Seattle Civil Rights and Labor History Project Special Section," http://depts.washington.edu/civilr/segregated.htm (accessed January 16, 2006).

42. For recent salient overviews, see Yong Chen, *Chinese San Francisco, 1850–1943: A Trans-Pacific Community* (Stanford: Stanford University Press, 2000); Madeline Yuan-yin Hsu, *Dreaming of Gold, Dreaming of Home: Transnationalism and Migration Between the United States and South China, 1882–1943* (Stanford: Stanford University Press, 2000); Adam M. McKeown, *Chinese Migrant Networks and Cultural Change: Peru, Chicago, and Hawaii, 1900–1936* (Chicago: University of Chicago Press, 2001); Erika Lee, *At America's Gates: Chinese Immigration during the Exclusion Era, 1882–1943* (Chapel Hill: University of North Carolina Press, 2003); and Sucheng Chan, ed., *Chinese American Transnationalism: The Flow of People, Resources, and Ideas between China and America During the Exclusion Era* (Philadelphia: Temple University Press, 2006). See also Chang, "Borderlands in a World at Sea," 384–403.

43. Arthur F. McEvoy, *The Fisherman's Problem: Ecology and Law in the California Fisheries* (New York: Cambridge University Press, 1986), 65–92; Chris Friday, *Organizing Asian-American Labor: The Pacific Coast Canned-Salmon Industry, 1870–1942* (Philadelphia: Temple University Press, 1994), 25–103. Patterns of racial segregation were consistent but often inverted elsewhere on the Pacific coast. Along the lower Fraser River and Strait of Georgia in British Columbia, Japanese immigrants dominated the fishery while cannery jobs were off limits for all but white Canadians. Similarly, Asian immigrants in Hawaii were relegated to harvesting sugar cane while white Americans ran the mills and plantation operations. See Patricia Roy, *A White Man's Province: British Columbia Politicians and Chinese and Japanese Immigrants, 1858–1914* (Vancouver: University of British Columbia Press, 1990), 64–268; and Ronald Takaki, *Pau Hana: Plantation Life and Labor in Hawaii, 1835–1920* (Honolulu: University of Hawaii Press, 1983).

44. Connie Y. Chiang, "'Monterey-by-the-Smell': Odors and Social Conflict on the California Coastline," *Pacific Historical Review* 73 (May 2004), 183–214; and *Shaping the Shoreline: Fisheries and Tourism on the Monterey Coast* (Seattle: University of Washington Press, 2008), 12–39.

45. Matthew Morse Booker, "Oyster Growers and Oyster Pirates in San Francisco Bay," *Pacific Historical Review* 75 (February 2006), 63–88.

46. For an overview of these hydrologic and social changes, see Klingle, *Emerald City*, 44–87; for the Duwamish River, see also George Blomberg, Charles Simenstad, and Paul Hickey, "Changes in Duwamish River Estuary Habitat over the Past 125 Years," *Proceedings: First Annual Meeting on Puget Sound Research* (Seattle: Puget Sound Water Quality Authority, 1988), 2:437–454.

47. For the original fisheries around Seattle, see Barton Warren Evermann and Seth Eugene Meek, "A Report upon Salmon Investigations in the Columbia River and Elsewhere on the Pacific Coast in 1896," *Bulletin of the United States Fish Commission for 1897* (Washington, DC: GPO), 34–47; R. Rathbun, "A Review of the Fisheries in the Contiguous Waters of the State of Washington and British Columbia," *Report of the United States Fish Commission for the Year Ending June 30, 1899* (Washington, DC: GPO, 1890), 251–350. For commercial fishing, see L. H. Darwin to Louis F. Hart, October 1, 1919, box 2J-1-18, Fisheries Commission File, 1919, Governors' Papers, Hart Group, Washington State Archives.

48. *Twenty-Eighth and Twenty-Ninth Annual Reports of the State Fish Commissioner, 1917–1919* (Olympia, WA, 1919), 10–13, WSA. For urban fishery politics, see Joseph E. Taylor III, *Making Salmon: An Environmental History of the Northwest Salmon Crisis* (Seattle: University of Washington Press, 1999), 166–202. For an overview of this conflict and the fishery closing, see Klingle, *Emerald City*, 173–176.

49. *Seattle Times*, July 31, 1928. For arrest records, see *Annual Reports of the State Fish Commissioner: Twenty-Eighth and Twenty-Ninth, 1917–1919* (Olympia, WA, 1919), 162; *Thirtieth and Thirty-First* (1919–1921), 202, 293–94; *Thirty-Second and Thirty-Third* (1921–1923), 44–45, 104; *Thirty-Fourth and Thirty-Fifth* (1923–1925), 63–64, 128; *Thirty-Sixth and Thirty-Seventh* (1925–1927), 123–124, 203, WSA. For other accounts, see *Seattle Times*, October 1, 6, 11, 1928.

50. Carl Abbott, *How Cities Won the West: Four Centuries of Urban Change in the North American West* (Albuquerque: University of New Mexico Press, 2008), 70–73; Berglund, *Making San Francisco American*, 171–217.

51. "The A.-Y.-P. Exposition," *World's Work* 18 (August 1909), 11890.

52. *Seattle Times*, August 29, 1909; Thrush, *Native Seattle*, 118–122. For world's fairs as racial exploitation, specifically along the Pacific Slope, see Robert W. Rydell, *All the World's a Fair: Visions of Empire at American International Expositions, 1876–1916* (Chicago: University of Chicago Press, 1984), 184–233.

53. *Seattle Times*, August 8, 1909. "Igorot" is one current and preferred term for this group of Philippines indigenous people. I use the 1909 original term in the main text as well.

54. Herbert C. Hoover to Charlie Field, April 29, 1912, as quoted in Rydell, 208. For another analysis of the connections between race, imperialism, and American frontier ideology, see Kramer, *The Blood of Government: Race, Empire, the United States and the Philippines* (Chapel Hill: University of North Carolina Press, 2006), 35–158, 229–284.

55. Abbott, *How Cities Won the West*, 73.

56. Frederick Jackson Turner, "The Significance of the Frontier in American History," in *The Frontier in American History* (New York: H. Holt and Co., 1899, 1920), 1–35. I borrow my analysis of Turner from Stuart M. Blumin, "Driven to the City: Urbanization and Industrialization in the Nineteenth Century," *OAH Magazine of History* (May 2006), 47.

57. Kerwin Klein, *Frontiers of Historical Imagination: Narrating the European Conquest of Native America, 1890–1990* (Berkeley: University of California Press, 1997), 78; see also Wrobel, 27–142.

58. Frank Norris, "The Frontier Gone at Last," *World's Work* 3 (February 1902), 1729–1730, also quoted in Wrobel, 73.

59. Wade, 1.

60. For the links between immigration restriction and overseas expansion in the United States and Canada, see Lee, *At America's Gates*; Adam M. McKeown, *Melancholy Order: Asian Migration and the Globalization of Borders* (New York: Columbia University Press, 2008); Kornel Chang, "Circulating Race and Empire: Transnational Labor Activism and the Politics of Anti-Asian Agitation

in the Anglo-American Pacific World, 1890–1910," *Journal of American History* 96 (December 2009), 678–701; and Andrea Geiger, *Subverting Exclusion: Transpacific Encounters with Race, Caste, and Borders, 1885–1928* (New Haven: Yale University Press, 2011).

61. Herbert Croly, *The Promise of American Life* (1909; reprint, Boston: Northeastern University Press, 1989), 22–23, 349–350; Wrobel, 79–80.

62. Theodore Roosevelt, "The Pioneer Spirit and American Problems," *Outlook* 96 (September 1910), 56–60, quoted in Wrobel, 80.

63. James Scott, *Seeing Like a State: How Certain Schemes to Improve the Human Condition Have Failed* (New Haven: Yale University Press, 1998), 2–3, 87–146. For the Owens River, see William L. Kahrl, *Water and Power: The Conflict over the Los Angeles Water Supply in the Owens River Valley* (Berkeley: University of California Press, 1983), 80–179. For city engineers, see Stanley K. Schultz, *Constructing Urban Culture: American Cities and City Planning, 1800–1920* (Philadelphia: Temple University Press, 1989), 153–205. For sanitarians, see Martin V. Melosi, *The Sanitary City: Environmental Services in Urban America from Colonial Times to the Present* (Baltimore: Johns Hopkins University Press, 1999).

64. For descriptions and analysis of the earthquake and fires, plus their aftermath, see Dyl, 27–77, 102–103; Philip L. Fradkin, *The Great Earthquake and Firestorms of 1906: How San Francisco Nearly Destroyed Itself* (Berkeley: University of California Press, 2005), 51–191. For the social ramifications of disasters on urban life, see Kevin Rozario, *The Culture of Calamity: Disaster and the Making of Modern America* (Chicago: University of Chicago Press, 2007).

65. Fradkin, 289–296; Dyl, 92–97.

66. Susan Craddock, *City of Plagues: Disease, Poverty, and Deviance in San Francisco* (Minneapolis: University of Minnesota Press, 2000), 1–123; and Nayan Shah, *Contagious Divides: Epidemics and Race in San Francisco's Chinatown* (Berkeley: University of California Press, 2001), 1–203.

67. Dyl, 190–228. See also Craddock, 124–160; Shah, 120–157.

68. Dyl, 226; see also "The War on Rats versus the Right to Keep Chickens: Plague and the Paving of San Francisco, 1907–1908," in *The Nature of Cities: Culture, Landscape, and Urban Space*, Studies in Comparative History Series, ed. Andrew Isenberg (Rochester, NY: University of Rochester Press in association with the Shelby Cullom Davis Center for Historical Studies at Princeton University, 2006), 38–61. For urban horses in their national context, see Clay McShane and Joel A. Tarr, *The Horse in the City: Living Machines in the Nineteenth Century* (Baltimore: Johns Hopkins University Press, 2007).

69. For ecological metaphors, see Peter A. Coates, *American Perceptions of Immigrant and Invasive Species: Strangers on the Land* (Berkeley: University of California Press, 2006), especially 18–21. For eugenics and immigration, see Mae M. Ngai, *Impossible Subjects: Illegal Aliens and the Making of Modern America* (Princeton: Princeton University Press, 2004), 15–90. For immigrants and disease, see Alan M. Kraut, *Silent Travelers: Germs, Disease, and the "Immigrant Menace"* (New York: Basic Books, 1994), 50–77.

70. For the Malthusian strain of frontier anxiety, see Wrobel, 112–121 (quotation at 117).

71. Shah, 158–258.

72. Daniel Johnson, "Pollution and Public Policy at the Turn of the Century" and Christopher G. Boone, "Zoning and Environmental Inequity on the Industrial East Side," in *Land of Sunshine*, 78–94, 167–178. For oil and beaches, see Paul Sabin, *Crude Politics: The California Oil Market, 1900–1940* (Berkeley: University of California Press, 2005), 53–78. For romanticizing California's Hispanic past, see William Deverell, *Whitewashed Adobe: The Rise of Los Angeles and the Remaking of Its Mexican Past* (Berkeley: University of California Press, 2004); and Phoebe S. Kropp, *California*

Vieja: Culture and Memory in a Modern American Place (Berkeley: University of California Press, 2006).

73. Steven Stoll, *The Fruits of Natural Advantage: Making the Industrial Countryside in California* (Berkeley: University of California Press, 1998), 124–154; and Douglas Cazaux Sackman, *Orange Empire: California and the Fruits of Eden* (Berkeley: University of California Press, 2005), 119–180.

74. George J. Sánchez, *Becoming Mexican American: Ethnicity, Culture, and Identity in Chicano Los Angeles, 1900–1945* (New York: Oxford University Press, 1993), 129–208; and Matt Garcia, *A World of Its Own: Race, Labor, and Citrus in the Making of Greater Los Angeles, 1900–1970* (Chapel Hill: University of North Carolina Press, 2001), 1–154.

75. Deverell, *Whitewashed Adobe*, 172–187.

76. Deverell, *Whitewashed Adobe*, 188–206. First quotation is from the *Los Angeles Herald Examiner*, October 17, 1958; second is from Samuel Holmes, "An Argument against Mexican Immigration," *Transactions of the Commonwealth Club of California* 21 (March 23, 1926), 23, both quoted in Deverell, *Whitewashed Adobe*, 188, 205. According to Deverell, the vast majority of those killed by the outbreak were Mexican.

77. Natalia Molina, *Fit to Be Citizens?: Public Health and Race in Los Angeles, 1879–1939* (Berkeley: University of California Press, 2006), 116–188.

78. Deverell, *Whitewashed Adobe*, 127–128.

79. Thomson to C. J. Moore, February 15, 1898, box 1, fol. 1, R. H. Thomson Papers, Special Collections Division, University of Washington Libraries. For demographics, see Thomson, "The Seattle Regrades," [c. 1930], 11, box 13, fol. 5, same location; and O. A. Piper, "Regrading in Seattle North District," [c. 1910], 1, Local Improvement District 4818, Letters, fol. 3, Seattle Engineering Department, Seattle Municipal Archives.

80. *Seattle Post-Intelligencer*, April 28, 1899.

81. Reginald Heber (R. H.) Thomson, *That Man Thomson*, ed. Grant H. Redford (Seattle: University of Washington Press, 1950), 63–70; Mary McWilliams, *Seattle Water Department History, 1854–1954* (Seattle: Water Department, 1954), 53–63. For a more sanguine overview of Thomson's tenure as city engineer, see William H. Wilson, *Shaper of Seattle: Reginald Heber Thomson's Pacific Northwest* (Pullman: Washington State University Press, 2009).

82. Thomson, "The Seattle Regrades," 3.

83. Thomson to Frederick J. Haskin, April 24, 1908, box 4, book 5, R. H. Thomson Papers, Special Collections Division, University of Washington Libraries.

84. R. M. Overstreet, "Hydraulic Excavation Methods in Seattle," *Engineering Record* 65 (May 4, 1912), 480–483. For an overview of early regrading, see Klingle, *Emerald City*, 98–104.

85. Arthur H. Dimock, "Preparing the Groundwork for a City: The Regrading of Seattle, Washington," *Transactions of the American Society of Civil Engineers*, Paper No. 1669, 92 (1928), 733.

86. Louis P. Zimmerman, "The Seattle Regrade, with Particular Reference to the Jackson Street Section," *Engineering News* 60 (November 12, 1908), 511; "The Jackson Street Regrade," 1.

87. *Wong Kee Jun v. Seattle*, 143 Wash. 505 (1927). The other "Jackson Street regrade cases" (as defined by the Court in *Davis v. Seattle*) were *Jorguson v. Seattle*, 80 Wash. 126 (1914); *Farnandis v. Seattle*, 95 Wash. 587 (1917); *Lochore v. Seattle*, 98 Wash. 265 (1917); *Blomskog, Erickson, and Cotton v. Seattle*, 107 Wash. 471 (1919); *Davis v. Seattle*, 134 Wash. 1 (1925); *Bingaman v. Seattle*, 139 Wash. 68 (1926); and *Hamm v. Seattle*, 140 Wash 427 (1926). Only in *Jorguson* did the Court find for the city.

88. Klingle, *Emerald City*, 181–185.

89. Roderick D. McKenzie, "The Ecological Approach to the Study of the Human Community," *American Journal of Sociology* 30 (November 1924), 298–301; Klingle, *Emerald City*, 192–197.

90. McKenzie, "Ecological Succession in the Puget Sound Region," *Publications of the American Sociological Society* 23 (1929), reprinted in *Roderick D. McKenzie on Human Ecology: Selected Writings*, ed. and intro. Amos H. Hawley (Chicago: University of Chicago Press, 1968), 243.

91. Donald Francis Roy, "Hooverville: A Study of a Community of Homeless Men in Seattle" (M.A. thesis, University of Washington, 1935), 1, 20–21.

92. *Seattle Star*, December 30, 1930; and Calvin Schmid, *Social Trends in Seattle*, Publications in the Social Sciences, vol. 14 (Seattle: University of Washington, 1944), 286–287.

93. "Protest against Shacks in the Interbay District," April 26, 1937, file 154992, Seattle City Clerk's (Comptroller's) Files, Seattle Municipal Archives; Berner, *Seattle, 1921–1940: From Boom to Bust* (Seattle: Charles Press, 1992), 183–187; Klingle, *Emerald City*, 197–201.

94. Paul Sabin, "Home and Abroad: The Two 'Wests' of Twentieth-Century United States History," *Pacific Historical Review* 66 (August 1997), 305–335, quotation at 318.

95. For energy and utility systems, see Bruce Stadfeld, "Electric Space: Social and Natural Transformations in British Columbia's Hydroelectric Industry to World War II" (Ph.D. diss., University of Manitoba, 2002); and Andrew Todd Needham, "Power Lines: Urban Space, Energy Development, and the Making of the Modern Southwest" (Ph.D. diss., University of Michigan, 2006). For weeds and other mobile biota, see Ian R. Tyrrell, *True Gardens of the Gods: Californian-Australian Environmental Reform, 1860–1930* (Berkeley: University of California Press, 1999); Klingle, "Spaces of Consumption in Environmental History," *History and Theory* 42 (December 2003), 94–110; Mark T. Fiege, "The Weedy West: Mobile Nature, Boundaries, and Common Space in the Montana Landscape," *Western Historical Quarterly* 36 (Spring 2005), 22–47; and Zachary J. S. Falck, *Weeds: An Environmental History of Metropolitan America* (Pittsburgh: University of Pittsburgh Press, 2011). For the challenges of identifying proper spatial and historical scales in environmental history, see Richard White, "The Nationalization of Nature," *Journal of American History* 86 (December 1999), 976–986; and Joseph E. Taylor, III, "Boundary Terminology," *Environmental History* 13 (July 2008), 454–481.

96. Dorothy Fujita-Rony, "Water and Land: Asian Americans and the U.S. West," *Pacific Historical Review* 76 (November 2007), 563–574; see also Patricia Nelson Limerick, "Disorientation and Reorientation: The American Landscape Discovered from the West," *Journal of American History* 79 (December 1992), 1021–1049. For environmental and labor history, see Gunther Peck, "The Nature of Labor: Fault Lines and Common Ground in Environmental and Labor History," *Environmental History* 11 (April 2006), 212–238; and Thomas G. Andrews, "'Made by Toile'? Tourism, Labor, and the Construction of the Colorado Landscape, 1858–1917," *Journal of American History* 92 (December 2005), 837–863.

97. For example, see Gunther Peck, *Reinventing Free Labor: Padrones and Immigrant Workers in the North American West, 1880–1930* (New York: Cambridge University Press, 2000); Fujita-Rony, *American Workers, Colonial Power: Philippine Seattle and the Transpacific West, 1919–1941* (Berkeley: University of California Press, 2003); Chen, *Chinese San Francisco*; Kramer, *Blood of Government*; and Geiger, *Subverting Exclusion*.

98. One suggestive study in this vein is Mansel G. Blackford, *Pathways to the Present: U.S. Development and Its Consequences in the Pacific* (Honolulu: University of Hawaii Press, 2007).

99. For landscape and forgetfulness, see Patricia Nelson Limerick, "Empire and Amnesia," *Historian* 66 (September 2004), 532–538; Don Mitchell, *The Lie of the Land: Migrant Workers and the California Landscape* (Minneapolis: University of Minnesota Press, 1996); and Dolores Hayden, *The Power of Place: Urban Landscapes as Public History* (Cambridge: MIT Press, 1995). For the frontier and the persistence of innocence, Patricia Nelson Limerick, *The Legacy of Conquest: The*

Notes to Pages 144–151

Unbroken Past of the American West (New York: W. W. Norton & Co., 1987), 35–54. For a compelling study of how certain frontier ideas about savagery and nature persist in a particular Utah landscape, see Jared Farmer, *On Zion's Mount: Mormons, Indians, and the American Landscape* (Cambridge: Harvard University Press, 2008). For a recent study of how past borderlands affect present-day borders, see Geraldo L. Cadava, "Borderlands of Modernity and Abandonment: The Lines within Ambos Nogales and the Tohono O'odham Nation," *Journal of American History* 98 (September 2011), 362–383.

100. For "metronatural" Seattle, see *Seattle Post-Intelligencer*, October 21, 2006; *Seattle Times*, October 21, 2006; and the Seattle Convention and Visitors Bureau web site at http://www.metro natural.com/ (accessed December 24, 2006).

101. Spencer Michaels, "Fear of SARS Hits San Francisco's Chinatown," *The NewsHour with Jim Lehrer*, April 25, 2003, http://www.pbs.org/newshour/bb/health/jan-june03/sars_04-25.html (accessed August 4, 2009); *Quarantine Stations at Ports of Entry Protecting the Public's Health* (Washington, DC: National Academy Press, 2005), 14–69. For how fears over SARS affected businesses and residents in Seattle's International District, the former Chinatown, see "SARS scare, economy keep Uwajimaya's sales flat," *Puget Sound Business Journal*, June 20, 2003. For pandemic disease monitoring, see Seattle and King County Department of Public Health, "Pandemic Flu Response Plans, Version 14," http://www.kingcounty.gov/healthservices/health/preparedness/pandemicflu/plan.aspx (accessed February 11, 2009); and Tom Costello, "Why Seattle Is Prepared for a Bird Flu Pandemic," *NBC Nightly News with Brian Williams*, April 26, 2006, http://www.msnbc.msn.com/id/12426421/ (accessed February 12, 2009).

102. For a small sample of the immigrant smuggling trade along the Pacific coast, see the following articles from the *Los Angeles Times*: "Smuggling of Chinese Ends in a Box of Death, Squalor," January 12, 2000; "Chinese Stowaways in Good Condition," April 4, 2001; and "Human Smuggling Operation Probed," January 17, 2005. For invasive species in California, see the web site for the intergovernmental agency, Invasive Species Council of California, established in 2009 to "coordinate and ensure complimentary, cost-efficient, environmentally sound and effective state activities regarding invasive species," http://www.iscc.ca.gov/ (accessed December 16, 2011).

103. Klingle, *Emerald City*, 263; for Portland, see Ellen Stroud, "Troubled Waters in Ecotopia: Environmental Racism in Portland, Oregon," *Radical History Review* 74 (Spring 1999), 65–95; for San Diego, see Kevin Delgado, "A Turning Point: The Conception and Realization of Chicano Park," *Journal of San Diego History* 44 (Winter 1998), 48–61; and J. Holtzman, "Barrio Logan, San Diego, California," www.umich.edu/%7Esnre492/holtzman.html#problem (accessed August 3, 2009).

104. For the quotation, see *Seattle Times*, January 4, 2009; for tribal recognition and opposition to it, see *Seattle Post-Intelligencer*, September 5, 2008, and July 15, 2009.

105. Wade, 342.

Chapter 8

1. Richard Wade, *The Urban Frontier: Pioneer Life in Early Pittsburgh, Cincinnati, Lexington, Louisville, and St. Louis* (Chicago: University of Chicago Press, 1959), 1.

2. Robert R. Dykstra, *The Cattle Towns* (New York: Atheneum, 1968), 99.

3. D. W. Meinig, *The Shaping of America: A Geographical Perspective on 500 Years of History*, vol. 1, *Atlantic America, 1492–1800* (New Haven: Yale University Press, 1986), 69; Carl Abbott, *How Cities Won the West: Four Centuries of Urban Change in Western North America* (Albuquerque:

University of New Mexico Press, 2008), 11, 44; Duncan Aikman, ed., *The Taming of the Frontier* (New York: Minton, Balch and Company, 1925), 204; Eugene P. Moehring, *Urbanism and Empire in the Far West, 1840–1890* (Reno: University of Nevada Press, 2004), 4, 13, 125, 128 .

4. Robert Bradford, Denver City, to W. B. Waddell, 18 January 1860, William Hepburn Russell, Alexander Majors, and William Bradford Waddell Papers, Huntington Library.

5. Abbott, *How Cities Won the West*, 21.

6. David Hamer, *New Towns in the New World: Images and Perceptions of the Nineteenth-Century Urban Frontier* (New York: Columbia University Press, 1990), 163.

7. D. W. Meinig, *The Shaping of America*, 69.

8. Abbott, *How Cities Won the West*, 24.

9. Bernard Bailyn, *The New England Merchant in the Seventeenth Century* (New York: Harper and Sons, 1964), 33.

10. Timothy R. Mahoney, *River Towns in the Great West: The Structure of Provincial Urbanization in the American Midwest, 1820–1870* (New York: Cambridge University Press, 1990), 209; Abbott, *How Cities Won the West*, 60–61.

11. Meinig, *The Shaping of America* , 66.

12. Mahoney, *River Towns in the Great West*, 210.

13. Bailyn, *The New England Merchant in the Seventeenth Century*, 34.

14. Bailyn, *The New England Merchant in the Seventeenth Century*, 60–74.

15. Virginia D. Harrington, *The New York Merchant on the Eve of Revolution* (Gloucester, Mass.: Peter Smith, 1964), 63–72.

16. Alan Taylor, *William Cooper's Town: Power and Persuasion on the Frontier of the Early American Republic* (New York: Alfred A. Knopf, 1995), 107–111, 437.

17. Mahoney, *River Towns in the Great West*, 110.

18. Timothy R. Mahoney, "Down in Davenport (I): Antebellum Town Economic Development in a Regional Perspective," *Annals of Iowa* 50 (Summer 1990), 457, 460–65.

19. Mahoney, "Down in Davenport (I)," 460–65.

20. Wilma Daddario, "Side by Side, the Stout Farmer and the Keen-Eyed Speculator: Founding and Shaping Nebraska City, 1854–1870" (M.A. thesis, University of Nebraska, 1992), 14, 25; Robert Bradford, Denver City, to W. B. Waddell, 19 October 1859, 3 November 1859, 29 November 1859, William Hepburn Russell, Alexander Majors and William Bradford Waddell Papers, Huntington Library, San Marino, California; Abbott, *How Cities Won the West*, 79.

21. Abbott, *How Cities Won the West*, 79–80.

22. *North American and United States Gazette*, 15 December 1853.

23. Lore Ann Guilmartin, "Textiles from the Steamboat Bertrand: Clothing and Gender on the Montana Mining Frontier" (Ph.D. thesis, Texas A&M University, 2002), 45–46.

24. Lewis Atherton, *The Frontier Merchant in Mid-America* (Columbia: University of Missouri Press, 1971), 98.

25. Abbott, *How Cities Won the West*, 46.

26. Gunther Barth, *Instant Cities, Urbanization and the Rise of San Francisco and Denver* (New York: Oxford University Press, 1975), xiii.

27. Abbott, *How Cities Won the West*, 12.

28. Abbott, *How Cities Won the West*, 32.

29. Moehring, *Urbanism and Empire*, 175.

30. Mark Eifler, *Gold Rush Capitalists: Greed and Growth in Sacramento* (Albuquerque: University of New Mexico Press, 2002), 56–60.

31. William Cronon, *Nature's Metropolis: Chicago and the Great West* (New York: W. W. Norton and Company, 1991).

32. Abbott, *How Cites Won the West*, 46.

33. Guilmartin, "Textiles from the Steamboat Bertrand," 2.

34. Don L. and Jean Harvey Griswold, *The Carbonate Camp Called Leadville* (Denver: University of Denver Press, 1951).

35. Henry Veith Papers, Nebraska State Historical Society.

36. Abbott, *How Cities Won the West*, 13.

37. Timothy H. Breen, "Looking Out for Number One: Conflicting Cultural Values in Early Seventeenth-Century Virginia," *South Atlantic Quarterly* 78:3 (1979), 342–360; Timothy R. Mahoney, "'A Common Band of Brotherhood': The Booster Ethos, Male Subcultures, and the Origins of Urban Social Order in the Midwest of the 1840s," *Journal of Urban History* (July 1999), 619–646; Robert R. Dykstra, *The Cattle Towns* (New York: Atheneum, 1968), 248.

38. Alexandra Fuller, *The Legend of Colton H. Bryant* (New York: Penguin Press, 2008), 84.

39. Dykstra, *The Cattle Towns*, 248.

40. Aikman, *The Taming of the Frontier*.

Chapter 9

1. Estwick Evans, *A Pedestrious Tour, of four thousand miles through the western states and territories, during the winter and spring of 1818 interspersed with brief reflections upon a great variety of topics* . . . (Concord, NH: Joseph C. Spear, 1819), 191.

2. Thomas Jefferson, *Notes on the State of Virginia*, in *Jefferson: Writings*, ed. Merrill D. Peterson (New York: Library of America, 1894), 291.

3. John William Reps, *Cities on Stone: Nineteenth Century Lithograph Images of the Urban West* (Fort Worth, TX: Amon Carter Museum, 1976); John William Reps, *John Caspar Wild: Painter and Printmaker of Nineteenth-Century Urban America* (St. Louis: Missouri Historical Society Press; distributed by University of Missouri Press, 2006).

4. For revealing studies of the ethnic and racial component of travel narratives, maps, and other forms of cultural production, see Wayne Franklin, *Discoverers, Explorers, Settlers: The Diligent Writers of Early America* (Chicago: University of Chicago Press, 1979); Thomas Hallock, *From the Fallen Tree: Frontier Narratives, Environmental Politics, and the Roots of a National Pastoral, 1749–1826* (Chapel Hill: University of North Carolina Press, 2003); Stephanie LeMenager, *Manifest and Other Destinies: Territorial Fictions of the Nineteenth-Century United States* (Lincoln: University of Nebraska Press, 2004); Elizabeth Vibert, *Traders' Tales: Narratives of Cultural Encounters in the Columbia Plateau, 1807–1846* (Norman: University of Oklahoma Press, 1997).

5. The scholarship on American print culture is both deep and rich. For selected studies that chronicle the growth, content, and circulation of that print culture, see Jeffrey L. Pasley, *The Tyranny of Printers: Newspaper Politics in the Early American Republic* (Charlottesville: University Press of Virginia, 2001); David Waldstreicher, *In the Midst of Perpetual Fetes: The Making of American Nationalism, 1776–1820* (Chapel Hill: University of North Carolina Press, 1997); Michael Warner, *The Letters of the Republic: Publication and the Public Sphere in Eighteenth-Century America* (Cambridge: Harvard University Press, 1990).

6. For the development of geographic publishing, see Martin Brückner, *The Geographic*

Revolution in Early America: Maps, Literacy, and National Identity (Chapel Hill: University of North Carolina Press, 2006). For travel narratives, see Bruce Greenfield, *Narrating Discovery: The Romantic Explorer in American Literature, 1790–1855* (New York: Columbia University Press, 1992); Hallock, *From the Fallen Tree*; Larzer Ziff, *Writing in the New Nation: Prose, Print, and Politics in the Early United States* (New Haven: Yale University Press, 1991); Larzer Ziff, *Return Passages: Great American Travel Writing, 1780–1910* (New Haven: Yale University Press, 2000).

7. Paul W. Mapp, *The Elusive West and the Contest for Empire, 1713–1763* (Chapel Hill: University of North Carolina Press for the Omohundro Institute of Early American History and Culture, 2011).

8. Peter J. Kastor, *William Clark's World: Describing America in an Age of Unknowns* (New Haven: Yale University Press, 2011), 62–67, 78–87.

9. Brückner, *The Geographic Revolution in Early America*; John R. Short, *Representing the Republic: Mapping the United States, 1600–1900* (London: Reaktion, 2001), 144–162.

10. For the role of landscape description (primarily surveying) in land ownership, see Edward T. Price, *Dividing the Land: Early American Beginnings of Our Private Property Mosaic* (Chicago: University of Chicago Press, 1995); Alan Taylor, *William Cooper's Town: Power and Persuasion on the Frontier of the Early American Republic* (New York: Norton, 1995).

11. D. A. Hamer, *New Towns in the New World* (New York: Columbia University Press, 1990).

12. Zadok Cramer, *The Ohio and Mississippi Navigator* . . . (Pittsburgh: Zadok Cramer, 1802), 20.

13. Cramer, *The Navigator (1802)*, 26.

14. Zadok Cramer, *The Navigator: Containing Directions for Navigating the Monongahela, Alleghany, Ohio and Mississippi Rivers* . . . (Pittsburgh: Z. Cramer, 1808); Zadok Cramer, *The Navigator: Containing Directions for Navigating the Monongahela, Allegheny, Ohio, and Mississippi Rivers, with an ample account of these much admired waters* . . . (Pittsburgh: Cramer, Spear, and Eichbaum, 1811); Zadok Cramer, *The Navigator: Containing Directions for Navigating the Monongahela, Alleghany, Ohio, and Mississippi rivers, with an ample account of these much admired waters . . . and a concise description of their towns* (Pittsburgh: Cramer, Spear, and Eichbaum, 1814); Zadok Cramer, *The Navigator...to which is added an appendix, containing an account of Louisiana, and of the Missouri and Columbia Rivers, as discovered by the voyage under Capts. Lewis and Clark* (Pittsburgh: Cramer, Spear and Eichbaum, 1817); Zadok Cramer, *The Navigator . . . To which is added an appendix, containing an account of Louisiana, and of the Missouri and Columbia rivers, as discovered by the voyage under Capts. Lewis and Clark* (Pittsburgh: Cramer & Spear, 1824).

15. In 1807, Cramer secured a plum contract when he published the journals of Patrick Gass, in the process releasing the first account of the Lewis and Clark Expedition based on the manuscript journals of one of the explorers. But even in this situation, Cramer included no illustrations or maps, and only in later editions did he begin to include crude woodcuts. More relevantly, however, there was no visual representation of frontier settlements like Pittsburgh that Cramer promoted so vigorously. See Patrick Gass, *A Journal of the Voyages and Travels of a Corps of Discovery: Under the Command of Capt. Lewis and Capt. Clarke of the Army of the United States, from the Mouth of the River Missouri Through the Interior Parts of North America to the Pacific Ocean, During the years 1804, 1805 & 1806* . . . (Pittsburgh: Zadok Cramer, 1807); Patrick Gass, *Journal of the Voyages and Travels of a Corps of Discovery Under the Command of Capt. Lewis and Capt. Clarke, of the Army of the United States, from the mouth of the river Missouri through the interior parts of North America to the Pacific Ocean, during the years 1804, 1805, and 1806* (Philadelphia: Mathew Carey, 1810 and 1812).

16. For studies of Filson and *History of Kentucke*, see Hallock, *From the Fallen Tree*, 56–76.

17. This was apparently the only major map published by Pursell, who remains something of mystery, leaving no record of his training or experience. While Pursell's map of Kentucky was widely distributed and featured prominently as a source for numerous other maps, none of the major map collections in the United States indicates that Pursell himself created other maps. Likewise, Pursell does not feature in the correspondence surrounding Filson's publication, or record or the work of other cartographers.

18. John Garretson Clark, *New Orleans, 1718–1812: An Economic History* (Baton Rouge: Louisiana State University Press, 1970); Daniel H. Usner, Jr., *Indians, Settlers, and Slaves in a Frontier Exchange Economy: The Lower Mississippi Valley Before 1783* (Chapel Hill: University of North Carolina Press, 1992).

19. Philip Pittman, *Plan of New Orleans* (London: J. Nourse, 1770); *The Isles of Montreal as they have been survey'd by the French engineers* (Montreal: n.p., 1761).

20. H. M. Brackenridge, *Views of Louisiana* (Pittsburgh: Cramer, Spear, and Eichbaum, 1814); Amos Stoddard, *Sketches, Historical and Descriptive, of Louisiana* (Philadelphia: Mathew Carey, 1812).

21. The debate over what constitutes a frontier has a rich history all to itself. My own working definition emerges from Greg Nobles's useful terminology of an intercultural contact zone where no one particular group wields political or cultural control. See Gregory H. Nobles, *American Frontiers: Cultural Encounters and Continental Conquest* (New York: Hill & Wang, 1997), Preface.

22. Jedidiah Morse, *Geography Made Easy* (New Haven: Meigs, Bowen, and Dana, 1784), 112–113.

23. For selected examples, see Pierre-François-Xavier de Charlevoix, *Journal of a Voyage to North-America.Undertaken by order of the French King. Containing the Geographical Description and Natural History of that Country, Particularly Canada . . .* (London: R. and J. Dodsley, 1761); Antoine-Simon Le Page du Pratz, *The History of Louisiana, or of the Western Parts of Virginia and Carolina . . .* (London: T. Becket and P. A. De Hondt, 1763); Thomas Jefferys, *The Natural and Civil History of the French Dominions in North and South America . . .* (London: T. Jefferys, 1760); James Pitot, *Observations on the Colony of Louisiana from 1796 to 1802* (Baton Rouge: Louisiana State University Press, 1979). In addition, many of the late eighteenth-century European travel narratives that circulated throughout the United States were later republished in Reuben Gold Thwaites, *Early Western Travels, 1748–1846* (Cleveland: A. H. Clark Company, 1904).

24. The European and Euro-American belief in Indian laziness has been a central concern of a vast literature on intercultural contact, European science, and federal policy. For examples, see Robert F. Berkhofer, *The White Man's Indian: Images of the American Indian from Columbus to the Present* (New York: Vintage Books, 1979); Terry Jay Ellingson, *The Myth of the Noble Savage* (Berkeley: University of California Press, 2001); Harry Liebersohn, *Aristocratic Encounters: European Travelers and North American Indians* (Cambridge: Cambridge University Press, 1998); John F. Moffitt and Santiago Sebastián, *O Brave New People: The European Invention of the American Indian* (Albuquerque: University of New Mexico Press, 1996); Bernard W. Sheehan, *Seeds of Extinction: Jeffersonian Philanthropy and the American Indian* (Chapel Hill: University of North Carolina Press, 1973), 102–105; Anthony F. C. Wallace, *Jefferson and the Indians: The Tragic Fate of the First Americans* (Cambridge: Belknap Press of Harvard University Press, 1999), 180–203.

25. Pitot, *Observations on the Colony of Louisiana*, 29.

26. Brackenridge, *Views of Louisiana*; Stoddard, *Sketches, Historical and Descriptive, of Louisiana*.

27. Thomas Jefferson to Meriwether Lewis, 20 June 1803, *Letters of the Lewis and Clark*

Expedition, With Related Documents 1783–1854, ed. Donald Jackson (Urbana: University of Illinois Press, 1978), 1:61–66; Jefferson to Lewis, 16 November 1803, *Letters of the Lewis and Clark Expedition*, 1:137; Jefferson to Thomas Freeman, 14 April 1804, *Papers of Thomas Freeman, 1796–1807*, Manuscript Division, Library of Congress; James Wilkinson to Zebulon Pike, 30 July 1805 and 24 June 1806, both in *The Journals of Zebulon Montgomery Pike*, ed. Donald Jackson (Norman: University of Oklahoma Press, 1966), 1:3–4 and 285–287.

28. *History of the Expedition under the Command of Captains Lewis and Clark, to the sources of the Missouri, thence across the Rocky Mountains and down the river Columbia to the Pacific Ocean: Performed during the years 1804-5-6 by order of the government of the United States* (Philadelphia: Bradford and Inskeep, 1814); Zebulon Montgomery Pike, *An Account of Expeditions to the Sources of the Mississippi: and through the western parts of Louisiana to the sources of the Arkansaw, Kans, La Platte, and Pierre Jaun Rivers . . .* (Philadelphia: C. & A. Conrad & Co., 1810); *Message from the President of the United States, communicating discoveries made in exploring the Missouri, Red River, and Washita, by Captains Lewis and Clark, Doctor Sibley, and Mr. Dunbar; with a statistical account of the countries adjacent. February 19, 1806* (Washington: A. and G. Way, 1806); *An Account of the Red River, in Louisiana, Drawn up from the Returns of Messrs. Freeman and Custis to the War Office of the United States, who Explored the Same, in the year of 1806* (Washington, 1806). The notion of Indian cities, and their connection to early western explorers, has been most thoroughly developed in Carolyn Gilman, *Lewis and Clark: Across the Divide* (Washington, DC: Smithsonian Books, 2003).

29. Jedidiah Morse, *A Report to the Secretary of War of the United States, on Indian Affairs, comprising a narrative of a tour performed in the summer of 1820* (New Haven: Converse, 1822). For Morse's travel and observations, see Richard Morse to Elizabeth Morse, 13, 22, and 23 June 1820, *Morse Family Papers, 1779–1868*, Beinecke Rare Book and Manuscript Library, Yale University.

30. For examples, see Henry Rowe Schoolcraft, *A View of the Lead Mines of Missouri . . .* (New York: Charles Wiley & Co., 1819); Henry Rowe Schoolcraft, *Travels in the central portions of the Mississippi valley: Comprising observations on its mineral geography, internal resources, and aboriginal population* (New York,: Collins and Hannay, 1825); Henry Rowe Schoolcraft, *Narrative of an expedition through the upper Mississippi to Itasca Lake: the actual source of this river: embracing an exploratory trip through the St. Croix and Burntwood (or Broule) Rivers: in 1832* (New York: Harper, 1834).

31. Schoolcraft, *Travels in the central portions of the Mississippi valley*, 51–52.

32. Kastor, *William Clark's World*, 233–244.

33. Peter J. Kastor, "'What Are the Advantages of the Acquisition?': Inventing Expansion in the Early American Republic," *American Quarterly* 60: 4 (2008), 1027–1030.

34. John William Reps, *John Caspar Wild: Painter and Printmaker of Nineteenth-Century Urban America* (St. Louis: Missouri Historical Society Press, distributed by University of Missouri Press, 2006); J. C. Wild, *The Valley of the Mississippi: Illustrated in a Series of Views* (St. Louis: Chambers and Knapp, 1841).

Chapter 10

1. For a list of McDermott's publications and scholarly collaborations see the calendar to his papers. Allan McCurry, *John Francis McDermott Research Papers: A Descriptive Inventory* (Edwardsville: Southern Illinois University, 1985).

2. Correspondence files, McDermott Research Collection, Lovejoy Library, Southern Illinois University at Edwardsville.

3. McDermott Research Collection; SIUE.

4. For a discussion of these issues, see Alden T. Vaughan, *New England Frontier: Puritans and Indians, 1620–1675* (Boston: Little, Brown, 1965); Douglas E. Leach, *Flintlock and Tomahawk: New England in King Philip's War* (New York: W. W. Norton, 1966).

5. McDermott wrote his seminal "The Confines of the Wilderness" as published in *The Missouri Historical Review* 29:1 (October) in 1934 and built upon similar research in the city's probate records throughout the 1930s.

6. For early St. Louis's history, see Charles E. Peterson, *Colonial St. Louis: Building a Creole Capital* (St. Louis: Missouri Historical Society, 1949); J. Thomas Scharf, *History of St. Louis City and County* (Philadelphia: Everts, 1883); James N. Primm, *Lion of the Valley: St. Louis, Missouri* (Boulder: Pruett, 1981). J. F. McDermott, *Private Libraries in Creole St. Louis* (Baltimore: Johns Hopkins University Press, 1938) gives an excellent rendition of St. Louis citizens and citations to the authors listed above.

7. McDermott, *Private Libraries in Creole St. Louis,* part 2, 23–169.

8. On the organization of early libraries in private hands on both sides of the Atlantic, see Helmut Lehmann-Haupt, *The Book in America* (New York: Bowker, 1951), 194–259.

9. McDermott, *Private Libraries*, 24; McDermott Research Collection, Southern Illinois University at Edwardsville, Box 43/20–21 and Box 49–54; St. Louis Probate Court Historical Records; French and Spanish Archives of St. Louis.

10. Ibid., 26.

11. Ibid., 62.

12. Ibid., 90.

13. Ibid., 128–166.

14. *Narrative on the Founding of St. Louis by Auguste Chouteau* (ca. 1806), St. Louis Mercantile Library Special Collections, University of Missouri, St. Louis.

15. It seems very possible that an audience of readers who were literate in both French and English existed in a variety of North American towns from Quebec City and Montreal to New Orleans—and including St. Louis and Detroit. The *Montreal Gazette/Gazette de Montréal*, for example, printed various sections in only one language (literature often in English, political items often in French). This suggests an audience that could read both languages, and we know that the fur trade in the late eighteenth and early nineteenth centuries promoted fluency in both languages for those employed in positions requiring literacy. Bilingualism in such frontier cities is a topic that has not been studied and would benefit from bibliographical investigations. For more on Montréal, see Yvan Lamonde and Patricia Lockhart Fleming, *Cultural Crossroads: Print and Reading in Eighteenth- and Nineteenth-Century Montreal* (Worcester, MA: American Antiquarian Society, 2004).

16. For information on the early imprints of early Missouri printers, such as Joseph Charless, see Viola A. Perotti, *Important Firsts in Missouri Imprints* (Kansas City: Perotti, 1967); also David Kaser, *A Directory of the St. Louis Book and Printing Trades to 1850* (New York: New York Public Library, 1961).

17. John Neal Hoover, *The First St. Louis Library: Books and People on the Missouri Frontier, 1811–1851* (St. Louis: St. Louis Mercantile Library, 1989); McDermott, "Private Libraries in Frontier St. Louis," *Papers of the Bibliographical Society of America* (March 1957), 21–37; McDermott, "The First Book Store in Early St. Louis," *Mid-America* (July 1939), 21–37.

18. Hoover, *The First St. Louis Library.* Additional records on the history of the St. Louis Lyceum are held by the Jefferson National Expansion Memorial Library.

19. McDermott, "Public Libraries on St. Louis, 1811–1839," *Library Quarterly* (January 1944),

9–27; Hoover, *Cultural Cornerstone, 1846–1998: The Earliest Catalogues of the St. Louis Mercantile Library* (St. Louis: University of Missouri, 1998).

20. Michael Winship, *A History of the Book in America*, vol. 3, *The Industrial Book, 1840–1880* (Chapel Hill: University of North Carolina Press, 2007), 129–130.

21. Winship, 130.

22. Records of the St. Louis Lyceum are in the Special Collection of the St. Louis Mercantile Library at the University of Missouri, St. Louis; additional bibliographical information has been gleaned from the accessions records of the Mercantile Library preserved in the Library's archives.

23. St. Louis Mercantile Library Accession Records, St. Louis Mercantile Library Archives.

24. Peterson, *Colonial St. Louis*.

25. See Aubrey Starke, "Books in the Wilderness," *Journal of the Illinois State Historical Society* (January 1936), 258–270. For further examples, the St. Louis Mercantile Library alone possesses three distinct "frontier" libraries: the earliest public library collection described above, the John Mason Peck collection of books and papers, and the Ethan Allen Hitchcock collection.

Epilogue

1. John Warner Barber, *History and Antiquities of New Haven, Connecticut, from Its Earliest Settlement to the Present Time* (New Haven, 1831); Leonard Bacon, *Thirteen Historical Discourses, on the Completion of Two Hundred Years: From the Beginning of the First Church in New Haven* (New Haven: Durrie and Peck, 1839). For more on this process, see Jean M. O'Brien, *Firsting and Lasting: Writing Indians out of Existence in New England* (Minneapolis: University of Minnesota Press, 2010).

2. See also more modern histories such as Rollin G. Osterweis, *Three Centuries of New Haven, 1638–1938* (New Haven: Yale University Press, 1953); and Floyd Shumway and Richard Hegel, eds., *New Haven: An Illustrated History* (Woodland Hills, CA: Windsor Publications, 1981).

3. Lauric Henneton, "Plots and Rumours of Plots: The Geopolitics of the Greater Long Island Sound in the Mid-Seventeenth Century," paper given at the Omohundro Institute of Early American History and Culture Conference, New Paltz, NY, June 17, 2011, 3.

4. Charles H. Townshend, *The Quinnipiack Indians and Their Reservation* (New Haven: Tuttle, Morehouse and Taylor, 1900).

5. For the best and only modern history of these events and the reservation, see John Mehta, *The Quinnipiac: Cultural Conflict in Southern New England* (New Haven: Yale University Publications in Anthropology, 2003).

6. Joanna Brooks, ed., *The Collected Writings of Samson Occom, Mohegan* (New York: Oxford University Press, 2006), 23, 162–164. See also John Mehta, *The Quinnipiac: Cultural Conflict in Southern New England* (New Haven: Yale University Publications in Anthropology, 2003), 179–180.

7. Brooks, *Collected Writings of Samson Occom*, 35. The town and Yale's other famous preacher and writer, Jonathan Edwards, spent a significant portion of his career as an Indian missionary in Stockbridge, Massachusetts. Though he never mastered an Indian language, his second son, also Jonathan Edwards, became fluent in Mahican and wrote a significant treatise on Indian languages. Jonathan Edwards, Jr., *Observations on the Language of the Muhhekaneew Indians, in Which the Extent of that Language in North America is Shewn, its Genius is Grammatically Traced, Some of its Peculiarities, and Some Instances of Analogy between that and the Hebrew are Pointed out* (New Haven: Josiah Meigs, 1787).

8. Unlike her brother and other Mohegans who joined the Brotherton movement and relocated

to upstate New York. As Joanna Brooks notes, "female-headed tribal factions tended to resist removal from traditional lands." Brooks, *Collected Writings of Samson Occom*, 28.

9. Brooks, *Collected Writings of Samson Occom*, 28. Gladys Tantaquidgeon was a descendant of Lucy Occom Tantaquidgeon.

10. See, for example, Jay Gitlin's Introduction to Margaret Van Horn Dwight, *A Journey to Ohio in 1810* (New Haven: Yale University Press, 1913; Lincoln: University of Nebraska Press, Bison Books, 1991).

11. New Haven merchants early on became involved with the local fur trade. By the early nineteenth century, a new generation had turned to the maritime version—a seal-hunting fleet in the South Atlantic—with such "success that one stretch of beach used to dry furs on the coast of Patagonia was known as the New Haven Green." Pelts were taken to distant markets such as Canton and accounted for a "considerable fraction" of the city's wealth. See Douglas W. Rae, *City: Urbanism and Its End* (New Haven: Yale University Press, 2003), 44.

12. Adam S. Horowitz, "Sí se puede (bailar) / Yes we can (dance): Stories of Performance and Migration in New Haven, CT" (Senior essay, Yale College, 2009), 10–12.

13. Rosanna Ensley, "Peerless Pageant: The First Ten Years of Tampa's Gasparilla Festival," *Tampa Bay History* 21 (2007), 20–35.

14. Canter Brown, Jr., *Tampa Before the Civil War* (Tampa, FL: University of Tampa Press, 1999), 7; Nancy Hewitt, *Southern Discomfort, Women's Activism in Tampa, Florida, 1880s-1920s* (Urbana: University of Illinois Press, 2001), 23.

15. Brown, *Tampa Before the Civil War*, 25–27.

16. Hewitt, *Southern Discomfort,* 23; Robert P. Ingalls, *Urban Vigilantes in the New South: Tampa, 1882-1936* (Gainesville: University Press of Florida, 1988), 2–3; Brown, *Tampa Before the Civil War*, 23 and 65.

17. W. H. Timmons, *El Paso: A Borderlands History* (El Paso: Texas Western Press, 1990), 12–14.

18. Marc Simmons, *The Last Conquistador: Juan de Oñate and the Settling of the Far Southwest* (Norman: University of Oklahoma Press, 1991), 99–101.

19. Timmons, 74.

20. Timmons, 183.

21. See Timmons, especially chapter 7, 169–206.

22. Yolanda Chávez Leyva, "Moments of Conformity: Commemorating and Protesting Oñate on the Border," *New Mexico Historical Review* 82:3 (Summer 2007), 343–367.

23. Abraham Zamora, "*Barrio de los Indios*: The Tiguas and the Urban Landscape of El Paso" (M.A. paper, University of Texas at El Paso, Spring 2011).

24. Howard Lamar and Leonard Thompson, eds., *The Frontier in History: North America and Southern Africa Compared* (New Haven: Yale University Press, 1981), 3–13.

CONTRIBUTORS

Adam Arenson is an assistant professor of history at the University of Texas at El Paso. He is the author of *The Great Heart of the Republic: St. Louis and the Cultural Civil War* and is currently researching the art, architecture, and urban context of the Home Savings and Loan buildings built between 1954 and 1990.

Barbara Berglund is associate professor of history at the University of South Florida and the author of *Making San Francisco American: Cultural Frontiers in the Urban West, 1846-1906*. Her work focuses on the intersection of cultural forms and social power—with particular attention to race, class, and gender— usually in the cities of the urban Far West.

Alan Gallay holds the Lyndon Baines Johnson Chair in American History at Texas Christian University. His most recent book is *Colonial and Revolutionary America*.

Carolyn Gilman is special projects historian at the Missouri History Museum and author of seven books on frontier and western history. She is currently working on a book about the American Revolution on the frontier.

Jay Gitlin has taught history at Yale University since 1985. He is the author of *The Bourgeois Frontier: French Towns, French Traders, and American Expansion*. The associate director of the Howard R. Lamar Center for the Study of Frontiers and Borders, he also serves as a faculty adviser in the urban studies program.

John Neal Hoover is the director of the St. Louis Mercantile Library Association at the University of Missouri–St. Louis, where he also is a member of the faculty of the Departments of History and Museum Studies. He is the immediate past president of the Bibliographical Society of America and author of

St. Louis and the Art of the Frontier and *Adventures and Sufferings: The Indian Captivity Narrative Through the Centuries*.

Peter J. Kastor is professor of history and American culture studies at Washington University in St. Louis. His most recent book is *William Clark's World: Describing America in an Age of Unknowns*.

Matthew Klingle is associate professor of history and environmental studies at Bowdoin College in Brunswick, Maine. He is the author of *Emerald City: An Environmental History of Seattle* as well as essays and articles.

Timothy R. Mahoney is professor of history at the University of Nebraska–Lincoln. He is the author of *River Towns in the Great West* and *Provincial Lives* and coeditor of *Regionalism and the Humanities*.

Karen Marrero is the 2012 Earhart Foundation Fellow in American History at the William L. Clements Library at the University of Michigan. She holds a Ph.D. in history from Yale University. She has published in the *Journal of Colonialism and Colonial History*, *Canadian Review of American Studies*, and most recently with the University of Missouri Press.

Brett Rushforth is an associate professor of history at the College of William and Mary, where he teaches courses on the history of early America, American Indians, comparative slavery, and the Atlantic World. He is the author of *Bonds of Alliance: Indigenous and Atlantic Slaveries in New France*.

Daniel Usner is the Holland M. McTyeire Professor of History at Vanderbilt University. He regularly teaches a course on the history of New Orleans and is currently writing a book entitled *From Bayou Teche to Fifth Avenue: Crafting a New Market for Chitimacha Indian Baskets*.

Elliott West is the Alumni Distinguished Professor of History at the University of Arkansas and author of several books on western social, environmental and American Indian history, including *The Contested Plains: Indians, Goldseekers and the Rush to Colorado* and, most recently, *The Last Indian War: The Nez Perce Story*.

INDEX

Abbott, Carl, 151, 154, 160, 163
Abenaki Indians, 59, 65
absolutism, royal, 51, 222 n.8
Acapulco, city of, 13, 21, 25
Acolapissa Indians, 33, 37
Africa, 7, 12, 14, 16, 42
African Americans, 28, 29, 138, 142; in Seattle, 140, 142; in slavery, 30, 34; in Tampa, 204
agriculture, 96, 97; California, 109–10, *111*; environmental effects of, 118; mechanized, 116
air travel, 119
Alaska, 130, 143
Albany (N.Y.), town of, 80, 156; fur trade at, 69; Iroquois traders and, 51, 69; Lamoureux in, 62, 64; liquor smuggling and, 51, 62, 64
Albuquerque, Afonso de, 16
Algonquian-speakers, 50, 56, 59–60, 62, 63, 75; Great Peace of Montreal and, 67–68, 69, 72; multi-ethnic and multilingual communities, 70
Alton (Ill.), town of, 154, 155
American Revolution, 39, 52, 84, 96, 231 n.17
amusement, place of, 5, 6
Anchorage (Alaska), town of, 162, 163
Anderson, John, 91
Anglicans, 96
Anglo-Americans, 87, 171, 183; British empire and, 93; Catholicism and, 165; Indians and, 87–88, 93–95, *95*; as majority, 189. *See also* whites
Anishinaabe language, 59
Apache Indians, 59
Appalachian Mountains, 87, 89, 92
Arapaho Indians, 132
Arrivé, Jacques, 61–62
Ashalacoa ("Long Knife") "tribe" (Virginians), 87, 88, 92, 95, 100, 102; Indians' view of, 101; U.S. Indian policies and, 103. *See also* Virginia

Atchatchakangouen (Grue [Crane]) band, 74
Atherton, Lewis, 159
Atlantic World, 30–31, 32, 35; Louisiana and New Orleans in, 39, 43, 45; migration in, 38
Audubon, John James, 190

Babis, Louis, 60
back-of-town collaborations, 33, 35, 36, 39, 40, 44, 45
Baltimore, city of, 170
barter, 153
Barth, Gunther, 126
Bates, Frederick, 191
Baynton, Wharton, and Morgan, 91, 99
Bayou St. John, 33, 34, 40, 44
Beauharnois, Marquis de, 77
Beaver Wars, 225 n.6
Bellini, Jacques Nicolas, 175, 177
Bienville, Jean-Baptiste Le Moyne de, 32, 33
Biloxi Indians, 34, 37
Bingham, George Caleb, 190
Black Majority (Wood), 35
Bocarro, António, 19
Bocquet, Simple, 78–79
boleta system, 22
Booker, Matthew, 126, 237 n.27
boom-and-bust cycles, 107, 159
boosters, 112, 121, 131, 162, 164; conquest of nature/savagery and, 132; legacies of dispossession and, 142; Mexicans viewed by, 138; moving frontier and, 149; postfrontier stage of development and, 157; representation of frontier cities and, 171, 172–73, 175
borderlands, 45, 124, 150, 209 n.6
Boré, Etienne Jean, 41
Boston, city of, 25, 26, 28, 35, 181; books and print culture in, 191, 196, 197; British blockade of, 100; merchants of, 155–56;

Boston, city of *(cont.)*
  representation of frontier cities and, 170, 171; as subject of representation, 188; as trade center, 192; trade with frontier cities, 154
Bouquet, Col. Henry, 89
Bradstreet, Col. John, 76
Brazil, 2, 14, 21, 107–8
Breslay, René-Charles de, 49–50, 51, 60, 62, 65, 221 n.1
British Columbia, 130
Broderick, Matthew, 27
Brooks, Joanna, 202, 251 n.8
Brown, Michael, 27
Building the Devil's Empire (Dawdy), 32
Bureau of Indian Affairs, 144
Burke, Thomas, 127
Butler, Richard, 91, 101
Butler, William, 91

Cabanné, Jean Pierre, 192
cabildos (Spanish municipal corporations), 24
Caddo Indians, 185
Cadillac, Antoine de la Mothe, 68, 69, 74, 228 n.43; Detroit envisioned as city by, 85; Native urban space in Detroit and, 70–72
California, 108, 116; agriculture, 109–10, *111*, 137, 237 n.27; ports of, 124
Californios, 124, 125
câmaras (Portuguese municipal councils), 16–17, 18, 24
Canada, 59, 76, 79, 191
capitalism, 160
Caribbean region, 7, 38
Carondelet, village of, 6
Cartier, Jacques, 52, 53–54, 57
cartographers, 171, 183
Carver, Jonathan, 194
catchment areas, 160
Catholicism, 54, 57, 61, 222 n.8; Anglo-Americans and, 165; French-Indian relations and, 60; Indians of Detroit and, 70; women and, 62
cattle industry, 129, 137
Cerré, Gabriel, 194
Champlain, Samuel de, 52, 54
Chaoucha Indians, 33
Charless, Joseph, 198
Charleston (Charles Town) (S. Carolina), city of, 25, 26, 35, 154, 170
Charlevoix, Father Pierre, 32

Chartier's Town, 88
Chauvin family, 75
Chemin de Lachine (Lachine Trail), 57, 60
Cheyenne Indians, 132
Chicago, city of, 113, 158, 161–62, 186
China, 12, 14, 144; Japan's trade with, 19; Philippines trade with, 20, 21; Portuguese empire and, 17–19; silver standard and, 12–13
Chinatowns, 129, 130, 135, 137
Chinese immigrants, 2, 126, 129, 207; in fishing industry, 130–31; industrial laborers, 130; in the Philippines, 20–21; San Francisco earthquake and, 134–35; in Southern California, 137
Chitimacha Indians, 33, 37
Chouteau, Auguste, 1, 190, 193, 194–95
Chouteau, Gabriel, 194
Chouteau family, 193, 194
Christianity, 55
Chumash Indians, 124
Cincinnati, city of, 31, 154, 161, 163, 173; books and print culture in, 196; incremental change and, 186; maps of, 180; resemblance to eastern cities, 188
cities: in American Far West, 122; defined, 4–5; eastern, 167, 182; economic role of, 8; empire-building and, 11, 14; establishment of, 7; gender composition of, 117; nation-making function of, 6; native and métis satellite villages, 5–6; Pacific Slope, 124, 130, 133, 142, 145; port cities, 45; in Portuguese empire, 14, 16–17; Progressive thinkers and, 134; river cities, 31, 173; in Spanish empire, 19–20; *urban* versus *metropolitan*, 234 n.2. *See also* frontier cities
citizenship, whiteness linked to, 6
City and the Country, The (Williams), 4
civilization, 1, 51, 134; "civilizing" of Indians, 70–71; nature and, 122; savagery and, 167, 172; Turner's frontier thesis and, 3, 121–22, 133
civil society, 183
Civitates orbis terrarumI (Braun and Hogenberg), 15
Claiborne, William, 41, 42–43
Clark, George Rogers, 100
Clark, William, 190
class, 7, 44, 84, 164, 202
Clatsop Indians, 185
Clements, Frederic, 136
clipper ships, 110, 113

Cody, William F. "Buffalo Bill," 122, 123, 143
Coeur qui Brule, 1–2, 209 n.2
Collot, Georges-Henri-Victor, 192
Colonial St. Louis (Peterson), 197
colonists/colonization, 7, 18, 26
Colorado, 112, 113, 116, 162
Columbus, Christopher, 121
communications revolution/technologies, 108, *111*, 118, 153, 232 n.5; differences among urban areas and, 163; frontier cities' growth enabled by, 112–13; outposts' link with metropoles and, 155
Compagnie de Colonie, 72
Company of the Indies, 75
Comstock Lode, 113
Connolly, John, 98–102
conquest, 4, 16, 168, 187; Iroquois claims around Detroit, 225 n.6; of nature, 122, 123, 132, 133, 143; by Virginians (Ashalacoans), 88, 103
Cooper, Frederick, 32
Cooper, James Fenimore, 188
Cooperstown (N.Y.), town of, 156–57
corporation, modern, 114
cotton, 12, 42
Couc, Isabelle (Madame Montour), 75
counterfeiting, 51
coureurs de bois ("runners of the woods"), 67
coureurs de villes ("runners of the city"), 67, 69–70, 71, 77; British rule and, 80–84; French imperial effort and, 85; fur trade and, 81, 228 n.43; *négociants*, 78–79; political-commercial interrelatedness and, 73–74
cowboys, 163
Craig, Larry, 28
Cramer, Zadok, 173, 175, 246 n.15
Crawford, William, 231 n.17
creoles/creole practices, 37, 38, 45, 67
Cresap, Michael, 100, 101
Crescent City. *See* New Orleans, city of
Croghan, George, 82, 89, 231 n.17
Croly, Herbert, 133–34
Cronon, William, 161, 235 n. 7
Cuillerier ("Beaubien"), Antoine, 80
Cuillerier ("Beaubien") family, 76
Cuillerier, Angelique, 80, 82–83
"cultural wetlands," 45

d'Abbadie, Jean-Jacques-Blaise, 37, 38
Dakota territories, 161, 162

Daman (India), city of, 17
Davenport (Iowa), town of, 157, 158
Davenport, George, 157
Davenport, Rev. John, 201
Davis, Mike, 124
Dawdy, Shannon, 32
Dearborn, Henry, 41
Deerfield, Mass., raid on (1704), 74
deforestation, 34
Delaware Indians, 87, 88–89, 91, 92, 100, 102
Del Veccio, Charles, 177, 179
democracy, 3, 40
Denver, city of, 155, 157, 162
Des Moines, city of, 154, 157
DesRuisseaux, Madame, 82
Detroit, city of, 64, 85–86, 177; British rule over, 80–84; *coureurs de villes* and, 69–70, 71; explorers' descriptions of, 186–87; French fort at, *68*, *68*, 69; fur trade and, 85; imperial rivalry and, 66, 67, 69–70, 225 n.1, 225 n.6; as Montreal of the West, 85; population of, 76–77; slaves at, 78, 80; small French population of, 72–73; as trade center, 72, 73, 76, 77, 192
Detroit-Kekionga corridor, *68*, 75
Detroit River, community at (map), *78*
Didier, Pierre, 194
diplomacy, 12, 14, 61, 209 n.2; *coureurs de villes* and, 73, 85; Pennsylvania state seal and, 96
Discovery, Settlement and Present State of Kentucke (Filson), 175
disease (pathogens), 17, 122, 123, 124, 202; pandemic flu, 144; plague, 135–36, 138, 139; yellow fever, 42–43
Diu (India), city of, 17
Dodge City, 163
Dubuque, town of, 154
Ducharme, Catherine, 74, 226 n.21
Dunmore, Lord, war of, 98, 100–103
Dutch empire, 17, 19
Duwamish Indians, 144
Duwamish River, 131, 142

Eastman, Seth, 190
Eaton, Theophilus, 201
Edmonds, Penelope, 210 n.13
Edwardsville Public Library (Illinois), 198
Elliott, Matthew, 100–101
El Paso (Tex.), city of, 206–8

empire: cities and, 11, 14, 52, 200; frontiers and, 3–4; military demands of, 26; in Ohio Valley, 103; power networks and, 7

English/British empire, 4, 14, 30, 88, 156; American Revolution and, 39; Anglo-American settlers at odds with, 93; Canada taken over by, 79; Detroit's Indians and, 79–84; frontier outposts of, 154; fur trade and, 69; invasion of New Orleans, 43; liquor trade with Indians, 64, 224 n.37; Pittsburgh and, 89; urbanization of little importance in, 25. *See also* French-English rivalry

English language, 197, 249 n.14

Enlightenment, 169

environmental changes, 33–34, 130, 140–41

Erie Canal, 156

Essex Book Shop (St. Louis), 195

eugenics, 136

Evans, Estwick, 165–66, 167, 183

exchange, cultural and economic, 3

explorers, 171, 185–86, 190

Fafard ("Macouc"), Marie-Anne, 63

families, frontier and, 116–17

farmers, 114, 172; Chinese, 20; Detroit and, 77; merchants and, 156, 158; New Orleans and, 38, 42; Pennsylvania land policy and, 97

Filson, John, 175, 181, 247 n.17

fishing industry, 130–31

Flagg, Edmund, 192

Flint, Timothy, 192

floods and flood-control, 34, 42

Florida, West, 39

Florissant, town of, 198

Formosa, 19

forts, 31, 67, 77, 85, 151, 154

Fort Stanwix, Treaty of (1769), 90, 92

Fox Indians, 59

Franks, David, 91

Franks, Moses, 91

Freeman-Custis Expedition, 185

free people of color, 28, 39, 42; incorporation of New Orleans into United States and, 41–42; militiamen, 41; restrictions on, 44

French and Indian War, 77, 81, 89

French empire, 4, 14, 88, 175; books and print culture in, 192–94; Detroit and forts of, 67; frontier outposts of, 154; relations with Indians, 49–50; smuggling in, 51; urbanization of little importance in, 25

French-English rivalry, 50, 51, 56, 64; Detroit and, 66, 67, 69–70, 71, 76, 225 n.6; French and Indian War, 77, 81; Virginians ("Long Knife" tribe) and, 92

French language, 1, 81, 197, 198, 209 n.2, 249 n.14

Friedlander, Isaac, 110, 112

frontier cities, 162–63, 172, 200–201, 208; chaos in, 51; civilization and, 181; commerce and, 25, 31; as commercial outposts, 151, 155, 158; comparison with modern cities, 200; cultural development of, 191; defined, 2, 152, 153, 160, 209 n.6; elusive character of, 164; European cities in Asia, 11–12, 156; expeditions into the West from, 184–85; global markets and, 120; histories connected by, 7; as imperial strongholds, 52; intermediary role of, 151; maps of, 169–70, 180–81, 187–88; as masculine spaces, 163, 164; metropoles' connections with, 52; paradox of, 149–50; railroads and, 159; representation in American culture, 168–70, 173, 175, 187–89; rivers and, 107; self-government in, 12; in Spanish empire, 23–26; suburbs of, 6; telescoped development of, 113; trade with metropolitan center, 152–53; white settlement and, 167–68; world market and, 107–8. *See also* cities

frontier exchange, 33, 35, 37–40, 43–44

Frontier in History, The (Lamar and Thompson), 208

frontiers, 164, 167, 172, 189, 208, 210 n.6; debate about cities and, 182; decivilizing elements of, 183; defined, 2–3; empire-building and, 6; frontier mentality, 113–14; global, 7; investors in booms on, 114; limits of imperial power and, 66; "near frontier," 150; as rural spaces, 5; towns as spearheads of, 31, 122; transportation revolution and, 116–17; Turner Thesis, 52; urban frontier anxiety, 133

Fujita-Rony, Dorothy, 143

Fuller, Alexandra, 163

fur trade, 52–53, 59, 68–69, 72, 227 n.23; bilingual fluency promoted by, 249 n.14; Coast Salish peoples and, 125; Detroit dominated by, 85; French-Indian kinship networks and, 76; in Montreal, 91; in New Haven, 251 n.11; in Pittsburgh, 91, 93; settler opposition to, 94–95, 95

Gage, Gen. Thomas, 91
Galena (Ill.), town of, 154, 155, 157
Gallay, Alan, 118, 153, 156
gambling, 44, 163
Gaspar, Jose, 204, 205, 206
Gasparilla Festival (Tampa), 203, 205
Gass, Patrick, 246 n.15
Gelves, Marques de, 22
gender, 7, 30, 84
geographers, 171, 187
George III, king of England, 87, 99, 103
Geronimo, 122
Gibault, Father, 198
Gibson, George, 91
Gibson, John, 91–92, 99, 100–101
Gitlin, Jay, 52
Goa, city of, 12, 13–14, 16–17, 25, 114, 200; Council of, 11; international trade system and, 156; Macau and, 18; military demands of empire and, 26; in sixteenth-century illustration, *15*; U.S. frontier cities compared with, 108
Godefroy family, 76, 82
gold rushes: California, 6, 109, 114, 126, 161; Klondike, 139, 162
Gouin family, 76
Gratiot, Charles, 192
Gratz, Bernard, 91
Gratz, Michael, 91
Great Depression, 123, 141
Great Lakes, 58, 66, 172, 225 n.2; concentration of Indians in, 77; *coureurs de villes* from, 70
Great Peace of Montreal (1701), 67–68, 72
Great Plains, 162
Greek immigrants, 131
Guadalupe Hidalgo, Treaty of, 109, 207
Gulf of Mexico, 25, 33

Hall, Basil, 192
Hamer, David, 152
Hansen, Cecile, 144
Hatian Revolution, 41
Hawaii, 109, 124, 131, 143
Hawthorne, Nathaniel, 188
Hinderaker, Eric, 103
hinterlands, 25, 33, 142, 152, 164; Chicago and, 161, 162; cities' relation to, 143, 153, 160–61, 163, 164; descriptive terms for, 150; of Detroit, 67, 83, 85–86; flow of trade and people into, 155; of Goa, 14; of Manaus, 107, 119; mining, 161; of San Francisco, 126, 161; settlers drawn to, 159; unruliness of, 51
hoboes, 139, 141
Hochelaga (Iroquoian town), 53, 54
Ho Chunk (Winnebago) Indians, 70
Hoover, Herbert, 132
Horse, John, 204–5
hotels, 6, 119, 137, 205
Houma Indians, 33, 37
Howard, Governor, 87
Hudson River valley, 156
Hudson's Bay Company, 124
Hunt, W. Price, 191
Huron Indians, 54, 55, 56
Huron-Petun-Wendat Indians, 70, 77, 80
hurricanes, 32

identity, American national, 3
Igrot people, 132, 239 n.53
Illinois and Michigan Canal, 161
Illinois country, 194
Illinois Indians, 63, 70
immigrants, 117, 163, 208; illegal, 144; in New Orleans, 32; restrictions on immigration, 133, 136–37; violence against, 129–30
indentured servants, 34
India, 7, 12, 13–14, 17, 22, 110
Indian country, 2, 102, 191, 198, 203, 225 n.1
Indian Ocean, 12, 14
Indians (Native Americans), 29, 40, 108, 235 n.16; alcohol consumption by, 49–50, 56, 62, 65; Anglo-Americans and, 87–88, 93–95, *95*; in California, 125; Dunmore's War and, 99–103; El Paso and, 206–8; English/British empire and, 69, 79–84, 93; explorers and, 185, 186–87; in fairs and expositions, 132; forced removal of, 187; French empire and, 53, 54–56, 63–64, 70–71; frontier cities and, 118–19, 153; fur trade and, 68–69; kinship networks with the French, 71; languages, 59, 81, 82, 203, 250 n.7; "laziness" of, 247 n.24; in Mississippi Valley, 31; New Haven and, 201–3; in New Orleans area, 33, 37; resources for worldwide trade and, 124; as slaves, 34, 62; in Spanish empire, 23, 24; territorial conceptions of, 68, 69; Turner Thesis and, 121–22. *See also individual and tribal names*
indigenous peoples, 3, 107, 210 n.13, 212 n.18

indigo, 42
individualism, 3, 134
industrialization, 201
"instant cities," 159
Inuit people, 132
investors, 114, 158, 163
Iowa City, 154, 157
Iroquois Indians, 51, 53, 54, 61, 75; as allies of the English, 69, 225 n.6; Anglo-Americans and, 87; attack on Montreal, 57–58; at Detroit, 66, 69; Great Peace of Montreal and, 67–68, 69, 72; Pittsburgh and, 88
Irving, Washington, 188, 190, 192
Italian immigrants, 131

Jamestown (Va.), town of, 30, 114, 163
Japan, 12, 13, 14, 19, 20
Japanese immigrants, 129, 137, 142, 238 n.43
jazz music, 45
Jefferson, Thomas, 42, 43, 103, 165, 167; culture of American West and, 182; Lewis and Clark Expedition and, 194
Jenkins, C. M., 129
Jesuits, 16, 18, 19, 56; in Detroit, 77; Indian converts and, 60; in Manila, 21; in New Orleans, 32
Jews, 91
Johnson, Sir William, 79–80, 82, 84, 91
Jones, David, 92
Joseph (slave of Lamoureux), 62

Kahnawake (Sault Saint-Louis), town of, 55, 58, 61, 64, 74
Ka-Lang-ad, 132
Kane, Joe, 119
Kansas City, 155
Kastor, Peter, 40
Katrina, Hurricane, 27–28, 29
Kekionga (Fort Wayne), 67, 75, 76, 80, 81, 84
Kelérec, Louis Billouart de, 37
Kenny, James, 89
Keokuk (Iowa), town of, 154, 163
Keskabikat, Michel, 60
Kickapoo Indians, 70
kinship, French-Native: *coureurs de villes* and, 71, 74, 78; Lamoureux and, 59, 60, 63. *See also* métis (mixed-race people)
Klingle, Matthew, 118, 153, 158, 162
Korean immigrants, 137
Kuskkuskies, town of, 89

Labbadie, Silvestre, 194
laborers, itinerant, 123, 126
labor unions, 136
LaButte (Chesne), Charles, 75
LaButte (Chesne), Pierre, 75–76, 78, 79, 83
Laclède, Pierre de, 1, 190, 192, 193, 194
Lafrenière, Nicolas Chauvin de, 36
Lakota Indians, 132
Lamoureux, François Charles, 65
Lamoureux, François ("Saint Germain"), 50–52, 56, 63, 222 n.4; French imperial state and, 59; French-Native intimacy and, 59–60; Native partners of, 58, 61–62; trial of, 61, 62, 64
Lancaster (Pa.), town of, 154
landscape paintings, 188
land speculators, 90, 92, 98, 163; moving frontier and, 149; in Portuguese empire, 17; representation of frontier cities and, 172; San Francisco tideland reclamation and, 126
land titles, 92–93, 96–98
Las Vegas, city of, 119
Latin America, 7, 13, 24, 212 n.18
Leadville (Colorado), town of, 113, 157–58, 162, 163
Le Blond de la Tour, 32
Le Claire, Antoine, 157
Lehmann-Haupt, Helmut, 193
Lepore, Jill, 35
Le Scel, Barbe, 60
Levy, Andrew, 91
Levy, Solomon, 91
Lewis and Clark Expedition, 185, 194, 246 n.15
Lexington (Ky.), town of, 31, 172, 175, 180
Lexington (Mass.), town of, 154
libraries, 190, 191, 193–98
liminality, 150
Lincoln (Nebraska), town of, 162
liquor trade, 49–50, 62
Livingston, Robert, 69
Logan, 92, 103
Logstown, 89
London, city of, 109, 115, 154, 197
Long, Stephen Harriman, 185
Lopez, Roberto, 4
Los Angeles, city of, 119, 122, 128–29, 134, 200; immigrants in, 143; Mexicans in, 137–38; sanitary campaigns, 138, *139*
Louboey, Lt. Henri de, 34
Louisiana, 64, 73, 192; colonial population

of, 34; "dysfunctional" reputation, 27, 35; economic weakness of, 36; incorporated into United States, 40–43, 177, 195; population of, 39; slavery in, 38; Spanish rule over, 1, 39; uniqueness in American history, 28, 30; wetlands of, 29
Louisville (Ky.), town of, 31, 173, 175, *177*, 180, 186
Louis XIV, king of France, 51

Macau (China), city of, 12, 13, 17–19, 114, 156; military demands of empire and, 26; Philippines trade with, 22
Makougan (Mak8a8an), 62
Malacca, 19, 22
Manaus (Brazil), city of, 2, 107–8, 119–20, 200
Manchu dynasty, 19
Mandan Indians, 185
Manila, city of, 12, 13, 19–22, 156; ethnic segregation of, 20; military demands of empire and, 26; silver from America in, 19; U.S. frontier cities compared with, 108
maps, 166–67, 170–71, 180–81, 188, 189; of American explorers, 185–86; Kentucky, *177*, 247 n.17; New Orleans, *176*; Ohio River and towns along, *174*; standard convention of urban maps, 175
marriage, mixed, 16, 214 n.15
Mascouten Indians, 70
Mason-Dixon line, 88
Maspero, P., 179
Massachusetts Bay Colony, 35
McClure, David, 89–90, 95
McDermott, John Francis, 190, 191, 193, 196, 197, 198
McKay, Aeneas, 91
McKenzie, Roderick D., 141
Meinig, D. W., 152, 155
Ménard, Marguerite, 59
Mercantile Library (St. Louis), 194–97, 198, 250 n.22, 250 n.25, 255, 257
merchants, 39, 151, 152–53, 155, 164; in Boston, 155–56; economies of scale and, 158–59; English, Scots, and Irish, 84; French, 51, 53, 56, 59, 64, 74; libraries of, 194; in Portuguese empire, 14, 17; postfrontier stage of development and, 157; records of, 190; of St. Louis, 193, 197; in Spanish empire, 13, 20, 21, 22
Mesquakie (Fox) Indians, 59, 70

métis (mixed-race people), 6, 60, 63, 75, 124, 189; British rule and, 81; Detroit-centered trade network, 67; Frenchmen married into networks of, 78; as wealthiest citizens of Detroit, 79
metropoles, 52, 153, 172, 185
Mexican-American War, 124
Mexicans/Mexican Americans, 137, 142, 203
Mexico, 13, 21, 25, 137, 192, 206
Mexico City, 25
Miami Indians, 67, 70, 72, 84, 86; British trade with, 83; Kekionga outpost, 75, 81; kinship networks with the French, 76
Michaux, André, 192
Michigan, 161, 187
Michilimackinac, 62, 67, 77, 80
middle class, 134, 164
Middle Ground, 91, 103, 150
militia: in New France, 55, 79; in New Orleans, 41, 43; in Pennsylvania, 97, 99, 102
Miller and Lux Company, 129
Ming dynasty, 18, 19
Mingo Indians, 87, 92, 101, 102, 103
mining, 5, 112–13, 118, 151, 161
Minneapolis, city of, 162
missionaries, 21–22, 49, 56, 89–90, 92, 95
Mississippi River, 33, 44, 67, 154
Missouri Gazette, 195
Missouri Indians, 1
Mobile, town of, 25
modernity, 133
Moehring, Eugene, 160
Mohawk Indians, 55, 59, 62, 74, 81
Mohegan Indians, 202–3
Moluccas, 22
Momauguin, 201
Montana, 108, 116, 117, 159, 162
Montreal, city of, 2, 7, 35, 49, 65, 69–70; Anglo-American views of, 183; books and print culture in, 191; empire and, 52, 63; French-Iroquois relations and, 54–56, 57–58; fur trade and, 52–53, 68, 91, 124; geography and, 53; Indian communities surrounding, 50, 55–56; liquor smuggling in, 50, 51, 62, 63–65; maps of, 175; plan of, *58*; population of, 55, 56; reach of Native representatives' voices and, 66; settlement of, 54; slaves in, 78; as trade center, 192; trade with west, 67, 80, 85; urbanization of, 57, 58; U.S. frontier cities compared with, 108

Moore, Marshall, 127
Morse, Jedediah, 181–83, 186, 187–88
Morse, Samuel F. B., 109
Muir, John, 126
Mullanphy, John, 191

Nashville, town of, 172
Natchez (Miss.), town of, 177, 186
nationalism, cultural, 171, 188
nation-making/building, 4, 6, 8, 200
Native Americans. *See* Indians (Native Americans)
nature, conquest of, 122, 123, 132, 133, 143
Navigator, The (Cramer), 173, *174*
Nebraska City, 157
négociants, 78–79
Nevada, 113, 116, 117, 164
Neveu family, 75
New Amsterdam, city of, 11
New England, 24, 170, 182, 192
New France, 55, 58, 64, 108, 192, 222 n.8; books on, 194; *coureurs de bois* in, 67; Detroit and, 73, 76; officers as nobility of, 74, 79; officials' tolerance of smuggling, 65
New Haven (Conn.), city of, 201–3, 208, 251 n.11
New Mexico, 207, 208
New Orleans, city of, 25, 44–45, 166, 186, 192; in American imagination and history, 28–30, 183; books and print culture in, 195; cultural refinements of, 192; founding of, 32; French regime in, 30, 32–38; as frontier city, 28, 30, 31, 165; Indian tribes and, 33; Katrina hurricane and, 27–28; maps of, 175, *176*, 177–79; mix of migrants in, 29; similarity to other Atlantic port cities, 35; slavery and, 39–40, 42–43; Spanish regime in, 30, 38–39; unique cultural heritage of, 45
New Salem (Ill.), town of, 154
New York, city of, 25, 35, 66, 67, 80, 181; books and print culture in, 196; as immigrant city, 28, 117; investors in, 158; price of staples in, 107; as subject of representation, 188; as trade center, 192; trade with frontier cities, 154; transformation of trade in, 156
New York Burning (Lepore), 35
Nipissing Indians, 49, 59, 60, 65; Lamoureux's trial and, 62–63; liquor smuggled to, 58, 62
Norris, Frank, 133
Northwest Territory, 98, 173

Notes on the State of Virginia (Jefferson), 165
Noyelles de Fleurimont, Nicolas-Joseph, 75

obedience, simulation of, 18, 26
Occom, Samson, 202, 203
Odawa Indians, 63, 65, 70, 75, 76, 79
Ohio Company, 99
Ohio River, towns along (map), *174*
Ohio Valley, 90, 103, 112; competing colonial projects in, 91; Indian tribes of, 87–88; river cities of, 173
Ojibwe indians, 70, 187
Omaha, city of, 155, 162
Onas ("bird quill") "tribe" (Pennsylvanians), 87, 88, 92, 95; Dunmore's War and, 102–3; Indians' view of, 101; U.S. Indian policies and, 103. *See also* Pennsylvania
Oñate, Juan de, 206, 207
Oneida Indians, 59
Onondaga Indians, 70
Oregon Treaty, 109
Orleans Territory, 39, 40, 41
Oronhoua, 62
Osbey, Brenda Marie, 39
Osceola, 204–5
Otermín, Antonio de, 206
Ouabankikoué, Marguerite, 74–75, 83
outposts, frontier, 25, 154

Pacific Ocean, 7, 12
Panama Canal, 132, 133
Panic of 1893, 122, 126
Parkman, Francis, 222 n.8
Pauger, Adrien de, 32
Paul, Moses, 202
Pawnee Indians, 122
pays d'en haut (upper country), 66, 68, 71, 72, 73, 85
Peck, John Mason, 198
Penn, William, 14, 87
Pennsylvania, 80, 87, 88; Quaker elite of, 96; Virginia in conflict with, 92, 95–103. *See also Onas* ("bird quill") "tribe"
Pensacola, 25, 34
Pequot War, 202
Perren, Barbe, 62
Perrin du Lac, François Marie, 192
Peru, 21
Peterson, Charles, 197
Peterson, Jacqueline, 225 n.2

Phelan, James D., 135
Philadelphia, city of, 14, 26, 154, 155, 181; books and print culture in, 196, 197; "Hell Town," 35–36; publishing industry in, 170; representation of frontier cities and, 170–71; as subject of representation, 188
Philip II, king of Spain, 20, 23
Philip IV, king of Spain, 22
Philippe, Odet, 205
Philippines, 12, 108, 132, 143; administered from Mexico, 21; Royal Ordinances followed in, 24; silver from, 13; Spanish colony building in, 19; U.S. acquisition of, 131
Philipson, Joseph, 198
Piankashaw Indians, 67, 70
Pigarouiche, Étienne, 60
Pigarouiche, Marguerite, 59–60
Pitot, Jacques, 183
Pitt, Fort, 80, 89, 92, 98
Pittsburgh, town of, 7, 31, 94, 97, 173; boosters and, 172; Dunmore's War and, 98–103; history of, 88–90, 230 n.7; population of, 90; urbanism and, 90; on Wingenund's map, 94
Plan of the City and Suburbs of New Orleans (map), *178*, 179
plazas, in Spanish cities, 23, 24
politics, 5, 8, 152, 168; machine politics in New Orleans, 28–29; racial, 5
pollution, 130, 131, 137, 141
Pontchartrain, Fort, 70, *78*
Pontiac's War, 75, 81, 89, 93
Popé, 206
population density, 5, 172
Portage des Sioux, village of, 6
Porteus, John, 83
Portland, city of, 144, 162
Portuguese empire, 21, 24, 25, 211 n.18; Goa and, 14, 16–17; Macau and, 17–19; as middleman in Asia trade, 12; Spanish rivalry with, 20, 22
postcolonial theory, 7
Potawatomi Indians, 70
Potosí, silver mines of, 13
Potter, David, 117
power relations, unequal, 3, 200
priests, 53, 78–79
Pritchard, James, 51
Private Libraries in Creole St. Louis (McDermott), 190, 191
probate records, 191

progress, idea of, 123, 133, 142
Progressive Era, 122, 133–34, 140
Promise of American Life, The (Croly), 133–34
property, private, 129
prostitutes, 163
public health, 134, 142
public works projects, 123
publishing industry, in early republic, 168–69, 171, 180, 189
Pueblo (Tigua) Indians, 206–8
Puritans, 14
Pursell, Henry, 175, 247 n.17

Quakers, 89, 91, 93, 95, 96
Quebec, 25, 72, 85
Queen Aliquippa's Town, 89
Quenet, Jean, 62
Quincy (Ill.), town of, 154, 155
Quinnipiac Indians, 201

race, 7, 42, 84, 132, 202; anti-Indian race hatred, 94–95; racial segregation, 125, 142, 238 n.43; racial stereotyping, 166
railroads, 108, 115, 129, 153, 154; Chicago and, 161, 162; Chinese immigrant workers and, 117; construction of, 109; in Florida, 205; Great Northern Railroad, 127, 128, 162; merchants and, 159; paths of settlement and, 157; Southern Pacific, 207
ranching, 115, 118
real estate, 115
Réaume, Simon, 63
religion, 51, 52, 90, 116
restaurants, 6
rice, 12, 42
Richter, Daniel, 225 n.1
roads, 23, 24
Rockford (Ill.), town of, 154
Rocky Mountains, 162
Roman Empire, 150
Roosevelt, Theodore, 134
Rothman, Hal, 119
Roy, Étienne, 75
Roy, François, 75
Roy, Marie Magdelene, 75, 83
Roy, Pierre, Jr., 74–75, 83
Roy, Pierre, Sr., 74, 226 n.21
"Royal Ordinances Concerning the Laying out of New Towns" (Philip II), 23, 24
Roy family, 74–76, 227 n.28

Rushforth, Brett, 118
Russian empire, 4

Sacramento, town of, 161
St. Ange de Bellerive, Louis, 194
St. Augustine, 25
St. Charles, village of, 6
St. Clair, Arthur, 98, 100, 102
St. Domingue, 64
St. Ferdinand de Florissant, village of, 6
St. Joseph (Mo.), city of, 155
St. Lawrence River, 53, 55
St. Louis, city of, 1–2, 7, 31, 154, 157; in American imagination and history, 183, 192; currency note issued by Bank of St. Louis, 179–180, *179*; as frontier city, 162, 186, 198; as global village, 209 n.4; investors in, 158, 162; libraries and print culture in, 190–99, 250 n.22, 250 n.25; Louisiana Purchase and, 177; resemblance to eastern cities, 188; satellite villages of, 6; trade shifted to Chicago from, 161, 162; waterfront, 180, *180*
St. Malo, Juan, 39
St. Martin (DesButtes), Jacques, 80
salesmen, traveling, 159
saloon, western, 5
San Diego, city of, 130, 132, 144
San Francisco, city of, 6, 7, 112, 158, 162; closing of frontier and, 122; earthquake (1906) in, 134–35; gold rush and, 109, 126, 159; "Grain King" of, 110; immigrants in, 143, 144; merchants of, 159, 161; Mining and Stock Exchange, 114–15; rapid development of, 112; urban space reconfigured in, 136; waterfront (tidelands), 126, 129, 236 n.26; world's fair in, 131–32
sanitation: in Los Angeles, 138, *139*; in San Francisco, 135–36; in Seattle, 139–40
Santa Fe, city of, 183–84
St. Domingo, slave insurrection in, 42
Sauconk, town of, 89
Saugrain, Antoine, 194
Sauk Indians, 70
"savagery," 94, 123; civilization in conflict with, 3, 122, 133, 167, 172; conquest of, 122, 132, 143
Savannah (Ga.), city of, 14, 35
Schenectady, town of, 156
Schoolcraft, Henry Rowe, 186–88
Scott, James, 134
sea-lanes, 12, 14

Seattle, city of, 7, 119, 143–44, 158; closing of frontier and, 122; as gateway to Alaska, 162; geography and, 124–25; Great Depression and, 141; Herring's House, 121, 125, 144; immigrants in, 143; Indians in, 121–22, *127*, 128, 132; population growth, 139; Skid Row district, 127–28, 141; urban space reengineered in, 131, 139–41; waterfront (tidelands), 126–28, *127*, 129; world's fair in, 132
Seminole Indians, 204–5, 206
Seneca Indians, 70, 80, 89
settler colonialism, 6, 8, 200
Seven Years' War, 92
Shah, Nayan, 137
Shannopin's Town, 89
Shawnee Indians, 87, 88, 91, 92, 100, 101
ship building, 113
"Significance of the Frontier in American History, The" (Turner), 3
Sigo8ch (Sigoouitz, Sigoouy), 62
Silègue, Thiton de, 38
silver, 12–13, 19, 21, 158
Simon, Joseph, 91
Single Whip Tax, 12
Sioux Indians, 59, 122
Sitting Bull, 122
slaves/slavery, 30, 31, 36–37, 183; from the Caribbean, 41; in Detroit, 78; Indians as slaves, 34; New Orleans as commercial center and, 39–40; official planners in New Orleans and, 32–33; restrictions on movements of, 39; runaway slaves, 35, 37, 39, 204; slave insurrections, 42, 43; in Virginia, 96
Slavic immigrants, 131
Smith, Jedediah, 190–91
Smith, Michael P., 45
smuggling, 21, 49, 50, 51, 58, 60, 63–65
Snowshoe (La Raquette), 61–62
sociology, 151
Sothern, Billy, 29
Spanish empire, 4, 14, 175, 211 n.18; Anglo-American views of, 183; British rivalry with, 39; California as part of, 125; frontier cities in, 23–26; frontier outposts of, 154; galleon trade, 21, 22; Manila and, 19–22; Pueblo Indians and, 206–7
Spear, Jennifer, 37
Spice Islands, 14
Springfield (Ill.), town of, 154

Springfield (Mass.), town of, 154
State of India, 14, 16, 18
steamboats, 154, 157, 159, 162, 163
Sterling, James, 81–83
Stevens, Isaac Ingalls, 125
Stevenson, James, 84
Stevenson, Robert Louis, 115, 119
Stoler, Ann Laura, 32
suburbs, 5, 6, 77, 121, 137
sugar, 42
Suzanne (slave of Lamoureux), 62

Tampa (Fla.), city of, 203–6, 208
Tantaquidgeon, Gladys, 202
Tantaquidgeon, Lucy Occom, 202
Tardiveau, Bartholomew, 198
Taylor, Paul, 237 n.27
telegraph, 108–9, 110, 113, 114, 154
Texas, 109, 114, 161, 201, 206
Thompson, Leonard, 208
Thomson, R. H., 139, 140
Thrush, Coll, 121
Tigua (Pueblo) Indians, 206–8
Tlingit Indians, 132
Tocqueville, Alexis de, 189
Tonty, Alphonse, and wife, 71–72, 74, 229 n.43
Townshend, Charles H., 202
trade, 5, 123, 200, 203; Detroit and networks of, 67; disregard of imperial trade laws, 21, 26; frontier cities in Asia and, 11; global networks of, 8, 13; mobility and, 84; sea-lanes and, 12; in spices, 12, 17; transpacific and transatlantic, 132–33
traders, 2, 17–18, 69, 80, 91–95, 151
trading posts, 31, 154
transportation revolution/technologies, 108, 111, 116, 153, 232 n.5; differences among urban areas and, 163; frontier cities' growth enabled by, 112–13; metropolitan growth and, 123
travelers, 171, 183, 189
travel narratives, 166, 169, 186–87, 188, 247 n.23
Travels in the Interior of North America (Carver), 194
Trois-Rivières, city of, 78
Trudeau, Laurent, 194
Trudel, Marcel, 78
Trumbull, George, 84
Tsimshian Indians, 124
Tunica Indians, 37

Turner, Frederick Jackson, 3, 52, 121, 122, 139; on cities, 133; as Malthusian, 136
Turner Thesis, 44, 121–22

United States, 115–16, 168; early republic, 167, 184; entry into World War I, 131; entry into World War II, 142; expansion of, 4; Florida acquired by, 204; Indian policies, 103; Louisiana acquired by, 40–43; Mexican border, 124, 207, 208; printing industry, 169; western territories annexed by, 108
Urban Frontier, The (Wade), 2, 31, 145, 149
urban history, 5, 210 n.12
urbanization, 5–8, 25, 57, 58
urban space, 5, 24, 37, 74
Usner, Daniel, 118

Vail, Albert, 109
Vandalia Company, 99
Vaudreuil, Philippe Rigaud de, 51, 64, 73
Vimont, Barthélemy, 54
Vincennes, Fort, 67, 75, 84, 176
Vincennes Library Company, 198
Virginia, 88, 90, 170, 175; founded as profit-making enterprise, 97; Pennsylvania in conflict with, 92, 95–103; Western settlers' gravitation toward, 96. See also *Ashalacoa* ("Long Knife") "tribe"
Virginia City, Nevada, 109, 113, 115, 118–19, 159, 164
voyageurs, 74

Wabanaki Indians, 70
Wade, Richard C., 2, 31, 44, 126, 145, 209 n.5, 257; on cities and western settlement, 52; on towns as spearheads of frontier, 122, 133, 149
Wampanoag Indians, 202
"warehousing cities," 159
water rights, 129
Wea Indians, 70
Webb, Walter Prescott, 114
West, American, 3, 8, 154, 158; annexation of, 108; Asian immigrants in, 143; class structure in, 164; development of culture in, 182; emergence as distinctive region, 109; European image of, 169; frontier in historiography of, 4; global history and, 7; images of West in American culture, 166; in Mississippi Valley, 31; Virginia's role in populating and governing, 170

West, Elliott, 122–23, 153, 203
wetlands, 29, 39, 45
wheat production, 109–10, *111*, 112, 161
White, Richard, 51, 71, 122
White Eyes, 92, 102
whites, 42, 44, 136, 205; Francophone, 183; frontier cities and white settlement, 167–68, 183; militiamen in New Orleans, 43; in Pacific Slope cities, 122; racial purity of, 95; whiteness, 6, 37. *See also* Anglo-Americans
Wild, John Caspar, 188, 189
Wild West shows, 122, 132
Wilkinson, Gen. James, 41
Williams, Raymond, 4
Wingenund, 94 (caption)
Winship, Michael, 196
Wisekaukautshe (Piedfroid [Cold Foot]), 74
women: Catholicism embraced by Native women, 62; city as frontier for, 117; single women in American West, 116; as victims in Dunmore's War, 101, 102; violence and, 118; wives of French colonial officials, 71–72
Wong Kee Jun v. Seattle, 141
Wood, Peter, 35
Worcester (Mass.), town of, 154
working class, 29, 134, 136, 164
world's fairs, 6, 131–32
World War II, 142
Wyandot Indians, 87, 88

Yakuts, 124
Yale University, 202, 250 n.7
Yellow Creek Massacre, 100, 102, 103
Yellow Hand, 122
Yellowstone Expedition, 185
Yesler, Henry, 127
Young, Mary Gamble, 141–42

zanja system, 129, 137
zones of emergence or transition, 150–51
zones of encounter, 3, 150, 153, 160

ACKNOWLEDGMENTS

From all three co-editors:
There are many people to thank for their support of the two conferences—held at the Howard R. Lamar Center for the Study of Frontiers and Borders at Yale and the St. Louis Mercantile Library at the University of Missouri–St. Louis—from which this volume originated. In New Haven, John Mack Faragher and George Miles provided thoughtful advice and excellent suggestions at every step of the way. It was Johnny's idea to establish the Center, and under his leadership, all of us have had the opportunity to think creatively about the history of the West, the result being symposia and conferences on such topics as "Global Oil Frontiers," "Ethnic Cleansing on the Frontiers of Europe and America," and "Women and Colonization on North American and Australian Frontiers." All was made possible by the generous support of the Lamar Center provided by Roland and Lois Betts and Jeremy Kinney and Holly Arnold Kinney.

Howard Lamar opened the conference and, as usual, created an environment of congeniality and shared intellectual endeavor. Edith Rotkopf handled all the arrangements with her usual thoroughness and care, making sure no participant ever missed a meal or a travel connection. Alan Gallay gave the keynote at Yale and even produced an additional paper when one of our presenters had to withdraw. Adam Arenson kept track of every word and thought. Without his careful stewardship, the crafting of this volume would have been infinitely harder.

In St. Louis, John Neal Hoover, Director of the St. Louis Mercantile Library at the University of Missouri–St. Louis, and his staff made us all feel like traveling rock stars. John and the Mercantile have supported every aspect of this project from planning to publication. Elizabeth Gentry Sayad and *Les Amis* were our gracious hosts at a reception and dinner. Barbara Berglund, formerly a fellow at the Lamar Center, joined us at the Mercantile, and Elliott West gave the keynote in St. Louis—or, as he described the city in one of his many delightful e-mails, "Cahokia's western suburb."

Other scholars who contributed to the conferences and other conversations that resulted in this collection included Gwenn Miller, Peter Silver, Carl Brasseaux, Fred Fausz, Carlos Schwantes, Bill Foley, Leo J. Garofalo, and Cory Willmott.

These conferences reoriented our scholarly work and that of this volume's contributors. We rediscovered that frontier cities provide a lens that allows us to view vital yet neglected everyday realities that shaped the lives of people in the past and provide intriguing precedents for our experiences in this age of increasing global integration.

We thank the anonymous reviewers for their kind and helpful suggestions. Above all, we thank Bob Lockhart at the University of Pennsylvania Press for his enthusiasm, encouragement, and editorial expertise. It has been an absolute pleasure to work with him, Erica Ginsburg, Julia Rose Roberts, and copyeditor Clia Goodwin, and we are thrilled to be part of the burgeoning list of Penn Press publications in the fields of American history and urban studies. We think this is a perfect fit.

Needless to say, we thank all of our colleagues whose work appears in this book. They have been patient and diligent in producing revised versions of their original papers. It was truly great and productive fun to have conversations that began with central-place theory and ended with casks of brandy being thrown over walls in eighteenth-century Montréal.

Many conference calls and perhaps thousands of e-mails later, we have made it to the finish line. Now a bit more from each of us, individually.

Jay Gitlin:
The idea for a conference on frontier cities had its misty origins in my undergraduate years at Yale. After taking a course with Roberto Lopez on medieval urban history, I began daydreaming about merchants and urban life in Genoa and Venice. And then I took Howard Lamar's legendary class on the American West and listened intently when he described an international West of shifting empires and people from diverse cultures, including French fur traders who learned native languages. Here was a West that a kid from New York could appreciate: a world of retail adventure and multicultural negotiations. Many years later, after conversations with Alan Gallay, who had a program at the Ohio State University entitled "Crossroads of Globalization: 'Hot Spots' in the Early Modern World," and Adam Arenson, then a graduate student at Yale finishing his dissertation on St. Louis, we began to plan the conferences in New Haven and St. Louis.

Origin stories aside, I thank my wife, Ginny Bales, and son, Basie Gitlin, for their indulgence while I snuck away from family vacations to answer e-mails about "FC." When the planning began, Basie was a history major at Yale. Now he has an M.Phil. in early modern history from Cambridge. I would like to offer my deepest thanks to Barbara and Adam, who have done so much of the work. Their vision and energy have made this book a reality. We have bonded over this project and have been quite the congenial team.

Barbara Berglund:

I thank Jay and Adam for allowing me to join them on this frontier cities adventure and I thank John Mack Faragher for his mentorship and encouragement that initially brought me to the project. *Frontier Cities* has been an enriching experience. Over the years that it has been in my life, it has taught me about writing and editing collaboratively and about the broadest implications of cities and frontiers. I would also like to thank Steve Dubb, my husband and in-house editor, for his loving generosity—he has read every word of many drafts of various incarnations of the introduction and epilogue with patience, care, and interest.

Adam Arenson:

I thank the University of Texas at El Paso Department of History for travel and indexing funds, and I thank my family for their support while I have made the transition, during this project, from graduate student to assistant professor, advising my own graduate students. I especially thank Rebecca Rosenthal for her forbearance as we have begun our careers together but have maintained our relationship long-distance, whether New York to New Haven, New York to St. Louis, New York to El Paso, or, now, El Paso to Los Angeles. The academic lifestyle has led me to many frontier cities already—and our son, Simon, thankfully, is still excited to hear about my travels to all of them.

We leave the last words for the late Richard Wade, who, along with John Francis McDermott, provided the inspiration for this work. Wade began work on his seminal book, *The Urban Frontier*, at the Mercantile Library in St. Louis. In the year before his death in 2008, Wade opined,

> The new generation of urban historians has an international dimension out of necessity. Globalization has spun an urban web around the world. Foreign scholars are already active on this task. We should be also—or risk our own irrelevance.

www.ingramcontent.com/pod-product-compliance
Lightning Source LLC
Jackson TN
JSHW020935150725
87619JS00002B/4